I0605289

CRUDE CREATURES

Crude Creatures

Confronting Representations of Black People in Yiddish Culture

Gil Ribak

NEW YORK UNIVERSITY PRESS
New York

NEW YORK UNIVERSITY PRESS
New York
www.nyupress.org

Library of Congress Cataloging-in-Publication Data
Names: Ribak, Gil, author.
Title: Crude creatures : confronting representations of black people in Yiddish culture / Gil Ribak.
Description: New York : New York University Press, [2025] |
Includes bibliographical references and index.
Identifiers: LCCN 2025004483 (print) | LCCN 2025004484 (ebook) |
ISBN 9781479837977 (hardback) | ISBN 9781479837984 (ebook) |
ISBN 9781479838011 (ebook other)
Subjects: LCSH: Black people in literature. | Yiddish literature—History and criticism.
Classification: LCC PJ5120.7.B53 R53 2025 (print) | LCC PJ5120.7.B53 (ebook) |
DDC 839/.1093552996—dc23/eng/20250626
LC record available at https://lccn.loc.gov/2025004483
LC ebook record available at https://lccn.loc.gov/2025004484

This book is printed on acid-free paper, and its binding materials are chosen for strength and durability. We strive to use environmentally responsible suppliers and materials to the greatest extent possible in publishing our books.

The manufacturer's authorized representative in the EU for product safety is Mare Nostrum Group B.V., Mauritskade 21D, 1091 GC Amsterdam, The Netherlands.
Email: gpsr@mare-nostrum.co.uk.

Manufactured in the United States of America

10 9 8 7 6 5 4 3 2 1

Also available as an ebook

To my parents Eliezer (z"l) and Bruria,

may she be set apart for long life

CONTENTS

A NOTE ON TRANSLITERATION AND ORTHOGRAPHY

Yiddish can be quite challenging to transliterate. In one Russian Yiddish newspaper, the very word "Orthography" appears in four different spellings in the same article! While the transliteration of names, words, and phrases in Yiddish usually follows the guidelines of the YIVO Institute for Jewish Research, certain titles are spelled as they appear in the original texts, e.g., *Yidishes tageblat* rather than *Yidishes togblat*. As for names, they are spelled as they usually appear: Shmuel Charney (not Tsharney) and Abraham (not Avrom) Cahan.

Introduction

The usually noisy and talkative classroom became suddenly quiet. An awkward silence continued for a few moments as a question I had asked sank like a stone. Students in the class "Introduction to Modern Yiddish Culture" had just read a short segment from *Motl, the Cantor's Son* by the famed Yiddish author, Sholem Aleichem (Sholem Yankev Rabinovitsh). As Motl and his family arrive in New York, he sees a Black woman and a Black man on the subway, and describes them: "Crude creatures. Frightfully thick lips. Big white teeth and white fingernails."[1] I asked the students whether they thought it was a racist portrayal. After the initial silence, several students argued it was racist; most believed it was not, since it is written from the perspective of an eight- or nine-year-old child from Tsarist Russia who sees a Black person for the first time in his life. Still, numerous questions remained, as a quote that is supposedly from a child's standpoint was written by an adult author—does Motl say openly what Sholem Aleichem would not or could not utter? Was Motl's take meant to be a comedic device or convey something else? And more importantly, does this example reflect a wider phenomenon?

The initial astonishment at different physical features is merely one facet in the multilayered encounter between African Americans and Yiddish-speaking Jews. Just as Black Christians often envisioned ancient Israelites and the story of the Exodus before seeing a single Jew, on the Jewish side an encounter of sorts also happened long before most had ever seen a single Black woman or man.[2] This book offers a new cultural history which both critically revises a topic that has received considerable scholarly attention and uncovers a wide array of previously unexplored materials. It looks at how Yiddish culture—the press, theater, literature, and other realms, both in Eastern Europe and later in the United States through 1929—depicted Black Africans and African Americans, and what can we learn from these portrayals about the intricate ways in which an immigrant group integrated its own cultures into the American racial hierarchy and vocabulary.

There is a vast scholarship about the relations between various immigrant groups and African Americans. In the ethnic and racial mosaic of American society, Black-Jewish relations have been notable not only due to the plethora of books and essays written about them, but also due to the defensive or polemical character of many of them. The tribulations of the Civil Rights Movement, and the rise of Black Power and various expressions of anti-Jewish sentiment among Black militants, mostly from the 1960s on, added much to the polarization in the literature on those charged relations.[3] Nonetheless, within that scholarship, until recently, there has seemed to be a near consensus when examining the descriptions of Black people in late nineteenth- and early twentieth-century Yiddish culture. Most scholars have argued that the Yiddish press repeatedly condemned discrimination and prejudice against African Americans and highlighted the similarities between the situation of Jews in Eastern Europe and African Americans. News items and editorials applied terms like "pogrom" and "blood libel" when covering race riots and lynching, while the white assailants were often described as bloodthirsty pogromists. Therefore, most scholars have agreed that Yiddish culture "sensed that a special relationship existed between blacks and Jews"; that "Blacks seemed, in the eyes of Yiddish writers, [as] America's Jews"; and "Unlike most White Americans of the early twentieth century, they [Jews] did not seek to distance themselves from African Americans."[4] Those inaccurate and self-congratulatory generalizations were then often adopted by scholars and observers outside Jewish Studies and congealed into a prevailing conventional wisdom.[5]

The last two or three decades have witnessed significant reexaminations of the celebratory narrative, which have exposed a more complex and troubled encounter between Jews and African Americans. Scholars including Marc Dollinger, Jeffrey Melnick, and Michael Rogin have shown Jewish immigrants' and their offspring's pursuit of fully-fledged status as whites and how they absorbed, internalized, and expressed various aspects of American popular culture's racial attitudes.[6] Yet those studies have usually not fully explored the wider ambivalent and often contradictory approach to racial issues that was part of the culture of

Yiddish-speaking immigrant Jews. As this book shows, moreover, negative racial concepts appeared in Yiddish-language sources that were created in the Old World, long before most Jews had encountered an actual Black person or attempted to situate themselves in America's racial hierarchy.

Furthermore, the strong denunciation of white brutality and racism in the Yiddish press does not tell us much about the portrayal of Black women and men, which was much more ambiguous. There was a gap—at times, a scathing gap—between the *genuine* condemnation of lynching, violence against Black Americans, bigotry, and racial segregation on the one hand, and the ways in which Yiddish authors, newspapers, playwrights, actors, and theater managers represented Black persons on the other. Those sources frequently represented Black people in general, and African Americans in particular, as a mixture of exotic people *and* a reincarnation of East European Slavic peasants, the *poyerim/muzhikes* (peasants), with many of their accompanying perceived traits: volatility, looming violence, coarseness, and drunkenness, together with directness and simplicity. In addition, a socioeconomic reality in which Jewish businessowners catered to a Black clientele and lived in Black neighborhoods reinforced the resemblance, in Jewish eyes, between the Jewish economic role in relation to Old-World peasantry and their role vis-à-vis African Americans.[7]

Thus, Yiddish writers were able to tap into stereotypes known to their audience while satisfying their appetite for the bizarre and the intriguing. In these literary illustrations, Black women and men came across less as "America's Jews," and more as the New-World embodiment of East European peasantry. At the same time, apart from the Old-World reservoir of images, Yiddish writers reflected the prevalent social and racial concepts of early twentieth-century Europe and America, which had put the "Nordic" race at the helm of human progress, augmented by the common representations of Black characters in popular culture. Therefore, Yiddish writers were fascinated with the ways Black people looked, walked, talked, and behaved. They also did not balk at describing Black characters as cannibals, oversexed, prone to violence, childlike, or just happy-go-lucky people. Amid the rise of American xenophobia during World War I and the ensuing Red Scare, recurring attempts to close America's gates as waves of pogroms swept the former Russian Pale of Settlement, and increasing antisemitism in the 1920s, the search for political allies became ever more urgent. In this context, American Jews would gradually come to see African Americans as potential allies.[8] Yet any improvement in the attitudes of Jews toward Black Americans would be neither complete nor instant, and much ambivalence remained. Yiddish culture distilled and exhibited those contradictory approaches.

Whereas any periodization has its weaknesses, 1929 is a useful endpoint in considering how Yiddish culture portrayed Black people for several reasons. 1929 signaled a watershed not only because of the crash of the stock market and the onset of the Great Depression, but also because it marked a transformation in Black-Jewish relations. Prior to the 1930s, the question of antisemitism among Black Americans was hardly mentioned (despite several anti-Jewish utterances by Black nationalist Marcus Garvey[9]). After 1929, however, a more bifurcated pattern emerged. On the one hand, the 1930s saw more cooperation between African Americans and American Jews, most notably in radical and bohemian circles; the 1931 case of the Scottsboro Boys—nine Black men and teenagers who were falsely accused in Alabama of raping two white women—was widely covered in the Yiddish press as a symbol of injustice and became a cause célèbre, especially among Jewish communists. On the other hand, urban malaise, the rise of several antisemitic Black demagogues, the Harlem race riot of 1935, and the pressures of the Great Depression brought about new flashpoints that heightened Black-Jewish tensions and changed the terms and dynamics of these groups' interrelations.[10]

Moreover, the 1930s' economic woes were compounded by the drastic restriction of immigration following legislation in 1921 and 1924 which cut off the stream of Yiddish-speaking newcomers. The demographic shift toward a majority of American-born, native English-speaking Jews occurred against a backdrop of universities' quotas, "Christians only" employment advertisements, residential restrictions, social exclusion, and Henry Ford's anti-Jewish campaign. An intensified clamor for "100 percent Americanism" accelerated the move to English, as Yiddish book sales plunged, Yiddish newspapers' circulation decreased, and audiences at Yiddish theaters shrank. While pockets of Yiddish speakers certainly remained, in such an atmosphere, even a Yiddish accent was a source of embarrassment.[11]

Capturing the Hearts of Women and Children

Why Yiddish? What is its significance? For a millennium, Yiddish has been the lingua franca of a minority—Ashkenazi Jews—who lived in various countries and continents, often under crippling legal restrictions. By 1939, approximately 11 million Jews spoke Yiddish, comprising more than two-thirds of world Jewry. Since the High Middle Ages, Yiddish had been intimately interwoven into Jewish life and closely involved in the evolution of Jewish religious practices, customs, and folkways. In more recent times, Yiddish served as the vehicle for the proliferation of an array of movements such as Hasidism, socialism, and nationalism. As Jewish immigration to Western Europe, the Americas, the Land of Israel, Australia, and South Africa created new centers of Yiddish-speaking populations, Yiddish educational institutions, literature, theater, and press developed and achieved a high level of creativity and ingenuity. Even a prominent detractor of Yiddish, the Hebraist lexicographer, Eliezer Ben-Yehuda, had to admit (1910) that Yiddish, "in its *liveliness*, in its embedded *clownishness* . . . it captures the hearts, especially of the laypeople, of women and children."[12]

Until the closing years of the nineteenth century, Yiddish was indeed seen as the language of the common people, women and men alike. Traditional Jewish society featured semi-bilingualism, if not multilingualism, where Yiddish served as the spoken vernacular, while Hebrew (or rather *loshn koydesh*, a mixture of rabbinical Hebrew and Aramaic) was the language of prayer and sacred texts. In addition, some Jews spoke varying degrees of other languages (German, Polish, Ukrainian, Romanian, etc.).[13] For observant Jews, Yiddish lacked Hebrew's religious authority; for modernizing Jews of various ideological persuasions, Yiddish was an obstacle to integration and progress, a corrupt "jargon." Despite its lowly status and the fact that it was rarely the first language of choice for nineteenth-century Jewish writers, Yiddish's earthiness, playfulness, and humor had made it a mirror of Jewish life. At the same time, Yiddish culture was seldom insular and commonly open to diverse external influences. As historian Kenneth Moss has noted, for many Yiddish and Hebrew writers those languages functioned as a "permeable membrane," absorbing and processing idioms, terms, and imagery from outside sources. Thus, as we shall see, early twentieth-century Yiddish writers would readily use American racial terminology, whether referring to "worthless coon nonsense" or quoting the lyrics of a popular tune such as *Hesitation Blues*.[14]

Apart from its historical centrality in the life of Ashkenazi Jews and its cultural vitality, Yiddish is important for another reason. Whereas there were a few Yiddish-speaking African Americans (akin to Yiddish-speaking Gentiles, mostly peasants, in the Old World), Yiddish was an internal Jewish language. Jewish anxieties usually defined the limits of the discussion in texts that were accessible to non-Jews. Hence, Yiddish enabled a freer, sharper, and more nuanced discourse than other languages, and race was no exception. The same was true for the less popular (in those years) Hebrew: Since numerous Yiddish authors wrote also in Hebrew, this book looks at several relevant Hebrew works written by them, too. There is no Hebrew-Yiddish "language war" in this study.[15]

The significance of Yiddish culture as a case study is quite pertinent to the larger context of immigration history as well. This book shows how would-be immigrants had preconceived imagery of Black Africans prior to setting foot in the United States and seeing a single Black woman or man. Yiddish-speaking immigrants came from Eastern Europe, a part of the world that in the nineteenth century had virtually no Black population at all. However, press reports, pulp fiction, translation of travel tales from other languages, and pseudoscientific texts (and in the Jewish case also rabbinical literature) already conveyed European culture's classification of Black Africans as savage, brutal, and animal-like creatures. Parallel developments can be found among other immigrant groups who also hailed from areas that had practically no Black population.[16] Those themes are especially relevant to studying the dynamics of racism. Rather than treating racism as a binary, dichotomous concept, where individuals, groups, and cultures are deemed as either racist or not, this book presents a spectrum of attitudes and values, where one can be genuinely anti-racist, yet harbor racist judgments or imagery.

Between Kushim, Moors, Shvartse, ניגער (Niger) and נעגער (Neger)

Some of the following terms may upset contemporary readers. Yet twenty-first-century sensibilities should not prevent the necessary clarification of the historical terminology at hand and its meanings. One of the earliest terms for Black Africans was *Kushi* (Kushite, Kushim in plural), which the Hebrew Bible usually designated as someone from Kush—the area south of Egypt, encompassing roughly the territory of modern-day Sudan, at times also parts of Ethiopia and Southern Egypt. In and of itself, Kushite was a neutral name, unless put in an unfavorable context of far-flung, primitive people. In ancient Jewish sources, Kushite was sometimes applied to other dark-skinned people, such as Arabs. That term would be used also in Yiddish texts through the twentieth century, yet other terms exceeded it; as before, Kushite was not negative in and of itself, yet was occasionally put within a derogatory framework. The term "Ethiopian" for Black Africans in general was less common in Yiddish-language sources, apart from references to Ethiopian Jews that became more common in the Yiddish press by the turn of the twentieth century.[17]

In Eastern Europe, Yiddish sources also termed Black people *Narapim* and *Murinen/Murines* (Moors). Those names reflect the ambiguity and porous nature of such classification, as they refer not only to Black Africans, but also to Arabs. *Narap* is derived from "Arab" (*Arapy* in Russian), which can be translated as "Black Moors" or "Blackamoors." Both Yiddish lexicographers and linguists Aleksander Harkavy and Nakhum Stutchkov grouped together those words with other terms for Black people, although the latter put Moors and Narap in the same sub-category as "Mulatto." The salient element is that all those terms, especially in a society that had barely any firsthand contact with any Black person, evoked mostly imagined generalizations.[18] As for the ubiquitous term *Shvartse/Shvartser* (Black woman/man), several scholars have argued that it was used pejoratively among American Jews by the mid-twentieth century. That seems to be a later development; among Yiddish speakers, the term also denoted Jews with a dark skin complexion. Through the 1920s, Shvartse was usually used neutrally. Journalist and civil rights advocate, Harry Golden, who was born in Eastern Galicia and grew up on New York's East Side, recalled that when his father wrote for the socialist *Forverts* (Jewish Daily Forward) about the heavyweight prizefight between Black pugilist, Jack Johnson, and his white rival, Jim Jeffries (1910), he referred to Johnson as the "shvartzer," but "He meant no disrespect to Jack Johnson." Even if Golden's sympathy for the cause of racial equality affected his recollection of a much earlier period, it was certainly the circumstance that set the tone of how Shvartse was used.[19]

Two of the most common terms in the period under review were *Neger* (נעגער) and *Niger* (ניגער). Whereas in the early twentieth century the hateful term "nigger" had not yet reached the level of vileness as the ultimate racist offence it has acquired by the twenty-first century, it already served as a strong anti-Black slur. As the Noble Prize laureate in literature, Toni Morrison, commented, the second English word after "okay" that European immigrants uttered was often "nigger."[20] Yiddish-language sources used both the word Neger, which corresponds to the German *Neger*, or the English "Negro," and Niger, which is similar to the racial insult. In English, the term "Negro" was not considered offensive by either Blacks or whites in the timeframe covered here (through the 1920s). While the German "Neger" was more offensive than the English-language "Negro," it was also acceptable until the late twentieth century.[21]

An indication of the level of sensitivity and shame surrounding the use of the N-word (or "nun-word" in this case) involves Yiddish literary critic Shmuel Niger (pseudonym of Shmuel Charney). Many scholars have interpreted that pen name as a sign of Charney/Niger's alleged identification and solidarity with African Americans. The fact that the pseudonym of a single Yiddish intellectual—as important as Shmuel Niger is—has received such scholarly attention demonstrates those scholars' pressing need to prove the critic's anti-racist credentials.[22] The reality seems to be more prosaic. Writing in his diary in 1933, Niger recalled that shortly after his arrival in America (1919), sweatshop poet Morris Rosenfeld paid him a visit. The first question Rosenfeld posed to him was, "What name will I adopt here in the [new] country, since Niger sounds so bad." In that diary entry, Niger did not refer to the meaning of Niger, nor to the reason for changing his last name or any relation to Black people; he just commented on how bad Rosenfeld looked, and speculated that the poet had syphilis, which made him paranoid, megalomaniacal, and insane. Yet apparently, Niger heeded Rosenfeld's advice, as his letterhead in the 1920s featured the name "S. Niger" in Yiddish and "S. Charney" in English.[23]

To a certain extent, Yiddish sources used *Niger* and *Neger* interchangeably, since at times both spellings appeared in the same text, and even referred to the same person. Thus, the moderate and mild-tempered *Yidishe velt* (Jewish World), which was established in New York by cautious established Jews, had a frontpage headline in 1902 "14 shot by a Niger," while the subtitle read, "A murderous Neger besieged by 20 policemen." The *Forverts* had a 1912 front-page headline, "Niger beats to death an old woman," yet the news item featured the spelling "Neger" more than "Niger." When the *Forverts* eulogized in 1922 the death of the Black comedian Bert Williams, it still mostly used the spelling "Niger" when lamenting "the tragedy of many comedians, and especially of Niger actors who play on Broadway." The reason is that "the vulgar audience in America is used to watch on the stage only comic Nigers." The Orthodox daily *Morgen zhurnal* (Morning Journal) reported on the 1912 convention of the Republican Party, describing a "Niger delegate from Kentucky," but when quoting his statement, it mentioned "the Neger delegates."[24]

Nevertheless, the terms *Niger* and *Neger* were not completely interchangeable. Their usage exemplifies how absorbed Yiddish culture was in contemporary American racial imagery and expressions and the depth of that terminology's influence. It is noteworthy that in Eastern Europe, Yiddish writers and periodicals hardly used "Niger" and opted for "Neger" or "Shvartse." When searching the Historical Jewish Press website, the use of "Niger" in East European Yiddish periodicals, from the 1860s through 1929 is reserved to S. Niger's name, or to texts by American-based authors (Sholem Ash, Borekh Glazman) whose writings were published in Eastern Europe. In America, the use of *Niger* was often utilized for sensationalist, comic, or crime-related news items, while *Neger* was reserved for more serious discussions, such as the "Negro question" or the "Negro problem." Therefore, Yiddish newspapers featured headlines such as "A 19-year-old Niger shoots his young wife in cold blood," "A rabbi stabbed by a Niger," "Crazy Niger shoots 2 people," "Crazy Niger stabs 2 men," "A Niger stabs a white girl," "A Niger kisses also the white bride," or "A Niger bandit stabs three Jews." On the other hand, while there were several articles with the headline "The Niger question," a more common pattern was "the Neger question."[25]

The important question is whether Yiddish writers knew about and understood the difference between "Negro" and "Nigger," or remained oblivious to it. It would be quite difficult to determine to what extent the

Yiddish *readership* was aware of such a difference; in respect to Yiddish writers and intelligentsia, nonetheless, there is much evidence to demonstrate that they knew well what each term signified, and the sociocultural differences between them. As early as 1890, a Lower East Side Jew complained in a letter to a New York Hebrew periodical *Ha-pisgah* (The Summit) about Jews who frequented a local vaudeville showplace called Grand Museum. There they watched a regular skit that presented an anti-Jewish stereotype of a Jewish storeowner on Baxter Street, who "flatters the Negro customer," yet after the customer leaves, the Jew "pokes out his tongue and calls out after him 'Niger!'" In 1906, the daily *Varhayt* (Truth), established a year earlier by a pioneer of the Yiddish socialist press in America, Louis E. Miller (formerly Bandes), as an independent socialist paper, emphasized the dissimilarities between Jews in Russia and Black Southerners; it put "Niger" in quotes as an offensive term used by white Southerners. In 1909, the weekly *Yidishe bine* (Jewish Stage) reported on "Negroes" (Negers), who protested against the Broadway show *The Nigger* by Edward Sheldon. The report mentioned that "the play itself is just friendly toward the Negroes," but the protesters came out "against the title of the play, 'the Niger,' which is offensive to them."[26]

More telling is what the longtime editor of the *Forverts*, Abraham Cahan, a monumental figure in the Yiddish press and the Jewish labor movement, wrote in his notes when covering the Leo Frank trial in Atlanta (1914). Frank, a Jewish pencil factory supervisor, was arrested and found guilty of the murder of his employee, Mary Phagan, a teenage white girl; subsequently (August 1915) Frank was snatched from his prison cell and lynched by a white mob. As Cahan was analyzing the letters sent by the initial prime suspect, a Black janitor named Jim Conley, Cahan noted that Conley referred to a Black man as "a 'Negro,' a word used by intelligent people. The common Black man says 'Niger,' not 'Negro.'" In his serialized novel *Where Is Her Child?*, published by the *Forverts* in 1923, Yiddish playwright and poet, Zisl Kornblit, remarked parenthetically, "(In the South people always call the Black man 'Niger,' both to his face and behind his back. But when they want to flatter him a little, instead of 'Niger' they say 'the colored man,' or the 'colored race')."[27] The spelling ניגגער ("Nigger"), however, remained quite rare, and might suggest awareness of its offensiveness. Hence, in this book נעגער is transliterated as "Negro" and ניגער as "Niger" in order to stay as close as possible to the Yiddish source; like "Black," it is capitalized (unless it is in lower case in an English-language original) since it denotes a racial/ethnic group. While textual consistency would call to capitalize "white" as a racial/ethnic group as well, its usage by white supremacists has rendered this approach problematic. There is no perfect solution. Ironically, white nationalists, who capitalize "white," are also those who have limited its use (e.g., excluding "non-Aryans"), thus illustrating the difficulty in utilizing the capitalized term.[28]

"Popularity Among the Ignorant Masses, Especially Women"

In addition to the abovementioned apologetic or celebratory approach that is noticeable in the scholarship about Yiddish culture's portrayal of African Americans, there are two lacunas in the study of that culture in general that have limited the scope of inquiry. The first involves a cultural hierarchy that separated highbrow, "proper" culture and what was termed *shund* (trash/pulp/schlock). It is not coincidental that in his pioneering study, "The Negro in Our Literature" (1945), Yiddish poet and critic, Yitskhok Rontsh, did not include a single work of what was considered *shund*. Despite its immense popularity, critics and scholars have often treated such lowbrow culture as not worth exploring. As late as the 1990s, Yiddish poet and academic, Irena Klepfisz, has argued that mid-nineteenth-century Yiddish works were "still 'low brow,' as evidenced by their popularity among the ignorant masses, especially women." All those distinctions ignore the fact that often the same authors produced both high- and lowbrow works; and that accusing a personal or ideological rival of being a shundist was a common tactic to settle a score with them.[29]

More importantly, lowbrow works were probably the bulk of what was consumed by the Yiddish-speaking public both in Eastern Europe and in the United States. By the mid-nineteenth century, a growing number of Jewish men and women in Tsarist Russia and Habsburg-ruled Galicia were reading religious and quasi-religious writings, alongside secular Yiddish literature, whether (freely) adapted or original, sold by *pakntreger* (traveling booksellers), often in the form of chapbooks. By the 1890s, a transatlantic Yiddish book industry emerged, where American publishers increased their sales in Eastern Europe while printing houses from Lemberg (Lviv), Vilna (Vilnius), and Warsaw sent Yiddish books to American bookstores. The modernization and improved efficiency of the transatlantic book trade brought Yiddish prose to an ever-growing number of readers in various countries. The development of the Yiddish press and theater both in America and in Eastern Europe further contributed to the mass dissemination of images about a host of topics.[30]

For example, one of the world's most popular Yiddish writers, Shomer (nom de plume of Nokhem Meyer Shaykevitsh), was denounced by so many critics that his name became synonymous with shoddily-written, sentimentalized, and plagiarized literature. Sholem Aleichem even published (1888) a pamphlet titled "Shomer's Trial," a dramatized trial of Shomer for his alleged crimes against Yiddish, literature, and the Jewish people. Regardless of the debate over Shomer's literary transgressions, it is quite clear that together with his predecessor, Ayzik (Isaac) Meyer Dik, Shomer's works (over 250 novels, novellas, and plays) created a modern Yiddish-reading public. Numerous memoirs describe how beloved Shomer was, and how customers in bookstores used to drop in to ask whether there was something new by him. In fact, Shomer's huge success brought about a wave of imitators, whose book covers featured, in a tiny font "like the novels" and in huge letters "by Shomer."[31] As we will see, in his writings Shomer both referred to the supposed savagery of Africans and created the character of an evil, apelike Jewish woman who looks like "a Negress."

This book focuses on Yiddish literature, press, and theater that drew tens, if not hundreds of thousands of readers and viewers. That is one of the reasons why poetry is not included here. To be sure, American Yiddish poems, such as Sarah Barkan's *A 'prayz-fayt'* (A 'Prizefight'), Moyshe Leyb Halpern's *Salut* (Salute), H. Leyvik's *Negershes* (Negroly), Rose Nevadovska's *Tsu di shvartse froyen* (To the Black Women), Berish Vaynshteyn's *Lintshen* (Lynching), and Yehoash's (Shlomo Bloomgarten's) *Lintshen* (Lynching) were filled with poignantly graphic depictions of Black suffering and horror at racist violence, and brimmed with sympathy. In Leyvik's words, "But to you [African Americans] my face looks no less horrifying/ Than the appearance of every face in a lynching mob." Whereas in the past, critics such as Yitskhok Rontsh viewed those poems as reflecting compassion and the shared experience of Jews and Blacks, in recent years scholars including Merle L. Bachman, Amelia Glaser, and Jessica Kirzane have shown the contradictory character of those and many other poems: Alongside empathy and commiseration, those immigrant poets often viewed African Americans through a perspective of racial hierarchy and stereotypical traits while stressing their own whiteness.[32]

One of the often-quoted examples of identification with African Americans is the Whitmanesque epic poem, *Kentoki* (Kentucky), by Yisroel-Yankev Schwartz (1925), which follows three generations of a Jewish family in Lexington, Kentucky. Schwartz, who lived in Lexington for over a decade, described how newly arrived Jews, without speaking English, "understood—or more clearly said—smelled, felt, the naked essence of the unfamiliar Niger"; and "it was natural" that Black Kentuckians also sensed that the newcomers "were somehow closer people; belonging indeed to the white race, but a white race of another kind." Other depictions in the book-length poem, however, disclose Schwartz's preconceptions, writing about naked Black kids who "Jumped over fires, like young, wild, forest monkeys"; and Black adults' "childish laughter." As Avraham Novershtern has justly commented, Schwartz also displayed stereotypical Black men, who are victims of their own erotic desires and overpowering primal urges.[33]

Whereas the representation of Black women and men in Yiddish poetry has received more scholarly attention than other genres of Yiddish culture, poetry seems to have been the least popular among Yiddish speakers. Poets habitually bemoaned the fate of the marginalized Yiddish bard. Mani Leyb's (Mani Leyb Brahinski's) poem *To the Gentile Poet* illustrated the "very happy" non-Jewish poet where "The earth is yours"; in contrast, "And here I am, unneeded, a poet among Jews." As Irving Howe, Ruth R. Wisse, and Khone Shmeruk have perceptively determined, modernist Yiddish poetry was "mainly of the little magazine and for the elite audience." Poet Aren Rapaport privately mocked (1926) the few readers of Yiddish poetry, terming them "fools" who will never understand poetry.[34] This book looks at the wider field of Yiddish culture, and especially at its most popular works, which touched many more Jewish women and men—however silly, hackneyed, abysmal, or lewd critics believed those works to be.

A second lacuna in the study of Yiddish culture relates to a political and ideological bent. For many decades, modern Yiddish culture has been studied as mostly a domain of the Jewish left (whether socialists, anarchists, or communists), whereas others were largely disregarded. That focus brought about a surfeit of studies of Yiddish on the left;[35] only recently have scholars begun to look at Orthodox, nationalist, and other non-radical varieties of Yiddish culture.[36] Jewish radicals have their rightful place in this book, and at times they featured the most fascinating incongruities about race. But there is so much more to popular Yiddish culture than the Jewish left. Furthermore, more recently, especially in the United States, Yiddish has emerged in a new, subversive garb, a culture—as its current proponents often believe—that supposedly has always been imbued with progressive, feminist, queer, and anti-imperialist sensibilities. While such beliefs may seem endearing, they have only a tenuous connection, at best, to the historical development of Yiddish: a rich and varied culture which encompassed the religious, the secular, and a whole range between them, the radical and conservative, the assimilationist and Jewish nationalist, the racist and anti-racist (categories that were hardly mutually exclusive). The present hip, "alternative" renditions of Yiddish have created, in the words of Ruth R. Wisse, "a debased image of Yiddish" that amounts to a "caricature."[37]

There is another specifically American element at play. The celebrated Black author and critic Ralph Ellison wrote, "You cannot have an American experience without having a black experience" and "I recognize no American style . . . which does not bear the mark of the American Negro."[38] Apart from the first chapter, which examines the imagining of blackness in Eastern Europe, this book mainly focuses on Yiddish culture that was produced in the United States. There were certainly other significant centers of Yiddish culture in cities including Berlin, Buenos Aires, Johannesburg, London, Mexico City, Melbourne, Montevideo, Montreal, Paris, Tel Aviv, and Vienna, as well as in smaller cities. Nevertheless, in America, Yiddish culture not only reflected the centrality of race, but also profoundly exhibited—sometimes against its authors' own intentions—the concepts of the surrounding white society.

For a better understanding of those concepts, we need to look at the elusive nature of representation. As sociologist Stuart Hall has mentioned, the word "representation" is "an extremely slippery customer." Hall argued that the term "black" is "essentially a politically and culturally *constructed* category" which cannot be reduced to "a set of fixed transcultural or transcendental racial categories." Thus, statements that there were incidents of cannibalism in West and Central Africa in the nineteenth century, or that African Americans had a higher level of illiteracy than white Americans in the opening years of the twentieth century do not in and of themselves establish such fixed racial traits.[39] Conversely, employing adjectives such as "savage" or "ignorant" communicates a congealed set of static attributes and constructs a deterministic racial category. Some cultural historians feel uneasy with the term representation, since it might suggest that texts and imagery merely reflect or imitate social reality; hence, they prefer "construction," "invention," or "production" of knowledge, identity, etc. In our context, representation is neither a replication of reality nor is it completely invented. It corresponds with existing assumptions, judgments, values, and beliefs, which by themselves are part of social reality.[40]

As historian David Lowenthal has reminded us, "The past is a foreign country," yet one "with a booming tourist trade." Before reaching for our passports, we should consider to what extent the past is an utter terra incognita. A general rule of thumb could be that references which might seem highly offensive and racist to twenty-first-century readers did not seem as such a century ago, and depend on the context in which they were written or expressed. When Yiddish writers mentioned Black women and men's physical characteristics, those were not necessarily offensive; allusions to Black people's purported lower cultural or moral level were denigrating, but at times were not deterministic, i.e., they suggested that improvement was possible. The most demeaning type of discussion linked physical appearance and ingrained savagery, ignorance, criminality, etc. In the first volume of his *Historye fun di fereynigte shtaaten* (History of the United States, 1910), Abraham Cahan dealt with the Old World, including Africa. In his description of the skin color of the people who live in southern Senegal, Cahan mentioned that they are taller than those north of them and their color is "black as a beetle/insect [*zhuk*]." Whereas today this description would be considered tasteless if not racist, it was more of Cahan's style of folksy explanation which did not link physical features to level of morality or development. Yet in his portrayal of the Portuguese explorers' encounter in 1498 with native populations in East Africa, Cahan ascribed markers of savagery to the latter's behavior: The Portuguese sailors offered them marmalade cookies, and after overcoming their initial fear, the Africans devoured them. "When a Negro asked another Negro for a piece, he angrily pushed him away." An example of a linkage between Black physicality and criminality was published in Cahan's newspaper, the *Forverts*, which depicted (1921) a New Jersey Black man charged with murder, saying, "The murderer looks more like a gorilla (a monkey) than a human being."[41]

"Your Hair Is Straight, Thin, and Silky": The Absorption of Racial Similes

We should bear in mind several significant factors. In the period under review, Jews did not govern countries, did not have a military, and had no sovereignty on any piece of land. In a sense, when discussing the Old World, it seems an unfair line of inquiry to examine what East European Jews, a minority living on a meager diet and under legal restrictions, thought about another vilified population—Black Africans or African Americans—with whom they had no contact. But this elucidation is needed to refute many myths and assumptions about the alleged historical experience or religious heritage of Jews that ostensibly caused them to sympathize with African Americans. In the case of American Jews, whose self-image as champions of the Civil Rights Movement and racial justice has been a compelling and lasting component of their identity, a critical examination of the culture produced by their immigrant ancestors is warranted. Second, when reading some of the more disparaging mentions in Yiddish sources about Black women and men, it is worthwhile to remember that those sources often had much to say—and often worse—about others, including the Irish, immigrants from Slavic countries, and even the more esteemed "Yankees" (the common term for old-stock, Anglo-Saxon, Protestants in many Yiddish sources).[42]

No less importantly, the Yiddish intelligentsia—whether radical or conservative, assimilated or nationalist—frequently viewed the *Jewish* masses with derision, regarding them as backward yokels, vulgar and in dire need of enlightenment. At times, the critique sounded like something antisemites would gladly adopt. One of the classic Yiddish writers, Sholem Yankev Abramovitsh (known after one of his literary creations as Mendele Moykher Sforim—Mendele the Bookseller) wrote in his 1869 novel, *Fishke der krumer* (Fishke the Lame), about the Jewish poor: "Today it's really easy to tell a Jewish house from the outside. There's a little pile of garbage, a little puddle of sewage. . . . The smell alone tells you that a Jew lives here." Elsewhere he wrote about the simple shtetl dweller, whose coat is "stained with kugel grease, rice, eggyolk, pus, snot, etc.," but for the Jew, "The stain is an ornament."[43] Other members of the intelligentsia, though perhaps less extreme than Abramovitsh, still fashioned themselves as a Yiddish "Talented Tenth."[44] Yiddish authors often related paternalistically to their readers as a simpleminded mass that needed both cajoling and education. Well into the twentieth century, Yiddish journalists such as Yankev Magidov and Dovid Shub relayed such attitudes toward "Moyshe," the symbolic common reader. Despite this masculine name, women were often those associated with ignorance; Shub described the success of Yiddish advice columns "among the women and non-intelligent male readers."[45] If that critical and elitist inclination, combined with an acute awareness of group image, was aimed at the Jewish public, it was even more evident when characterizing Black people, who were already defamed in European and American culture.

Within the sources presented in this book, there is a relative paucity of female writers. The reason is not the lack of Yiddish-writing women, but rather the range of presumably feminine topics. As historians Ayelet Brinn, Nurit Orchan, Shmuel Werses, and others have shown, either due to decisions of male editors and publishers, or commercial preferences of the authors themselves, women writers tended to address subjects that had to do with the domestic or immediate sphere—love, matchmaking and marriage, family matters, education, charity, and communal needs.[46] Not only in Eastern Europe, where Black Africans were mostly an abstraction, but also in the United States, where African Americans were part of daily life, there was a relatively low number of women (apart from poets) who wrote about them before 1929. Still, the memoirs of Yiddish actress Bertha Kalish (Kalich) and African American singer and actress Ethel Waters, Yiddish columnist Sadie Vinokur's portrayal of a forlorn Black elevator man, the impression of poet Malka Li (Lee, born Malka Leopold) when seeing Black people for the first time, and the facial expressions of Yiddish actress Anna Apel as Aunt Jemima are all an important part of the story.

Moreover, the fairly low number of Yiddish female authors below notwithstanding, gender is integral to the framework under discussion. As scholars including George M. Fredrickson, Sander L. Gilman, Kali N. Gross, Beverly Guy-Sheftall, bell hooks, Jan Nederveen Pieterse, and others have thoroughly demonstrated, assumptions and generalizations about Black women and men's ostensive oversexed urges, innate violence, and parental inadequacy were deeply entrenched in European and American cultures. While Yiddish writers often argued for ideals of a common humanity, they, too, shared such assumptions. Gendered descriptions of Black bodies and Black masculinity and femininity appeared frequently in the Yiddish press, literature, and theater both in Eastern Europe and the United States.[47]

Recent decades have witnessed the proliferation of Whiteness Studies, where scholars have looked at the ways European immigrants came to identify as white while using whiteness as a vehicle for social integration and upward mobility. Yet critics have pointed out that many Whiteness Studies have neglected to account for the heterogeneous historic experience of different immigrant groups, as well as ignored religion as an important factor in intergroup relations in American history.[48] Another critic has argued that when looking at East European Jewish immigrants before the 1920s, many could hardly use basic English, and therefore absorbed only limited impressions of American racial imagery.[49]

This book is enriched by both Whiteness Studies and their critics. In Eastern Europe, categories of black/white were meaningless for Jews and their neighbors. In the United States, in the period leading up to 1929, Yiddish-speaking Jews' racial status was unstable and they—alongside other immigrants, such as Greeks and South Italians—constituted an "in-between" classification, neither Black nor white. Yet as Toni Morrison's quote above shows, you need not be white to absorb white racial attitudes toward Black Americans, nor do you need to understand English to absorb racial similes. As early as 1892, a feuilleton in a conservative Yiddish newspaper urged immigrant Jews in America to naturalize; it sardonically linked race to political rights: "The Niger may be born in America ten thousand times, but his skin is black, his hair woolly." In contrast, "Your [Jews] skin is white as was George Washington's, your hair is straight, thin, and silky as [Presidents] Cleveland's and Harrison's." Even with such sarcasm, the advantages of whiteness preceded English literacy.[50]

Some readers might object to confronting the very questions that are raised here. For several generations of American Jews, liberal/progressive causes became inseparable from their Jewish identity. Within that set of selective assumptions, support for the Civil Rights Movement and racial justice seemed to be an extension of Judaism's religious values and Jewish historical experience. Many rabbis and communal leaders backed such beliefs and constructed a powerful narrative of a Black-Jewish alliance. The disproportionate number of Jews active in the founding of the National Association for the Advancement of Colored People (NAACP) in 1909, cooperation between Jewish labor unions and their Black counterparts, and the amicability of Jewish and Black musicians and bohemians preceded the heyday of the Civil Rights Movement: voting registration volunteers Andrew Goodman and Michael Schwerner, who were murdered with their Black colleague, James Earl Chaney, in Mississippi (1964); the battered face of Rabbi Arthur J. Lelyveld of Cleveland, who was beaten in Mississippi (1964) by white segregationists; and Rabbis Abraham Joshua Heschel and Maurice Eisendrath marching with Martin Luther King, Jr., from Selma to Montgomery, Alabama (1965) comprise the highlights of that collaboration. As several historians have concluded, though, there was never a Black-Jewish alliance, but rather situational cooperation between Black and Jewish elites.[51]

The absence of an alliance does not convey the full complexity of this subject. Black leaders, ministers, and newspaper editors recurrently differentiated between Jews and white Americans, as well as between Jews and other immigrant groups. Biblical stories about the ancient Israelites' slavery and the exodus deeply affected African American commentators; as late as 1935, African American mathematician and essayist Kelly Miller remarked, "the Negro takes to the Hebrew Scripture as [a] duck to water." Prominent leader and educator Booker T. Washington, who expressed an anti-Jewish sentiment early in his career, praised (1899) Jews' "unity, pride, and love of race" and called fellow Black Americans "to imitate the Jew in these matters." Reverend T. Jefferson Goodall of Savannah's First African Baptist Church hailed (1915) Jews, since they live according to the "laws of health and nature. . . . They furnish a fitting example for life along these lines." On the other hand, viewing Jews as avaricious businessmen and those who murdered Jesus was also common. As acclaimed writer Richard Wright reminisced, Black Americans hated Jews "not because they exploited us, but because we had been taught at home and in Sunday school that Jews were 'Christ Killers.'" Growing up in West Helena, Arkansas, Wright remembered chanting with other children, "Bloody Christ Killers/Never trust a Jew/Bloody

Christ Killers/What won't a Jew do?" The distinction between Jews and Gentile whites did not always carry with it positive tones.[52]

On their end, white supremacists also sensed there might be a special connection between Blacks and Jews. Whether because they saw Jews as racial mongrels, subversive radicals, callous financiers, or simply resolved to undermine Christian civilization, white bigots singled out Jews not just as generic "Negro lovers," but as the brains and money behind the Civil Rights Movement or any challenge to the existing racial status quo. In 1868, Ku Klux Klan riders murdered S. A. Bierfield, a Russian-born young Jew who ran a dry-goods store in Franklin, Tennessee, for socializing with local Black men and allegedly selling them ammunition. In 1930, a Miami Jewish tailor by the name of David Weinberg was tarred and feathered and thrown injured from a car for being a communist and "associating with Negroes." Among Henry Ford's antisemitic fulminations was his newspaper's charge that jazz was "Yiddish moron music." That accusation was embodied in the Nazi "Degenerate Music" exhibition (1938), whose catalog's title page featured a derisively-shaped Black musician, playing the saxophone and wearing a Star of David on his lapel. In a similar vein, Southern white segregationists referred to racial integration, in the words of a South Carolinian Citizens' Council member (1956) as "part of an international communist plot made and being executed by the Jews."[53]

When it came to Yiddish (sans "Moron") music, several Black performers argued that they were drawn to Yiddish songs since they reminded them of Black spirituals. Louis Armstrong, Cab Calloway, Duke Ellington, Ella Fitzgerald, Paul Robeson, Ethel Waters, and many more performed Yiddish songs before diverse audiences. The song "Eli, Eli" received much attention—it first appeared in a Yiddish operetta in 1896, with lyrics by the star of the Yiddish stage, Boris Tomashevsky (Thomashefsky), and music by Jacob Sandler. This mournful Yiddish song would become popular with African American performers, as it begins with a verse from Psalms 22:2 ("My God, my God, why have you abandoned me"), which was also Christ's last words in the New Testament's gospels of Mark and Matthew. Poet Maya Angelou remembered, "A Black singer had recorded 'Eli Eli' and I listened to the song carefully. The beautiful high melodies and the low moaning sounded very close to the hymns of my youth." Angelou pointed out that for centuries, "Black American slaves had seen the parallels between their oppression and that of the Jews in Biblical times." That song was included in the all-Black Broadway show *Rhapsody in Black* (1931); by that decade, Black musicians were using Yiddish words as a form of "jive," for those "in the know."[54]

And here is the rub. Even the cultural harvest of East European Jewish immigrants, a group that arguably displayed the highest level of sympathy with Black Americans—a sympathy for which it was singled out—had shown the systemic and enduring effects of European and American racism. That pattern is relevant to the controversy over critical race theory. The last years have seen a reawakened dispute over critical race theory, its definition, and teaching in public schools. The term itself became a rallying cry where opposing sides clashed over a host of public policy issues revolving around the implementation, meaning, and social effects of that theory. This book provides historical and cultural context to that significant debate via a case study. Regardless of whether one agrees or not with the legal and political agenda of some advocates of critical race theory, the historical weight of the imagery of Black women and men must be reckoned with (see figure I.1).[55]

Figure I.1. The historical weight of imagery—Members of Brooklyn's Young Men's Hebrew Association (YMHA), 1929, Call # I-337.B10.F012.0126. Photo Courtesy of the American Jewish Historical Society.

The following chapters proceed thematically and to some extent geographically. The first chapter deals with Eastern Europe. Although most of them would never see a Black person in real life (unless they immigrated to America), East European Jews had already acquired some level of information—however skewed or incoherent—that served as a basis for imagining Black persons. Focusing mostly on the nineteenth century, this chapter looks at a wide range of materials, including rabbinic exegesis, pious advice, travel narratives (either original or adapted from other languages), folklore, reports of scientific explorations, pulp literature, press reports, political rhetoric, and educational materials. Whereas those sources were far from monolithic, they ascribed to Black Africans characteristics of savagery, primitiveness, less-than-human nature, cowardice, heightened or depraved sexuality, and absence of familial feelings.

The second chapter provides a historical background of the actual interactions between African Americans and Jewish immigrants. Once Yiddish-speaking Jews arrived in the United States, Black women and men were no longer an abstraction; now they were clients, neighbors (at certain locations), and at any rate an integral part in the mosaic of American society. After delineating recollections of seeing a Black person for the first time, the chapter focuses on the multi-layered encounter of Yiddish-speaking Jews with African Americans, where economic realities reinforced the images of Black Americans as America's reincarnation of East European peasants. The chapter also examines residential patterns and labor issues. The coalescence of Old-World attitudes toward the peasantry and white American modes of relating to African Americans brought about a combination of empathy and distance.

The following chapter is dedicated to the American Yiddish press's attitudes toward Black people and its conflicting trends. The violence and discrimination against America's Black population deeply upset Yiddish writers and editorial staff and forced them to consider whether Jews would be next to bear the brunt of prejudice. Nonetheless, the Yiddish press communicated—frequently by the same writers who fiercely attacked white racism—the whole array of traits ascribed to Black people (not only to African Americans) at the time: Alleged criminality and depravity, violent tendencies, alcoholism, volatility, ignorance, backwardness, and childlike character. Representations were not limited to editorials and news items: Feuilletons, jokes, cartoons, short literary sketches, and advertisements are no less important in the final analysis.

The fourth chapter looks at the performance of race on the Yiddish stage, first in Eastern Europe, then in the United States. Even if the Yiddish stage in America was not as extreme as its English-language counterpart in performing live racial caricatures, popular Yiddish shows did not shy away from parading stereotypical Black characters, who were dull-witted, clownish, savage, or animal-like. There was undoubtedly a contextual difference between showing a Black character in Bucharest or Krakow and performing race in New York or Chicago. Yet in both cases, Yiddish playwrights, directors, managers, and actors utilized the existing conventions of European and American theaters when displaying Black individuals.

Finally, the fifth chapter illustrates the growing nuance in the depiction of Black characters and increased sympathy for them in the critically respectable Yiddish fiction of the 1920s in comparison with the widely circulated pulp literature of the 1890s and 1900s. As in other branches of Yiddish culture, however, the ambivalence did not vanish, as certain literary conventions about alleged Black behavioral traits, such as being childlike, found their way into writings that sought to humanize African Americans. The contrast between many authors' principled denunciation of racism and the often-disparaging esthetical depiction of Black characters was a hallmark of many of the works under review. The first half of this chapter analyzes the writings of lowbrow writers such as Avner Tanenboym, whose adaptations into Yiddish of Jules Verne's *Voyages extraordinaires* proved to be bestsellers both in Europe and America. The second half concentrates on more critically acclaimed authors such as Sholem Ash (Asch), Borekh Glazman, and Yoysef Opatoshu.

Each of those chapters could have been developed into a book-length study in its own right. I have chosen to offer a comprehensive new history of this topic and assembled ample evidence to support my conclusions. Hopefully, this book will assist further research that will expand our understanding and suggest a paradigmatic shift.

1

"Mothers Sell Their Little Children"

Imagining Blackness in Eastern Europe

In the spring of 1871, the first sustained Yiddish newspaper in Tsarist Russia, the weekly *Kol mevaser* (Heralding Voice, 1862–1873), published a serialized story titled, "The Negro Trade or the Slaves' Ship." Supposedly translated from the German by one Abraham Shpiegelthaler of Nikolayev (in modern-day Ukraine), the narrative described how hundreds of African women, men, and children were lying tied up near the shoreline in Zanzibar, where those "unfortunate creatures . . . mothers and daughters, fathers and sons" were crying and lamenting their misfortune. While the writer sympathized with the suffering of the captured Africans and their desperate revolt, he also remarked, "the greatest pain [for the enslaved] to bear is to be quiet. . . . The Negro is afraid to be silent: when he is alone, he talks to himself . . . he would rather die ten times than not talk for an hour."[1]

Mostly from the mid-twentieth century on, a long line of Jewish leaders, rabbis, thinkers, and scholars have argued that Jewish identification and sympathy with African Americans derived from the enduring tenets of Judaism that supposedly emphasized social justice, or from the Jewish historical experience as a marginalized minority, or from a combination of the two. The ancient Israelites' bondage in Egypt and their exodus served as a powerful symbol that amalgamated religious and historical elements. It was not only communal leaders or rabbis who invoked what they saw as essential Judaic doctrines and the common historical experience of Blacks and Jews as oppressed minorities: One historian has claimed that "the historic roots of Jewish culture" were at the root of Jewish "involvement with blacks," whereas another has maintained that Jews identify "with people more marginalized than themselves." Much has been written about the Judaic values of *tzedakah* (charity) and *tikkun olam* (repairing the world), and the resulting

Jewish attitudes of kinship with Black Americans due to suffering and shared experience.[2] To what extent can we identify these themes in nineteenth-century East European Yiddish culture's portrayal of Black people, a population that scarcely existed in that region, with which Yiddish-speaking Jews had virtually no contact? Did Yiddish-language sources exhibit such affinity or view the situation of Jews as analogous to that of Black people?[3]

Several pertinent facts about Yiddish writers and readers should be kept in mind. Yiddish texts circulated in a Jewish society bedeviled by grinding poverty, economic and residential restrictions, and the internal oligarchy of the *Kehile* (the legally mandated Jewish community with its administration, taxes, and courts). Most Jews in Tsarist Russia and Habsburg Galicia lived on a meager diet, often based on potatoes, buckwheat, and bread, while their communities were repeatedly plagued by epidemics and disease.[4] Under such living conditions, the situation of other maligned populations—Black Africans and African Americans—with whom they had no contact was probably the least of their concerns. Still, an examination is warranted to dispel any myths and exaggerations about purported Jewish religious or historical heritage that caused Jews to sympathize with African Americans.

As the opening example demonstrates, many references to Black Africans in Yiddish were adapted, often quite freely, from other languages. Yiddish-language texts that depicted Black persons fall into three broad categories. The first consists of translations of Talmudic, medieval, and early modern rabbinic literature, written originally in Hebrew, Aramaic, and Judeo-Arabic. Though not religious per se, the tales of medieval Jewish travelers, such as Benjamin of Tudela, belong to this category as well. A second category is made up of European and American literature, adapted—with varying degrees of accuracy or proper attribution—usually from the German or Russian, although the original texts might have been in English or French. Those adaptations into Yiddish were hardly translations but rather reworkings that added and removed materials, Judaized the original characters and setting, and changed the plotlines. Finally, there were original secular writings in Yiddish, whether fiction or nonfiction. At the same time, the distinctions between religious and worldly and even between fiction and nonfiction were not always clear-cut.[5]

When looking at the representations of Black Africans and African Americans in Yiddish culture in nineteenth-century Eastern Europe, with significant precursors beforehand, the idiom *Vi es kristlt zikh azoy yidlt zikh* (As the Christians do, so do the Jews) is suitable. Concepts from the surrounding society, transmitted in Yiddish, continually pervaded Jewish culture, bringing with them whatever was in vogue at the time, from religious discourses, travel literature, folklore, anti-slavery writings through works of scientific racial determinism. Whereas all those influential sources were barely monolithic and at times contradictory, they included certain threads that would repeatedly appear in the portrayal of Black people. Finally, the dissemination of those texts shows that East European Jews who immigrated to America and elsewhere were not a blank slate about dark-skinned people. Several American Jewish memoirists mentioned that in the Old World they read about Black folks and saw pictures in books and newspapers.[6] While most of them would not see a Black person in real life before their arrival in America, they already acquired certain information—however biased—that served as a basis for imagining Black people.

Rabbinic Musings

When considering what attracted the Yiddish reader, the assertion of the prosecutor in Sholem Aleichem's denunciation of Shomer, *Shomer's Trial* (1888), rings true: "People are always fond of hearing a tall tale. . . . On the Sabbath day after the *tsholent,* [a popular stew for the Sabbath] when one can cast aside momentarily the burden of worrying about a living, when it is possible to forget that there are such things as a shop or a store to run, a broker to whom one owes money . . . at that moment women, teenage boys and young girls gather round to hear" such tales.[7] In addition to such tales, the sanctity assigned to biblical, Talmudic, and later rabbinic texts in traditional Jewish societies assured that they would be continually recycled and cited. A Jew's ability to quote a proverb in its original Hebrew/Aramaic both showed one's erudition and reaffirmed the high place of the proverb in the hierarchy of Jewish knowledge. Sholem Aleichem personified and parodied that phenomenon in his character Tevye the Dairyman, a simple country Jew, with his frequent quotes (accurate and mistaken alike) from Jewish sources.[8]

Hence the handful of biblical verses that deal explicitly with either Black Africans or people with a darker skin color have received abundant interpretations and commentary—e.g., the mythological "Curse of Ham" (Genesis 9:18–27), in which Ham was the one who saw his father, Noah, naked and drunk, or, according to Talmudic sources, engaged in sex in the ark, yet Noah's curse was actually aimed at Canaan, the non-Black son of Ham. Other examples include Miriam and Aaron speaking against their sibling, Moses, for marrying a Kushite woman (Numbers 12:1), and verses such as "Can the Kushite change his skin?" (Jeremiah 13:23), "Are you not like the Kushites to me, O Israelites?" (Amos 9:7), and "I am black but comely. . . . Don't stare at me because I'm swarthy" (Song of Songs 1:5–6). Until fairly recently, those verses were usually construed as conveying a negative meaning. Observers and scholars alike saw the "Curse of Ham" as a biblical justification for the enslavement of Black Africans, viewed Jeremiah as equating blackness and sin, and believed, in the words of bible scholar William R. Harper, that Amos was denigrating the Israelites by likening them to "the far distant, uncivilized, and despised black race of the Ethiopians." As for the maiden who sang to the daughters of Jerusalem in *Song of Songs*, whereas that segment is not about Black Africans, it imparted ancient Israelites' standards of feminine beauty regarding skin color. In recent decades, however, scholars have offered more nuanced ways of understanding those and other verses: They showed that the "Curse of Ham" includes no linkage of Black Africans with slavery, and that the negative readings of some of those verses reveal more about the context of the commentators than about racial attitudes in antiquity.[9] Our main interest is not in what are the accurate readings of those verses, but rather the themes and patterns that were absorbed and transmitted in Yiddish texts.

As historian David M. Goldenberg has justly pointed out, it is absurd that scholars have "ransacked" ancient Jewish texts in order "to find racist sentiment," while much better places to explore such sentiments are in Christian and Muslim societies that had well-established systems of enslaving Black Africans. If anything, the attitudes of those societies deeply permeated and affected the Jewish minorities residing among them.[10] Medieval Jewish luminaries who lived under Muslim rule, such as Yehuda Halevi and Maimonides, wrote in different places—Halevi in Spain of the early to mid-twelfth century and Maimonides in Egypt of the late twelfth century—and held different theological perspectives. Yet both wrote about Black people as having inferior mental capacities and being less than fully human, or in Maimonides's words, "lower than the rank of a human but higher than the rank of apes." In this categorization, it must be said that Maimonides referred to all people who live in extreme climate regions, south and north, and included also "Turks." At any rate, those philosophical treatises were hardly comprehensible to most readers: As Yiddish satirist Aren-Dovid Ogez (Ogus) noted in his abridged and redacted rendering into Yiddish of Maimonides's *Guide to the Perplexed*, the book "is not accessible for simple people, and even for Talmudists it is difficult to study and thoroughly understand it."[11]

Much more accessible to traditional East European Jews were the multi-volume editions of the Hebrew Bible called *Mikra'ot gedolot* (Great Scriptures/Anthologies), which first appeared in the early sixteenth century and include Aramaic translations and biblical commentaries by prominent medieval rabbis. That rabbinic Bible came out in dozens of editions and was highly authoritative among Ashkenazi rabbis and Talmudists who pondered endlessly over it.[12] In the commentary for the verse, "Are you not like the Kushites to me, O Israelites?" (Amos 9:7), readers encountered the claim by twelfth-century Rabbi Eliezer of Beaugency (Northern France), "After all, when you sin against me, you are to me like the Kushites, the lowest of all nations." An even more notable Bible commentator and Hebrew grammarian, David Kimchi (RaDaK), who lived in Southern France the late twelfth and early thirteenth centuries, linked Black people and slavery: He interpreted the verse that the Israelites would be "like Kushites, who are slaves . . . as they are sold as slaves—so should you [Israelites] be slaves." Other rabbis, such as the towering rabbinical authority of Ashkenazi Jewry, eleventh-century Rashi (Rabbi Shlomo Yitzchaki), as well as his contemporary, Rabbi Joseph Kara (both lived in modern-day France), connected "I am black but comely" (Song of Songs 1:5–6) and ugliness. Rashi believed that the woman's husband left her because she became too suntanned and therefore unattractive, while Kara asked, "if she is Black, how can she be comely?," answering it, "Even though I'm Black—I'm comely, since I can adorn and spruce myself up."[13]

Apart from Black individuals' alleged inferiority and unsightliness, it was another odious reference—probably a misquote—in rabbinical literature which made its way into the most popular Yiddish book ever published, the *Tsene-rene* (Come Out and See). This popular anthology of stories and commentaries on the Bible, organized according to the weekly Torah readings in the synagogue, appeared in more than two hundred editions since the early seventeenth century. Though widely known as the "women's Bible," the author, Yankev ben Yitskhok Ashkenazi of Janów (Poland), aimed the book at the majority of Jews, women and men alike, who could read little Hebrew.[14] In many editions of *Tsene-rene*, the *Haftore* (public readings in the synagogue from the biblical prophetic books, which follow the Torah reading every Sabbath and Jewish holidays) that relates to the verse from Amos contained a view ascribed to the prominent twelfth-century Jewish philosopher and Bible commentator, Abraham ibn Ezra. Ibn Ezra quoted, without necessarily agreeing with, a tenth-century Karaite commentator, Japheth ben Eli, who supposedly argued, "Kushite women are wanton [*hefker*] and nobody knows his father." Whereas the *Mikra'ot* acknowledged that ibn Ezra quoted ben Eli—a Karaite, and therefore an unauthoritative source—*Tsene-rene* differed in two important respects: It quoted the above sentence as if ibn Ezra himself said it, and added that Black women were "free for adultery/prostitution [*znus*]." As early as 1711, an Amsterdam edition of *Tsene-rene* included that sentence, and subsequent editions, such as the ones published in Vilna and Grodno (1827), and Warsaw (1849 and 1859), comprised either an identical or nearly identical quote. Later editions, such as those printed in Vilna (1865 and 1895) did not include that reference, yet the one that came out in Lublin in 1910 still contained it.[15]

The significance of such characterization lies not only in the immense popularity of *Tsene-rene*, but also in its canonical status and continued reading and recitation. It is unclear whether the removal of the derogatory quote was linked to the emancipation of the serfs in Russia (1861) or derived from heightened awareness about the horrors of slavery and the spread of abolitionist literature among *maskilim*, i.e., Jewish proponents of the *Haskalah* (Jewish enlightenment) by the early nineteenth century, if not earlier. Yet even the *Tsene-rene* editions that omitted the sentence about Black women's ostensible promiscuity repeatedly included the myth that explains not only black skin but also the related agony of all Black people as a result of Noah's curse on Ham's descendants. In the text that relates to the Noah weekly Torah portion, *Tsene-rene* editions from 1865, 1895, and 1910, repeated, "Noah said to Ham, 'your children will be darkened [*farfinstert*, which also means "embittered"] and blackened [*farshvartst*, also "shamed/disgraced"] those are the Kushites, the Narapin, who came out of Ham due to the curse."[16]

Regarding Miriam and Aaron speaking against Moses for marrying a Kushite woman (Numbers 12:1), nineteenth-century *Tsene-rene* editions reveal the strangeness of black skin to Ashkenazi Jews. Rashi interpreted the verse by concluding the woman was called Kushite "as a man calls his beautiful son 'Kushi' to ward off the evil eye," i.e., using the opposite term. Different editions of *Tsene-rene*, that were published in Vilna and Grodno (1827), Zhitomir/Zhytomyr (1859), Lemberg (1865), Vilna (1865 and 1895), and Warsaw (1890) all reproduced Rashi's explanation, but with one notable addition. Their text reads, "Because he [Moses] took a beautiful wife who is beautifully shaped and beautiful in good deeds . . . the verse says Kushite as you would say gypsy about a beautiful child in order not to give him the evil eye." Adding "gypsy" served as an elucidative measure for Yiddish readers, for whom the looks of a Black person was an abstraction; that term provided a negative benchmark both in the esthetic and sociocultural sense.[17]

Unfavorable representations of Black people appeared in other Yiddish religious texts, which were constantly reprinted and disseminated. Perhaps the first iconographic portrayal of Black people in modern Jewish culture appeared in the illustrated Venetian *Haggadah* (1609), which was simultaneously printed in Judeo-Italian, Judeo-Spanish, and Judeo-German. The page that begins with "Pour out Thy wrath upon the nations that know Thou not" shows both white and Black men, presumably Pharaoh's sorcerers, engaging in idolatry and magic; yet only on the side of the turbaned Black men there are also little Black children, who represent demons, dancing around the fire. Though all the characters under the main text are idolators, the Black ones are set apart by the dancing children/demons and the exotic clothing of the Black elders.[18]

More widely spread in Central and Eastern Europe was a collection of more than 250 pious tales called the *Mayse bukh* (Tales Book), which first appeared in 1602, and came out in dozens of editions through the early twentieth century. Just like *Tsene-rene*, it was meant to provide access to revered Jewish texts—in this case mostly Talmudic and later rabbinic sources—for the majority of Ashkenazi Jews, who could not read Hebrew or Aramaic. While anchored in Jewish traditions, the stories also reflected the influence of European folk literature with both its didactic and entertaining themes. Though it does not refer to Black Africans, at least one tale mentions blackness as an affliction or blemish. When one rabbi, Elazar Ben Shimon, meets "a large, Black man," he offends him, saying "tell me you despicable man, are all the people in your town as black as you?" The Black man answers, "I don't know, but go to the master who made me and ask him why you have made such a black contemptible tool." The rabbi then recognizes his wrongdoing, begs the Black man for forgiveness, but the latter refuses and reiterates his reply. The rabbi learns from his mistake, preaches to others not to do it, and the tale ends with Rashi's interpretation that the Black man was the prophet Elijah, whose task was to teach Elazar not to be arrogant. Whereas the tale is meant to elucidate a Talmudic warning against haughtiness even by those who master the Torah, it treats blackness as the ultimate sign of inferiority: Rabbi Elazar undergoes a test, which he initially fails, when encountering what he deems to be the lowest form of humanity. Moreover, the Black man reaffirms his lowly status and repeats thrice his question why God has made him so black and therefore despicable.[19]

"Strange and Savage Creatures": Travel Narratives

Though not religiously authoritative texts, the accounts of medieval Jewish travelers such as Eldad ha-Dani (ninth century) and Benjamin of Tudela (twelfth century) spread across Ashkenazi Jewry, where they sparked much interest. They depicted exotic, far-flung Jewish communities and the Ten Lost Tribes of Israel, who live beyond the legendary River Sambatyon, which supposedly does not flow on the Sabbath. Eldad recounted how he was captured by "tall Black Kushites, with out any clothing on them, because they are like beasts and eat human beings." Those Africans slaughter and devour Eldad's Jewish fellow traveler, who is "fat," but find Eldad to be too emaciated, and subsequently fail to fatten him enough. Eldad's tales circulated for centuries among Yiddish-speaking Jews and became a staple of folkloristic discussions. In his satirical novel, *Travels of Benjamin the Third* (1878), Mendele Moykher Sforim acerbically portrayed the shtetl's Jewish backbenchers, paupers, and idlers, and their fierce debates behind the oven of the house of study. There "they mixed in the regular chat about the ten tribes, how happily they live in those faraway places, with great glory, wealth and honor; naturally Eldad Ha-Dani was also mentioned with that." The novel's main character, Benjamin, becomes absorbed with such books that "open his eyes" to the world's "strange and savage creatures."[20]

Where Eldad's imagery conjured "strange and savage creatures" with their cannibalism, Benjamin of Tudela also characterized *some* Black Africans ("Bnei Kush"), who lived south of Egypt, as beasts, yet not cannibals but rather grass eaters: "Some of them are like beasts in all their ways, eating grass on the bank of the Pishon [probably the Nile River or one of its tributaries] and in the fields they go about naked and they have no intelligence like other people. They lie with their sisters and whoever they find." Although he indirectly mentioned that there are other Black Africans, Benjamin's description focused on the savage ones. He combined various traits that other authors mentioned above, such as animal-like nature, lack of fully human capacities, and sexual lust that recognizes no family relations or incestual taboos.[21]

Benjamin's *Travels* became part of the Jewish literary canon and was translated into Yiddish in Amsterdam in 1691. The book spread across Ashkenazi Jewry both in its Hebrew original and Yiddish rendition, and similarly to Eldad ha-Dani's stories, it sparked the imagination of Jewish women and men. By the mid-nineteenth century, Benjamin's tales were so famous among East European Jews that a Romanian-born Jew, Israel Joseph Benjamin, self-importantly fashioned himself Benjamin II, and like his medieval predecessor he set out in a search for the remnants of the tribes of Israel. Between 1859 and 1862, Benjamin traveled across the United States, publishing his impressions in a German-language book, *Drei Jahre in Amerika* (Three Years in America, 1862). Benjamin II was surprised when, in Aspinwall (modern-day Colón, Panama), "a Black man greeted me as a [fellow] Jew"; after learning that the man was from Jamaica and there is an entire Black Jewish community there, Benjamin concluded, "it is very likely that they are descendants of slaves who converted to Judaism."[22]

Though he traveled across a country on the eve of a civil war, Benjamin II had little to say about the sectional rift. Still, he praised the Antebellum South for what he saw as the region's better treatment of Jews, brushing aside the peculiar institution of slavery. Benjamin enthusiastically reported that Southern states "for natural reasons, surpassed by much in their liberality the Northern states" and "it was only the South which sent Jews to the Senate." The reason for Southern "liberality," according to him, was both racial and class-based: "The white man feels himself united with, and more intimate with, other whites—as opposed to the Negroes. Since the Israelite there does not perform the lower kinds of work that the Negro does, he was quickly absorbed among the upper classes." Benjamin's stories circled in Eastern Europe through German-reading maskilim, to the extent that by the 1870s, Mendele Moykher Sforim could rely on his readers' knowledge of the earlier two travelers to create a satirical genealogy based on the Benjamins. That is merely one indication of the wide diffusion of imagery relating to Black people among nineteenth-century Yiddish-reading Jews.[23]

Alongside religious and quasi-religious writings, Black characters appeared in secular Yiddish literature, both in (often free) adaptation and in original works. As with the religious texts, traveling booksellers distributed that literature, often in the form of chapbooks. Books such as *A Thousand and One Nights* and *Tsenture venture* (the Yiddish title given to the *Adventures of Sinbad the Sailor*, which is a part of *A Thousand and One Nights*) were in such high demand that they became a household item among traditional Jews who did not view it as a transgression. Growing up in Neshwies (Niasviž) in Byelorussia in the mid-nineteenth century, one of the world's most popular Yiddish writers, Shomer, recalled finding *A Thousand and One Nights* "in Jewish Ashkenazi language" (Yiddish) on his mother's bookshelf. The young boy read the book in hiding for fear that his mother or melamed would catch him, yet the mother read the book out loud to the family.[24]

As several scholars have shown, in those tales, Black characters serve largely as negative stereotypes, as slaves with depraved sexual potency. Short-story writer and champion of Yiddish cultural renaissance, Hersh Dovid Nomberg, translated *A Thousand and One Nights* in the early 1900s; as in the original, the Yiddish version abounds with Black slaves who commit adultery with white women. In the story about the petrified prince, the reader encounters a Black slave, who is in "a miserable state" and "licks the sand off the floor" with "his lips, where the upper one is hanging down over the lower lip." He is angry and impatient with the princess who has an affair with him; "The [other] Black men were here with their lovers and drank," but as she was late, "I had no desire to drink." He tells her, "you're telling lies, hussy!" and threatens her, "as true it is that Blacks are head and shoulders above whites," he would leave her if she is ever late again.[25]

Within the corpus of translated secular texts which became extremely popular among nineteenth-century Yiddish readers, Joachim Heinrich Campe's adventure book, *Die Entdeckung von Amerika* (The Discovery of America, 1782) took a central place. Yiddish lexicographer and historian Zalmen Reyzin illustrated how that book was closely linked to the beginning of the Haskalah literature in both Hebrew and Yiddish. Indeed, a leading figure in the Haskalah movement in Russia and a prolific recorder of Jewish life, Avrom Ber Gotlober, claimed that when he grew up (1820s), the book became so popular that "almost all the Jews, even the most pious, read it" and "needless to say the women": They closed their *Tsene-rene* and other religious books "and read only Columbus" (Gotlober called Campe's book by the title of one of its Yiddish adaptations). Gotlober recalled that his imagination carried him with Columbus, and he "was amazed by the savage people in America." Campe's book exemplifies the duality in many late eighteenth-century philosophers and intellectuals' calls against slavery in the name of freedom, equality, and humanity: The objection to the enslavement of non-European people was often a fashionable intellectual convention that hardly meant the abolitionists viewed those people as equal to Europeans. Gotlober's fascination with the "savage people" echoed the mixture of curiosity and derision that European writers such as Campe expressed toward non-Europeans in America.[26]

The earliest reworkings into Hebrew and Yiddish of *The Discovery of America* (1807 and 1817, respectively) differed in their portrayal of Black women and men. While Campe condemned slavery as "a disgrace to mankind" that subjugates and kills "our Black brothers," the translator into Hebrew, Moses Mendelsohn-Frankfurt (who had much admiration for, but no family connection to Moses Mendelssohn) did not use those words, but enthusiastically elaborated on the latest news in abolitionism. Still, Mendelsohn-Frankfurt described how slave traders "tempted the innocent" Africans, so "fathers sold their sons and sons [sold] their fathers" into slavery. Furthermore, "the mother shall not have mercy on her own son" and sold him to slavery for trinkets such as "bells, glassware, and mirrors." In another segment, Campe depicted the adventures of the Portuguese explorer, Vasco da Gama, while sailing near the coastline of East Africa; da Gama was "most pleasantly surprised" to see that apart from "the barbaric people" he met earlier along the coast, there were also the "well-behaved" residents of Malindi (Modern-day Kenya), who were "closer to the Asians" in their level of developed commerce. Again, Mendelsohn-Frankfurt added his own touch: "[Da Gama] said, all the residents of the African coast I've seen so far are savages, ignorant like wild beasts."[27]

Whether it was due to growing awareness of the evils of the slave trade, or to the need to publish more succinct versions of Campe's book, the translations into Yiddish omitted most of the above offensive references, whether from the German original or the Hebrew version. The first reworking of *The Discovery* into Yiddish by Khaykl (Khayim) Hurvits, titled *Tsofnas paneyakh* (Revealer of Secrets, 1817), did not mention da Gama's encounter with the "barbaric people." Still, as historian Rebecca Wolpe has remarked, Hurvits's repeated denunciations of the conquering Spaniards' cruelty toward Native Americans did not extend to Black slaves, where he dryly described the reality: "Until this very day people are always used to selling black people from Africa to AMERICA; and all the harsh labor in America is done by the Blacks, and they are called NEGROES" (emphasis in the original). A few years later, Mordecai Aaron Guenzburg of Vilna translated *The Discovery* into both Hebrew (1823) and Yiddish (1824). As in Hurvits's translation, Guenzburg's version included no mention of African women who sell their children to slavery nor anything about the "barbaric" people that da Gama encountered. Unlike Hurvits, Guenzburg attacked the "disgraceful human trade."[28]

The renditions of Campe's book to Hebrew and Yiddish illuminate how early nineteenth-century Jewish enlighteners' opposition to slavery fitted well within the earlier framework of European enlightenment. The support of abolitionism by Jewish maskilim (modernizers) did not articulate identification with enslaved populations but rather with the European advocates of the oppressed. Moreover, there are no indicators that those Jewish authors and translators viewed the situation of slaves, Black and others alike, as equivalent to the status of Jews in Eastern

Europe, however limiting it was. Africans' seeming low level of development, which many authoritative Jewish sources set forth, also militated against drawing parallels between European Jews and Black slaves. As early as 1795, a Polish-born maskil, Isaac Satanov, exemplified that ambivalence, writing about, "internal speech, which is intelligence, which is very lacking in the Kushite. And because of this it was seen fit to allow them to be maltreated and to be sold as animals." Yet "the philosophers of our time have signaled that they are human beings like us. Therefore they banned mistreating them."[29]

"Mothers Sell Their Little Children"—Ayzik Meyer Dik

Opposition to slavery, of any race, and support for abolitionism appeared several times in the writings of the first modern best-selling Yiddish author, Ayzik (Isaac) Meyer Dik. A Vilna maskil who published over two hundred works of fiction and nonfiction in Hebrew and Yiddish, mostly in the second half of the nineteenth century, Dik's career as a "women's writer"—read by many men as well—enabled him to sell thousands of chapbooks, where each copy circulated widely. Both entertaining and didactic, Dik's encyclopedic scope of writings aimed at fighting superstition and disseminating knowledge, drawing from Jewish, European, and American sources, including Harriet Beecher Stowe's *Uncle Tom's Cabin*.[30] While Dik was well aware of Tsarist censorship and usually included praise for Russia's emperor, the political mood among mid-nineteenth-century Russian radical intelligentsia constituted a significant source of influence: Russian intellectuals drew a direct parallel between the situation of serfs in Russia (emancipated in 1861) and that of Black slaves in the United States (emancipated in 1863) to underline the evils of enslavement.[31] No less important, the late 1860s and early 1870s witnessed the beginning of more substantial Jewish immigration from Russia to the United States, when famine and a cholera epidemic struck the Pale of Settlement. The numbers grew considerably after the pogroms of 1881–1882, increasing Jewish interest in "Columbus's country" and its inhabitants.[32]

Scholars have examined Dik's reworking of *Uncle Tom's Cabin*, published (1868) in Vilna under the title *Di shklaveray oder di laybeygenshaft* (Slavery or Serfdom). The book starts and ends with clear denunciations of slavery, and in its historical and moralistic introduction, Dik negotiated the incongruous influences of European racial discourse and traditional Jewish sources in his conceptualization of skin color. In Dik's version, Uncle Tom's owners are Jewish, and he is not martyred but ends up a free man, working with his family at a multiracial Jewish village in Canada.[33] Much less consideration has been given to original works by Dik that portray Black Africans. In 1856, Dik's *'Iyey hayam* (Island of the Sea) was published, where the main character is a French Jew, a surgeon who travels to desolate regions. As the book condemns the slave trade, it presents a harsh imagery of Africans—"mothers sell their little children [as slaves] for pins and glass beads and moreover rejoice, thinking they tricked the Europeans" in such a deal. Dik's depiction is very similar to that in Mendelsohn-Frankfurt's Hebrew translation of Campe's *The Discovery of America*, and both echo *Tsene-rene*'s characterization of defective African familial emotions.[34]

Dik's use of a European racial vocabulary about Black Africans while arguing for their shared humanity is more evident in a travel novel, *Di vistenay zahara* (The Desolate Sahara), which was published in the same year (1868) as *Di shklaveray*. The main plot follows the journey of the narrator, a French Jew by the name of Yaacov Shalita, on his way home from Senegal back to France through the Sahara Desert. As in *Di shklaveray*, the book contains harrowing descriptions of the enslaved who were trafficked from Africa to America, the violence of slaveowners, the argument that Jewish planters treat their slaves much better than Christian owners, and praise for Tsar Alexander II, who liberated the serfs in Russia without violence, in contrast to the American Civil War.[35]

More revealing, however, is the encounter between Shalita and a seventeen-year-old African girl, when he and fellow travelers camp outside the city of Timbuktu (modern-day Mali). The beautiful girl's name is Nae'ere, and her family includes "a father with ten wives and twenty children" as well as many slaves. She is about to be married to a young local wazir, and though "she was indeed savage and ignorant (plain)," she "was by nature very clever" and spoke Portuguese well. After comparing the color of God and standards of beauty in each culture and laughing at the diametrically opposed postulations, Shalita shows Nae'ere pictures of Paris and tells her, "look at the palaces, the carriages, our soldiers . . . with your black faces you all look like apes compared to us. Well, my dear fool? Say now who is more respectable?" Nae'ere replies that Europeans "are more powerful and braver than us, and more learned"; she and her people believe, nevertheless, "it is a sin for people to pretend to be the masters over a world which is not theirs." Nae'ere sees Europeans as "heretics" who focus on this world while her people are "devout Muslims" who view this world as a corridor where one just passes through: "Therefore we are born black so we would not need to wash and dye ourselves." The narrator is astonished that "a young child of semi-savage parents could talk so philosophically" and explains it by reference to Nae'ere's Portuguese governess, who gave her "a degree of education."[36]

Unquestionably, Dik accepts the concept of European superiority over Black Africans in nearly any sphere, and the novel displays his dabbling with Western stereotypes of African women's debauched sexuality or African men's cowardice. When the local king in Timbuktu holds a banquet to honor the European visitors, ten beautiful teenaged concubines dance before them. The guests admire the dancers' skill and agility, but they notice that often the dancers repeat two movements which "presented only the highest degree of love [making]" and that was "offensive to respectable people." Later the travelers encounter a hyena which terrorizes the locals, and "the red lips of the Negroes turned white due to great fear." When the convoy's pasha orders several slaves to help shoot other wild animals, "their teeth were chattering with fear," and one of the Europeans asks why the pasha needs such "good-for-nothings [*shlimazelnikes*]." *Di vistenay zahara* also includes numerous descriptions of Black African appearance. When a huge convoy camps near the Europeans' encampment outside Timbuktu, the narrator details the color diversity among Africans—Nubians, Abyssinians, Murzukians [from Southwest Libya], etc., some of whom are "black as pitch, some brown, some dark yellow." Only "our five Europeans were fully white and looked like bright stars in a dark night." In a different part, a footnote tells, "The Nubians [of North Sudan/South Egypt] are very ugly people, large and strong as giants. Their noses are bent and twisted like a river when it flows into the sea." Dik's descriptions—by a writer who never left Russia's Pale of Settlement—echo sexualized imageries of the Black body that were prevalent in nineteenth-century Western culture, which ascribed oversexualized, animalistic traits to Black Africans and African Americans. The same is true for accounts of Black men's alleged cowardice or outlandish appearance.[37]

All the same, there are aspects that were clearly meant to endear some characters to Yiddish readers. In some books, Dik addressed his female readers directly, opening with *Mayn tayere lezerin* (My dear female reader); in *Vistenay zahara*, he highlighted Nae'ere's female piety, values, and *tsnies* (modesty) in an appealing way, especially for traditional Jewish readers. When detailing the Muslim wedding ceremony between Nae'ere and her bridegroom, Bakhori, Dik remarked that from a certain point it "was almost as by us Jews." After Shalita returns home at the end of the story, Dik ends the book with a quote from a Muslim credo, "God is great, and great is his mercy." In a sense, Dik was writing implicitly about Jewish sensibilities when describing African Muslims. *Vistenay zahara* would become so widely read that it was mistaken for a genuine scientific account. In 1875, the Warsaw Hebrew weekly, *Ha-tsefirah* (The Dawn), which aimed at popularizing the knowledge of sciences among East European Jews, published a serialized report titled "Travel through the Sahara Desert" by a young maskil, Nekhemye-Dov Hofman. Hofman referred to "two wise and world-famous men," "Yaacov Shalita of Orleans" and "Daniel Hof" (the latter was a fellow traveler in the novella) and quoted Shalita as a nonfiction, independent source of information about Africa.[38]

Dik would continue to write against the enslavement of Black Africans in later books, such as *Der opekun* (The Guardian, 1872), and the posthumously-released *Di amerikaner geshikhte* (An American Story, 1899). Whereas Dik's works were highly successful, as they were geared toward both enlightening and entertaining of the masses, other maskilim (proponents of Jewish enlightenment) were more didactic. A pioneer of the Jewish press in Russia and an untiring maskil, Aleksander Tsederboym, who established in Odessa the leading Hebrew paper of the period, *Ha-melits* (The Advocate, 1860–1904), had often used both *Ha-melits* and its Yiddish supplement, *Kol mevaser*, to enlighten the Jewish masses. As with the publications of other maskilim, Tsederboym's newspapers took their cue from European writers' representations of Black individuals, which combined inquisitiveness and disdain. Tsederboym seemed to be unsure wherefrom the Black slaves in America originally came. In the first issue of *Kol mevaser* (1862), he explained to his readers that the "Negroes" were "the Black people who are born there [United States] since the days of yore." Tsederboym strongly denounced the slaveholders: In such a "free country," where "nobody asks whether . . . [you are] a Jew or a Christian," they still "torment them [slaves] mercilessly." Nonetheless, Tsederboym noted that Black people "understand this hard work and how to go about the plants . . . no European can do that," and that "only they [Black people] are fit for that work." In its report about the Civil War in 1862, Tsederboym's *Ha-melits* commented that the Northerners wanted to set free the slaves "without paying heed that a great calamity might happen to the savage slaves themselves, because they are unfit for freedom anymore."[39]

To be sure, like other maskilim, Tsederboym and other writers in *Kol mevaser* strongly deplored slavery and extolled the United States for its abolition. A maskil and teacher in Tsarist crown schools, Shmuel Resser, translated (1865) an article from a German illustrated newspaper about the cruelty of the slave trade in Africa, which he called "a disgrace to humanity" where "people are traded like cattle." Resser mentioned that "the goodhearted Northerners in America want to liberate the Blacks" for a good reason, and provided graphic details of how a local ruler in modern-day Senegal butchered anyone deemed too weak to be sold as a slave. Interestingly, Resser contrasted the ruthlessness of the African king with a European slave trader, whom Resser termed a "kind slave broker," who saw the mangled bodies and "regretted the whole deal." In 1870, the paper (probably Tsederboym himself) contradicted what it wrote several years earlier (quoted above) and attacked those who believed that "only Black Negroes in America know how to handle cotton"; Southern planters failed to understand that "these days it is very wrong to enslave people."[40]

At the same time, as the opening paragraph of this chapter demonstrates, *Kol mevaser* exhibited the attitudes embedded in contemporaneous European culture toward Black people, which classified them as savage and inferior. In 1869, Tsederboym wrote a book review of a Yiddish book titled *Der lufballon* (The Hot Air Balloon), originally written in English by Dr. Samuel Fergusson. Tsederboym did not seem to realize that the book was fictional, a reworking of Jules Verne's *Cinq semaines en ballon* (Five Weeks in a Balloon, 1863), where Fergusson is the main character. Tsederboym praised the educational qualities of the book, where readers can learn about "the customs of totally or semi-savage peoples, the Negroes, and the slave trade." In the same year, a reader by the name of A. Vohliner complained about the dishonest practices of the matchmaking business in Jewish society, which he deemed to be worse than slavery. To make his point, he mentioned the "Negro trade, that is with Black savage people," where it is easy "to catch a crude person and sell him like an ox." As European countries sought to abolish the slave trade, Vohliner believed that Jewish society must terminate the matchmaking "bazaar."[41]

"A Carriage Can Drive Through Each Nostril": The Growing Influence of Pseudoscientific Racism

Kol mevaser began as a Yiddish supplement to the Hebrew-language *Hamelits*, and it was in the latter newspaper that a young writer by the name of Nokhem Meyer Shaykevitsh published (1870) one of his first columns, titled, "Cannibals on the West African Coast." Supposedly translated from the English, Shaykevitsh argued that despite British efforts, "the fierce bloodthirstiness of those savages" does not allow them to coexist peacefully with each other. Even though "they are cowards, scared of the sound of a rustling leaf," one tribe, residing in New Calabar (modern-day Nigeria), launched a surprise attack against its neighbors, killing several of them and taking prisoners. Europeans who live nearby went to the local leaders to ask for the release of those captured, and to their horror saw one of the leaders' wives "carrying a basket with cooked human hands and legs that she handed out to her guests, who quickly devoured that meat"; in another house the Europeans found "a cooked human head" on a table. When the Europeans complained to the king (whose house also served human meat) about that custom, he was puzzled, and mentioned that Britain just banned the slave trade "but not eating their enemies' flesh, which has been holy to my people since the days of yore." In subsequent years, under the pen name Shomer, Shaykevitsh would become arguably the world's most popular Yiddish writer in the late nineteenth century—though critics often maligned him as a plagiarizer, a tacky writer, whose hackneyed characters and melodramatic stories were as bad as his pompously Germanized Yiddish.[42]

Whereas the juxtaposition of African savagery with European humanism and civility dovetailed many other European texts at the time, it was a later book by Shomer that reflects the growing influence of pseudoscientific racism. In 1888, he published the novella *Halb mentsh halb affe* (Half Human Half Ape), where the main villain is an intelligent yet corrupt woman, Rachel Flefen (Flefen is close to the Yiddish *plefen*—to stupefy/shock). Flefen, who had a child with another man, threatens the narrator, Yitskhok Fiktel, that if he would not declare that he was married to her, fathered the child, and now would give her a divorce, she would make a scandal; that would surely destroy Fiktel's recent marriage to the young and beautiful Anna. Flefen even goes to the authorities and a rabbinical court to complete the frame-up, which ultimately ruins Fiktel's life and brings about Anna's early death. While the novella takes place in Eastern Europe and has no Black or African characters, the depiction of Flefen's physical appearance as an ape is telling: "The title orangutan (an ape) would fit her better than a woman," as "never in my life have I seen such ugliness." Flefen looks "Black like a Negress" and has "a nose (no Jewish house should witness such as nose) where a carriage drawn by four horses can drive through each of its nostrils." Prior to his marriage to Anna, as Fiktel feels that "the orangutan has a desire to marry me," the very thought strongly "nauseated" him. The narrator mentions how Flefen "held out her large, black hand" before bidding him farewell; after his marriage to Anna, when Flefen surprisingly visits the newlyweds, Anna is not enthusiastic to shake "the black hand of the ape," but she still does it.[43]

It is worth mentioning again that Rachel Flefen is an East European Jew; the fact that already in 1888, a highly popular Yiddish writer could link apelike physical traits to Black-like appearance epitomizes how such imagery, which by the nineteenth century was well-embedded in European culture and deterministic discourses about polygenesis, permeated the Yiddish intelligentsia. Nonetheless, Flefen is no primitive simian; she is a writer, an intelligent and strong-willed woman, well-versed in philosophy and the Talmud, and fluent in German, Hebrew, and Russian. Interestingly, while Shomer was considered a "women's writer," especially the "new reading women," a conspicuous aspect in *Half Human Half Ape* is its unabashed misogyny and gendered moralism: Fiktel and an acquaintance talk about Flefen's novel's "grammar mistakes, which can be forgiven since she is a woman." What cannot be forgiven, however, is Flefen's immorality, since "such shameless words should not be allowed to come out of a woman's pen, the heroine of her novel comes across as one of the streetwalkers." Throughout the novella, Flefen herself appears as sexually forward, and Shomer links her apelike physiognomy to her oversexed depravity.[44]

By the time *Half Human Half Ape* came out, Shomer's writings were reaching an expanding audience. If in 1864 the estimated number of bookstores in Russia was 63, by 1903 it grew to about 3,000. The number of public libraries in Russia also increased, yet censorship and other restrictions stymied its growth among Jews; they often turned to book peddlers or informal reading circles, which then evolved into book clubs and eventually into unofficial lending libraries. The rapid development of the transatlantic Yiddish book industry in the 1890s and marketing innovations increased the availability of Yiddish books. While acculturated Jews and/or Hebraists still sneered at Yiddish as a vulgar *zhargon*, by the 1890s it began to emerge as a respectable vehicle for literature and science. Whether or not Sholem Aleichem's frontal attack against him was the main cause for his departure to America in 1889, Shomer remained more successful than his detractors and, together with Dik, helped to create a Yiddish reading public.[45]

Shomer was not the first in utilizing a deterministic vocabulary. Its effect among East European Jewish modernizers was evident already in 1841 in a Hebrew-language natural science book penned by Yoysef Sheynhak (Joseph B. Schönhak) of Suvalk in Northeastern Poland. When warning about head lice, Sheynhak noted, "the louse on the kushi's (neger's) head is black, and our land's louse would also appear black if it is found on his head." More influential among East European maskilim were the popular science books of German Jewish author Aaron Bernstein: In 1862, *Ha-tsefirah* dedicated an issue to Bernstein and lauded him as "the sage whose wisdom in the natural sciences quenched many people's thirst for knowledge." A Yiddish translation (1910) of Bernstein's *Aus dem Reiche der Naturwissenschaft* (From the Field of Natural Sciences, 1853–1856) followed the author's anthropological assertions about racial differences, "[the gap between Europeans and Black Africans] is greater than the difference between the Negro-races and the most capable ape species."[46]

A more neutral portrayal, which was still riddled with many of the period's assumptions, was written by poet and editor Avrom Reyzin (also spelled Reyzen/Reisin). Reyzin, whose lyrics often became beloved

Yiddish folk songs, edited a chrestomathy (a collection of learning materials) that came out in Warsaw in 1908. In the collection's segment about nature and geography, Reyzin wrote a short chapter titled "The Negroes," where he detailed their physiognomy: "The nose is flattened, the lips are thick and the teeth—very white." Since Africa is very hot, "they go around almost naked," but for esthetics, "they don a piece of fur over their shoulder or put on a belt." African women usually till the fields, while "the men occupy themselves with hunting or do nothing." Reyzin wrote, "The Negroes buy wives. But despite it, the woman is respected by the Negro." After describing how Africans "deify different animals and large trees," Reyzin concluded that "Negroes are very strong and can endure a lot"; since "they are very good workers," they were shipped off and sold as slaves, but now slavery is abolished. One has to keep in mind the purpose of chrestomathies, which were meant to provide general knowledge of various topics, mostly for young people. Reyzin's own ambivalence, nevertheless, will be more apparent in a poem, "A Little Negro" that he wrote after his immigration to New York in 1911: Upon seeing a young Black child, the poet is struck by his color, "My God! How ugly your creature looks!" But later, as the child laughs, the poet realizes that "my white little brother" laughed in the same way and instantly "the Black kid became beautiful to me."[47]

The Symbol of the Kushi

The significance of racial thought notwithstanding, sympathy for the plight of Africans and appreciation of their courage in their fight against European conquerors did manifest itself. The Egyptologist, explorer, poet, translator, and pioneer of Yiddish journalism in America, Getsil Zelikovitsh, served (1884–1885) as an Arabic-English interpreter in the British military's expedition to Sudan. Zelikovitsh published (1886–1887) a serialized travel log (later issued as a book) in East European Hebrew newspapers, where he empathized with the local population. In "The Death of a Little Savage," Zelikovitsh lamented the death of fifteen-year-old Ibrahim, shot to death by British soldiers as he tried to visit his father, who was incarcerated in British death row. Ironically referring to Ibrahim's purported savagery, Zelikovitsh wrote, "Kushi boy! It's not good to be a savage these days. Why did you go to kiss your father and bid him farewell? This is appropriate only to savages like yourself." Referring to the real savages—the British soldiers who jeer at Ibrahim's body—Zelikovitsh sarcastically argued that Ibrahim "should extol them [the British] for eradicating a savage and sanctifying the goddess 'civilization.'" In another article, Zelikovitsh ridiculed those who think Europeans are more advanced: "Are the Kushites savages because they do not put on a tall hat like us? . . . Are they savages because they refuse to put their feet in the chock of small and narrow shoes?" Yet when it comes to honor and bravery, Zelikovitsh observed how "those savages were willing to shed the last drop of their blood for their ancestral home." According to Zelikovitsh, his compassion for the African population led the British commander, Lord Kitchener, to accuse him of sympathizing with the enemy and terminate his military position.[48]

Concomitantly, even a sympathizer such as Zelikovitsh, a pioneer of Yiddish erotic literature, conveyed a highly sexualized imagery of Africans, and especially of African women. In one segment he described two wailing African women who followed the British soldiers, since Saeed, the respective son and fiancé of the two, was arrested by the British, and the women pleaded for his release. Zelikovitsh paid attention mostly to the fiancée, Aisha, a tall, young woman of about seventeen years old: "Her lovely, healthy waist was girdled in leather loincloth, and both of her perfect breasts poured out love sparks." In an encounter with two other Sudanese teenage sisters, Karima and Halima, "the most beautiful women I have seen in the Land of Kush," Zelikovitsh noted that Karima's "see-through white silken sash was wrapped around her chest and did not cover its secrets." Those physical descriptions suited well Zelikovitsh's view that, unlike Europeans, Africans were inherently sexual. Africans "do not need to read lustful books to stimulate love like the Europeans, since the principle of pure love is well known to them and embedded in their hearts since birth."[49] In 1887, Zelikovitsh immigrated to the United States, where he developed a successful career in Yiddish journalism alongside other popular East European-born Yiddish writers who immigrated to America in the 1880s, such as Dovid Hermalin, John (Yoyne) Paley, the abovementioned Shomer, Avner Tanenboym, and Yisroel-Yoysef Zevin (under the pen name Tashrak). Their writings circulated among hundreds of thousands of Yiddish readers, both in America and in Eastern Europe, and communicated numerous portrayals of Black people. Their works are discussed below in the context of American Yiddish culture.[50]

Despite the sympathetic stance of writers such as Zelikovitsh and some of the earlier maskilim, by the late nineteenth and early twentieth centuries the very term *Kushim* marked an undesirable, lowly metaphor in internal Jewish squabbles. In 1875, the Hebrew weekly *'Ivry 'anokhi* (A Hebrew I am), that came out in the Austrian city of Brody (modern-day Ukraine), published a letter by 130 Jews from the Land of Israel, pleading with British Jewish financier Moses Montefiore to continue programs that encouraged productive labor among local Jews. The plea mentioned that local Jewish leaders tyrannically "oppressed the poor as if they were Kushites." In 1880, the moderate-orthodox Hebrew periodical *Ha-magid* (The Herald) published a similar complaint about the distribution of charity funds for Jewish residents in the Holy Land: Writing from Bucharest, Elazar Roke'ach, a proto-Zionist activist and pioneer of Hebrew and Yiddish press in Romania, argued that Jews in the Land of Israel seek productive work and not charity, so "we shall not be oppressed like Kushites" under communal leaders. Two years later (1882), Kiev-based Hebrew educator and writer Yitzhak Yaacov Weissberg, who opposed Jewish mass migration to the New World, claimed that Jewish migrants who returned from America say that "they were treated there like Kushites," since "their beneficiaries [American Jews] sold them to the Yankees as slaves and maidservants."[51]

The above quotes did not necessarily express any disdain toward Black Africans per se; they did reflect internalization of the imagery of them as the most oppressed and despised population—which Jews must not resemble in any shape or form. In 1883, a leading figure in the East European Jewish press and an eventual Zionist leader, Nahum Sokolow, decried what he saw as Jewish assimilationists' submissive behavior, who seek to placate and imitate the Gentiles. Yet, he claimed, antisemites reply, "and you [assimilators] are like Kushites and apes, who all they do is to mimic others." In 1901, Yiddish literary critic Yisroel Isidor Elyashev (writing under his pseudonym Bal-Makhshoves—"A thinker") criticized the Jewish Colonization Association (JCA), established to assist the mass migration of East European Jews to the New World or the Land of Israel. Writing in the Krakow weekly *Der yud* (The Jew), Elyashev directed his attack at the rich Western European leaders of JCA, "who look at you, the Russian Jew, as a Negro [*Neger*] from Africa, with whom there is no accountability." A year later (1902), the Zionist thinker Ahad ha'am ("The Commoner," the pen name of Asher Ginzberg) mocked Theodor Herzl's utopian novel *Altneuland* (The Old New Land), arguing that Herzl's vision for a Jewish state is so foreign to Jewishness that a Nigerian could have written it. In response, Zionist leader Shmaryahu Levin, who gained a reputation in Tsarist Russia (and later in America) as a charismatic Yiddish orator, defended Herzl: "We have such an immense belief in the character of the Jewish people that we are certain a large population of Jews in their own state cannot become a population of Kushites—a free man does not free willingly accept slavery." More than in earlier examples, Levin drew a stark distinction between Jews and Blacks, and intrinsically linked the latter to slavery.[52]

A Greeting from Our Farthest Brethren

There is little doubt that the above conceptions of race, hierarchy, and difference became enmeshed with religious aspects in the discussion about Ethiopian Jews, a topic which began to receive more attention in the Yiddish press by the opening years of the twentieth century. The reports of French-Jewish scholar Joseph Halévy, and especially of his student, Jacques Faitlovitch, who became Ethiopian Jews' champion among world Jewry, drew interest in the Jewish press. As early as 1864, *Kol mevaser* informed its readers that the *Falashim* (a common term for Ethiopian Jews that is considered offensive today) are charitable and industrious, but "in general they are very ignorant and rarely you find someone who knows the content of the Torah." *Der yud* lauded (1901) Ethiopian Jews who "sacrificed themselves for their belief" yet argued that their religion "took on many foolish things and superstitions," and they have the bible "only in a Kushite language."[53]

The question whether Ethiopian Jews were actual Jews gained noticeable coverage in the first Yiddish daily in Tsarist Russia, *Der fraynd* (The Friend), which first appeared in 1903 and reached a circulation of close to 50,000 during its peak in 1905.[54] That year, the daily published several articles by Yishaye Uger (later organizer of the gymnastic clubs' movement among Polish Jews) dedicated to Faitlovitch and Jews in Ethiopia. Uger presented different hypotheses about the origin of Ethiopian Jews and leaned toward the idea that they are local Africans who converted to Judaism, "but they do not originate from the same race [*shtam*] as Jews." Still, those Black Jews "lead a moral and virtuous life, unlike the other peoples of Abyssinia that are semi-savage." A humoristic feuilleton poked (1908) fun at Jewish organizations which competed for influence over the issue of Ethiopian Jews, unintentionally revealing its skepticism that those Ethiopians are genuine Jews; the sketch termed them "Abyssinian Subbotniks," in reference to Russian Christian Sabbatarians, who adopted certain elements of Judaism. Also in 1908, the popular Warsaw daily *Haynt* (Today) published a talk with Rabbi Haim Nahum (future grand rabbi of Turkey) who led an expedition to Ethiopia, titled "a greeting from our farthest brethren." Nahum clarified what he believed to be the differences between Ethiopians and other Africans, as well as between Jewish and not-Jewish Ethiopians: The Ethiopian "is not savage, not bloodthirsty, and cannot be compared at all to a Negro." Nonetheless, "While Ethiopians are lazy by nature, the Falashim among them excel in their diligence."[55]

Undoubtedly, during the opening years of the twentieth century, most East European Jewish prayers, dismay, and focus were not dedicated to Ethiopian Jews, but rather to the calamities at home: A wave of pogroms, beginning in Kishinev (April 1903), continuing through the Russo-Japanese War (1904–1905), and peaking during the abortive Russian Revolution (1905) and its aftermath. Between 1903 and 1906, more than seven hundred pogroms broke out in Russia, in which more than three thousand Jews were murdered. Those ordeals brought about an increased flow of Jewish emigration from Russia, as close to 700,000 Jews immigrated to America between 1904 and 1908.[56] Amid the tumultuous and violent episodes in Russia, *Der fraynd* overall conveyed a positive depiction of the United States and of Americans in general. However, the popular daily did not shy away from critically exploring themes of racial injustice and violence in American life. Apart from real alarm over such inequities, it is quite conceivable that due to Tsarist censorship, it was easier for the pro-Zionist daily to attack foreign countries. In 1903, the paper published a long, unsigned article, titled "The Persecution of Negroes," which compared lynchings and race riots to pogroms, and noted that a false accusation of rape against a Black man in Kentucky was a "blood libel." The writer used an unfavorable quote by Abraham Lincoln about African Americans to show that "Even the best and most enlightened Americans do not doubt that the Negroes are an inferior kind of people," and whites believe Black people are "liars, cowards . . . among them there are many thieves . . . they are lazy, drunkards." Whereas the writer clearly condemned "such deep hatred," he added, "you cannot deny that some of those traits can be found indeed among the Negroes," since they were enslaved until forty years ago, and treated "not better than work livestock." When describing the response of the local Black population in Wilmington, Delaware, to a lynching case (1903) and subsequent violence against Black communities, the article noted that "their hot African blood boiled" and they responded with violence.[57]

The writer was probably Kh. Aleksandrov (pseudonym of Khaim Miller), a socialist who immigrated to America in 1889, where he was active in New York's socialist Yiddish press, and served as an American correspondent for the *Fraynd*. His approach to racial questions resembled what the Yiddish press in America, especially on the left, began to impart in those years: an unequivocal denunciation of white racism while ascribing inferior attributes to Black individuals owing to their history, culture, race, or a combination thereof. In 1904, Aleksandrov published a series of articles about Black Americans, where he fiercely attacked white violence and its crippling effects on African Americans. Slavery was a curse both to slaveowners and slaves; "the Negro . . . became lazy, reckless, ignorant." Furthermore, "by nature, he is a born-farmer, and city life has the most destructive effect on him." Aleksandrov commended Black educator and leader, Booker T. Washington, as "in none of his books did he keep quiet about the faults of his race," and quoted Washington's argument about the comparative growth of literacy among various countries, maintaining, "The local Negro is even more capable of studying than the Spaniard, Italian, or South American." In 1905, Aleksandrov lambasted the increasing racial segregation, mentioning how painful it was for Black students and theatergoers to be summarily excluded only because of their color. That was the reason, he asserted, for the pervasiveness of "thousands of charlatans" who offer Black customers "powders, drops and other remedies, which can allegedly turn a Negro into white as snow." A persecuted Jew did not face those problems, "as he could convert to Christianity; but what could do the poor Negro, who is persecuted for nothing other than the color of his skin"?[58]

The *Fraynd* continued to publish articles that condemned racism by whites and mocked the concept of white superiority. Some of those articles were translations, such as the writing of Dutch anti-colonialist writer Eduard Douwes Dekker (Multatuli); others were originals, as an article by Yehoshua Podruzhnik, who was active in Yiddish journalism in Belgium and Britain. Reviewing weddings among Black Africans, Podruzhnik argued that among Central African tribes, principles of gender equality "are observed more punctually than in Europe," and European attempts to civilize Africans result in "a barbaric and sometimes savage attitude of whites toward Blacks."[59] As with many Yiddish texts beforehand, the translations were hardly precise. In 1910, as Booker T. Washington visited Europe, he gave an interview to the Viennese paper *Neue Freie Presse* (New Free Press) during the Austrian leg of his tour. A free and redacted Yiddish translation of that interview appeared in the *Fraynd*, where the unnamed translator wrote a sentence that did not appear in the German original, in which Washington "seeks to put in their [African Americans'] Black bodies a pure, white soul." The Yiddish article mentioned that Washington's "face color is not so black" (omitting the original text's comment that Washington's face color was "comparable to that of South Italians"), and that "only his curly hair and the form of his face show that he is descended from Blacks." The Black leader's "intelligent appearance is another sign that he is the best child of the Black race." In that respect, too, the *Fraynd* bore a resemblance to American Yiddish newspapers in those years, which celebrated Black leaders and achievements.[60]

It is worth mentioning that throughout the period covered here—through the opening years of the twentieth century—the sight of a Black man or woman remained a rare, memorable, and exotic occurrence in Eastern Europe. Socialist writer and translator Uriah Katzenelenbogen, who grew up in Vilna in the 1890s, recalled hearing stories about Africans from Jews who migrated to South Africa and came back to Lithuania (to look for a wife), and imagined them as "a race of big, sturdy children." One day a circus came to town, and Katzenelenbogen saw "a real colored man, strong, half-naked," who conducted himself "With how much dignity!"; "This poor wandering wrestler was the first living Negro that I had ever seen." The sight of Black people was still a newsworthy item in 1912: The Warsaw Yiddish daily, *Der moment* (The

Moment), reported that "many Negroes come to Warsaw and hire themselves out for various jobs." As the ten-year-old Elias Newman was en route to America (1913) from his native Polish hometown of Stashov, he saw a Black man in Krakow, and the spectacle was so extraordinary that it was engraved in his memory half a century later.[61]

* * *

When examining the above representations—expressed both in religious and worldly writings, adapted and original, fiction and nonfiction texts alike—is there any basis to the claim that the tenets of Judaism and/or Jewish historical experience as a marginalized minority made Jews likelier to identify and sympathize with Black people? Did Yiddish-language sources show affinity with them, view similarity in their experience or see the situation of Jews as akin to Black Africans or African Americans? As the above source material demonstrates, there is little ground to conclude that such attitudes existed.

Among advocates of Jewish enlightenment (maskilim), condemnations of the enslavement of non-Europeans and support of its abolition usually served as a fashionable cultural precept that did not exclude viewing the enslaved as savage and inferior. Identification was not extended to the enslaved but rather to the European proponents of abolitionism. Moreover, regardless of how restrictive the status of East European Jews was, there are hardly any signs that those Jewish writers saw their situation as comparable to non-European populations. The exhortations against slavery had to do with Jewish enlighteners' desire to immerse their readers in the latest tenor of European culture; another motive was to praise the Tsar, who prevented bloodshed as he emancipated the serfs, as opposed to the violence elsewhere by both slave traders and extreme abolitionists. Only at the turn of the twentieth century, as immigration to America mushroomed and the country's importance grew for the Jewish readership, some voices appeared (such as Aleksandrov), which offered a more systemic critique of white racism, while maintaining some ambivalence.

The abolition of slavery, however, was not the main dimension where references to Black African and African Americans arose. A mash-up of rabbinic exegesis, pious advice, travel narratives, folklore, tales of scientific explorations, literature, press reports, political quarrels, and educational materials communicated imagery of Black people—whether they were termed Kushites, Narapim, Moors, or Negroes—that contained certain themes. Whereas those sources were far from monolithic and at times contradictory, they imparted characteristics of savagery, primitiveness, less-than-human nature, cowardice, heightened or depraved sexuality, and lack of familial feelings. As their Yiddish readership had hardly ever seen a Black person, some of the texts offered graphic details—not necessarily derisive—about Black physiognomy, including lips, nose, hair, and skin tones. Furthermore, it is instructive that in the debate about Ethiopian Jews, writers who accepted their Jewishness underlined the qualities that they saw as distinguishing Black Jews from other Black Africans, e.g., higher levels of industriousness and civilization. That discussion, just as the political dispute among Jewish nationalists utilized the term *Kushim* as a symbol for undesirable, lowly attributes, shows that by the late nineteenth century, the imagery of Black women and men solidified into a set of objectionable traits.

The above suggests that the Jewish immigrants who made their way to America were not a *tabula rasa* about Black people. While the vast majority of them would not see a Black person until their arrival in the Golden Land, they already had somewhat of an idea of them—as imagined, incoherent, and imprecise as it was—and an array of characteristics to ascribe to Black men and women. Once they encountered African Americans, the latter would cease to be a nonconcrete concept, about which they had read in the above-discussed assortment of sources; in America, the Black population would soon be likened to the East European peasantry with whom Jews were used to dealing. No less important, in their new land, the immigrants would live in a society with long-held, entrenched modes of describing and behaving toward Black Americans, which would have a lasting impact on the newcomers.

2

The Negro Took the Place of the Peasant

The Encounter Between East European Jewish Immigrants and African Americans

Writing in early 1903, the editor of the New York orthodox Yiddish daily *Morgen zhurnal*, Peter (Peyrets) Wiernik, tried to explain to English-language readers the acute predicaments faced by Jews who live among Russians. Wiernik referred to the Russian masses as "the unhappy medium between the Asiatic and the European," and argued that "the Russians—that is eighty-five or ninety per cent of them—are so much below everything we know here that *we would have to go to the illiterate Southern negro for a familiar example of their mental capacity*." Twenty years later (1923), Yiddish socialist poet and editor, Avrom Lesin (originally Valt), who held very different views from Wiernik, conveyed a similar impression. In an editorial that lambasted the Ku Klux Klan, Lesin equated the Polish nobility to Southern former slaveowners, and the "dull-minded, dejected peasants" to the "dull-minded, dejected Negroes."[1]

Once Yiddish-speaking Jews arrived in the United States, Black people were no longer an abstraction, the topic of religious commentaries and musings, exotic travel accounts, journalistic reports, folktales, or works of fiction. Now African Americans were clients, neighbors at certain places, and at any rate an integral part of a diverse American society. Even when there were no direct contacts between the groups, Jewish immigrants lived now in a society that had deeply ingrained ways of representing and practicing racial hierarchy and differentiation. After the initial astonishment at seeing a Black person diminished, as they became a mundane reality for Jewish immigrants, certain attitudes became discernible. Those attitudes involved cultural and socioeconomic patterns which had Old-World roots, combined with American ways of relating to African Americans. In Eastern Europe, Jewish society featured identifiable modes of thought and behavior toward various strata among the non-Jewish population, and distinguished between the surrounding peasantry and those seen as carriers of higher culture. As scholars Israel Bartal, Ewa Morawska, and David Roskies have shown, Jews differentiated between what they saw as high-cultured and low-cultured Gentiles: As a result of the Jews' economic position in Eastern Europe, the non-Jews normally encountered by most Jews until the mid-nineteenth century were usually limited to peasantry (Belarusian, Lithuanian, Polish, Romanian, Ukrainian, etc.), Polish *pritsim* (lords, landowners), and Russian or Habsburg officialdom.[2] At the same time, whereas Jewish immigrants often cast other low-status groups, such as the Irish and East European immigrants, as America's peasantry, those groups were not Black. Jewish newcomers did not remain oblivious for long to white racial etiquette, which would also affect their interactions with Black women and men.

The rise of American nativism during World War I and the ensuing Red Scare led to increasing antisemitism in the 1920s, and recurring attempts to close America's gates even as waves of pogroms swept the former Russian Pale of Settlement. In this environment, American Jews would gradually come to see African Americans as potential allies.[3] Yet any improvement in the attitudes of Jews toward Black Americans would be neither complete nor instant, and episodes of lingering suspicions remained. This chapter examines salient features such as residential patterns and socioeconomic relations in the historical encounter between Yiddish-speaking Jewish immigrants and African Americans.

Old-World Connotations—The Peasantry

By the late nineteenth century, certain stereotypical images of non-Jews were widespread throughout East European Jewish society. The basic image of the Gentile in Yiddish folklore was that of a peasant, portrayed as inherently Jew-hating, strong, coarse, drunk, illiterate, dumb, and sexually uninhibited. That attitude yielded songs like "oy, oy, oy/ shiker iz a goy/ shiker iz er/ trinken muz er/ vayl er iz a goy" (drunk is a goy/ drunk is he/ drink must he/ because he is a goy), and sayings like "a Gentile remains a Gentile," "when the Gentiles have a feast, they beat up Jews," "when the Jew is hungry he sings. When the Gentile is hungry, he beats up his wife," and "the Jew is small and Vasil (a common Ukrainian name) is big."[4] Countless accounts and folktales by East European Jews illustrated Gentiles as dull-witted peasants whose ignorance could only compete with their promiscuity.[5]

Numerous memoirs and accounts by Jews from different regions in Eastern Europe, and with different political convictions, invoked that basic image. Avrom Ber Gotlober, who lived as a (married) teenager in the town of Chernikhov (in modern-day Ukraine) in the 1820s, remembered the peasants who frequented his father-in-law's tavern: "[A]nyone who beat up his wife when he cheated on her or she cheated on him" visited the inn. The peasants imbibed "until they were drunk and exposed themselves." After drinking and hugging each other, they usually began to fight amongst themselves "until blood was spilled." A similar description appeared in the memoir of Avrom Lesin, who did not grow up in a shtetl but in a city (Minsk) in the 1870s and 1880s, and had a completely different background from Gotlober. As a child, he visited a local tavern whose owner he knew. There he saw that "[Gentile] drunkards lay around on the dirty floor, embracing and jostling one another, singing with hoarse voices, snoring" as the Jewish owner stood at the door and "laughed with such deep contempt that his whole body shook." The Yiddish author I. J. Singer, who grew up in a Polish shtetl at the turn of the twentieth century, described how during Christian holidays thousands of peasants swarmed into town: Right after the religious ceremonies, the peasants "got drunk, danced, and beat each other up." Singer mentioned the alarm of the Jewish merchants in the shtetl's market square when fights broke out between drunken peasants, who used to crack each other's skull with big wooden rods: The Jews used to pack their goods, fearing that "it's starting" again.[6]

Those examples suggest that, while the peasant's basic image was not divorced from a certain socioeconomic reality, it often congealed into a fixed set of traits: Whether the memoirists accurately described actual events is less important than their portrayal of Jewish attitudes in their respective hometowns toward the peasantry. Furthermore, the fact that immigrants of different backgrounds, regions, and political convictions ascribed similar basic characteristics to the peasantry attest to the potency of the latter's image. The peasant was so closely associated with rudeness and dullness that, as late as 1952, Yiddish linguist and folklorist Hirsh Abramovitsh argued that one should not use the word *poyer* (peasant) when referring to Jewish farmers or agricultural workers: "[M]y pen does not let me write down the word poyer" when discussing Jewish farmers. The image of the peasant was deeply rooted in Yiddish language and folklore, where the words *poyer* or *muzhik* denoted coarseness, blockheadedness, and small-mindedness.[7]

At the same time, however, Yiddish folklore portrayed peasants as down-to-earth, no-nonsense people, whose directness and simplicity were not corrupted, in contrast with the Jews' tortuous ways, casuistry, and nervousness. Peasants were coarse and simple, but they did not suffer from *goles* (exile) complications and lived happily on their land.[8] More importantly, even when expressing suspicion and fear of peasants, East European Jews' attitudes were often tempered and accompanied by pity for the peasants' miserable conditions. Irving Chait, who grew up in today's Latvia of the 1900s, recalled how his innkeeper grandfather felt sorry for the peasants, and even if "a peasant would get so drunk" that he was willing to sell his horse for more vodka, the grandfather would not let him pay. A journalist of Soviet affairs, Maurice Hindus, who grew up in the Pale of Settlement in the 1890s, mentioned that "left to himself the Russian peasant is a stranger to racial prejudice," yet "free vodka, the promise of government protection and the lure of loot" caused some peasants to go out on a pogrom. In some Jewish homes peasant women served as maids, and growing up in such circumstances, Jewish children like future real estate developer Louis Horowitz remembered fondly the presence of those women in their childhood.[9]

In the United States, too, Jews continued to categorize the surrounding Gentile society according to strata and national origin, and African Americans were frequently seen as the new country's reincarnation of peasant folk. A reality where Jewish storeowners, tavern keepers, peddlers, and landlords dealt with Black clientele, and some Jewish business owners resided in Black neighborhoods, strengthened the similarity between the old Jewish economic role vis-à-vis East European peasantry and their subsequent role in relation to African Americans. Moreover, the rural origins of recent Black migrants from the South deepened their similarity to the peasantry in Jewish eyes.[10]

Absolute Beginners—First Impressions

To Jewish immigrants from Eastern Europe, African Americans looked exotic and novel. When a newly-arrived immigrant by the name of Dave Pearlman began peddling (1884) in the town of Americus, Georgia, the first house he visited was the home of a Black family; when the door opened, Pearlman found himself staring "into the eyes of a large, smiling black woman." As he had never seen a Black person before, he briefly could not tell apart her skin from the dark background of her home's interior, so he believed he saw "two bodiless eyes and an empty, floating dress." He screamed, "A dybbuk [an evil spirit]," and fell flat on his back; later he made sure to spit in the air to fend off the evil eye. A Lithuanian-born Jewish immigrant by the name of Menachem Mendel Frieden immigrated to America in 1904, arriving in Norfolk, Virginia; he recalled, "I feared whenever I saw them, since one has to become accustomed to these black-skinned people. I had never before seen people of this color, their behavior brutish and lacking in manners." When a young immigrant by the name of Sam Carasik arrived in Baltimore in 1906 from Bobroysk (in modern-day Belarus), he saw many African Americans. Carasik told his friends that one of the Black men looked like a "polished boot"; as had been the case with Pearlman, Carasik's more experienced family members or friends laughed at him for being a "greenhorn."[11]

A more learned immigrant, the Hebrew educator Zvi Scharfstein, who would later become active in communal schooling initiatives and a professor of education at the Jewish Theological Seminary in New York, arrived in the city in 1914. On his third day in America, as he and his wife were walking down the Bowery, they saw African Americans: "It was the first time we saw Black people. Beforehand we saw them only in books and newspapers' illustrations. Now they actually passed by us, showing their white teeth and pouting their thick lips, whose strong redness lit their faces' blackness. With each encounter or brushing elbows against them—my heart quivered." Scharfstein admitted that ". . . woe to my disgrace! Even now, after living for forty years in America, after spending time with Black men and women who are servants in my house . . . I cannot remove completely the traces of that hidden fear from my heart." Yiddish poet Malka Li arrived in New York in 1921 at the age of seventeen and, as with Sholem Aleichem's Motl the Cantor's Son, her first encounter with Black people was on the subway: "There I saw Negroes and Negresses for the first time. [Previously] I have seen them only in geographical pictures and now I do not take off my eyes from them."[12]

Neighbors and Strangers

As historians Robert G. Weisbord, Arthur Stein, and Seth M. Scheiner have demonstrated, until World War I contacts between Jews and African Americans in New York City remained rather sporadic.[13] A Yiddish journalist and labor organizer, Menakhem-Mendel Tsipin, traveled (1914) to Detroit to write about Jewish life there: Though the two groups rarely socialized, Tsipin was surprised to report that Jews and Blacks lived "in very close proximity" that "I have never seen before." Tsipin's description suggests that while Jews indeed lived not far from African Americans in New York of the 1910s, the immediate vicinity of the two groups in Detroit was still a noteworthy phenomenon for a New York-based Jew. Another factor was sheer numbers—more than 1.3 million Jews lived in the Empire City in 1914, compared to slightly over 100,000 African Americans.[14]

Immigrant Jews in New York, Chicago, Atlanta, and other places proved to have less compunction than most white Americans—both native-born and immigrants—about living alongside African Americans. Hailing from a society where it was common to trade with peasants and others of different backgrounds, Yiddish-speaking Jews were quite willing to conduct business and live close to their Black customers. By the turn of the twentieth century, there was a noticeable population of Jewish immigrants in Manhattan's Black neighborhood of San Juan Hill. In Atlanta, Russian and Polish Jews usually clustered near but not within Black neighborhoods, except for Jewish grocers, who lived above their stores located within Black sections of the city. As an African American newspaper in Savannah, Georgia, commented in 1923, Jews were not too proud to live in a Black district.[15] Jews remained an identifiable minority within the Black section of Harlem (north of 130th Street and west of Park Avenue) throughout the 1910s; and though their numbers began to decline after the massive influx of Southern African Americans into Harlem during World War I, by 1920 Jews made up nearly the entire white population in that district of Harlem. A cofounder of the NAACP, Mary Ovington, observed that in New York, "Jews and Italians prove less belligerent tenement neighbors than Irish."[16]

Jewish immigrants, however, had their own reservations and did not always welcome Black neighbors. Sociologist Thomas Jesse Jones, who studied an East Harlem block between 1897 and 1901, reported that the "pressure to leave has been heavy" on the block's "remaining negroes," as "The mutual hatred of the Jew and negro is hearty. Once they separate, they never meet again." Several Black families "expressed their regret at seeing Jews come into the street, while they lived on good terms with the Italians." Jewish landlords were concerned that their property would be devalued if Black residents would settle in or near it. An African American newspaper, *New York Age*, complained in 1908–1909 that the property owners' West Side Improvement Association, an organization formed (among other reasons) to bar Black encroachment in West Harlem, was "composed in the main of Jews," among them East-Side banker Meyer Yarmulovsky (Jarmulowsky). In 1913 a Jewish landlord, Raphael Greenbaum, sued another (white) landlord for violating a restrictive covenant by renting to Black tenants. A real estate ad in a Yiddish newspaper (1914), which listed an apartment for sale or lease on West 133rd Street between Lenox and 7th Avenue, noted, "in a Niger neighborhood, but the house is in good condition."[17]

There were certainly pull factors—better housing and economic opportunities—in the process by which almost all of Harlem's Jewish residents left the neighborhood between 1917 and 1930. The influx of African Americans into the neighborhood during World War I and the 1920s, nevertheless, also played a crucial role in the Jewish exodus. Distinguished sociologist Irving Louis Horowitz, who grew up in Harlem in the 1930s, remembered how other Jews looked at Jews who stayed in Harlem "as dregs—social scourges and economic failures—simply by virtue of the fact that they remained" in what was quickly becoming a deteriorating Black neighborhood. Just north of Harlem, in Washington Heights, where former Jewish Harlemites settled, Jewish landlords implemented racially restrictive agreements, which barred Black residents. The Windy City witnessed a pattern of ethnic succession similar to that of Harlem: While East European Jews replaced the Irish and Germans in Chicago's Maxwell Street section, Jewish exodus from the area began already around 1910, as African Americans started moving in. In the 1920s, Jews left Grand Boulevard (today's Dr. Martin Luther King Jr. Drive) and Washington Park, and by 1930 Black residents comprised over 90 percent of the population in each of those two neighborhoods.[18]

Patterns of ethnic residential succession were closely tied to class difference and social distance, which often affected the images of African Americans among immigrant Jews. Russian-born physician and economist, Isaac M. Rubinow, wrote in 1902 that the emerging Jewish immigrant middle class aspired to reside in the new buildings, "with an elevator and a 'nigger boy' on the stoop." In 1917 the *Forverts* published a feuilleton that humorously depicted how Jewish families were moving uptown and reminded its readers of the "Negro who operates the elevator," who, with air of authority, "stands like a captain and hands out a timetable to each new neighbor" on moving day. Longtime civil rights activist, Rabbi Israel Goldstein, who grew up in a Yiddish-speaking community in South Philadelphia in the 1900s, mentioned how Jews took it "for granted" that "our Black fellow citizens were mostly engaged in menial occupations." Goldstein, who from 1918 served as the rabbi of Manhattan's prestigious synagogue B'nai Jeshurun and later headed the American Jewish Congress, reminisced that "Jews probably sinned less against the Negro than others." Nonetheless, Goldstein argued that "Jewish belabastas [sic] [proprietors, bourgeois] looked down upon the schwartze [Blacks]." So even if someone among them "may have been very nice personally to his Negro chauffeur or servant or whatever it was, [he] had a contempt for him which showed through inevitably, he regarded him as a lower species of human being."[19]

Beyond residential or class differences, Jewish immigrants also viewed African Americans with trepidation. A Board of Education plan (1904) to send Jewish pupils from overcrowded schools on the East Side to the West Side drew some two thousand angry Jewish parents, who protested against the plan. Whereas the racial aspect was not necessarily the chief cause for alarm, it did come up. The moderate *Yidishe velt* reminded its readers that the proposed plan would send Jewish children into "a Negro neighborhood, not far from the Tenderloin [district]," where they would face "Negroes and painted-up hussies." Abraham H. Fromenson, President of the Zionist Council of Greater New York, who was also involved in working against Christian missionaries, and served as coeditor of the conservative *Yidishes tageblat* (Jewish Daily News), warned that the children would be sent to a school on West 46th Street, "a street infested with the dirtiest rabble, the scum of the colored race."[20]

Furthermore, for Yiddish-speaking Jews the very look of Black people immediately put the latter under the category of non-Jews. Small groups of African Americans who termed themselves "Black Jews" appeared in Harlem circa 1915, but at that time Jewish immigrants scarcely knew anything about them and if they did, regarded them as Gentiles. The poet and novelist, Harry Roskolenko, who grew up on the Lower East Side in the 1910s, told his immigrant mother during World War I that there were "Negro Jews" in Harlem: "[S]he was astonished at first and later insisted that I had invented them." When he asked her what she would do if her daughter married a Negro Jew, "she slapped my face and that ended my sociological explorations." Communist writer Michael Gold (pseudonym of Isaac Granich), who grew up on the Lower East Side about a decade earlier than Roskolenko, recalled in a semi-autobiographical novel how his Romanian-born father "fetched a Negro to supper," who was "tall, stiff, unsmiling, mysterious as death." The father reassured his wife, "Katie, do not be frightened. . . . This black man is one of us. He is an African Jew." Yet the mother sneaked out to inform the neighbors and they "came in to witness the miracle." Overall, among Yiddish-speaking Jews, the idea of Black Jews was met "with incredulity or amusement."[21]

The skepticism about whether Black Jews were genuinely Jewish was far from being merely a religious concern in early twentieth-century America. Even Jews who sympathized with African Americans felt the need to denote a clear racial differentiation between Jews and Blacks. At a time of growing xenophobia and antisemitism, any recognition of Black individuals as Jews could have cost dearly in undermining the Jewish claim for whiteness. In 1924, Romanian born Jewish writer and journalist, Konrad Bercovici, published an ethnographic report about the Black population of Harlem. Whereas he used stereotypical terms to describe Black "naïve merriment" and "gaiety," his nuanced text distinguished between various points of view and factions in Black Harlem and expressed sympathy for the plight of African Americans. Bercovici depicted the "Jewish Negroes—Abyssinian Jews, squat and long bearded, hooknosed *falashes*, real Jews—who because of their color are compelled to live among people of an alien faith instead of among their own co-religionists." Several Black Jews told him that they wanted "to live among the other Jews," but the latter did not want to socialize with them. Black Jews resented "their inability to mingle with their white brethren of the same religion," and it made them "bitter against their privileged co-religionists." In 1929, the *New York Sun* published a story in which a downtown kosher butcher was chuckling as he told a customer, "Funny thing. . . . Some colored people came in this morning and wanted some kosher meat. Real negro people from up in Harlem." The butcher laughed as he said, "They say they are Jews!"[22]

Socioeconomic Relations

Unlike Italian or Slavic immigrants, Jews rarely worked as common laborers or menial workers; thus, there was barely any job competition between them and African Americans. Before 1920, the numbers of African Americans in New York's garment industry remained very low. As more and more Black workers entered the needle trades, Jewish labor unionists attempted to organize them, departing from the exclusionary practices of most American unions. In the context of the labor market, Mary Ovington noted (1911) that in dealing with Black coworkers, "Jewish girls are especially tolerant. They believe that good character and decent manners should count, not color." Moreover, Jewish unions assisted the establishment of Black workers' unions, such as A. Phillip Randolph's Brotherhood of Sleeping Car Porters. Jewish labor organizers and socialists were aware that employers in various industries, including the garment industry, often hired Black workers as strikebreakers. In 1920, the president of the largest Jewish-dominated labor union in America, the International Ladies' Garment Workers' Union (ILGWU), Benjamin Schlesinger, reported that African American women had "begun invading" the ladies' needle trades in several cities, where employers used them "as a club" against the unions; nonetheless, Schlesinger promised, the union was making inroads in educating and organizing this incipient Black constituency.[23]

Like other socialists and labor leaders, Schlesinger presented future plans as if they were achieved goals. The reality is that the low number of the union's Black members declined even further after 1920: In

1929, approximately 4,000 Black women worked in dress shops in New York City, of whom only 200 were union members. The numbers of African American workers in men's clothing were even lower, since that industry required less semi-skilled workers; therefore, the other predominantly Jewish labor union, the Amalgamated Clothing Workers of America (ACWA), developed less extensive efforts to organize Black workers. Still, ACWA's Yiddish organ, *Fortshrit* (Progress), consistently and strongly condemned racism and violence against African Americans: After the East St. Louis race riots in 1917, the paper sarcastically noted that many white Americans believe the "pogrom" against Black Americans "was a just one," since "they should not have had black skin." Despite the ACWA's miniscule number of Black members, an organizer for the ACWA, S. Drobkin, praised in 1917 African American strikers, "whose eyes glistened with fire of enthusiasm and faith in their just cause." To be sure, Jewish union leaders and organizers were habitually self-congratulatory and exaggerated the level of interracial solidarity and cooperation. Yet they made constant efforts to organize Black workers even though the latter's small numbers in the needle trades (among other reasons) rendered such efforts nearly ineffectual.[24]

As the upcoming chapter about the Yiddish press demonstrates, the ideal of racial equality and nondiscrimination would remain central among Jewish labor organizers and socialists, *alongside* remarks that highlighted African Americans' alleged backwardness and inferiority. Russian-born labor lawyer Meyer London, the first East Coast socialist elected (1914) to the U.S. House of Representatives, who represented Manhattan's Lower East Side, spoke in January 1922 in support of the Dyer anti-lynching bill. London said, "We owe to the Negro our love because of the martyrdom to which we have subjected him." The *Forverts*'s Yiddish summary of London's speech began with another sentence from it: "I look upon the colored man as my weaker and younger brother. I owe him the duty of defending him." Whereas there is no doubt about London's empathy and sincerity in fighting against racism and lynching, and being ahead of his time, casting African Americans as the "weaker and younger brother" reflected underlying assumptions and expectations that would bedevil Black-Jewish relations for decades to come.[25]

Another example of such duality was articulated in 1926 by Abraham Revusky, a Labor Zionist who immigrated to America two years earlier and wrote profusely about American socialism. Revusky hailed the progress made by Black Southerners in terms of increased literacy levels and obtaining college degrees and unambiguously denounced the racism of white labor unions. A compassionate observer who was in touch with Black socialists, Revusky also noted that from the employers' viewpoint, Black workers "excel not only in lower material needs, but also in greater mental servility and subordination to the 'boss.'" Revusky lamented the paucity of a revolutionary Black leadership, and in his reference to communism, he described the "lack of truly capable persons" among Black radicals, except for Lovett Fort-Whiteman (who would later perish in a Soviet Gulag).[26]

Whereas contacts between Jewish immigrants and African American workers in the garment industry were largely intermittent in the period up to 1929, many Jewish peddlers, storeowners, pawnbrokers, and saloonkeepers met and dealt daily with Black clients. Scholars have mentioned cases that exhibited amicable and even intimate relations between Jewish peddlers and merchants and their Black clients. Not only were Jews more willing to conduct business with Black buyers, but some of them also remained oblivious to white racial codes, staying overnight at African American homes, eating meals with those families, or just greeting Black fieldhands. While non-Jewish white merchants talked rudely to their Black customers, "Well, boy, what do you want?," Jewish traders addressed them as "Mr." or "Mrs.," and asked, "What can I do for you?" Jewish storekeepers in the South allowed Black clients to try on clothes, something that other stores would never do, as white buyers would deem such clothes unwearable. One Jewish storeowner recollected, "We took no chances. We did not even offer any of this ready-to-wear apparel to our white customers, so they could never say a Negro had tried it on." Furthermore, unlike American-born and established Central European Jews, many East European Jews' language, accent, and clothing relegated them to the margins of white Southern society. As a historian of Southern Jewry noted, since Jewish immigrants had not met Black people before, they were more likely to behave according to their actual experience with African Americans rather than out of the history of slavery and hatred: "When the Negro smiled at the Jew, the Jew smiled back."[27]

Nevertheless, the relations between Jewish peddlers and merchants and their Black clientele should not be romanticized, as they were beset with suspicions and prejudice. That antagonism had to do not only with Blacks' and Jews' respective views of one another, but also with the prevalent effects of white racism. Arriving in America mostly with little capital and little knowledge of English, East European Jews turned to seek the patronage of customers—namely poor African Americans—whose business was often shunned by more established merchants. Already in 1898, famed author Mark Twain, whose own portrayal of Jews was slanted, noted that the Jewish merchant "supplied all the negro's wants on credit," and "Before long, the whites detested the Jew, and it is doubtful if the negro loved him." Jewish newcomers were soon warned by family and friends not to transgress racial etiquette. More than half a century after Dave Pearlman's death (1916), his family members remembered his stories about what happened in 1884, when his cousin, Sam, first learned that Dave stayed overnight in the homes of his Black customers; Sam's "face suddenly turned ashen white." In a loud voice, Sam said, "It is forbidden. . . . You can't associate with them in that way. Sell to them—yes. Take their money—yes . . . but do it all outside." What terrified Sam was that Dave told white farmers that he stayed overnight in the homes of Black customers, hence confirming that Jews broke racial codes. An apparent violation of such codes could have endangered not just the livelihood but also the lives of Jewish communities. After a race riot erupted in Atlanta in September 1906, local newspapers and public figures accused mostly Jewish saloon owners, who allegedly emboldened Black depravity and drunkenness. In the wake of the riot, city authorities shut down several dozen saloons owned by Jewish immigrants.[28]

Commercial relations and physical proximity were accompanied by cases in which Jewish peddlers, pawnbrokers, and storeowners fell victim to Black perpetrators. Fear of violence by Black offenders or assumptions about purported Black wantonness made its way into Jewish descriptions of African Americans. In 1897, *Harper's Weekly* published a story by Edwin Emerson Jr. about Jewish immigrants on Manhattan's West Side (between 28th and 42nd Streets). Barely concealing his own hatred of both Jews (whose accent his report mimicked) and African Americans, Emerson conveyed the feelings of a Jewish garment storekeeper toward his Black clientele: The Black man "is unclean and all vot he touches is unclean." The storekeeper told how occasionally he and his family had to flee to "where we be noddings but white peoples" when the typical Black man “fight and scream ofer his wifes and childrens, and cuts and hacks mit razors and knifes.” Emerson observed “the stoic scorn of the Hebrew” toward “the happy-go-lucky joyousness of his dusky neighbor,” scorn that was curbed by the Jewish “pizzness is pizzness” dictum. As one scholar has justly noted, Emerson revealed his own “maliciousness,” yet the sentiments he portrayed “have an authentic ring.”[29]

If Emerson’s perspective was that of a hostile outsider, Jewish sources affirmed his impression. When Menachem Mendel Frieden arrived in Norfolk, Virginia (1904), he joined his brother, who resided where his store was located, at the heart of a Black neighborhood. Frieden recalled that he could not understand “why behavior was different towards the ‘niggars,’ as they were called there” and asked his brother about that. The brother replied, “Wait till you get to know them and then talk about it.” New to America and hardly speaking any English at all, Frieden soon realized that a “‘black’ store did not cost much” and opened a grocery store outside Norfolk, which served Black clients in that area. Frieden mentioned that among his family members and friends, “The assumption was that every black was a thief and a murderer,” and “one had to keep a careful watch around them.” Frieden described dealing with Black customers and how he “shook all over with fear”: “Their faces were the faces of savages, their eyes protruding and frightening,” and “these blacks will take advantage of you when they see that you’re afraid. They steal merchandise and tell you to shut up.” Yet Frieden admitted that they were excellent buyers, as “they can easily be convinced of almost anything. They have faith in the white man, especially in the South, a legacy of years of slavery.” According to him, African Americans “want to buy everything they see,” and “They are among the best of customers; they don’t have the inclination to save. Everything they earn they spend immediately.”[30]

Socialist Zionist leader Borekh Tsukerman, who emigrated to the United States from his native Lithuania in 1904, pointed to a specific form of economic activity among Jewish immigrants as a potential source of friction with Black clients—the customer peddler. Those peddlers sold their customers almost anything—clothing, furniture, home equipment, and other products, carried no merchandise with them, but rather sent their clients to pick up the wares from wholesalers. The buyers paid off the peddler in weekly installments, and as Tsukerman travelled across the country in 1907–1908, he noticed such peddlers “in almost every city and town." Tsukerman noted, "the exploitation of the buyer was enormous. The [peddler's] profits had to be very high to cover damages when buyers ceased paying and legally you could not collect from them" as the clients were so impoverished. Somewhat disclosing his own bias, Tsukerman claimed, "the customers were among the poorest and most backward element," since "most of them [customer peddlers] peddled among Negro families." In his view, "the anti-Jewish sentiment that grew in the hearts of the non-Jewish buyers" of customer peddlers caused much damage, as clients "began regarding him as an exploiter, which unfortunately was not far from the truth."[31]

"Much Poorer, More Ignorant"—Impressions of Visitors and Locals

What most of those sources point to is a continuation of an East European Jewish pattern in dealing with peasant clients: intensive economic relations combined with minimal social intermingling. Traveling across the Mississippi Valley in 1916, Yiddish journalist H. Levin published his impressions in the nonpartisan, liberal Yiddish daily *Der tog* (The Day). Levin berated what he saw as the bigotry of Southern Jews—the Jewish merchant in the South "makes a living of the Negro but *liking* the Negro—no." Black observers seemed to admire Jews' group cohesion and anti-assimilationism, noticing the mixture of physical proximity and social distancing. An African American newspaper in Atlanta, *The Voice of the Negro*, praised (1906) Jewish "self-respect" and how miscegenation was rare among Jewish storekeepers who resided "right in the middle of a strictly colored neighborhood." A Black minister in Norfolk, Virginia, Richard Bowling, commented in 1928 about the Jewish businessowner, "Six days out of seven he, his wife, and his children will see more of colored people than . . . even their fellow Jews. Howbeit, they all remain Jews. Neither does colored blood filter into their family nor does any of the Jewish blood filter into the veins of Negroes. They are in the Negro world but not of it."[32]

If Levin's report focused on the attitudes of Southern Jews, an ambivalent approach toward African Americans was noticeable also among Jewish radicals who visited the South. One of the leaders of the Jewish socialist Bund in Tsarist Russia was Borekh Charney Vladeck, who immigrated to America in 1908. In later years, he toured across the country as a Yiddish public speaker and advocate of socialism, and witnessed Jewish life in the South as well as racial violence and abuse. Vladeck recalled how in Savannah, Georgia, he protested (1911) the abysmal violence against the city's Black population before the local police chief. The latter laughed, and told him, "you don't belong here—go back to your goddam New York." At the same time, Vladeck wrote in 1911 that for Jewish peddlers and storeowners, "the Niger here took the place of the peasant in the old home," with the difference that the Black Southerner "is much poorer, more ignorant, and dejected" than the Old-World peasant. The socialist leader maintained, "The Jew does not really hate the Black so vehemently as the Christian white. But in general . . . [the local Jew] shows no sympathy with him." Vladeck noted how the Jewish grocer resided in Atlanta's Black section, and his children "are under the influence of the Black Street, which is still half-savage and barbaric." Interestingly, while Vladeck condemned Southern Jewish businessowners' treatment of African Americans, he also argued that local Black people "entirely deny our 'white' privileges and say: You are no white—you're a Jew." The reason for it, Vladeck believed, was that Black locals "had less fear of the Jew than of the [white] Christian" since they came in close contact with Jews and "feel less hatred from the Jew than from the white Christian."[33]

The ambivalence toward African Americans was evident in the reports and impressions of one of the most prominent figures in the Yiddish press and Jewish socialism, the editor of the *Forverts*, Abraham Cahan. Cahan recalled that around 1900 he attended a "cake walk" show at Madison Square Garden (which he explained as "a kind of a Negro sport"), and noted, "In their way, they [Blacks] are very musical." Cahan believed that Black people were easily moved by dramatic effects: "[T] hey easily let out soulful sighs and hearty laughs just like children." In 1914, Cahan traveled to Atlanta to cover the trial of Leo Frank, and his reports from Atlanta drew an interesting parallel between white Southerners and Gentiles in Eastern Europe (particularly Polish lords, the *pritsim*). Southerners were "not so petty, enthusiastic about the cent, and grudging" as were Northern businessmen, but rather "hospitable" and relaxed. But Cahan believed that those very features were closely associated to the fact that local whites were used to have Black slaves perform all the hard work, and therefore lived "like the Russian or Polish pritsim used to live before serfdom was abolished"; carrying on that transnational analogy, Cahan wrote that Southern whites "had other traits of the Polish lords' character," such as being hotheaded and "more primitive" than Northerners.[34]

While writing that whites and Blacks were separated "just as people are separated from cattle," another thing that caught Cahan's eye was how "The streets were full of Negroes, mostly filthy and ragged." Commenting on the relations between Black women and men, Cahan noted that many couples were not married, and "the moral concepts among Negroes are not as strict . . . as by the whites," but the Black public opinion was "more sincere" than that of whites. During Frank's trial, Cahan detailed the testimony of the Black janitor, Jim Conley: He was the initial prime suspect, and testified against his employer (Frank). Most contemporary scholars believe that Conley was, in fact, the real murderer. Cahan enlightened his readers on the manner in which the "sly" Conley convinced the white jury: Black people had "fantasy power," and "talent for music and poetry," and "many of them are great liars." "When a Negro tells a lie, he always tells it with details, so it would seem true"; even "the most savage person from Africa is cunning," and Conley "was more cunning than the average Negro."[35]

Similar to Vladeck and Cahan, another socialist, Labor Zionist educator and writer Yoel Entin, who traveled (1924) across the South, also communicated an ambivalent picture of African Americans. Entin decried "the exploitation of the Negro" and "the whole cursed 'race problem' with all its painful and miserable ramifications," and remarked that the Black population gave the south much of "its special color and sound." Nonetheless, Entin portrayed the "dirty streets" where the Black population lived, "with its carefree joy of life, with its childish laughter, with the spicy tease of its mulatto daughters, a tease that already the old French 'decadents' understood well." Entin associated Black people not only with childlike behavior and unconfined sexuality, but also with looming violence: Entin spoke to a Jewish storekeeper in an undisclosed Southern city, who "sits in a little, dark, filthy Negro alley" and all his customers are Black. But the storekeeper was deeply frightened, since in the past "he testified against a Negro, and his [the Black man's] friends have plotted revenge."[36]

The reports of journalist Shmuel Blum revealed similar contradictory feelings. Blum immigrated from Byelorussia in 1909, and by 1920 was studying at the University of South Carolina; that year he recounted how African Americans performed most of the backbreaking jobs, only to be called "lazy" by the local whites. Blum argued that despite the profound Jewish misery, "we [Jews] still have hope," but "the Negroes' sufferings are deeper and graver, and without any hope." In a remark on Blum's essay, the editor, Avrom Lesin, exemplified the analogy between East European Jews and Southern Blacks, writing that you could believe what a white teacher said about Black pupils "exactly as you could believe what a Pole says about Jews." Yet apparently Lesin had no qualms about publishing other aspects of Blum's impressions in the socialist monthly *Di tsukunft* (The Future), which he edited. On the one hand, Blum deplored white racism in the South, shown also by Jews, like an unnamed Texas rabbi who told Blum that Black individuals "are not human beings, they are not descended from Adam." On the other, Blum claimed "the brain matter of a Negro skull is on average much smaller than the brain matter of a European skull." Blum believed that "in general, the Negro is ignorant . . . his childishness is very vivid in his anger: When a Negro becomes angry . . . he is ready to commit the most terrible crimes. An hour later the same hot-tempered guy is quiet as a lamb." Blum also maintained that African Americans "are very unsanitary in their way of life" and contrasted Black districts' "unpainted, windowless, collapsed" houses with the "Negro's love of lavish, loud clothes" and being wasteful. Blum criticized what he saw as African Americans' preferences: "[D] ress up well—yeah. But keeping yourself clean, what for?" A local businessman intimated to Blum that Black customers do not spend much on underwear—"why wear a costly undershirt that nobody can see?"[37]

The complex, nearly tortured, ambivalence of East European Jews toward African Americans, where empathy coexisted with reserve, appears clearly in the writing of Reform Rabbi Max (Mordecai Ze'ev) Raisin. Born in Byelorussia to a distinguished rabbinic family, he arrived (1893) in New York City at the age of eleven. One of the first East European Jews to study and be ordained (1903) at the Reform movement's Hebrew Union College, Raisin served as the rabbi of various congregations in Stockton, California; Meridian, Mississippi; Brooklyn, New York; and finally in Paterson, New Jersey. Raisin also served as the American correspondent of several Hebrew newspapers in Europe. While serving as a rabbi in Mississippi, Raisin supported equal rights for African Americans and traveled to the state capital, Jackson, to advocate for them. By the mid-1930s, Raisin expressed deep concern about the suffering of African Americans, writing, "I bow before Blacks in respect." As he pondered over the hatred toward Black Americans, Raisin admitted "and then I thank God that we Jews have at least white skin and are able to intermingle among whites." Yet immediately as this thought crossed his mind, "a feeling of self-disgust attacks me, and I bury my face in the ground in burning shame." Despite that shame, in the same place Raisin also penned, "Negroes must not be likened to Jews. They never wrote a bible, did not give prophets and messiahs to the world." The rabbi also commented, "only white trash will agree to marry Blacks" and believed that Jews (among others) left Harlem because of the influx of Black population.[38] Raisin's argument that Blacks "must not" be equated with Jews paralleled the recollection of a prominent Jewish figure, veteran Tammany Hall Judge, Jonah J. Goldstein. Goldstein, who was involved in many downtown associations, recalled an instructor at the Educational Alliance (an organization established by uptown Jews to Americanize Jewish immigrants) by the name of Mr. Davis. In one of his classes (1904), Davis mentioned "how ridiculous" was the idea there could be any similarity between Jews and Blacks.[39]

Raisin's gratitude to God for giving Jews a white skin reflected keen awareness of Jews' precarious situation in America's racial hierarchy. That recognition and the anxiety about the dangerous repercussions of not following white society's racial principles manifested itself in a 1928 exchange between Jewish intellectuals in the monthly *The Reflex*, which served as a forum for contemporary American Jewish life. That year, Lithuanian-born playwright Emanuel Jo Basshe and film producer and literary critic Bernard Smith severely criticized American Jews' behavior toward African Americans. They argued that not only established Jews, but also among "the newer immigrants, the Polish and Roumanian Jews of New York," once "the immigrant establish[es] himself economically and socially . . . than he begins to sneer at the 'nigger' and regard him as an object of exploitation, a creature good only for the dirtiest of jobs." Apart from being afraid to rock the boat, Basshe and Smith maintained, Jews' "insistence upon superiority to the Negro is the Jew's compensation for his own traditional inferiority." A quick reply was penned by the founder and editor of *The Reflex*, Shmuel M. Melamed. A former yeshiva student from Lithuania who studied in Germany, Melamed immigrated to the United States in 1914 and became a prolific writer in a host of German and later American newspapers, as well as in the Yiddish and Hebrew press. During World War I, his anti-Russian writings in Yiddish carried with them a negative and racialized imagery of all Slavs as "Asiatic." Melamed lampooned Basshe and Smith as having "a maximum of idealism and a minimum of experience" and soberly cautioned, "it would be criminal folly on the part of the American Jew to provoke the Gentile by treating the Negro as an equal." As "the racial line of demarcation is drawn very sharply" in America, "the Jew is a white man" and must follow the majority; to do otherwise "would be suicidal," and the Jew "can not afford to be less barbaric than his [white] neighbors."[40]

Potential Allies—Neither Immediately nor Completely

Several scholars have seen the Frank case as a starting point for alliance-building between African Americans and Jews in America. According to that interpretation, the lynching was a wake-up call for Jewish leaders, who were shocked to see that "an established Jewish merchant could be more vulnerable than a Black janitor." Thus, not only did the murderous wickedness of lynching in general dawn on those leaders: They began to see that Jews and Blacks shared a history of oppression and marginalization, and that as long as Blacks were lynched, disenfranchised, and discriminated against, American Jews were not safe either.[41]

Nonetheless, the period following Frank's murder did not display immediate signs of Jewish kinship with Black Americans. As historian Eugene Levy has rightly concluded, the Frank affair was the first incident that drew national attention, where the needs of African Americans and American Jews seemed to have been in direct conflict. The testimony of Jim Conley, the Black janitor, was a key factor in the prosecution's case, while Frank's legal team hoped to make the most of the Southern Black–White divide by employing an overtly racist language: One of Frank's attorneys referred to Conley as a "dirty, filthy, black, drunken, lying nigger." Many Jews believed that Conley was the real murderer, who heaped on lies about Frank to exculpate himself. The Anglo-Jewish press across the country widely reprinted editorials from various American newspapers that termed the janitor "depraved negro" or "black human animal," a fact noted and resented by the African American press. Furthermore, as discussed in chapter 3 below, the Yiddish intelligentsia's notions of civilization and savagery—in part influenced by prevailing concepts of racial hierarchy in American society—was evident in its portrayal of black-skinned people.[42]

Rather than Frank's lynching in and of itself, it was the changing conditions in the United States and in Eastern Europe during and after the Great War which would lead to the beginning of an attitudinal change among immigrant Jews toward African Americans and viewing them as potential allies. The emergence of American xenophobia during World War I and the ensuing Red Scare was intensified by the early 1920s, a decade that historian John Higham has called "The Tribal Twenties" for its crop of bigotry: On top of Henry Ford's anti-Jewish campaign came immigration restriction, universities' quotas, "Christians only" employment advertisements, a resurgent Ku Klux Klan, residential restrictions, and social exclusion.[43]

The question of restricted immigration became acute especially from 1917 on, as a civil war wreaked havoc (1917–1922) on the former Pale of Settlement, where Reds (Bolsheviks) fought Whites (counterrevolutionaries), Poles fought Ukrainians, Poles fought Bolsheviks, and Ukrainians fought amongst themselves. White armies, Polish forces, Ukrainian nationalists under Semyon Petlyura, and marauding bands of peasants and Cossacks attacked hundreds of Jewish communities, massacring unarmed, non-combatant Jewish families. Most estimates of Jews murdered or succumbing to disease and hunger mention a death toll of between 100,000 and 150,000, with many more injured and orphaned. Famed Russian-Jewish writer Isaac Babel, who traveled with a Red Army cavalry unit as a war correspondent, saw "naked seventy year-old men with their skulls bashed in and tiny children with their fingers hacked off."[44]

The news about the horrors that befell East European Jewry and the need to work for an immediate relief for one's family members engulfed nearly every Jewish immigrant family and raised relief work to a fever pitch. Under such domestic and international circumstances, the search for political allies became ever more pressing. Jewish unions would turn to organizing Black workers in the postwar years; another arena was civil rights. Although most of the Jews who were involved in civil rights organizations were not immigrants, several prominent East European Jews, like Henry Moskowitz and Jacob Billikopf, were active in the NAACP. More than before, the Yiddish press emphasized the parallels between the Jewish and Black historical experience, strongly condemned white racism, and applauded African American achievements.[45] Still, those changes did not occur at once and much ambivalence remained. The next three chapters demonstrate how the Yiddish press, theater, and literature continued to exhibit contradictory representations of Black Americans into the 1920s, in which sympathy and alienation coexisted.

* * *

Yiddish culture reflected the multi-layered encounter of Yiddish-speaking Jews with Black Americans. The type of characteristics that were often assigned to African Americans reflected a combination of two sources. One consisted of Jewish patterns of behavior and thought in Eastern Europe; the second was American racial attitudes. Class discrepancies sharpened the image of the Black population as the equivalent of the low-class Gentiles that Jews used to deal with in the Old World. The nature of economic relations with Black clients, added to the latter's low socioeconomic status and certain fears about their volatility and violence, paralleled Jewish attitudes toward a well-defined stratum in Eastern Europe: the *poyerim/muzhikes* (peasants). The images of peasants were interwoven in the way many immigrants perceived African Americans, with all the associated traits. As Jews in Eastern Europe differentiated between what they saw as high-cultured and low-cultured Gentiles, the peasantry was categorically cast as the latter.[46] Whereas there were other low-status groups, e.g., the Irish, Italian, and East European immigrants, those groups did not occupy the same place in American society's racial order. Jewish newcomers would soon become aware of white racial etiquette and that would have a deep impact on their dealings with Black Americans.

Economic realities in the United States, where Jews had Black clients in their clothing and dry goods stores, Black clients in their bars, Black maids in their homes, and Black tenants in their buildings, intensified the image of Black people as America's peasants. Like the Slavic peasantry, Black women and men were seen as simple and direct, sexually freer (or promiscuous), at times childlike, yet also volatile, potentially dangerous, and prone to violence. The Jewish merchant, journalist, or commentator expressed a mixture of pity for the Blacks' suffering and fear of their purported wantonness. The economic role played by Jews and the rural background of Black Southerners intensified the attitudinal similarity to the peasantry. Some of those attributes resembled the traits that American white society ascribed to African Americans; even if Jewish newcomers did not recognize instantly the racial codes, family members and friends were certain to enlighten them, especially if their line of work involved dealing with Black customers.

The amalgamation of Old-World attitudes toward the peasantry and white American modes of relating to African Americans brought about a combination of empathy and distance. Despite the sporadic use of a rhetoric about African Americans as "America's Jews," Yiddish-speaking Jews saw the country's Black population as the New-World incarnation of East European peasantry *and* a racial other.[47] That blend of influences and ambivalence would be well evident in one of the main pillars of Yiddish culture in America—the press.

3

"They Deserve All the Political and Economic Rights"

Contradictory Attitudes Toward Black People in the Yiddish Press

In 1888, the centrist, liberal Yiddish weekly *Der folksadvokat* (The People's Advocate) published "two children's questions" on its back page. One was "Mama! When a Niger cries, does he cry out ink?" The second joke was, "Mama! How is it that the Niger doesn't stain his white collar?" Forty years later (1928), choirmaster, conductor, and publisher Yitskhok Pirozhnikov described African Americans as a musical "genius people," who overcame immense repression and hatred and developed "magnificent, noble music." Writing in the socialist monthly *Di tsukunft* (The Future), which popularized literary, historical, and scientific themes, Pirozhnikov emphasized not only jazz music and ragtime, but also "Negro spirituals," which have "*no equal among any other nation.*" What is even more incredible, he argued, is that African Americans received "no encouragement and no help" from the surrounding white population, and "the Negroes were able to derive their music only from their own source." When Pirozhnikov compared Black spirituals to Hasidic melodies, he concluded that the spirituals sounded more "aristocratically refined."[1]

A Kingdom Unto Itself

How did the Yiddish press represent African Americans and Black Africans in the late nineteenth and early twentieth centuries, and what can we learn from it? The two examples above demonstrate the considerable distance made by the press over those decades, with growing sympathy for African Americans and a more nuanced understanding of their culture; at the same time, much ambivalence would remain well into the 1920s. To comprehend better the important developments in the Yiddish press's characterization of Black women and men, we need to grasp the functions of that press. The significance of Yiddish papers in immigrant Jewish life can hardly be overstated, and the press offers one of the best sources of information on Jewish life, a source that both reflected and influenced Jewish immigrants' attitudes and worldviews. By the turn of the twentieth century, Yiddish newspapers exerted immense influence and played a key role in the larger burgeoning settlements of Yiddish-speaking immigrants in America. The American-bred expression "*Di prese iz a melukhe far zikh*" (The press is a kingdom unto itself) had been born out of a reality in which the Yiddish newspapers offered another avenue to power and constituted new communal authorities. Those newspapers represented the wide spectrum of political opinion among East European Jews after the turn of the twentieth century: Orthodox, conservative, Zionist, liberal, anarchist, socialist, and later communist (categories that were not always mutually exclusive).[2]

For the immigrants, the Yiddish paper, regardless of ideological bent, was the most accessible and authoritative source of information, guidance, and news. Journalist Hutchins Hapgood, who portrayed New York's Jewish quarter in *The Spirit of the Ghetto* (1902), concluded that the Yiddish press had largely displaced the rabbi as the teacher of the people. Twenty years later, it was sociologist Robert E. Park who asserted in his groundbreaking study of immigrant newspapers, "In the Yiddish press the foreign-language newspaper may be said to have achieved form. . . . No other press has attained so complete a simplification of the racial language, nor created so large a reading public. No other foreign-language press has succeeded in reflecting so much of the intimate life of the people which it represents." The circulation of Yiddish dailies in America surpassed any other foreign-language newspapers in absolute numbers during and after World War I, peaking at nearly 650,000 in 1916. As each sold copy circulated widely, and as alongside those dailies operated a range of Yiddish weeklies, monthlies, and other periodicals, the estimated readership of the Yiddish daily press was two million in those years.[3]

The success and influence of the Yiddish press are even more impressive when one considers the obstacles it overcame. Only a minority among the immigrants who came to America before the Kishinev pogrom (1903) and the abortive revolution in Russia (1905) had seen a Yiddish newspaper in Russia (the first Yiddish daily in Russia was established only in January 1903, mainly due to prior government censorship). Moreover, according to the Yiddish theater historian and critic, B. Gorin (pen name of Yitskhok Goydo), most Jewish immigrants in the 1880s and 1890s had limited reading skills: "The common Jewish workers back then . . . [constituted] a very coarse element, the roughest people you could meet among Jews . . . many could not even read Yiddish." Thus, reading a Yiddish newspaper was a new cultural practice, which necessitated changes in one's daily habits and literacy level.[4]

The centrality of Yiddish newspapers in immigrant Jewish life has made the press a keystone of Yiddish culture in America. The scholars who have concentrated on the Yiddish press concluded that those papers repeatedly condemned discrimination and prejudice against African Americans and underscored the similarities between the situation of Jews in Eastern Europe and African Americans in America. News items and editorials applied terms such as "pogrom" and "blood libel" when covering race riots and lynching, while the white assailants were often described as bloodthirsty pogromists. Therefore, as one of those scholars has claimed, all Yiddish papers, "despite their ideological differences . . . stressed the close parallels between them [African Americans] and Jews"; according to that view, Yiddish papers believed "there was an emotional and psychological bond which drew the two groups together," and thus, "Blacks seemed, in the eyes of Yiddish writers, [as] America's Jews."[5] Focusing on the years between 1915 and 1935, historian Hasia Diner has examined three leading Yiddish dailies—the socialist *Forverts*, conservative *Yidishes tageblat*, and Orthodox *Morgen zhurnal*—and argued they all featured "uniformity" in relation to African Americans and highlighted their uplifting attitudes toward Blacks: the unequivocal denunciation of attacks against African Americans and white racism, praise for Black achievements, critique of Jewish misbehavior toward Blacks, and viewing Black Americans as America's Jews.[6]

Whereas those observations are indeed significant, they offer a static model that does not trace changes over time in the portrayal of African Americans (and Black people in general) and does not distinguish between various Yiddish publications. In addition, such interpretations treat one segment of the multifaceted and conflicting representations of Blacks in the Yiddish press. Yiddish newspapers' sensationalism, contradictory character, and contentiousness may weaken the scope of any sweeping statement. If one can generalize, nonetheless, the best and most ennobling references were aimed at notable Black figures, as well as to the abstract, suffering Black masses, while much more critical or even dismissive allusions were made toward actual Black women and men. Furthermore, the representations of African Americans did not remain static: the last stages of World War I and its aftermath, and the unprecedented mass murder of Jews during the Russian civil war and the Polish-Soviet war (1917–1922) coincided with a strain of domestic xenophobia that underlay the Red Scare, the "Red Summer" of race riots in 1919, university quotas, the singling out of minorities, immigration restriction, and Henry Ford's antisemitic campaign (1920–1927).[7] The convergence of those events would gradually lead Yiddish writers to look at African Americans as potential allies in the struggle against America's inequities and to compare antisemitism and anti-Black racism. Yet they hardly became enamored with African Americans, and that ambivalence would continue throughout the 1920s. The opening jokes above are merely one example of the fact that the representation of Black persons in Yiddish newspapers was not limited to front-page news and editorials, but also included caricatures, jokes, advertisements, and literary pieces. Though no single chapter could cover completely how the Yiddish press in America—across its remarkable length and breadth—portrayed Blacks through 1929, this chapter examines the major features and concepts in those depictions.

In the early years, when the sight of Black people still constituted somewhat of a bemused novelty, their appearance was the topic of jokes and commentary. In 1888, an anonymous reporter from Philadelphia wrote for the *Folksadvokat* about the visit to the Quaker City of the new Chief Rabbi of New York City, Jacob Joseph. As some synagogues used to be Black churches, the writer joked that "the Nigers were forbidden to show up" when the rabbi is around, "so he wouldn't stare at a Niger and God forbid is stricken with black bile [melancholy]." Another reference utilized the black body as a yardstick: M. Lefkowitz's second-hand clothing store on Lower Manhattan's Bayard Street published a recurring advertisement (throughout 1893) in the conservative weekly *Yudishe gazeten* (Jewish Gazette). Aimed at Southern storekeepers who dealt with Black clients, the advertisement boasted that it has "large sizes with long sleeves that should fit the largest Niger," or "the right sizes that should fit the largest Niger." (See figure 3.1).[8] A different allusion,

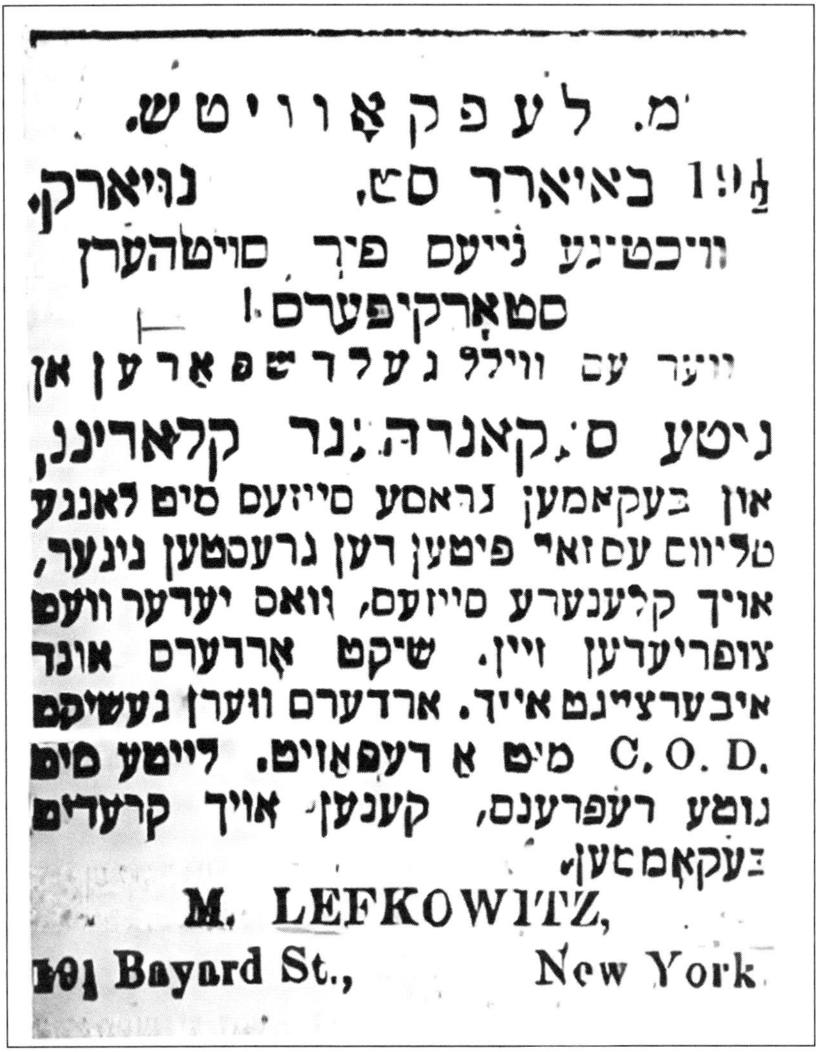

מ. לעפקאָוויטש.

101 באיארד סט. נויארק.

וויכטיגע נייעס פיר סויטהערן

סטאָרקיפּערס!

יוער עם וויל געלד שפּאַרען אן

ניטע סעקאנדהענד קלאָדינג,

און בעקאמען גראסע סייזעס מיט לאנגע

טליוס עס זאל פּיטען דען גרעסטען ניגער,

אויך קלענערע סייזעס, וואס יעדער וועט

צופריעדען זיין. שיקט אָרדערס אונד

איבערצייגט אייך. אָרדערס ווערן געשיקט

מיט א דעפּאָזיט. C. O. D. לייטע מיט

גוטע רעפערענס, קענען אויך קרעדיט

בעקאָמען.

M. LEFKOWITZ,

101 Bayard St., New York.

Figure 3.1. "That should fit the largest Niger," *Yudishe gazeten* (1893), advertisement for the Lefkowitz secondhand clothing store. Courtesy of the Historical Jewish Press Digital Collection, National Library of Israel and Tel Aviv University.

which foreshadowed Yiddish writers' critique of racism in America, is the abovementioned feuilleton in the *Yudishe gazeten* (1892), allegedly a letter from a Lithuanian Jew from Ireland, which sardonically mentioned "Your [Jews] skin is white as was George Washington's" and their hair "straight, thin, and silky"; in contrast, "The Niger may be born in America ten thousand times, but his skin is black, his hair woolly . . . he must always remain a Niger."[9]

Such an early, sarcastic comment about the ingrained racism in American society would soon be joined by one of the most important themes that recurred, albeit unevenly, throughout the Yiddish press: genuine horror and disgust with lynching, and a position that strongly protested against violence toward Black Americans, racial segregation, disenfranchisement, and racial injustice. Already in 1880, the *Yudishe gazeten* supported an African American campaign over the beating of a Black cadet by his white colleagues at West Point: "Black cadets should not be treated worse than white cadets." In August 1900, following a race riot in New York's Tenderloin district, the Yiddish newspapers expressed an uncharacteristic agreement with each other, attacking the racism that underlay the violence. The conservative *Yidishes tageblat* thought the riot was "a sad sign for Jews," while the anarchist weekly *Fraye arbeter shtime* (Free Voice of Labor) mockingly pointed to the "white man's burden," according to which the "unfortunate whites" must "civilize the savages, the Blacks" by assaulting them. Six years later, the *Yidishes tageblat* lambasted (1906) bigoted Senator Ben Tillman, comparing his racism to a "Russian Police officer, or a pogrom agitator," and blamed "those barbarians, those fanatics . . . the antisemites, the anti-Negroes, and all 'antis.'"[10]

The notion that violence against Black Americans ultimately endangers Jews was manifested early on. The *Yidishes tageblat*'s ominous statement that a race riot was "a sad sign for Jews" was echoed by its rival from the left, the socialist *Forverts*. One of the pioneers of the Yiddish socialist press in America, Louis E. Miller, observed (1903) that in the South, the attitudes of whites toward Blacks is that "of slaveowners to the slaves . . . the lyncher to the lynchee, hangman to victim." Miller cautioned that Jews "must be very careful, since next to the 'Niger' comes the Jew, and next to the 'Niger' question can pop up a 'Jews question.'" Later that year, a widely-covered lynching took place in Wilmington,

Delaware, where a Black man, George White, was burned alive for allegedly raping and murdering a white woman. In response, the moderate *Yidishe velt* warned, "The lynching of Blacks has become a horrifying epidemic," and asked, "is the soul of such white folks not blacker than the skin" of their victims when they behave "barbarically savage." In a different reaction to that lynching, the *Fraye arbeter shtime* claimed that the country lives in "a state of barbarism" and wondered "with what can the American population pride itself in comparison to the agitated, blind, and drunk peasants of Bessarabia" (where the Kishinev pogrom happened shortly beforehand).[11]

Fear of Perceived Black Volatility and Violence

Subsequent lynchings and race riots met not just wall-to-wall denunciations of violence and racism by all Yiddish newspapers, but also editorials about how such assaults blemished the very ideals at the foundation of the republic. Yet those condemnations focused on the cruelty and inhumanity of the white attackers, while African Americans often remained faceless victims. When Yiddish newspapers did describe Black women and men more directly, an ambiguous picture emerged. The sensationalist character of the Yiddish press, especially before World War I, and the fact that many news items were translated from local English and German-language newspapers, lent themselves to phrases such as "Black beast" in reports about Black suspects. The *Teglikher herold* (Daily Jewish Herald), a successful centrist daily established in 1894 by the publisher of the *Folksadvokat*, Michael (Mikhael) Mints, covered that year a race riot in Washington Court House, Ohio; the smaller headline read, "A Black beast the reason." Reporting that the state militia shot and killed several rioters as they attempted to break into the courthouse and grab a Black man convicted of rape, the paper commented, "All of that happened only because of a Black beast." In another case, where a Black man was lynched (1895) in Tennessee, the paper headlined the item with "Quick and just punishment." The Orthodox *Morgen zhurnal* put the headline "Black beast" in a 1906 report about a suspected Black attacker in Bay Ridge, Brooklyn. In 1910, the same daily published another story that mentioned a "Black Beast," the 65-year-old Allen Brooks, who was lynched in Dallas, Texas. The *Morgen zhurnal*'s "special correspondent," one Israel N. Mehl, explained, "In the South we are used already to crimes by Nigers. . . . The Nigers are especially dangerous as attackers of white women. The lynching and killings do not stop them from their devilish lust." In line with other American newspapers at the time, those Yiddish papers usually identified the race of lynching victims and suggested their culpability.[12]

Left-leaning Yiddish papers were somewhat less susceptible to the racial discourse that linked lynching to Black culpability. The socialist weekly *Arbeter tsaytung* (Worker's Paper) was established in 1890 as the organ of the United Hebrew Trades, an alliance of over twenty labor unions. It was edited for several years by Filip Krants (Philip Krantz, the pseudonym of Yankev Rombro), whose own writings about race and culture included both a sharp critique of white racism and a hierarchical view of civilization in which "low-cultured" nations, such as Black Africans, were at the bottom. The first issue of *Arbeter tsaytung* featured a rendition by the weekly's cofounder, Abraham Cahan, of an article by British explorer Herbert Ward, which Cahan titled "The Savages in Africa." Whereas he tried to argue that American capitalists were no less cruel than "their friends from wild Africa," Cahan ascribed to Africans many of the period's oversimplifications, such as bloodthirstiness and cannibalism. Perhaps to mitigate Ward's racist portrayal, Cahan reminded his readers that civilization "did not fall down from the skies" but developed gradually: "[A] thousand years ago our great-great-great-grandfathers were such savage creatures as the Black Africans" today.[13]

In 1901, after five Black laborers were lynched in Harrison County, Texas, for refusing to harvest cotton fields they rented from white planters, the *Arbeter tsaytung*'s coeditor, Herman Simpson, expressed his dismay—"five Negroes were lynched in Texas not because they committed horrible crimes against women, a claim which has become the common made-up story in every lynching, but because they refused to work" and be exploited. When a Black man, George Ward, was arrested in 1901 in Terre Haute, Indiana, for the murder of Ida Finkelstein, a Jewish teacher, the *Forverts* mentioned the suspect's race and certainty of his guilt yet warned that a lynching was imminent. After Ward was lynched, the paper termed it "Barbarism in civilized America," noted that "the mob became wild," and condemned the police, who did not stop several spectators from cutting off toes from Ward's charred body and selling them as souvenirs. After a white mob lynched (1908) nine African American men near Hemphill, Texas, the *Forverts* wryly remarked, "All whites think that you have to lynch Nigers—whether guilty or not."[14]

Nevertheless, fear of perceived Black volatility and violence crept into press reports, especially when the victims were Jewish. In 1899, the *Forverts* covered the stabbing of rabbi and meat market owner, Louis Ginzburg, in Binghamton, New York, by a Black assailant, Robert Russell. In a subheading, the paper mentioned that the rabbi "falls victim to a Niger's bloodthirst." In 1909, four Black men were lynched in Kemper County, Mississippi, after they were suspected of robbing and murdering a Jewish peddler. Both the *Yidishes tageblat* and the *Morgen zhurnal* detailed that the peddler was well known and liked by the white farmers. The *Yidishes tageblat* speculated the peddler "was murdered by Nigers. Four Nigers, probably the Jew's murderers, were lynched for it by the outraged farmers." When the peddler's body was found, the farmers "understood immediately that was the work of Nigers because none of the whites could have committed such a gruesome murder." The *Morgen zhurnal* relayed the story in a similar manner, yet did not include the word "probably." Later that year, the same daily reported, "a Niger bandit stabs three Jews" in Philadelphia, mentioning how the "wild Niger" also fought a policeman, but the latter subdued the "wild animal." In 1914, the left-leaning satirical Yiddish weekly *Der groyser kundes* (The Big Stick) presented its version of a brutal Black man in a comic strip by animator and Yiddish actor Isidore Buzet (see figure 3.2). It showed the pitiful Shmerel Pitem, who mixes up the address of his date, a blond girl, with that of "a Niger, who welcomed him holding a razorblade." The cartoon shows a baldheaded Black man with enormous lips, who brandishes a razorblade, kicking out the terror-stricken Shmerel.[15]

The subject of African Americans and crime drew much attention in the Yiddish press. Several newspapers, especially those on the left, pointed to Black poverty rates, surrounding racism and the anti-Black bias of the judicial system as the root causes that yielded African American offenders. In 1911, The daily *Varhayt* (Truth), established by Louis Miller in 1905 as an independent socialist paper (which gradually became a mouthpiece for secular Jewish nationalism and the Democratic Party's Tammany Hall), explained to its readers the misconception of linking race and crime. After John Cain, a Black man, stabbed to death

Figure 3.2. Shmerel Pitem walks into the wrong house, *Der groyser kundes*, 1914. Courtesy of the Dorot Jewish Division at the New York Public Library.

two people in a brawl that began when Cain refused to stop smoking on a platform of Manhattan's elevated train, the *Varhayt* argued that he defended himself against a hostile crowd and hinted that Cain might be mentally unbalanced. That case led the paper to publish an unsigned opinion column that contended, "Where the Black man lives under the same normal condition as the white, he has no more criminal tendencies than the white"; you find more Black criminals in some areas because "A large number of Blacks reside in the worst parts of every city, since whites refuse to have Blacks as their neighbors." In 1921, The *Forverts* ridiculed the concept of Black criminality in the South: In Georgia, a Black man was lynched "because he contradicted in a conversation the holy opinion of a white man," while another was lynched "for making an unreasonable comment about the pogrom against Negroes in Chicago."[16]

At the same time, Yiddish newspapers repeatedly portrayed what they saw as Black brutality and impulsiveness. Often copying items from English-language newspapers and receiving news via wire services, the Yiddish press abounded with sensationalist news items such as "Crazy Niger shoots 2 people," "Crazy Niger stabs 2 men," "A wild Niger jumps from a corner with a revolver in his hand," "Wild Niger holds up in forest," and "A Niger kisses also the white bride."[17] Beyond sensationalism, however, was genuine anxiety about Black offenders. In 1906, a shooting incident in Brownsville, Texas, in which Black soldiers were framed as culpable, resulted in President Theodore Roosevelt's order of a dishonorable discharge of 167 Black soldiers (decades later, all the men were pardoned and awarded an honorable discharge). At the time, the *Morgen zhurnal* lamented, "the Negro soldiers got a punishment that is too lenient for their pogrom. . . . And we believe that they deserve to be punished as harshly as all Jews would have believed they should be punished had they murdered several Jews" in Brownsville, Brooklyn. In 1921, *Yidishes tageblat* reported on the robbery and murder of a Jewish landlord in Harlem by two Black youths, and how "a group of Negroes, who instead of helping the victim, went through his pockets" and stole his money.[18]

Moreover, even when Yiddish newspapers emphasized the racial injustice in American society and the judicial system, they revealed much ambivalence. In 1918, the *Forverts* published a short sketch titled "The Innocent Negress" by playwright and satirist Berl Botvinik, describing the case of "a middle-aged, fat Negress . . . poor, shabby, and dirty-clothed," who is arraigned for stealing dry goods. Since the woman cannot afford a lawyer, the court appoints a public defender, who hardly speaks to her, but rather starts off with a readymade emotion-laden plea: "Here stands before you a mother, whose children wait for her at home. . . . Is this woman a thief? No! . . . As her skin is black, her soul is pure, white as an innocent dove." The defender claims the woman never went near the dry-goods store on that day, and calls to release her immediately, so she can go home "to her good, poor children." Still, when answering the judge's question, the woman calls out, "Guilty, guilty, your Honor! I stole the dry goods." She says that she was never married, and her son is in prison in Chicago. When she leaves the courtroom and passes by the defender, "who defended her so forcefully," the woman spits and says, "A big fool and a big liar." It is noteworthy that on different occasions Botvinik attacked racism (including by fellow Jews) and positively portrayed a Black character in one of his plays. Here, nonetheless, as Botvinik was denouncing the inherent injustice plaguing the judicial system, he ridiculed the defender's cliched speech about the suffering Black mother, who is really a criminal and a criminal's mother. Like many contemporary journalists and commentators, Botvinik's depiction remained deeply rooted in the contemporary concept of Black criminal pathology and inferiority.[19]

A similar mixed attitude appeared in the *Forverts* in an interview with the mother of Luther Boddy, a Black ex-convict, who killed (1922) two white New York City detectives. Writing under the pseudonym L. Malkes, journalist Leo Robins (originally Eliezer Rabinovitsh) wrote about the mother, "The old Negress is illiterate, she speaks with a deep Negro accent . . . but in her simple words there is a sea of thought." The mother said, "I raised my child right," but when her son went to the military, "they taught him how to shoot and murder." Robins even sympathized with Boddy, despite the press's "horrible tales" about him, since previously Boddy was constantly harassed and beaten up by the cops. On the other hand, Robins's impression of Boddy was that of "an ordinary Negro-boy" whose "facial features are regular and nobler than those of the ordinary Negro." Robins added that you see "hundreds of neatly-clothed young Negroes in New York," and often it happens "you stop and wonder that a Black guy does not have the face of a Negro despite the color of his skin." The allusion to Boddy's "nobler" facial features (as opposed to the "ordinary Negro") does not only illustrate the permeation of racial thought into the Yiddish intelligentsia, but also a linkage to the Yiddish journalist's overall positive assessment of Boddy. A different example of the connection between Black physical appearance and criminality was published in the *Forverts*—a newspaper that critic Cornel West has justly characterized as showing "genuine empathy" for African Americans—described (1921) a Black man charged with murder in New Jersey as follows, "The murderer looks more like a gorilla (a monkey) than a human being." Whereas the report might have been copied from an English-language wire service, the "explanation" of what a gorilla is seems to be an addition by the popular Yiddish daily.[20]

Furthermore, the belief, widely held in nineteenth-century America (and later), that alcohol was especially dangerous in the hands of African Americans, as it might unleash their ostensible inborn savagery, found its way into the Yiddish press. In 1907, *Yidishes tageblat* published an editorial titled, "The War against Drunkenness," written probably by the editor, John Paley. The writer sought to inform its readers about the effect of regional differences on the success of the anti-saloon movement: Whereas the push for prohibition had weakened in the Northeast, "the South is still different: millions of Negroes reside there, an inferior race, which becomes wild when drunk." The editorial argued, "It is certain that drunkenness has a great influence on the Negroes' savagery, as it is with any barbaric people who come in close contact with booze." Two years later, the *Morgen zhurnal* related (1909) to the debates in Alabama about a prohibition law, explaining that the state's "fanaticism" is not due to hatred of alcohol, but rather because of "the very serious Niger question." The writer (most likely the chief editor, Peter Wiernik) maintained, "All Southern observers realize that the Niger sinks morally and bodily" when drinking, as he is "too weak. . . . The Black man does not have the resolute will and ambition of the white man," and therefore drinking "makes him reckless to a degree that is rare among others." The editorial opposed prohibition as it is "against the principles of freedom" and thus unconstitutional; those who understand this problem are "The liberal residents of Alabama and the smaller percent Nigers who can understand such a question."[21]

Anxiety about assumed Black impulsiveness and aggression found its way into the discussions of lynching and race riots, even when the violence against African Americans was strongly deplored. Such trepidation was more noticeable in the conservative press. During the "Red Summer" of 1919, when lynchings peaked and race riots broke out in over thirty cities across the country, the *Morgen zhurnal* reported that placards were posted in Black neighborhoods in Washington, D.C., with the warning, "White residents! We are warning you not to go out of your homes tonight." Contrary to the claim of one historian, the Orthodox daily did not watch this "with enthusiasm," as "a positive step," or paint "Negro aggressiveness . . . in heroic terms"; the report mentioned that while many of Washington's Black dwellers are affluent, there are many others, who are so poor that they live "like common animals." The situation has worsened, since "certain Negroes" made "four criminal attacks against white women." In its report about the racial violence in Chicago that summer, *Yidishes tageblat* mentioned the fear of the general population and business owners that "wild Nigers" might rob them. In a short report on a mass meeting of "about 2,000 Nigers" in Harlem (1919), where speakers "threaten with power," the latter daily alluded to the "New Negro" movement among African Americans to improve their conditions. Whereas many whites support those demands, the paper mentioned that "others see in that propaganda the work of American 'reds,' who seek to converts the Nigers to Bolshevism."[22]

Such ambivalence toward African Americans was articulated in the major conservative Yiddish dailies' coverage of the race massacre in Tulsa, Oklahoma (1921). All Yiddish papers decried the bloodshed and graphically described how Black families had to flee their homes that white mobs torched. Yet as one historian has demonstrated, there were important differences between the socialist *Forverts* and the conservative *Tageblat* and *Morgen zhurnal*. The *Forverts* movingly reported, "the scenes among the wretched Blacks were heartrending," where injured Black women, men, and children were scattered on the floor of a hall where they found refuge. The daily also refrained from assuming the culpability of Dick Rowland, a young Black man accused of attacking a white woman, whose arrest ignited the riots. Whereas the *Tageblat* and *Morgen zhurnal* also covered the anguish of Black victims, they struck a more severe tone toward the city's African American population. The managing editor of *Morgen zhurnal*, Yankev Fishman, believed that Tulsa's white folk "exploited a single case of a brutal Niger to assault all the city's Nigers"; but he also commented, "A report that says the Nigers started the trouble by arming themselves and marching to the courthouse" to protect Rowland "sounds unbelievable." The *Tageblat* was harsher, writing that "an insolent Niger and a hysterical woman" caused the riot and falsely claiming that Black residents shot at the firefighters who tried to put out the fire in the Black district. It was white rioters, however, who forced out the firefighters at gunpoint, as the *Forverts* correctly reported. A few days after the riot, the *Tageblat* published a column by Yiddish poet and humorist Leo Kesner, who condemned the "wrong, inhumane and uncivilized" violence of white Tulsans against Black Tulsans, saying that the behavior of the former was more befitting "illiterate Ukrainian peasants" than "free American citizens." Yet Kesner also argued, "we have to admit" that "nearly all race riots in America" broke out as a result of a crime "which a Black man committed or tried to commit against a white person."[23]

As mentioned in the previous chapter, apprehension and assumptions about the danger posed by African Americans were also evident in the responses to the Leo Frank case (1913–1915). The Yiddish intelligentsia's conceptualization of civility and barbarity, which was informed by predominant notions of racial hierarchy in American society, left an unmistakable mark. When attacking (1915) Frank's murderers and their "barbarian customs of former slaveholders," the *Forverts* likened them to "The savage tribes of Africa," which "always do the same when they catch a stranger and prepare to roast and eat him." The left-leaning weekly *Bronzvil un ist nu york progres* (Brownsville and East New York Progress) contended that Frank was found guilty because he was a Jew, and determined that the "savage mob" of Georgia exceeded with its cruelty the "savage tribes of Africa," since the former "pretend to be civilized." The editor and publisher of the *Groyser kundes*, Yankev Marinov (Marinoff), wondered if "America is Africa—deep, deep Africa" and whether Americans were "civilized" or "just cannibalized African Zulus." The same weekly published a cartoon by Lola (Leon Israel), titled "Back into savage Africa!" in which all other states of the union point fingers at a wild-looking, apish monster, representing Georgia, holding a hangman's rope and a bludgeon; the caption says, "All states of America: look, look, here is the wild beast that strayed from deep Africa into our civilized country!!!"[24]

Jim Conley's likely guilt notwithstanding, it is significant that Yiddish newspapers usually referred to him as the "Niger Conley," "Conley the Niger," or just "the Niger." The New York correspondent of the Warsaw Yiddish daily, *Der moment* (The Moment), critic and poet A. Almi (Elye Sheps), wrote sarcastically that Atlanta's whites, "for whom a dog is more respected than a Negro," suddenly believe Conley, "a Black beast." A decade later, even the communist *Frayhayt* (Freedom, later *Morgn frayhayt*, Morning Freedom), which championed the cause of African Americans, used (1923) the term "Niger" in reference to a Black inmate who admitted that he saw Conley struggling with someone on the day Mary Phagan was murdered. As mentioned in the previous chapter, Abraham Cahan's comments about Black people's "fantasy power," "many of them are great liars," and "When a Negro tells a lie, he always tells it with details, so it would seem true," should be understood in this context.[25]

One of the angriest responses in Yiddish to the lynching of Leo Frank, which reflected the influence of racial concepts on the Yiddish intelligentsia, appeared in no other than the anarchist *Fraye arbeter shtime*. Whereas that weekly generally took a strong stand—often sardonic—against racism and violence, under the editorship of Shoel (Saul) Yanovsky (1899–1919), it served as a forum for diverse opinions, including views opposed to the editorial line. A few weeks after the lynching of Leo Frank, the weekly published a long tirade signed by the name "Dril.," who argued that "Frank did not know the Nigers as ungrateful and treacherous. He befriended the Niger Conley, and with that buried himself." While the writer claimed that "the Jew does not miss the opportunity" to take advantage of African Americans when he lives in their midst, "the Jews educate the Niger, they dress him up," and Southern whites "cannot tolerate it." The writer continued with a callous description of what he saw as typical Black traits: "The Niger is savage, servile . . . he is ashamed of himself and suspects anyone who treats him courteously. . . . No Niger knows his father, whether he's the mother's brother, son, or father." "Dril." contrasted the situation of Southern Blacks and Jews in Russia—"here [in the South] a lowlier race is oppressed by a higher race, there [in Russia] the opposite."[26] Although this writer's level of explicit racism was an outlier in the Yiddish press, the other examples demonstrate that if one looks for the roots of a nascent cooperation between Jews and Blacks, the Frank case in itself did not seem to have an immediate positive impact on the images of African Americans.

The Misconception About "America's Jews"

The contrast that "Dril." drew between Jews and Blacks is pertinent to one of the main and frequent assertions in the scholarship about the portrayal of Black people in the Yiddish press: According to it, Yiddish writers viewed African Americans as "America's Jews" since "Jews and blacks had endured similar suffering and similar persecution" and therefore "Yiddish newspapers knew that a special relationship existed" between African Americans and Jews.[27] Even if such expressions were made from time to time, especially in the years following World War I, we need to understand both the evolution of such rhetorical equations and their limitations. An early voice that opposed the comparison between Jews and African Americans was Vilna-born Leon Zolotkoff, who wrote for the Hebrew press in Russia and later for socialist papers, settled in Chicago in 1888, and became one of the pioneers of the Zionist and conservative Yiddish press in America. In 1900, he criticized an unnamed Reform rabbi, who focused on the emancipation of Black Americans in his Passover sermon. Zolotkoff wrote, "I have nothing against Blacks, God forbid," but since they are not mentioned in the Haggadah, "the emancipation of Blacks is a better topic for the Fourth of July," while in Passover one should speak about the liberation of Jews.[28]

A starker differentiation between Jews and Blacks was articulated in 1903, during a period of increased violence against Jews in Tsarist Russia: Socialist essayist and critic, Karl Fornberg (pseudonym of Yishaya Rosenberg), came out against anyone who tried to liken the situation of the Black population in America to that of Jews in Russia. Writing in the *Forverts*, Fornberg mentioned the economic differences between the groups, but focused more on Jews having "not only a large intelligentsia, but also a large intelligent *revolutionized mass*." He blamed white Southerners for their hate and oppression of African Americans, "but the Negroes themselves are not better because of that." According to him, most of the Black public is "poor, ignorant, without energy, without knowledge. They don't know what to do and how to help themselves." Fornberg claimed that only if African Americans leave the rural environment and occupations and move to the cities will they be able to advance their spiritual level.[29]

Another example of the *Forverts*'s version of anti-racism shows why it did not consider Jews and Blacks as comparable. Following a scandal in which Hannah Elias, a biracial affluent proprietor and former sex worker, was accused (1904) of blackmailing her benefactor, a wealthy white businessman, the daily published an unsigned column titled, "What the Nigers Say." It fumed against the references to Elias's race and the white public's belief "that only Niger women are capable of cheating money out of old millionaire revelers"; unlike their treatment of white women, the police did not hesitate to "snatch a Niger woman from bed in the middle of the night and drag her to the police station." The writer maintained that the woman "is not a Nigeress at all. She is an 'octoroon'—seven eighths white," but anyway this case "proves that Nigers are oppressed" in America and when "one Niger in a hundred thousand rapes a woman, everybody shouts that all Nigers are disgraceful criminals." The column emphasized African Americans' hard work that led to the establishment of schools, charitable societies, and hospitals. The conclusion was, "Naturally they are still not on the same level as whites, but how long is it since they were liberated from slavery?"[30]

Two years later, during a period which had witnessed (1903–1906) more than seven hundred pogroms in Russia, in which more than three thousand Jews were murdered, the *Varhayt* sought (1906) to provide a legalistic elucidation as to why the situation of African Americans and Jews under Tsarist rule must not be equated. The writer of an editorial (probably the editor Louis E. Miller) claimed that Southern whites' animosity toward any Black person "is now not more than a pure social hatred, which has little to do with the political and legal situation of Blacks." Whereas Black Southerners are persecuted and murdered, it was a specific segment of the white population that committed those crimes, and "The government does not help to persecute the Negroes." Furthermore, despite the violence against African Americans, "the law in America, even in the South, makes little differences between Blacks and whites." Thus, "Nothing can be more laughable, more foolish than to compare the race war in the American South with the race war in South, North, East, and West Russia."[31]

An illustration of the concept that African Americans were anything but "America's Jews" came in 1908 from socialist Zionist leader Nachman Syrkin, who like the *Varhayt* was an ideological foe of the *Forverts*. In that period, Syrkin became alienated from the Zionist movement and wrote for a short-lived monthly, *Dos folk* (The People), which was put out by socialist diaspora nationalists (territorialists). In an article that differentiated between groups' national identities, Syrkin claimed that African Americans "have no national consciousness. They have no distinct culture, language, religion" and no interest in a "national revival." Since "due to their race, they are social pariahs," Syrkin predicted that "with the cultural rise among them," Black Americans will "start dreaming about their own land and freedom." While at that time Syrkin had not yet moved to America and had no firsthand experience with American society or African Americans, the same cannot be said about his colleague Yekhezkl Vortsman. Vortsman, who together with Syrkin was active in early socialist Zionist circles in Switzerland, later wrote for Yiddish newspapers in Russia, Romania, and Britain, and after his immigration to America (1907), served as the editor of several Yiddish newspapers in Atlanta, Los Angeles, Montreal, and San Francisco (among others). Following the race riots in East St. Louis (1917), Vortsman wrote in *Der tog* about the "Negro Problem," where he, like many other Yiddish writers, likened the Russian peasantry to African Americans. Vortsman strongly attacked white racism, especially Jim Crow segregation, and condemned Southern Jews "who feel—or convinced themselves they feel—a deep hatred toward those oppressed souls." At the same time, he wrote that "The Negro is lazy" (since Black laborers are underpaid) and warned that even if the whites will not initiate "pogroms" against African Americans, "sooner or later, the Blacks will commit them [pogroms]" against whites.[32]

It was a sharp opponent of Zionism, however, the influential socialist activist and Yiddish journalist Tsivyen (pen name of Ben-Tsiyen Hoffman), who inadvertently exhibited his views about Black Africans. In 1917, Tsivyen lambasted the burgeoning Zionist movement, which had become a mass movement in America in those years under the leadership of progressive attorney Louis D. Brandeis. Tsivyen argued that Zionism cannot solve the Jewish problem in the Diaspora, exactly as "The Negro-republic 'Liberia' did not solve the Negro-question in America." The socialist essayist acerbically noted that some Zionists might "see it as a great disgrace to compare Jews and Negroes at all" without a *lehavdl* (differentiation); still, Tsivyen revealed his own partiality, asserting there is no question "whether Jews stand on a higher level than Negroes. Certainly Jews stand higher" in the same way that "the Jewish people stands much higher than other nations in its culture, development, and abilities."[33]

Tsivyen's notion of Jewish cultural superiority exemplifies how Jewish attitudes toward African Americans emanated not only from the latter's race and skin color but also from the fact that Yiddish writers often saw them—as they viewed other low-stratum Gentiles—as culturally backward. Hence there was some paternalism within the Yiddish press among people who truly sought to alleviate the plight of African Americans. Such an approach appeared in the writing of playwright and travel writer Perets Hirshbeyn (Peretz Hirshbein), whose writing often humanized non-Europeans. In 1917, Hirshbeyn published in *Der tog* his impressions of traveling across America, writing movingly about a case in Alabama, where a white mob forced a Black man to eat watermelon before he was hanged, "so people can amuse themselves." Hirshbeyn's text was a strong plea against violence, racial segregation, and the dehumanization of African Americans: "Here, in the South they say that the Negro is regarded like a dog. This is not true. With a dog, there is a relationship, you smile to him, show affection to him." Nevertheless, Hirshbeyn criticized what he saw as Black Southerners' submissiveness, and lack of understanding of their own situation, when they say, "they are treating us like dogs." That is, "Even they [African Americans] think that a dog is the most wretched creature in the United States of North America, and not the Negro." A few years later, Hirshbeyn chronicled (1920–1921) the lives of different ethnic groups in South Africa. Alongside his fascination with the Zulus, whom he called "the bravest of all Negroes," saying that they are "the most beautiful tribe . . . the Zulu is the true child of the country. Strong, gigantically built," Hirshbeyn stressed "the Kaffir's [Black African's] primitive soul," and determined that racial mixing was harmful, as "[the white man's] degeneration is easier when it is joined with the blood of a primitive human being."[34]

Another writer who found fault with Black Americans' alleged lack of awareness or resolve was A. S. (Avrom Simkhe) Zaks, a former rabbinical student from Lithuania, who came to America in 1908 and became active in the Jewish labor movement and socialist Yiddish press. During and after the "Red Summer" of 1919, Zaks published in *Der tog* a scathing attack against anti-Black "pogroms" and Jim Crow segregation, contending that the "same reasons" led to the violence against Jews in Europe and African Americans. He believed the two minorities should respond in the same way—"an eye for an eye . . . violence should be answered with violence." Still, Zaks passed judgment on the Southern Black populace, since "they are not even bothered by the small number of schools for Blacks" and their "servile obedience to the whites did not dissipate. . . . Negroes regard themselves as inferior, ugly creatures."[35]

A similar lack of understanding, or underestimation of the structural power disparity and long-terms effect of racism on African Americans, was at the core of a 1928 report by labor organizer and Yiddish journalist Harry (Herts) Lang. Lang wrote in the *Forverts* about local organizers in New Orleans's Black neighborhoods, who were trying to motivate people to protest the increasing cost of utility gas. Most Black residents opposed the agitation, as they feared losing future municipal or gas company jobs. According to Lang, the opposers distrusted the protest organizers, saying, "A Niger is a Niger, and Nigers can't expect anything from a Niger"; Lang wrote, "We should keep in mind that when a Negro calls a fellow Negro 'Niger,' he means it to ridicule and curse him." According to him, such attitudes represented "an inborn slave feeling among the Negroes here"; to exemplify how such a feeling manifests itself, Lang transcribed into Yiddish a Southern ditty—"Have you ever/in your life/ seen a Niger/kiss his wife?" For Lang, this ditty illustrated that "[f]or a Negro, a Negress is not a person . . . his Negro wife disgusts him. He craves a white face, white skin."[36]

It was not just the inability to understand fully the differences between the situations of African Americans and American Jews that produced some of the dismissive or patronizing comments above. Jewish preoccupation with Jewish public imagery among non-Jews, and a reluctance to wash dirty linen in (non-Jewish) public were certainly behind the critique of African Americans, who purportedly failed to follow suit. A colleague of Lang was the managing editor of the *Forverts*, Hillel Rogoff, who came to the U.S. (1890) at the age of eight, wrote in English for socialist newspapers, and became Abraham Cahan's right hand. In 1926, Rogoff extolled *The New Negro*, an anthology of poetry, fiction, and essays, edited by Alain Locke, that included the leading writers who were associated with the Harlem Renaissance. Rogoff sympathized with the young Black intelligentsia, and equated what Harlem was for its Black residents with what the Lower East Side had been for Jewish immigrants a generation earlier. Rogoff included translations into Yiddish of poems by Countee Cullen, Langston Hughes, and Claude McKay. Two years later (1928), however, Rogoff disagreed with Black reviewers who celebrated McKay's novel *Home to Harlem*, bemoaning, "If all the Negroes are like the men and women that are depicted in McKay's novel, then it is very sad." In Rogoff's view, all the characters' lives revolve around "debauchery, sex, and depravity," and in all the plotline's "obscene tangles," Black women and men "are only looking for pleasure, [and] the satisfaction of their lust."[37]

Putting Black Notables on an Equivocal Pedestal

Rogoff's expectation that Black artists would refrain from presenting negative aspects of fellow Black Americans and parade their achievements instead surely conveyed Jewish concerns about self-representation. One of the important features of the Yiddish press, especially after World War I, was to lionize prominent Black leaders such as Fredrick Douglas, Booker T. Washington, W. E. B. Du Bois, and A. Philip Randolph (among others), as well as to applaud Black achievements in various fields such as education, arts, and science. African American leaders were repeatedly lauded for their courage and vision. Even so, newspapers did not serve as merely cheerleaders, and their praise often disclosed underlying critique. In 1906, the coeditor of the *Yidishes tageblat*, Abraham H. Fromenson, came out against anti-Black racism, in response to an attack on Booker T. Washington by a St. Louis-based Jewish weekly, *The Modern View*. Washington had likened Blacks to Jews; the St. Louis newspaper condemned him, responding that, unlike Jews, "by carnal crimes [African Americans] bring their people into disrepute" and "the ignorance and idleness that makes for criminality in the negro" must be stamped out via education and work. Fromenson criticized that approach, complimented Washington as "good and worthy," and commended President Theodore Roosevelt for inviting (1901) Washington to dine with him at the White House. In his critique of *The Modern View*, Fromenson still exposed his own ambivalence, reminding his readers, "if he [the Black man] manifests evil inclinations we should not wonder at it, seeing the many years of slavery his race has gone through." In the same year, the *Tageblat* berated Washington for supposedly claiming that in their own land, Black Africans attained a higher civilization than white Europeans. An editorial proclaimed, "The Africans' honesty is because they had nothing to steal from one another. . . . We do not even want to talk about their approval of eating white [people's] flesh." The unnamed writer advised Washington to focus on the future rather than on the African "past pedigree." In 1912, a Chicago Yiddish weekly, *Der yidisher rekord* (The Jewish Record) favorably mentioned Washington's learning, and expressed the hope that "the time is not far when the Negro race will reach the level of all civilized nations."[38]

After the Black leader's death (1915), the coeditor of *Der tog*, Moyshe Kats, called Washington "the Negro Messiah" who understood that "before anything else, Negroes must be led out of their childlike condition." Kats equated Washington with Russian maskilim, who tried to integrate Jews into the surrounding society and teach them practical vocations. *Morgen zhurnal* also likened (1915) Washington to the maskilim in Russia, and reflected its own racial pecking order, wondering how a "born slave [Washington] . . . [could] speak and write like a white person" while Du Bois, "who has more white than black blood in his veins" was able "to speak and write from a pure Negro viewpoint." Journalist and chronicler of the Yiddish press, Yoysef Khaykin, hailed (1921) Du Bois as "a talented essayist . . . a highly-intelligent, sensitive, and gifted man" with clear goals, as opposed to Marcus Garvey and his supporters, "who have no practical program."[39]

Coverage of Marcus Garvey and his Back-to-Africa movement was indeed more critical: Several Yiddish writers drew parallels between Garvey's program and Zionism, which was a positive comparison for the *Yidishes tageblat* and *Morgen zhurnal* yet detrimental in the eyes of the *Forverts* through the 1920s. Others simply disliked the pageantry and rhetoric of the "Negro Moses." After Garvey's arrest and conviction (1922–1923) for mail fraud, Yiddish papers mostly deplored him for misleading and manipulating his supporters. Journalist and traveler Ben-Tsiyen Goldberg (originally Benyomen Veyf), who was Sholem Aleichem's son-in-law and would become a major figure in Jewish cultural organizations, described (1925) Garvey in the *Der tog* as "A short, fat, coarse Negro." Goldberg was confident that those whose money "Garvey squandered" still believed him and would continue to give him money. More tellingly, Goldberg analyzed why Garvey attracted so many African Americans: Garvey "played upon the fantasy of his people, to its longing and its primitive dreams."[40]

"A Sleeping Giant": Gradual Improvement and Its Discontents

It is hardly coincidental that praise for prominent African Americans intensified after World War I and into the 1920s, when the representations of African Americans had generally improved (though not overturned) in the Yiddish press. The rise of intolerance and xenophobia in wartime America, the ensuing Red Scare (1919–1920), and the "Tribal Twenties" made Black Americans appear—in Jewish eyes—as potential allies and fellow sufferers. Yiddish newspapers deepened their coverage of African American life, culture, and struggles, pointing to some parallels between the experiences of Black Americans (mostly Southern) and those of East European Jews. As the Yiddish press increasingly portrayed African Americans as allies to Jews, Black characters were cast in a more positive light. In May 1919, hundreds of thousands of New York Jews took to the streets to manifest their anger and frustration in mass parades and demonstrations against the continued slaughter of Jews in Poland. In his coverage of the protest for the *Forverts*, labor organizer and journalist Shmuel Kremer met non-Jewish workers who joined their Jewish colleagues' march. The attention of the Odessa-born writer was drawn to the young Black women: "It is pleasant yet odd to see Black women in the march of Jewish protestors." Kremer wrote that one of the Black women told him, "The dirty Poles lynch the Jews. The Jewish girls threw away their work and organized a protest. I also threw away the work, I also want to protest." A year later (1920), the *Tageblat* published the "travel impressions" of Hebraist and Zionist critic Re'uven Brainin, who explored Upstate New York. Upon his arrival in the town of Potsdam, he met a friendly Black porter in a local hotel, who "spoke to us in Yiddish, and not bad Yiddish at all." Brainin's friend and driver remarked that Yiddishist Chaim Zhitlovsky "would have been deeply delighted to hear how a Black man speaks pure Yiddish and doesn't want to speak in any other language with us." Yiddish-speaking African Americans (akin to Yiddish-speaking peasants/servants in the Old World) constituted an endearing and recurring topic in the Yiddish press, as well as on the Yiddish stage.[41]

As the previous chapter mentions, by 1920 poet and editor Avrom Lesin drew an analogy between East European Jews and Black Southerners, writing that you could believe what a white teacher said about

Black pupils "exactly as you could believe what a Pole says about Jews." In the same year, the Orthodox *Morgen zhurnal* featured an opinion column by essayist Dovid Leyb Mekler, titled "The unjust treatment of the Black race." Mekler blasted different European colonial powers for their crimes in Africa, and how both sides in World War I fooled Black recruits with false promises. Mekler marveled at African American advancements since the Civil War, and positively equated Jewish Zionism with the Back-to-Africa movement. Mekler went further than Lesin, arguing "in a certain sense, their [African American] situation is worse than . . . Jews in Poland." The latter could escape, whereas "the Negroes already found out that when they try to immigrate to other parts of the United States," hatred follows them and leads to massacres. Mekler described the world's Black population as a "sleeping giant," and they "will no longer allow to be ignored."[42]

No less important, after the Great War and in the 1920s, Yiddish newspapers gradually dedicated more space to Black literati and artists, not only highlighting their accomplishments, but also providing greater detail about African American life in general. In 1920, *Der tog* published a report about "the remarkable growth of the Negro colony in New York," which focused on Harlem. Besides description of Black churches and Black-owned banks, the report mentioned that "among them [Black Harlemites] there is a considerable number of artists, singers, musicians, lawyers, doctors, and other professionals." In the same year, a *Yidishes tageblat* editorial referred to Marcus Garvey's Universal Negro Improvement Association's conference in Madison Square Garden, noting that Black people were advancing "as all the other races, though at a slower pace." Still, the writer (probably the editor Gedalya Bublik) noted, "Among America's colored you find all sorts of cultured people, doctors, lawyers, teachers, politicians, businessmen, etc." who were becoming ever more politically aware. Similarly, in 1923, the *Forverts* published Leo Robins's accounts of New York's African American population, which stated, "In the last two decades a class of 'intellectuals' appeared among the Negroes." Robins likened the Black intelligentsia to the Russian *narodniki* (populists) of the 1870s—university-educated idealists who lived amongst the masses to "enlighten the people." Robins interviewed and lauded labor organizer and newspaper editor, A. Philip Randolph ("a slim young Negro with an intelligent face"), who would become a key figure in the cooperation between Black unions and the Jewish labor movement. Robins mentioned that "there are 300 Negro journals and newspapers in America" as an example of how culture spread in African American communities, and concluded that "little by little, the Negroes also create their own literature about the race question and their own history."[43]

Specialized and nuanced attention to African American life and creativity appeared in communist Yiddish publications, namely the daily *Di frayhayt* (published first in 1922 and in 1929 renamed *Morgn frayhayt*) and the monthly *Der hamer* (The Hammer, which began publication in 1926). Like their non-Jewish comrades, Yiddish-speaking communists saw America's Black populace as the quintessential oppressed masses which needed to be awakened and organized politically. *Frayhayt* was mostly careful not to use the spelling "Niger," and vehemently admonished any type of racism, including by Yiddish-speaking Jews. In *Frayhayt*'s early years (early 1920s), it was journalist Lilliput (pen name of Gavriel-Hirsh Kretshmer) who wrote extensively about African American culture. In 1922, Lilliput wrote a review of the ways Black characters were represented in the theater, from William Shakespeare's *Othello* through minstrelsy, Eugene O'Neill's *The Emperor Jones* (1920), and Eubie Blake and Noble Sissle's all-Black musical *Shuffle Along* (1921). In the spirit of the communist demand for artistic realism, Lilliput saw the latter two shows as "the first earnest attempt to bring the Negro onto the American stage as he really is" and was delighted that *Shuffle Along* "is typically Negro from start to finish." In his review of Clement Wood's novel, *Nigger: A Novel* (1922), Lilliput argued that other literary portrayals of African Americans "are all either filled with sentimental nonsense, or they're idealized depictions . . . or caricatures." Alongside his commendation of Wood's realistic sketch of African American life and speech, Lilliput extolled the book as it "shows us the patriotism of the Negro, his belief in a better world." Lilliput's serialized translation of this novel into the Yiddish appeared in *Frayhayt* in 1923. In later years, the Communist Party held "public trials" for its members suspected of racism; *Frayhayt*'s longtime editor, Moyshe Olgin, wrote scathing condemnations of Jewish party members who doubted the intellectual equality between whites and Blacks, opposed to their daughter going out or marrying a Black man, or avoided cooperating with Black members.[44]

In September 1926, the more literary and art-focused communist monthly, *Der hamer,* featured a column titled "Negro literature" with a translation of the story "The City of Refuge" by African American author Rudolph Fisher. An unsigned introduction (either by editor Leon Talmy or translator William Abrams) mentioned, "The wider public is familiar with Negro music, especially jazz. But they know little about Negro literature, Negro poetry, and Negro painting." Fisher's story gives readers "a look into Negro life in America—a field that needs to be artistically discovered by the conscious proletarian reader." Three months later, the editor disclosed that the column "was a tryout," and due to readers' enthusiastic responses, more segments would follow. In October 1928, *Hamer* published translations of "Negro poems" by Langston Hughes, William Waring Cuney, Helene Johnson and others. *Hamer* also published many Yiddish poems by poets such as Malka Li and Leonid Faynberg, who dealt directly with the predicament of Black Americans.[45]

"I'se in Town, Honey!"—Immersion in American Racial Vocabulary

Nevertheless, even in newspapers that had an ideological concern for the oppressed and prided themselves as bulwarks against capitalist ploys to divide the proletariat along religious, ethnic, and racial lines, the concept of African Americans as backward and childlike was still evident. In 1923, *Frayhayt* published a serialized report titled "Slave hell in sunny Florida" by one A. H. Schwartz, who was arrested (1921) for vagrancy on board a train in Florida and sent to a segregated county prison in Tallahassee. Schwartz graphically described the horrible food, the lice, and how a Black inmate was beaten to death. Schwartz also wrote that one night he was awakened by the sound of a man weeping in one of the cells of the lower floor (reserved for Black prisoners only): "A Negro was crying . . . [later] I heard how he was praying to God, praying gently in a simple childish manner that is so characteristic of Southern Negroes." Already in 1919, the prospective archenemy of *Frayhayt*, the socialist *Forverts*, drew a similar picture in its women's section. It published a piece by Sadie Vinokur about a Black elevator man, the "squirming, lively" John, who fell in love with a Jewish worker, Lily, who broke his heart. Vinokur's text brims with sympathy to "poor John . . . a heartrending longing look is seen in his big Negro eyes. Poor John!" Despite the overly compassionate depiction of John, some of Vinokur's description evokes her editor Abraham Cahan's portrayal of African Americans' "fantasy power": She wrote how John used "to talk to himself . . . imitating a girl's voice" and then answering with his own voice, laughing and dancing "as if Lily were really next to him."[46]

Such examples were hardly isolated cases but rather part of a wider pattern. Alongside the postwar gradual improvement in the description of African Americans, viewing them as potential allies and focusing more on Black writers and artists, the Yiddish press largely remained immersed in American racial imagery. In the years following World War I and into the 1920s, Yiddish newspapers ran a host of advertisements, mostly copied from English-language newspapers with Yiddish inscriptions added, which portrayed African American characters in domestic and servile roles. As historian Eric Goldstein has aptly noted, those ads used racial images to impart ideals of whiteness and upward mobility. In 1919, *Forverts* ran teaser advertisements for Aunt Jemima products with her image above the caption, "A new guest arrives in town on FRIDAY." When she arrived, the ads included the English-language tagline which became Aunt Jemima's catchphrase years beforehand, "I'se in town, honey!" (See figure 3.3). That year, *Groyser kundes* published a full-page ad for "Murad—The Turkish Cigarette," displaying two female Black servants in oriental clothing tending to the needs of a white woman, who has a stylish flapper hairdo (see figure 3.4). African American domestics appeared in ads for FLIT insecticide and laundry soap. In 1929, cigarette ads in *Morgen zhurnal* showed Jewish stars Eddie Cantor (see figure 3.5) and Al Jolson promoting the merchandise while in blackface. The racialized meaning of such ads was not lost on Yiddish writers: In 1927, *Der tog* published a skit by M. Ayzman about a Black elevator man who stands trial for striking a Jewish tenant; the tenant had humiliated him frequently in front of other tenants, calling him "darky" and "Niger," and asking him "if I like chicken, [or] whether 'Aunt Jemima' is my relative."[47]

Advertisements were not the only segment that reflected the profound impact of the surrounding racial imagery. One of the most successful characters in early twentieth-century American Yiddish culture was Yente Telebende. From 1913 through the mid-1930s, she appeared in

Figure 3.3. Advertisements for Aunt Jemima Pancake Flour, *Forverts*, 1919–1920. The heading of the one on the left is "Hanukkah Latkes"; the one on the right is captioned "A new guest arrives in town on FRIDAY." Courtesy of the Historical Jewish Press Digital Collection, National Library of Israel and Tel Aviv University.

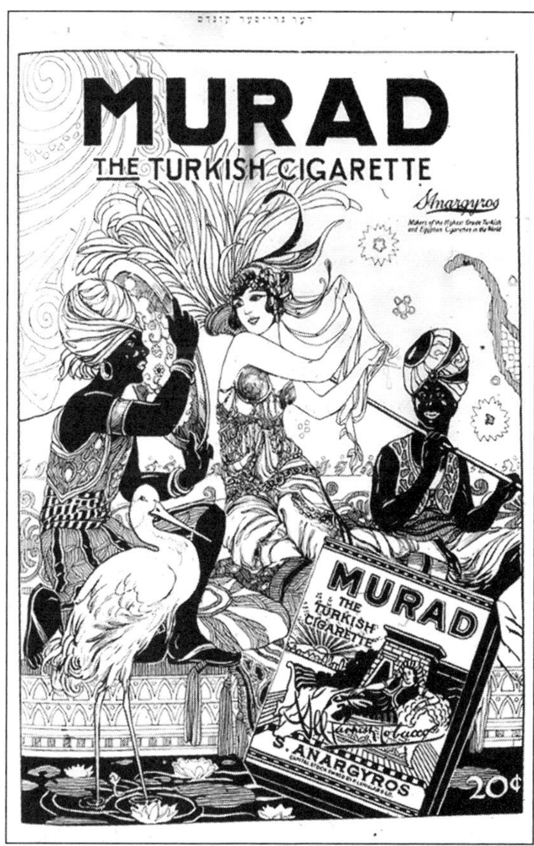

Figure 3.4. Murad cigarettes advertisement in *Groyser kundes*, 1919. Courtesy of the Dorot Jewish Division at the New York Public Library.

Figure 3.5. Advertisement for "Old Gold" Cigarettes, *Morgen zhurnal*, 1929, featuring Eddie Cantor. The title says, "Friends, how can I make yourselves crazy [entertain you] when the 'coughers' here in the front are making me crazy with their coughs?" Cantor is described as "The great American comedian who plays the main role in Ziegfeld's magnificent production 'Whoopee.'" Courtesy of the Dorot Jewish Division at the New York Public Library.

comical sketches by Yiddish humorist B. Kovner (pen name of Yankev Adler[48]) in the *Forverts*; the skits portrayed the overbearing and nosy Yente, her subdued husband Mendel, and their son Pine. Several highly successful theater productions would be based on Yente and her family on the Yiddish stage, which are discussed in the next chapter. With her opinionated tongue-lashing and crude behavior, the name Yente soon became an everyday term in American Yiddish, denoting a busybody, old-fashioned, loud-mouthed woman, and superseded the similar term *yakhne*.[49] A recurring character, though fairly marginal, was Pine's friend, the "Little Niger," a teenaged Black boy—the only nameless character in Kovner's sketches. After the first stage production of *Yente Telebende* (1917) increased the Black kid's visibility, Kovner penned a sketch in 1919, in which Yente complains that she expected Pine to become better and stop socializing with the Black boy. Yet Pine has become even worse: "The street has more influence over the local kids than the parents. A word from the little Niger is for him, Pine that is, much holier than my word." A year later, Kovner published a humoristic column dedicated to the "Little Niger." Kovner claimed that he received many letters from readers asking him why he refrained recently from mentioning the Black kid anymore. Kovner replied, "the little Niger is no small matter! With what didn't he assist Pine? He helped him in all his ventures: When Pine wanted to break windowpanes, tug at the beards of Jews, pelt Jewish women with 'snowballs,' prevent Jewish girls from walking through the street . . . in all those various ventures the little Niger was Pine's partner." Kovner teased his readers about the whereabouts of the Black kid, "Is he alive? Is he dead? Or maybe he has grown up and a 'mob' of white Americans lynched him?"[50]

Kovner's characterization of the Black kid is quite revealing. More than just signaling a different race and culture, the "little Niger" symbolizes the American environment, the crude American street with its pranks, vulgar behavior, and violence. The Black boy is the quintessential *sheygets*, a term that means not just a rascal Gentile boy, but also a misbehaved Jewish kid.[51] More significantly, Kovner's jokes seem odd, if not callous; they were published in a socialist daily which was committed to racial equality and devoted much space to condemning lynchings and racism in the strongest terms. Kovner's questions about the disappearance of the Black kid, whether he was dead, or a white mob lynched him, were published only a few months after the "Red Summer" of 1919, which was marked by lynching and race riots across the country. The gap between the *Forverts*'s ideological commitment against racism and Kovner's jokes shows the acute impact of American popular culture's prejudiced formulation of Black characters on Yiddish cultural expressions. It is important to bear in mind, however, that Yente Telebende sketches normally carried the subheading *shtiferay* (mischief/frolic). As entertainment, they constituted a separate genre, with much more artistic license (for commercial purposes). Kovner's highly popular skits show yet again that Yiddish papers conveyed their attitude toward race and African Americans in a myriad of ways that every so often challenged the formal editorial line.

The combination of passionate condemnation of racism and internalization of surrounding attitudes toward Blacks was unmistakable in the longest-existing satirical Yiddish newspaper, *Der groyser kundes* (1909–1927). The successful weekly, whose circulation was estimated at approximately 35,000 copies during its early years, repeatedly excoriated violence against African Americans as a betrayal of everything America represents. In 1921, it quipped that it is tough to be Black in the Congo, "but it's a thousand times bitterer to be Black in the State of Georgia!"[52] Concurrently, though, the weekly published several cartoons with jokes about African cannibals: A 1916 caricature showed an "African cannibal-chief" writing to "dear mother England" and complaining about the wartime scarcity. The chief asks, "Send us immediately a transport of missionaries! P.S., see to it that they are fat." (See figure 3.6). A year later (1917), a cartoon showed a half-naked witch doctor examining a cannibal patient, telling him, "You have been poisoned. The young man you ate yesterday must have been a decadent poet." (See figure 3.7). In 1920, the weekly showed a cartoon titled "In Africa," where two cannibals with shopping bags (one of them with a human foot inside) are complaining about the cost of living—"a pound of skinny missionary flesh costs 7 cents today!" (See figure 3.8). Whereas those caricatures seem to be copied from English-language newspapers, *Groyser kundes* published in 1926 a Yiddish poem and a cartoon titled "Tsebebe-Kebebe: An African Ballad" by "A. People Expert" (probably Leo Kesner, who used a proximate pen name). The poem played with making "Africa" sound like "Afrikake" (Afri-feces), and depicted Kebebe, the "naked daughter" of an African king. A prince from another tribe, "pere-odem Tsebebe" (savage/imbecile Tsebebe) wants to marry her, but the king demands a hundred oxen as a dowry. Since the prince has only ninety-nine oxen, a shaman advises him and the princess not to worry, since the king is nearsighted; at the end Tsebebe and Kebebe marry, and at the wedding everyone is eating "African wedding cakes." The accompanying cartoon shows the nearly naked bespectacled African king, his daughter, and several oxen (see figure 3.9).[53]

Figure 3.6. An “African cannibal-chief” writes to “dear mother England,” asking her to send missionaries that are fat, *Groyser kundes* (1916). Courtesy of the Dorot Jewish Division at the New York Public Library.

Figure 3.7. A caricature titled “The punishment for carelessness”: a witch doctor tells his cannibal patient, “You have been poisoned. The young man you ate yesterday must have been a decadent poet,” *Groyser kundes* (1917). Courtesy of the Dorot Jewish Division at the New York Public Library.

Figure 3.8. "In Africa"—two cannibals are complaining about the cost of living, *Groyser kundes* (1920). Courtesy of the Dorot Jewish Division at the New York Public Library.

Figure 3.9. "Tsebebe-Kebebe: An African Ballad," *Groyser kundes* (1926). Courtesy of the Dorot Jewish Division at the New York Public Library.

Other jokes in *Groyser kundes* showed Black persons as parallel to the dull-witted and sometimes ruthless peasants that populate the tales of Yiddish folklore.[54] A 1919 cartoon showed a feverish Black patient who says that the "doctor" who visited his home did not take his pulse but took everything else in the house. Another joke (1922) told of Black railway workers out West who telegraphed the company's headquarters in New York with a question: "The boss is dead. Should we bury him?" The company answered that they may bury him if they are certain he is dead. The workers replied via telegraph, "The boss is buried. We are certain that he was dead. Before we put him in the ground, we hit him over the head with pickaxes several times. Send us a new boss."[55]

Perhaps more damning was a cartoon (1925) that showed two pictures: "How they played and danced—once upon a time—and today." The upper picture shows the past: a man and a woman dancing, only their hands touching, as a classical-style orchestra plays by their side. The lower picture shows the present: Women (in flapper hats and hairstyles) and men are holding one another, and the men's hands are on the women's behinds. A jazz band plays next to them, featuring a heavyset Black drummer with exaggerated facial features (see figure 3.10). The

Figure 3.10. "How they played and danced—once upon a time and—today." The upper cartoon shows the past, and the lower shows the allegedly lewd present, *Groyser kundes* (1925). Courtesy of the Dorot Jewish Division at the New York Public Library.

Figure 3.11. "A summer tragedy in five pictures" (from right to left), *Groyser kundes* (1926). Courtesy of the Dorot Jewish Division at the New York Public Library.

message is clear; the Black drummer represents the immorality of the present dance and music, which white racialists dubbed "jungle music."

A few months later (1926), the satirical weekly published an animated sketch by one A. Yakobi, titled "A summer tragedy in five pictures." The sketch shows Mr. Weiss (White) who travels to the country and sunbathes. As the sun darkens his skin, Mr. Weiss's face turns black, and upon returning home, his wife does not let him in, "thinking he is a Negro." Mr. Weiss's boss "thinks the same" and does not give him his job back. The fifth and final picture shows the black-faced Mr. Weiss working as an elevator operator: "[B]efore he'll become white again, Mr. Weiss has no choice and must work as an elevator man in a hotel." (See figure 3.11).[56]

"Every Civilized Human Must Admit": The Readership

What about the millions of readers of those Yiddish newspapers? While it is empirically impossible to discern the responses of those readers, there are several indications that the readership shared the Yiddish press's utter condemnation of racist violence and discrimination alongside its internalization of white society's racial codes and assumptions. In 1910, a reader from Dallas, Texas, by the name of Yoysef Rudnitsky described in the *Forverts* the "barbarity" of "bloodthirsty two-legged animals" who lynched 65-year-old Allen Brooks. Rudnitsky mentioned how the lynchers tore into small pieces both Brooks's coat and the rope with which they hanged him, so many people could take them home as souvenirs. Rudnitsky also spotted "a Jewish boy" who proudly showed him a piece of the coat and rope "that he packed in a pouch and highly treasured." A few years later (1918), a reader by the name of Y. Meltzer wrote to the *Varhayt* to remonstrate about "the attitude of some Jews against the Negroes." Meltzer relayed that in Red Bank, New Jersey, Jewish business owners joined other owners and refused to serve Black customers in restaurants and ice cream parlors. He commended African Americans, asking "Weren't they the first to protest the pogroms?" adding that they were the Jews' "best friends" in America. Meltzer's call against racism was echoed in the *Morgen zhurnal*, which published a column titled "The Curious Reporter" from 1919 to 1922, where a journalist posed one question to five random Yiddish-speaking pedestrians on the street. After the Tulsa race massacre in 1921, five men near Thompkins Square Park and 7th Street were asked about it. All five castigated the violence; Alex Horowitz of Brooklyn said the attacks on Tulsa's Black community were "maybe worse" than the pogroms against Jews in Ukraine. Nathan Zilbershtok believed, "it's possible the Nigers also had a part in why such a massacre took place, but the whites are certainly guiltier." A worker by the name H. Vinkler praised African Americans' bravery in defending themselves, noting "I wish Jews in war zones were as daring as the Nigers in Tulsa," something that would have reduced the number of pogroms.[57]

Nonetheless, there were other examples of racialized assumptions about the African American character. In 1911, after popular columnist Dovid Hermalin published an article in the *Varhayt* against racial segregation in schools, a reader from Washington, D.C., by the name of Louis M. Ginzburg begged to differ. He pilloried the rich and "allegedly educated Nigers, who are ashamed of their poor brethren and their own race," and call poor Black people "no other name than 'Niger'" while they "always fawn on whites." Those wealthy African Americans would do anything "just to be near whites" and "push themselves into white society." Ginzburg believed Black elites should work among fellow African Americans rather than seek white acceptance, and his de facto defense of segregation in the name of Black solidarity led him to a set of rhetorical questions: "Why should a white person love the Negro when the Black [elite] hates him like it hates death? Why should a white person associate with the Negro when the educated Black man runs away from him?"[58] A different take came from Alter Rosen (née Rosenborsht), a newspaper agent and book dealer based in Syracuse, New York, who later served as a traveling agent for the Jewish Publication Society. Rosen wrote occasionally in various Yiddish papers, and several times railed against the Slavic people for their purported backwardness in comparison to "high-civilized Anglo-Saxons." In 1918, Rosen wrote a letter to the *Fraye arbeter shtime*, in which he declared, "I wholeheartedly believe that there are higher and inferior races" and "Every intelligent person must admit that the Negro race stands much lower than the white race." However, "every civilized human must admit that they [African Americans] deserve all the political and economic rights and privileges that Yankees get."[59]

* * *

There can be little doubt that violence and discrimination against America's Black population deeply unsettled Yiddish writers and editorial staff and forced them to consider whether Jews would be the subsequent victims of racism in America. The chasm between the republic's noble ideals of liberty and equality and the appalling treatment of millions of African Americans was repeatedly discussed in the Yiddish press. The horror expressed at lynchings and race riots and the utter condemnations of such acts were unequivocal across the spectrum of Yiddish newspapers (the rare exceptions mostly appeared when Jews were reported as victims of Black offenders). Especially after World War I and into the 1920s, Yiddish newspapers drew *certain* parallels between the situation of African Americans and that of East European Jews. In the discussion about racism and the situation of African Americans, Yiddish writers created a medium to talk—via another group—about Jews' place in America and their expectations, needs, and concerns.[60]

Nevertheless, that was one dimension out of many. When one reads beyond the denunciations of white assailants, the laudations for prominent Black figures, and the often-abstract descriptions of suffering Black masses, a more complex picture emerges. No reading against the grain is needed; the Yiddish press presented—frequently by the same writers who fiercely attacked white racism—the whole array of traits ascribed to Black people (not only to African Americans) at the time: criminality and depravity, violent tendencies, alcoholism, volatility, ignorance, backwardness, and childlike character. Jokes and commentary about cannibalism and skin color were present in the period through 1929, both in materials copied from English-language publications and those originally in Yiddish. Furthermore, in the years prior to World War I, Yiddish papers still exhibited considerable resistance to equating Jews, whether in the Old World or in the New, with African Americans.

The characterization of Black Americans in the Yiddish press was not merely an echo of the larger white society. Time and again, Yiddish newspapers cast African Americans as America's peasantry, with all its accompanying traits. Hailing from a society that used to distinguish between different strata in the surrounding gentile environment, Yiddish journalists attributed to African Americans characteristics similar to those of the Slavic peasantry. They described Black women and men as simple and direct, sexually freer (or promiscuous), and childlike, yet also volatile, lawless, potentially threatening, and prone to violence. Hence, despite mentioning certain parallels in the historical situation of Black Southerners and East European Jews, for the Yiddish press African Americans were the archetypical, autochthonous peasantry.[61]

Whereas viewing African Americans as fellow victims of hatred and possible allies certainly improved their representation after the Great War, it did not reverse the basic imagery, and much ambivalence remained. An interesting and recurring aspect was paternalism toward Black society that derived from a lack of understanding of the difference between the Jewish and Black experiences in the United States. The underestimation of the structural power disparity and long-term effect of racism on African Americans led Yiddish writers to chastise them for ostensibly lacking self-respect or pride. Apart from this incomprehension of the uniqueness of the Black experience, some of the critique of African American behavior stemmed from the Jewish preoccupation with public image; those writers would have denounced any Jews whose conduct might disgrace Jews as a whole.

While several of the abovementioned sources utilized pseudoscientific vocabulary, all in all the more deterministic facets of racism were not voiced by Yiddish writers. When they referred to African Americans as culturally backward and inferior, they believed that America's Black population could become civilized, or was already on that path. Another important distinction involves political and ideological differences: Even though non-radical newspapers showed less hesitation than their socialist, communist, or anarchist rivals to engage in racial discourse, it is important to recognize that representations of Black people were not limited to editorials and news items. Feuilletons, jokes, cartoons, short literary sketches, and advertisements are no less important in the final analysis, all the more when they are in discord with a newspaper's official line.

The Yiddish press's attitudes toward Black individuals and society encapsulate conflicting trends. On the one hand, they expressed a strong opposition to racism and violence, and true sympathy to African Americans born out of ideals such as *mentshlekhkayt* (humanity) and *mentshlekhe bahandlung* (humane treatment).[62] On the other hand, even when writing against racism, Yiddish journalists and essayists were immersed in its underlying assumptions and esthetics, which then affected their overall judgments and representation. Many of those writers were active in another major venue of Yiddish culture—the Yiddish theater. Just as in the press, the Yiddish theater would vividly capture those contradictory tendencies.

4

"My Mom Drank Ink"

The Performance of Race in the Yiddish Theater and Drama

In the first production of *Yente Telebende* on the Yiddish stage in New York (1917), the character of the "little Negro/Niger" performs a duet with Yente's son, Pine, in the beginning of the second act, titled, "Washington, Lincoln, and Moshe Rabeiny." Yiddish lyricist and actor Louis Gilrod wrote the lyrics, where the Black character sings, "I have a good heart just like you/even though I'm a Niger." Later he sings, "Why am I a Niger child? I'll tell you now/my mom drank ink/when she was pregnant with me." A few years later (1925), theater critic Y. Mar lamented that "The Yiddish theater assimilates in a scary hastiness" and gives its audience "what they can see and hear in the cheap English-language theaters" and "vaudeville houses."[1]

The Yiddish theater has always been bursting with ethnic characterizations—and caricatures. Stock types of Yiddish-speaking *Litvakes*, *Galitsyaner*,[2] Hungarian and Romanian Jews, as well as non-Yiddish-speaking, stiff German Jews, served as a comedic index of in-group differences. Similarly, many nationalities paraded on the Yiddish stage, where they were often cast as villains, as Yiddish plays used the stage as the place to get even with all the tormentors and persecutors of Jews over the centuries. In dozens of plays and operettas, non-Jews were typically reduced to negative caricatures, whether as evil Greeks fighting the Maccabees' rebellion, Romans who besiege Jerusalem and destroy the Temple, Frenchmen who persecute Jews in the Middle Ages or frame Captain Alfred Dreyfus in the 1890s, Spanish Inquisitors who torture heroic Jews, vile Hungarians who fabricate a blood libel, or drunk Russian peasants and soldiers who murder Jews in a pogrom. On stage, viewers saw uneven mixtures of tragedy, comedy, variety show, vaudeville and farce, free adaptations of famous plays, dramatized "current affairs," and especially pompous and nationalist versions of Jewish history, where actors with golden paper crowns and tin swords orated bombastic and heavily Germanized texts. But Jewish audiences adored those plays, which aligned with their concept of cultured and dignified art that highlighted Jewish sufferings and triumphs, while providing folksy comedy and music.[3] Indeed, in his analysis of an American Yiddish play from 1895, which includes a dim-witted Black fieldworker, ethnomusicologist Mark Slobin has aptly recognized not only "The brash language, racial stereotyping, and crass commercialism" of that piece, but also that it "is not an anomaly."[4]

When focusing on the United States, there was perhaps no other form of Yiddish culture which reflected the influence of prevalent American popular culture so vividly as the theater, with its vaudeville acts, "coon shouting," "Negro dialect" characters (some in blackface), and minstrelsy. Apart from that source of inspiration, however, was the portrayal of Black characters as a reincarnation of East European Slavic peasants, the *poyerim/muzhikes*, as they appear in Yiddish folklore with their volatility, coarseness, and mindlessness, together with straightforwardness. Those influences enabled Yiddish plays to mix the familiar and the exotic, American and Old-Country idioms, in a way that tapped into archetypes known to their viewers/readers, while satisfying their appetite for the bizarre and the intriguing.[5] Still, historians have argued that "The Yiddish theater remained free of plays and musical productions lampooning blacks"; and even viewed the abovementioned *Yente Telebende* as an example of how Yiddish culture "sensed that a special relationship existed between blacks and Jews."[6] However, examining a host of productions in the Yiddish theater and other pieces by Yiddish playwrights demonstrates how their performance of race was deeply rooted, especially in the American context, in the surrounding culture's idioms and imagery. As in other arenas of Yiddish culture, the 1920s would witness a gradual amelioration in the representation of Black characters on the Yiddish stage, and even several Yiddish-singing Black thespians.

East European Antecedents

Characters who were supposedly "Negroes," or those described as having a dark skin, appeared already in the nineteenth-century Yiddish theater in Eastern Europe. In 1868, the man who is considered as "father of the Yiddish theater," Avrum Goldfaden, published the lyrics of a song, "The Watchmaker," taken from the fourth act of his comedic play *Di mume Sosye* (Aunt Sosye, 1869). The song parodied the concept of time and why one should have a watch. At one point, as young folks are playing cards and drinking, someone "crawls out of the house/all smeared in black like a Negro/it doesn't matter to me that he's drunk/but oh no! Where is his watch?" A few years later (1877), according to the historian of the Yiddish theater, Zalmen Zilbertsvayg, when Goldfaden's troupe was based in Bucharest, Romania, he translated into Yiddish a play by German dramatist August von Kotzebue, *La Pérouse; or, the Desolate Island* (1795). In Goldfaden's production, titled *Di vilde inzel* (The Savage Island), young actor Zelik/Zigmund Mogulesko played the tragic role of a "Negress," presumably in blackface, who lives with a European man even though he is married to another (European) woman. Mogulesko enjoyed local success in that role and would later become one of the most popular pioneers of New York's Yiddish theater until his untimely death in 1914.[7]

Aunt Sosye's link between dark skin and some kind of mischief continued in Goldfaden's two historical-national plays, *Shulamis, oder bas-yerushalayim* (Shulamit, Or the Daughter of Jerusalem, 1880), and *Bar Kokhba, oder di letste teg fun yerushalayim* (Bar Kokhba, or the Final Days of Jerusalem, 1882). Most critics deem those plays to be Goldfaden's masterpieces, and the playwright himself wrote in private that only those plays remained "classic." In *Shulamis*, the protagonist Avsholem, a noble young man of Maccabean ancestry, is accompanied by his "savage servant," the dark-skinned Tsingitang, a comic figure who throughout the play speaks in a broken language ("I—tree go—big, branch?"), and growls "ooh, ooh." At one point, when Avsholem kisses his wife, Avigayil, Tsingitang comes between them and declares, "like that also for me!" Avsholem ridicules him, saying that he will have a bride "when you become white." Tsingitang laughs, "hee, hee, I become white? . . . I has bride, I devil" (a wordplay on *shvarts-yor* which means "devil" but literally a "black year"); in the same scene, Tsingitang can be heard "bellowing like a beast."[8]

Like *Shulamis*, *Bar Kokhba* is also set in ancient, post-biblical Zion. The main villain in the play is Papus, a wealthy Samaritan who is lame, half-blind, and Black. When Papus courts Bar Kokhba's bride-to-be, the beautiful Dina, he tells her, "Although I'm Black . . . my heart is red as fire." Dina rejects Papus's courting, and laughs at his "ugly, dirty, detestable figure," leading Papus to plan his revenge against her, Bar Kokhba, and Jews in general. A more multi-layered character than Tsingitang, Papus tells himself, "Under my black skin beats the heart even stronger" and sings "with me, everything is concealed behind the black mask." Papus helps the Romans enter the Jewish fortress and slaughter women, children, and old men. Both *Shulamis* and *Bar Kokhba* were highly successful, shown across Europe, the United States, and other countries before hundreds of thousands of viewers, continuing for decades after Goldfaden's death (1908). There were many anecdotes about those shows, such as Yiddish actress Bertha Kalish's recollection of a production of *Shulamis* in Budapest (1889), when the actor who played Tsingitang in blackface, Avrom Fishkind, screamed in fear when seeing a real Black man behind the stage. In later years, the portrayal of those characters was seen as disparaging to the extent that by the 1930s, productions of those plays in the Soviet Union and Poland sought to blunt the racial stereotypes, showing Tsingitang and Papus in a more positive light.[9]

It is noteworthy that both Tsingitang and Papus are depicted as "Black"—sometimes entailing Jewish actors in blackface—yet not necessarily Black Africans. Goldfaden's romantic imagining of the people who populated the Land of Israel in ancient times had more to do with nineteenth-century European culture's orientalized renderings of the Levant. When those plays were shown in the United States, they would take on new cultural contexts. Between 1877 and 1883, Goldfaden's troupe toured Romania, the Habsburg Empire, and Russia, and that period was perhaps the playwright's most creative period. In 1883, the Tsarist government decreed a ban on Yiddish theater, which damaged Goldfaden's career, and sent him wandering across Europe and the United States. While he lived in New York City for short periods (circa 1887–1889, and from 1903 until his death in poverty in 1908), during the Spanish-American War (1898) Goldfaden wrote an arch-patriotic poem for America, titled "To War!" In it, Goldfaden echoed European maskilim's support for the abolition of slavery. He implored fellow Jews to support fully "your brethren the Americans," and pointed to what he saw as American righteousness, mentioning the liberation of slaves and welcoming Jews from Eastern Europe: "And thousands of wretched Black slaves . . . who once liberated them from the vise? Also you [Jews] were oppressed by tyrannical Slavs! How do you feel now [living] at Uncle Sam's?!"[10]

New Land, Old and New Imagery

As the Yiddish theater in Russia was facing immense difficulties in the wake of the ban, it was thriving in New York. Starting in the early 1880s, the Yiddish theater became a leading cultural medium among the city's Yiddish speakers, serving as a fantasy weaver, educator, social gathering place, recreational center for the family, agent of charity, and a barometer of the public mood. By the 1890s there were already three successful Yiddish theaters on the Bowery, to which thousands of enthusiastic Jewish immigrants of all classes and ages flocked every week. The leading playwrights were Morris (Moyshe) Hurvits (a self-styled professor) and Joseph Latayner, who were extremely prolific in writing—and plagiarizing—dozens of plays and operettas. According to the historian and critic B. Gorin, in the late 1880s Hurvits penned *Shloymeh ha-meylekh* (King Solomon), which became "the most important part" of his oeuvre, i.e., "historical operas." In that play, which was produced for several years at various theaters, the character of Shulamis (not to be confused with Goldfaden's play), who is a "Shepherdess," complains to Elkhonen (her limping employer), that the sun had burnt her so badly, "I'm as black as the tents of a grave." But her love interest, Sholem, calms her down, saying that for him she is "so white, like the tapestries of King Solomon."[11]

Hurvits played to the sensibilities of his Jewish audience by referencing the *Song of Songs*, and conveyed whiteness as an ideal of feminine beauty. Yet there was a wider milieu to the early Yiddish theater, which started out in New York before branching out to Chicago, Philadelphia, and other cities. Those theaters operated in a popular culture that was saturated with the ethnic and racial imagery of many groups. Vaudeville and variety performances brimmed with drunk Irish acts and foolish Dutch (Germans) played by amusingly-accented comedians, alongside dancing, black-faced "Negro dialect" actors. Undeniably, not all representations were negative: Jewish singer and actress Belle Baker (born Bella Becker), said in 1919, "I was born in New York. . . . All my impersonations are real. When I sing an Italian or Irish or Yiddish song, I have a definite character in mind that I've known for years." Another group of characters that appeared on stage, mostly from the late 1870s on, were Jews themselves—big nosed, gesticulating, portrayed as greedy, cowardly, argumentative, and speaking with an outlandish accent. Interestingly, Jewish audiences were among those who attended and seemed to enjoy such shows, including those with Jewish characters. The complaint (1890) by Shmuel Nehemia Liebowitz about Jewish viewers who flock to watch shows with grotesque anti-Jewish motifs, cited in the introduction, was an early indication.[12]

As mentioned in an earlier chapter, for virtually all Yiddish-speaking immigrants, the first sight of African Americans was novel and striking. Actor and playwright Rudolf Marks (originally Radkinson) satirized that encounter in his successful comedy *Khaim in amerike* (1891), the title of which is a word game, as Khaim is both a common first name and a word meaning "Life" in Hebrew. That play was performed for decades in various theaters in the U.S. and later in Europe. Many of the recurring jokes in the play revolve around the "greenhorn" (i.e., newcomer) protagonist's misunderstandings about his new country. In one scene, Khaim sees a Black man for the first time, so he runs outside terrified in an undershirt and yells out "shma-yisroel!"—"Hear, O Israel," the credo that is supposed to be recited before death (among other liturgical uses). In 1896, when the play was shown at the Windsor Theater in the Bowery, it featured not only stars such as renowned actors Boris and Bessie Tomashevsky and Marks himself, but also "Mr. Perlmutter" (probably Efraim Perlmutter) as "Charlie the Niger."[13]

If *Khaim in amerike* good-naturedly related to a central theme in American Yiddish culture—acculturation difficulties of Jewish newcomers—rather than to African Americans, another play, which its author dedicated to Marks, exhibited a much more disdainful approach. In April 1895, the Yiddish play *Tsvishen indianer* (Among Indians), written by labor organizer, critic, and journalist Khonen-Yankev Minikes, was shown at New York's Windsor Theater. The play, which was an advertisement for a downtown clothing and dry goods store, features an Indian chief as a "cannibal" and a laughable character of a Black fieldhand by the name of Dixon. Dixon, who speaks broken English, listens to a Jewish peddler's prayer, starts singing while imitating the Hebrew words in gibberish, and leads all the other Black workers in dancing. When another character, Miss Mayzel, angrily tells them (in bad English), "sharap [sic], your [sic] blag [sic] creatures!" Dixon replies, "is very nice song, Miss Mayzel. Is a very nice song!" When she tells him, "Go in the hell, Black devil!" Dixon says, "I wouldn [sic] go, Miss Mayzel! I want a new suit to the Christmas! Hee! Hee! Hee! (he laughs loudly)." When Mayzel offers Dixon a suit that one of the peddlers gave her, Dixon examines it, "makes a sour face" and says, "Rags! No good! Hee, hee! (he laughs idiotically)."[14]

While it is unclear how many times that play/commercial was shown, it is important to remember who the author of that minstrel-infused play was. Minikes, who termed his play "comical vaudeville," was not an obscure writer, but rather a figure who bridged between different facets of the Jewish immigrant world, such as lowbrow and highbrow art, and labor unionism and journalism, as well as left-wing and right-wing. From 1897 through his death in 1932, Minikes edited and published the biannual *Minikes yontef bleter* (Minikes Holiday Newspaper), which became an eclectic and successful publication, featuring both lowbrow and highbrow literature, folk songs, and modernist poetry, in addition to conservative, socialist, and communist writers. Due to Minikes's many activities, famous Yiddish novelist Sholem Ash eulogized him as "the sexton" of the Jewish community. Critic S. Niger commented that while he would not praise the literary quality of the *bleter*, Minikes brought literature to thousands and thousands of readers (well beyond its circulation of up to 30,000 copies per issue).[15]

In 1897, Minikes edited a volume about the Yiddish theater that revealed some of the concepts that shaped the performance of race on the early Yiddish stage. One of the volume's authors, Moyshe Zeyfert, who wrote numerous successful historical novels and operettas, claimed that it was the eminent actor, Jacob P. Adler, who first "baptized the Yiddish stage" and turned it "Gentile." According to Zeyfert, Adler introduced "Eskimos, Zulus, Hottentots," and other groups onto the stage. In those years, the term "Hottentot" served as a catchall phrase for anything savage or menacing; it is hardly surprising that when mentioning Adler's version of *Othello* (1893–1897, intermittently), Zeyfert described Othello as speaking "in a Hottentot language." The mention of presenting Africans on stage as an imitation of American vaudeville theater implies not only the use of blackface, but also "speech" patterns that are associated with savages (in line with Tsingitang's growling). Nevertheless, we should remember that at the time of writing, Zeyfert's critique of Adler was informed by commercial rivalry, since in 1893 Zeyfert's translation of *Hamlet* for Tomashevsky's production competed against Adler's *Othello*. That rivalry would not prevent Zeyfert from having his play *Malkes shva* (Queen of Sheba) produced at Adler's Grand Theater a decade later (1906–1907), with Frida Zibel as the African queen.[16] In that same 1897 book to which Zeyfert contributed, John Paley argued that as Yiddish theatergoers want "to cry and especially to laugh," playwrights feel compelled to write historical plays with various nationalities, "and even Chinese and Hottentots." Paley acknowledged the influence of American burlesque shows on Jewish audiences, which compelled actors to "paint themselves like Nigers and dance on stage with cushioned bellies." Interestingly, both Zeyfert and Paley were regarded as writers of the same commercialized shund they were criticizing.[17]

Undoubtedly, not all Black characters on the Yiddish stage were Hottentots, Zulus, or black-faced dancers with cushioned bellies. Despite Zeyfert's and Paley's claims, historian Joel Berkowitz has shown that Yiddish productions of *Othello* in the 1890s tried to avoid abrasive racial stereotypes.[18] Another set of Black characters on the Yiddish stage appeared in productions based on Harriet Beecher Stowe's *Uncle Tom's Cabin*. After Stowe's novel was adapted and serialized by B. Gorin in the *Arbeter tsaytung* (1900–1901), two rival Yiddish theaters in New York, the Thalia and the People's, opened with almost simultaneous productions (1901) of that story. Thalia's version was translated by playwright Isidore Zolotarevsky, who left certain songs, such as "Down on the Swanee River," entirely in English, but let Topsy (an enslaved girl) sing "Shoo, Fly, Don't Bother Me" and other songs in Yiddish with English-language refrains. In its advertisements, the Thalia promised "Extra! 200 well-rehearsed Nigers!" and "no bluffs." People's Theater opened with Boris Tomashevsky's version, featuring "an ensemble choir from a Niger troupe, for the first time on the Yiddish stage." At one of the shows, Yiddish-speaking audience hissed when the villain Legree whips Tom. *Uncle Tom's Cabin* appeared occasionally for many years on the Yiddish stage across the country. In February 1915, when an English-language minstrel skit at Astor Theater was scheduled under the title *Uncle Thomashefsky's Cabin*, Tomashevsky was reportedly angered by the unauthorized use of his name and demanded that it be cancelled. The skit, starring Jack Curtis, was immediately canceled; Tomashevsky's protest against that skit would not prevent him from displaying minstrelsy in *Yente Telebende* two years later (1917).[19]

The 1890s also witnessed the rise of a playwright whom many critics view as the one who transformed the Yiddish theater from its vulgarity and clownishness into serious drama—Jacob Gordin, who arrived in New York in 1891. The famed playwright, who felt much more at home in Russian than in Yiddish, was a talented feuilletonist as well, and published insightful sketches about Jewish life. In his "travel pictures" from Berlin (1907), Gordin described seeing a Black man who walked past him, "looking around with big, white, frightened eyes." Gordin wondered, "How did he come to Germany? Did a 'gentleman,' who wanted to surprise Europe with his Black slave lead him on to here? Or did he run away from slavery, humiliation, lynch laws?" Gordin immediately moved to depict a group of Russian Jews he saw nearby: "And here go Russian Negroes. They are not Black but blackened [suffering]. . . . They are also running away from slavery, humiliation, lynch laws." Though in that text Gordin drew a direct parallel between the agony of any Black person and that of Jews in Russia, a feuilleton he published in 1906 illustrated a different attitude. In that piece, titled, "The Pipe Organ Blower, or the Comical Strike," Gordin ridiculed the *yahudim*—a pejorative used by Yiddish-speaking Jews to label acculturated Jews, mostly of German origin—with their Uptown Reform Temple, a pompous "Reverend," Christian-like services, and a pipe organ. However, the organ functions only when someone stands in the attic and pumps air into the organ by hand. In that temple, that someone is "an old, good, a little dull-witted Negro by the name Joe-Lincoln-Washington-Jefferson-Brown." After working in silence for years, old Joe, "who blew air and bowed like a slave before all the temple's officers," goes on strike and demands a raise, saying "what's the matter with the Jewish God" who is willing to pay him only 75 cents for all prayers?[20]

"I Have a Good Heart Just Like You/Even Though I'm a Niger": Parading Stereotypes on the Yiddish Stage

As in many other sources under review, although Gordin probably wrote approvingly about Joe's newly-acquired assertiveness, the Black character's servility and dullness are a side issue in the text—Gordin focused on mocking assimilated Reform Jews. In another case, the highly successful theater productions of *Yente Telebende*, a Black character also had a minor yet telling role. As mentioned in the previous chapter, for about two decades from 1913 onward, *Yente* was one of the most popular characters in American Yiddish culture. The first play based on her opened in November 1917 at Boris Tomashevsky's National Theater in Lower Manhattan and ran for about five weeks. One "Miss Winters" was mentioned in the role of the always-nameless "little Niger," who is one of Pine's (Yente's son's) best friends, though often Winters's name did not appear in the advertisements.[21] The Black kid appears mainly in the first two acts. At the start of the first act, he teaches Pine how to play the drums. At the beginning of the second act, the Black kid comes to Yente's home to call for Pine and soon they start the duet "Washington, Lincoln, and Moshe Rabeiny." (See figure 4.1). Pine and the Black kid sing together the first four lines in English: "Eeny-meeny-miney-mo/ catch a Niger by the toe/if he hollers let him go/ eeny-meeny-miney-mo." Then the song continues in Yiddish as follows:

NIGER: Forget that my skin is black/and don't be too clever/I have a good heart just like you/even though I'm a Niger.

PINE [in a wordplay on the verb *farshvartsn*, which means both "blacken" and "suffer/miserable"]: In America, my friend/you've been already for many years/therefore you seem to me/so blackened [miserable].

NIGER: Why am I a Niger child? I'll tell you now/my mom drank ink/when she was pregnant with me.

PINE: You are Black and I am white/we whites are alright/the white man can be everything/he can even become a policeman.

NIGER: The Niger can dance and make fun/the Niger can gobble up watermelon/the Niger can shoot crap with dice/the Niger can make goo-goo eyes.

Figure 4.1. On the left, the cover of the score for the show *Yente Telebende* (1917). On the right, a page from the sheet music, showing part of the song "Washington, Lincoln, and Moshe Rabeiny." Courtesy of the Library of Congress.

PINE: We whites are at the helm/we take pride in George Washington.

NIGER: The greatest man of all great people/is Abraham Lincoln who liberated us from slavery.

PINE: Definitely, definitely, it's not bad/you're really so right/but tell me Black fella, is there among you such a noble man as Moshe Rabeiny?

TOGETHER: Washington, Lincoln and Moshe Rabeiny/these are the honorable, beautiful names/the names will forever, forever live/because freedom they have given/and the whole Jewish people ought to appreciate and love endlessly/always and all the time/a teaching they gave us in a red, white and blue.[22]

It is highly likely that none of the viewers contemplated the lyrics or tried to read between the lines. After all, the stage production of *Yente* was meant to provide light, popular entertainment, and for seasoned theater figures such as Louis Gilrod, who wrote the lyrics, Joseph Rumshinsky, who wrote the music, and Boris Tomashevsky, who incorporated the song into the show, the main goal was to entertain the viewers and sell as many tickets as possible. The racial stereotypes in *Yente* were mild in comparison to those in contemporary American popular culture, with its depiction of Black youths as "pickaninnies," the imagined tattered Black juvenile who is mostly outdoors, ready for any kind of fight or mischief while gorging on watermelons. *Yente* does not stumble into all of those racial pitfalls, as it celebrates the friendship of Pine and the Black kid, the abolition of slavery, and America's freedom.[23]

All the same, the lyrics disclose deeply-embedded racial attitudes that correspond with those that spawned the stereotypical pickaninny, and that situate Jews and Blacks as diametrically opposed. Even as the song acknowledges Black Americans' centuries-long suffering, applauds the abolition of slavery, and mentions they could be good-hearted, it jokes about Black physical traits. More importantly, on one level the song parades many of the common racist tropes of the time, such as watermelon-eating, black skin and ink-drinking, and hints at Blacks' alleged oversexed attributes ("goo-goo eyes").[24] On another level, the song affirms purported white superiority, stresses Jews' whiteness, and sets "Jews" and "Blacks" apart as mutually exclusive categories. The rhetorical question of whether there is a Moshe Rabeiny among Black people cements the idea of Jewish cultural superiority. All of that occurs in a show where the Black kid is the only nameless character, an effacement that strengthens the racial stereotype. In addition, the song in *Yente* played on the association from *Song of Songs*—despite the color of his skin, the Black kid has a good heart; yet that skin color puts him at an inferior starting point, especially when compared to Jews like Pine, who are white.[25]

Yente's success and popularity brought about unauthorized Yiddish stage productions with the title *Yente Telebende* in Baltimore and Toledo, Ohio. *Yente*'s success led Tomashevsky to show it also at various cities in Massachusetts in June 1918.[26] In 1921–1922, additional theater productions of *Yente* opened in New York City, first at Lyric Theater in Brooklyn, later at Lenox Theater in Harlem, then short stints at other theaters. One of the new highlights in the 1921–1922 productions was the performance of African American singer Thomas La Rue (sometimes described as Thomas La Rue Jones), who had already become an attraction among Jewish audiences, especially in Brooklyn, where he appeared as "Tevye der shvartser khazn" (Tevye the Black Cantor), or just "Der shvartser khazn." La Rue sang before sold-out concert halls an assortment of Yiddish classics, both secular and cantorial, ending with "Eli, Eli." By early 1920, La Rue had appeared at the Liberty Theater (Brownsville) as a "great attraction," and later he would become a regular feature in the 1921–1922 stage production of *Yente Telebende*. In October 1921, B. Gorin remarked that the Black cantor caused the "biggest furor" in the show.[27] La Rue appeared in the third act, but advertisements and reviews usually described him as a special guest, or an "extra treat." All reviewers favorably mentioned La Rue's performance and the audience's enthusiasm about it. Abraham Cahan mentioned that the Black cantor came on during the last act, sang in Yiddish and Russian "exactly as it was at the Lyric Theater," and that "you can really admire him." It is noteworthy that La Rue was an addition to the show, and never replaced the "Little Negro." Another important change was that whereas the 1917 show included four acts, all the 1921–1922 productions had three acts.[28]

Did the performances of La Rue reveal that "a special relationship existed" between Blacks and Jews? As *Yente*'s playwright B. Kovner wrote jokingly in 1920, the spectacle of a Black man singing cantorial classics in Yiddish still seemed out of place to a degree that created amusement. As late as May 1920, the *Forverts* itself published a cartoon in its satirical section titled, "Both are singing . . ." which juxtaposed a Jewish cantor who sings bareheaded from Verdi's opera *Aida* and "the Negro wears a yarmulke and sings 'Eli, eli.'" Therefore, it was "a topsy-turvy world." The Black man in the cartoon, with a gaping mouth and grossly caricatured features, was none other than Thomas La Rue; that depiction changed more than a year later, when the *Forverts* began promoting La Rue and became invested in his performance as part of *Yente Telebende*. In March 1922, the *Forverts* showed a portrayal of La Rue which was much more dignified and esthetically pleasing (see figure 4.2).[29]

Furthermore, it is quite probable that many audience members believed La Rue was not Black, but rather a Jew in blackface. In April 1922, the manager of Liberty Theater in Brownsville, William Rolland, recounted that many people came to him, "willing to bet that the Negro cantor is no Negro but rather a disguised Litvak." Rolland sought to assure the public that La Rue is "a real Negro, even though he sings and speaks with such a tasteful Lithuanian accent." Rolland warned the public not to be "fooled into betting that the Negro is not a Negro at all." In 1923, popular Yiddish humorist Tashrak (pen name of Yisroel-Yoysef Zevin) published a feuil-

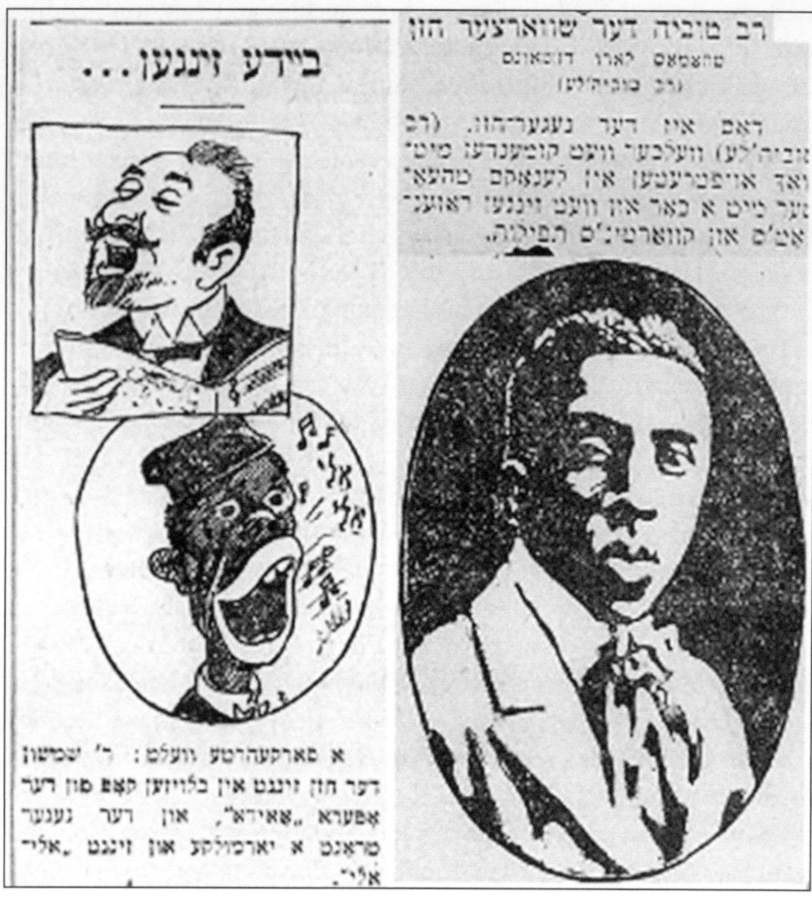

ביידע זינגען...

א פארקערטע וועלט: ר' שמשון
דער חזן זינגט אין בלויזן קאפ פון דער
אפערא „אאידא", און דער נעגער
טראגט א יארמולקע און זינגט „אלי־
אלי".

רב טוביה דער שווארצער חזן
(רב טוביה'לע)

דאס איז דער נעגער־חזן. (רב
טוביה'לע) וועלכער וועט קומענדע מיט־
וואך אויפטרעטען אין לענאקס טהעא־
טער מיט א כאר און וועט זינגען ראזענ־
בלאט'ס און קווארטין'ס תפילות.

Figure 4.2. Before and after—both images are of Thomas La Rue. The cartoon on the left is in the *Forverts* (1920), "Both are singing. . . ." The picture on the right is also from the *Forverts* (1922), "Reb Tevye the Black cantor." Courtesy of the Historical Jewish Press Digital Collection, National Library of Israel and Tel Aviv University.

leton that spoofed the Litvak-cantor-in-blackface story: He told of a friend of his from Kapule (Kapyl/Kopyl in modern-day Belarus, the birthplace of Mendele Moykher Sforim) who went to America, became a cantor, but later took the position of an opera singer. When the narrator and his family went to see him at the opera, they hardly recognized him, as he was "black as dirt." One family member said he had to be in blackface, since he played Othello. Still, the storyteller believed, "the goyim are those who blackened him/made him suffer in such a way."[30]

It is of note that La Rue was not the only Black performer who appeared as a cantor before Jewish audiences in the 1920s. In 1920, Hebrew and Yiddish educator and essayist, Shimshen Erdberg, presented two Black men to the readers of the *Yidishes tageblat*: One was "Mendel the Black Cantor," a "real goy" who said he was born in British Guiana and performed at Dovid Kesler's Theater on the Lower East Side. Erdberg's feuilleton took an affable and light approach, mentioning it is an "eye for an eye" that since a cantor's son, Al Jolson, "disguises himself as a Niger, a Niger disguises himself as a cantor." Like Rolland, Erdberg mentioned the incredulity of Jews about a Yiddish-speaking Black man, as someone asked Mendel, "Are you really Black?" Yet when Mendel sang, it was "not like a Black cantor but like a white Jew." Erdberg also wrote about David HaCohen, an Ethiopian-born Jew who claimed he was educated in France and in the Land of Israel before continuing to Tsarist Russia, where he was a cantor in training and married a local Jewish woman, Rokhl Rabinowitz. Erdberg added a little jab, asking HaCohen whether his two children were Black or white. The cantor replied, "They are white. But they are mine, I'm sure." More popular was Goldye Steiner, billed as a female Black cantor at a period when there were hardly any female cantors, whose performances (1925) in Yiddish, Hebrew, and other languages throughout the Northeast and Midwest drew thousands of Jewish viewers.[31]

On the one hand, those shows endeared those Black performers to Jewish audiences, who were moved to see them sing liturgical melodies and "Eli, Eli." Ethel Waters, one of the earliest Black pioneers to star on Broadway, recalled, "Jewish people in every town seemed to love the idea of me singing their song. They crowded the theaters to hear it, and they would tell one another: 'The *schwarze* sings 'Eili, Eili'! The *schwarze*!'" On the other hand, Waters's impression dovetails those of Rolland and Erdberg, showing how such performances served as both an attraction and an oddity for Yiddish-speaking Jews. Erdberg quoted HaCohen's Ethiopian family, who argued that "white Jews are no longer Jews, they're fakers" to demonstrate the abyss between Jews of different colors. In 1925, translator and critic Leyb Kristol excoriated Yiddish vaudeville for being inferior even to its English-language counterpart: It opened 1925 with "'Goldye the Black cantor,' a 'star' in the vaudeville theaters. The hackneyed, foul couplets and duets, and the foolish sketches" are all that Yiddish vaudevillians could offer. While it is unclear why Kristol focused on Goldye, it is apparent that the idea of a Black woman as a cantor seemed like a cheap stunt to him.[32]

La Rue's singing took place at the end of *Yente Telebende*. How did the 1921–1922 productions, which were somewhat different from the 1917 show, portray the "little Niger" (played by William Hughes[33])? (See figure 4.3). In his review of the show, Abraham Cahan mentioned a duet between Pine and the Black kid: Each of them stands in his own box above the stage, and they "take turns singing" to Yente, who is dancing and singing below them on the main stage. That setup resembles "Washington, Lincoln, and Moshe Rabeiny" from the 1917 production. In the 1921–1922 play, however, the most substantial dialogue between Pine and the Black kid appears in the second act, in English (written as a Yiddish text), where they have a deal with someone "who fixes broken panes": The kids will break windows, and "Afterward he'll come around with his pushcart and panes and fix them."[34]

Just as in Kovner's column in the *Forverts*, the Black kid in this context represents the outside world's intrusion into the immigrant Jewish family, and the vulgarizing and rough effect of the American street on Jewish children. At the same time, the Black kid is a good and loyal friend, who remains courteous toward other members of the Telebende family. In that respect, his character parallels American literature's trope of the Black friend, perhaps best known from Mark Twain's character of Jim in *The Adventures of Huckleberry Finn*, where a main theme is the clash between racial prejudice and individual judgment based on behavior.[35] Yet there is another important, Old-World element at work here: The Black kid's mischiefs, such as breaking windowpanes, tugging at the beards of elderly Jews, and harassment of Jewish pedestrians are the trademarks of the prototypical *sheygets*, who, in blessed America, joins forces with a Jewish lad. Just as Yiddish folklore associated the peasant lad with both negative and positive traits, the Black kid symbolizes negative influence over Pine, but he shows loyalty and directness.[36]

Another theater show, which was based on a play by Kovner (written together with Berl Botvinik), also featured the character of a Black teenager as a loyal friend. Originally titled *Shayke der bal-ago'le* (Shayke the Coachman), it opened in St. Louis in early 1921 and a year later played at the Lyric Theater in Brooklyn under the title *Shayke fun bronzvil*

Figure 4.3. Detail from a cartoon depicting (right to left) actress Diana (Dina) Goldberg as Pine and an unnamed actor as "his little Niger," *Tog* (1922). Courtesy of the Historical Jewish Press Digital Collection, National Library of Israel and Tel Aviv University.

(Shayke of Brownsville). An archived copy of the original play includes "a young Negro" by the name of George Washington, who speaks fluent Yiddish and remains amicable. When he and an old, nearly deaf melamed, Shmaya, try entering through the same door simultaneously, Shmaya becomes angry and says to anyone present, "he is really black like a Niger" and threatens Washington with his cane. Washington remains friendly, and speaks Yiddish to the old man, who then smiles, thinking Washington is Jewish, and says to Washington, "You don't say, a Jewish Niger?" Washington explains patiently that since he grew up on Cherry Street, "I speak Yiddish exactly like any Jew in New York. I can sing Yiddish songs." Washington proceeds to singing "Eli, Eli," and then puts Shmaya's hat on his head and recites the "shma-yisro'el." By the end of the play, after Shayke/Sam loses his fortune and returns to his job as a stableboy, Washington and Shayke's employer, "Charlie the expressman," drive a wagon through Brownsville, singing "vos mir zaynen, zaynen mir/ober yidn zaynen mir" (What we are, we are/but we are Jews); Washington "sings especially tastefully." The play corresponds not just to La Rue's popular performances, but also to the sight of Yiddish-speaking Black men and women (similar to Yiddish-speaking Gentiles, mostly peasants, in the Old World), who were becoming an established category in Yiddish culture. Washington's endearing role notwithstanding, it seems that his character was removed from the theater productions of the play, at least those in New York.[37]

The New World's Peasantry

If *Shayke der bal-agole* lionized the friendship and loyalty of the Black teenager in a less ambivalent form than *Yente Telebende*, other plays included minor Black characters that were peasant-like, usually in servant roles, with their associated simplicity and practicality. Abraham Schomer's play *Stayl* (Style) was shown (1913) at the Arch Street Theater in Philadelphia, and later that year at Kesler's Second Avenue Theater in New York, as well as at the Brownsville Liberty Theater (1915–1916). Schomer, who was the son of the famed writer Shomer, wrote a small role of a Black maid by the name of Elsie; Elsie silently follows the instructions of her employer, Mrs. Fayner, saying "alright ma'am" and "yes ma'am." She is silent and efficient, and at one point she reminds Mrs. Fayner that a guest is waiting for his drink—"well, ma'am?" That seemingly small and submissive role, nonetheless, should be weighed against the major (Jewish) characters, who exhibit madness, lust, and criminality. While her role is obedient, Elsie is one of the straightest characters.[38]

A somewhat larger role, that of Aunt Jemima, appeared in Osip Dymov's (pen name of Yoysef Perlman) 1919 satire about Americanization and consumerism titled *Bronks ekspres* (Bronx Express). In this play, the main character, Khatskl Hungershtolts (hunger-proud), a garment worker, falls asleep on his way home aboard the Bronx Express train. In his dream, all the characters from the overhead advertisement posters come to life, interacting with Hungershtolts and each other—among them an insect from a FLIT insecticide ad; Mr. Pluto, a devil figure in red, advertising mineral water; and Aunt Jemima in an apron, advertising her pancake mix. As she offers her pancakes, Hungershtolts says, "I never tasted you, auntie, but I'm very glad [to meet you]." Jemima continues to offer her product, saying, "delicious, economical, convenient, special for you sir." At one point, the insect from the FLIT ad says to Jemima, "He's after me auntie!" to which she replies, "(with contempt)," "What kind of aunt am I to you? Leave me alone." Like Elsie in Schomer's *Style*, Aunt Jemima is in a domestic, deferential role, yet her simplicity is sincere (despite Dymov's critique of the mass consumption products that her character promotes). To be sure, she is still a racial stereotype: As the show opened on December 31, 1919, at the New Yiddish Theater (on Madison Avenue), reviewer Zisha Landoy commented that "Madam Apel is a lively Jemima." Romanian-born Anna Apel played in numerous Yiddish vaudevilles and was known for the range of her mimics and facial expressions; according to the reviewers, she played in blackface in this production. In his review of the show, Abraham Cahan wrote, "Anna Apel . . . (as a Negress) has justly earned the applauds she received." In April 1922, *Bronx Express*'s English-language version opened in New York's Astor Theater, with Margaret Sullivan (daughter of Tammany Hall politician "Big Tim" Sullivan) playing Aunt Jemima in blackface. *Groyser kundes* published cartoonist Saul Raskin's caricature of the whole cast, including Sullivan smiling in blackface (see figure 4.4.). However, the Broadway production of Dymov's play was less successful than the ones in Yiddish theaters.[39]

In his assessment of *Bronx Express*, Cahan extoled Dymov for creating "something exceptional" that does not fit any of the Yiddish theater's categories of drama, comedy, farce, or vaudeville. There was certainly no shortage of comedies and vaudevilles in the Yiddish theaters well into the 1920s. In the same month that *Yente Telebende* premiered at the Lyric Theater in Brooklyn (October 1921), lower Manhattan's Second Avenue Theater opened a successful comedy, written by William Siegel with music by Joseph Rumshinsky. Lithuania-born Rumshinsky, who wrote the music for "Washington, Lincoln, and Moshe Rabeiny," was one of the most popular and prolific composers of the Yiddish theater, working closely with Molly Picon in the 1920s and early 1930s.[40]

The comedy by Siegel and Rumshinsky was titled *Hello Shmendrik* (that term means a stupid or unfortunate person) and it featured an unnamed "vaudeville Negro," who had a small role as a shoeshine boy

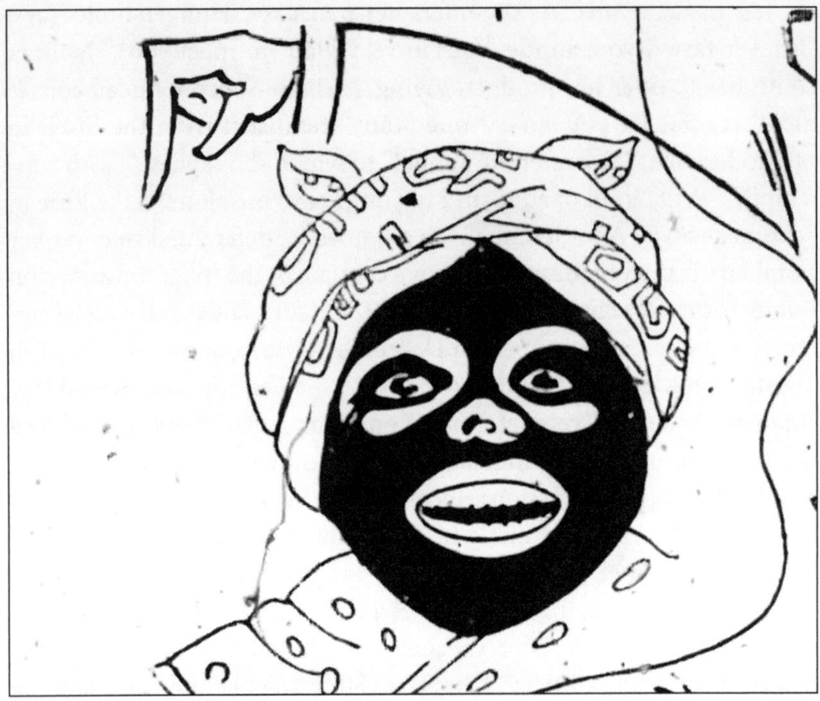

Figure 4.4. Detail from Saul Raskin's caricature of Aunt Jemima (played by Margaret Sullivan) in the Broadway English-language production of *Bronx Express*, *Groyser kundes* (1922). Courtesy of the Dorot Jewish Division at the New York Public Library.

(see figure 4.5). That Black actor, though, had a special talent—he could knock his head against the floor, and then spin on it. That scene turned out to be the show's greatest attraction, and critics such as "Yisroel der yankee" (Yisroel Friedman) scoffed at the play, which "pushed in a Niger," and even more so sneered at the "valued, praiseworthy, beloved Jewish public that goes mad over such 'exalted art.'" Friedman noted sarcastically that "an overturned Niger" was "the highest level that the Yid dish theater lived to see in forty years!" The *Forverts*, which promoted *Yente* at the same time, was quick to lambast *Hello Shmendrik* and what it saw as that show's racism. In a column by Berl Botvinik, he admitted the huge success of "the Niger who dances on his head." Botvinik joked that as "the Niger is the bigshot of the play," Rumshinsky and the theater manager, Joseph Edelstein, were "both anxious that the Niger would forget to show up for his performance." But since they did not really know how he looks, and since to them "all Negroes . . . have the same face," they go out to the street, "and when they spot a Niger, they run after him and shout, 'hey, don't forget to come to the show.' In each Niger they see only one. It seems to them that this is their Niger, their precious treasure of 'Shmendrik.'"[41]

One should take Botvinik's railing against Rumshinsky's and Edelstein's supposed racism with a grain of salt, considering both the *Forverts*'s interest in denigrating any competition with *Yente Telebende*, and Botvinik's own uneven record in portraying African Americans.[42] At any rate, despite the critics' disapproval, both *Yente Telebende* and *Hello Shmendrik* were box office hits. The same cannot be said about a one-act play by celebrated writer Yoysef Opatoshu, titled *In a Saloon* (1922). When Opatoshu first published this Prohibition-era drama (March

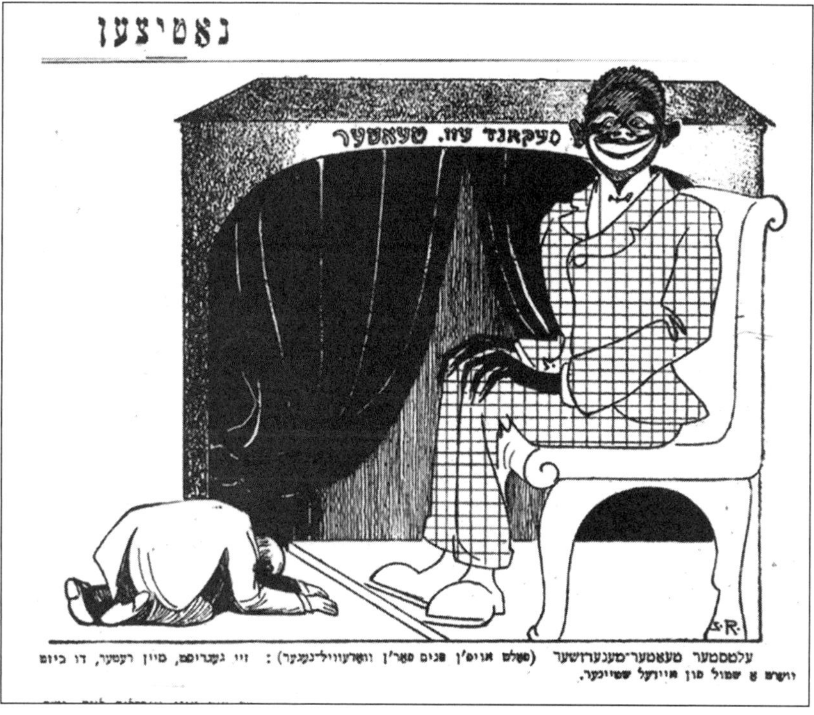

Figure 4.5. The caption reads, "The most senior theater manager (drops to the floor before vaudeville-Negro): Hail to Thee, my savior, you are worthy of a chair made of gemstones" (cartoon probably by Saul Raskin), *Unzer teater* (1921). Courtesy of the Historical Jewish Press Digital Collection, National Library of Israel and Tel Aviv University.

1922), the portrayal of a "Niger" was revealing not only due to his lines, but also the parenthetical stage directions. After two men fight over a woman in a saloon, a Black man, Jim, stands in the corner, "with a lip hanging down," and another character, Jake (who is Jewish), offers him a drink. Jim smiles, approaches Jake cautiously; then Jim "takes the glass with his apish hand," drinks, then "spits out left and right two yellow globs." Jim wants to buy the next round, but Jake "feels offended that a Niger treats him" and wants to pay again. Jim says, "No, brother, I must pay! Though admittedly, I'm a Niger. . . ." The two hug and kiss, and then Jim offers to take Jake home and introduce him to his wife: "She is a good girl, I'm telling you! Strictly kosher! Hee, hee, hee! She is an angel, come! You are my friend, everything belongs to you, even my wife." Jim says, "People are people, aren't they? For me it's all the same, a white person, a Black person, even a Jew. . . ." Jim and Jake proceed to talk about God, and Jim quotes his minister, who said, "There cannot be a shop without a foreman. That's true!" While talking, Jim "leans his neck on Jake's shoulder like a cow leans on another and moos."[43]

The character of Jim demonstrates Opatoshu's complex treatment of African Americans in his long career, a topic that will be discussed in the next chapter. Whereas he wrote passionate pleas against lynching and racism, one of his Black characters comes across not just as a simple-minded peasant who believes his minister, but also as animal-like. Jim's conviviality is interwoven with apelike or bovine-like features, and with debased morality when offering his wife to another man.[44] *In a Saloon* was shown on stage at least once in New York (May 1922), as a performance of the drama school at Maurice Schwartz's Yiddish Art Theater; one Velvel Stein played "A Niger"—as in the original play, the cast list did not mention Jim by name. Either because the play got an unenthusiastic reception or for some reason, Opatoshu reworked *In a Saloon* into a four-act play titled *Heys blut* (Hot Blood), which played in November 1922 at Warsaw's Yiddish "Central Theater." That production was also, in the words of one critic, "a stillborn child" and was summarily terminated.[45]

Vaudeville-like black-faced characters continued to appear on the Yiddish stage throughout the 1920s.[46] Yet it seems that the more callous and buffoonish stereotypes of Black women and men were declining. That development was surely linked to the gradual improvement in the representation of African Americans and growing awareness of their predicament that were evident in other venues of Yiddish culture during that time. In 1928, renowned Yiddish playwright and novelist, Leon Kobrin, published his play *Riversayd drayv* (Riverside Drive). The play, which premiered in 1931 at Maurice Schwartz's Art Theater, includes a minute, wordless role of a Black porter. Whereas Schomer's Elsie and Dymov's Aunt Jemima are simple and honest, albeit in servant roles, Kobrin lent more insight to the nameless porter. Early in the play, the porter carries the luggage of the Yaffes, an older couple who just arrived from the old country, into the lavish home of their son, Herman Jaffe, on the eponymous street of Manhattan's Upper West Side. As he puts down the bags and looks at the house, the porter "glances at the greens [newcomers], covers his mouth with his hand, chokes off a squeaking laughter and runs out." Although "merely" a Black employee in a menial job, with one quick look the porter sees the abyss between the traditional old couple and the assimilated, affluent environment of their son and his family. The decline of Jewishness, growing assimilation among the offspring of Jewish immigrants, and a looming generational clash are at the core of *Riversayd drayv*. In a sense, the play demonstrates the cultural contours in which even a socialist such as Kobrin functioned. He still utilized certain conventions about the porter, who remains nameless and wordless, and somewhat childlike; nevertheless, this character is perceptive and quickly exposes the crux of the matter.[47]

* * *

In 1918, there were eight Yiddish theater houses in Manhattan. A decade later, that number was cut in half; the theater season of 1929–1930 witnessed two 2nd Avenue Yiddish theaters put up for sale. Throughout the 1920s, Yiddish theater audiences dwindled. Still, the American Yiddish theater remained a vibrant and diverse arena well into the next decade.[48] That background is important when considering the argument that the typical recently-arrived Jewish immigrant, whose English was basic at best, was "able to absorb only a very limited and highly localized set of impressions of American life." Thus, as one historian has argued, scholars who have focused on the role of Jewish performers such as Fanny Brice, Eddie Cantor, Al Jolson, and Sophie Tucker (among others), dealt with "very uncommon people" in the reproduction of racial imagery (see figure 4.6). For most Jewish immigrants, "nothing could have been farther from their minds" in relation to those entertainers.[49] This evaluation of those Jewish performers' effect on Yiddish-speaking Jewish immigrants is probably correct. Beyond those individuals, however, remains the vast field of the Yiddish theater, which was both accessible to the immigrants and immensely successful among them.

We should also remember that there was never a single "Yiddish theater," but various institutions, often competing, which included a broad range of styles, and stretched across different countries.[50] Even if the Yiddish stage in America was not as extreme as its English-language counterparts in performing live racial caricatures, popular Yiddish shows did not shy away from presenting stereotypical Black characters, who were dull-witted, clownish, savage, or animal-like. There was unquestionably a significant difference between showing a Black character in Eastern Europe and performing race on the American Yiddish stage. Yet in both cases, Yiddish playwrights, directors, managers, and actors utilized the existing conventions of European and American theaters when displaying Black people. Still, if in Europe a Black person remained mostly an abstraction for Yiddish-speaking viewers, in America they were an immediate social reality; while contacts between Jews and African Americans in New York City remained sporadic prior to World War I, one did not have to live next to African Americans or work alongside them to absorb a host of images about them. Whether or not the Yiddish-speaking immigrant was exposed to English-language performers such as Brice, Cantor, Jolson, and Tucker, imagery of Black Americans was widely available on the Yiddish stage.

Perhaps even more than other branches of Yiddish culture such as newspapers and literature, the Yiddish theater strove for commercial success by appealing to the tastes of its audience. The dual sources that informed the portrayal of Black people—Old-World Yiddish folklore about the peasantry and American performance of race in minstrelsy and vaudeville—suited well the purpose of Yiddish theaters. Whereas scholars have romanticized Yiddish culture and viewed it as resistance to the cruder forms of Americanization,[51] the Yiddish stage proved to be part and parcel of American urban culture and fully immersed in American racial idioms. Even respected authors such as Gordin and Opatoshu, whose works critics considered more refined than the reg-

Figure 4.6. The title reads, "Found a compatriot" (i.e., a fellow Jew). The caption reads, "Jew: I thought you are a stranger! Now I see, black on white, that you are one of us!" The newspaper that is next to Jolson on the ground reads "Al Jolson resigns from an aristocratic club due to antisemitic deed," *Groyser kundes* (1926). Courtesy of the Dorot Jewish Division at the New York Public Library.

ular coarse repertoire of commercial theaters, and who found some commonality between African Americans and Jews, still shaped Black characters as laughable stock figures.

The performance of race in many of the aforesaid plays illustrates how large areas of Yiddish culture remain understudied or unstudied altogether and offer promising directions for future research. In conjunction with the success of the Yiddish theater, by the closing decade of the nineteenth century technological and commercial innovations made Yiddish literature much more affordable and accessible to Yiddish readers, both in Eastern Europe and in the United States. That literature, whose popularity and purportedly low quality won it the title of an "epidemic,"[52] abounded with depictions of both Black Africans and African Americans and would become a distinct feature in the Yiddish cultural sphere.

5

"A Heavy Bodily Scent"

Black Characters in Yiddish Prose

In 1929, Yoysef Opatoshu published a sarcastic short story titled *Zind* (Sin), in which a Bronx family of Jewish communists faces the fact that their teenaged daughter, Hannah, is socializing with John, a young Black man. While the father, "Comrade Gross," is on a three-month visit to the Soviet Union, the mother, "female Comrade Gross," is unhappy with her daughter's new friend, whom Hannah met at a communist Young Workers League's activity. The mother reproaches Hannah, "Couldn't you find any other friend apart from a Negro? And with such a pair of lips to boot?" and tells her, "Better look for a white lad!" Hannah angrily replies, "You taught me yourself that all people are equal." When the mother, Hannah, and John go to the harbor to welcome the father upon his return home, Comrade Gross tells them about his adventures, but "from time to time the sorrow from the Negro's eyes stood in the way of his talk." When they are back home, the father asks his wife about John; the mother says she advised Hannah to choose a white fella, and mentions Hannah's answer that "we have taught her that all people are equal . . ."; as the mother says that, both parents "burst out laughing." At night, the father cannot sleep, since he is troubled by his daughter's relationship with John, although "it's not pretty to think that way, it's a sin."[1]

Opatoshu's sardonic tone and his description of Jewish communists as racist hypocrites did not escape the notice of poet and critic Yitskhok Rontsh, who argued that anyone familiar with Jewish communists at the time would recognize that "Opatoshu's analysis is false." Rontsh called upon readers not to believe that communist parents' "attitude toward a Negro youngster would be so appalling as Opatoshu presented it." According to him, Opatoshu's resentment toward Jewish communists was related to the Arab anti-Jewish riots in the Land of Israel that year (August 1929), in which 133 Jews were murdered. The pro-Arab stance of the Communist Party and its Yiddish organ, *Morgn frayhayt*, which declared that the riots were "anti-imperialistic," alienated many Yiddish readers, who dropped the paper and party alike.[2]

Whether Rontsh's claim is accurate or not, Opatoshu's own ambivalent portrayal of African Americans, as shown in the previous chapter and below, demonstrates the contradictory nature of Yiddish prose in its treatment of race. This chapter delineates the growing nuance in the depiction of Black characters and increased sympathy for them in the critically respectable Yiddish fiction of the 1920s, especially in comparison with the widely circulated pulp literature of the 1890s and 1900s (including nonfiction texts by writers who were also journalists and essayists). By the late 1920s, as *Zind* exemplifies, the very accusation of racism could be used as a weapon in an intra-Jewish dispute. As in other branches of Yiddish culture, however, the ambivalence did not vanish, as certain literary conventions about alleged Black behavioral traits, such as being childlike, found their way into writings that sought to humanize African American women and men. The contrast between many authors' principled denunciations of racism and their often-disparaging esthetical depictions of African Americans was a hallmark of many of the works under review.

Those authors were also reaching increasing numbers of readers. The rapid development of the transatlantic Yiddish book industry in the said period was quite remarkable. From the "booklets epidemic" of the 1890s (see below) through the works of the 1920s, American publishers expanded their sales in Eastern Europe, while printing houses from Lemberg, Vilna, and Warsaw continued to send Yiddish books to American bookstores. Sometimes it was cheaper for American authors to have their books printed in Eastern Europe. The modernization and growing efficiency of the transatlantic book trade brought Yiddish prose to a growing number of readers in various countries. Even an author such as the discussed-below Borekh Glazman, who did not enjoy the same commercial success as the pulp writers or, later, as Sholem Ash, still reached tens if not hundreds of thousands of readers.[3]

Masters of Lowbrow Fiction

In the late 1880s, several Yiddish writers or future writers immigrated to America, and their writings would circulate among hundreds of thousands of Yiddish readers, in the United States, in Eastern Europe, and in other centers of Yiddish-speaking Jewry. That group included Dovid Hermalin, John Paley, Avner Tanenboym (Tanenbaum), Getsil Zelikovitsh, and Tashrak (Zevin). Their arrival coincided with that of Shomer, who was already a best-selling author in Eastern Europe before his arrival in New York (1889). Their works, whether original or adapted (or plagiarized) from other languages, included numerous renderings of Black Africans and African Americans.

The initial success of some of those writers derived from what critics termed the *heftn epidemye* (booklets epidemic): In 1892, a New York immigrant businessman, Sigmund Kantorowitz, contracted Avner Tanenboym to write a Yiddish adaptation of a German serial novel about the secrets and conspiracies of the Russian royal court. That book was serialized and sold as booklets in installments; Tanenboym reportedly received $4,000 from the profits of the novel's eighty-one booklets. This huge success revolutionized not only Yiddish book publishing but also the readership, which snapped up those booklets from dozens of bookstores and candy stores in New York and other cities. The popularity of this new format led other writers such as Dovid Hermalin and Getsil Zelikovitsh to publish similar dime novels that mixed intrigue, erotica, adultery, crime, and adventurous voyages. That trade soon spread across Eastern Europe, and as in America, readers could also borrow the booklets. The Yiddish press quickly picked up the idea and began publishing serialized novels, offering more venues for writers.[4]

Avner Tanenboym

Tanenboym, who immigrated to America in 1887, would establish a reputation on both sides of the Atlantic as an essayist and translator of popular novels and scientific texts. His ability to convey technological and philosophical topics in plain Yiddish made him popular not only among the readers of pulp fiction, but also in socialist and anarchist circles (Tanenboym was an anarchist in the 1880s, yet later became a

Zionist); a pioneer of Jewish libraries and catalogs in Russia, Avrom Kotik, estimated that Tanenboym was fivefold more popular than any other Yiddish writer.[5] An author whose works Tanenboym often "freely adapted" to Yiddish was French novelist Jules Verne. In his *Voyages extraordinaires*, Verne exhibited a dual approach toward Black Africans and African Americans that was characteristic of numerous nineteenth-century European and American writers. On the one hand, intense opposition to slavery and abstract declarations about the shared humanity of all races, and on the other, casting Black people as inferior and using a scornful vocabulary to describe them.[6]

In Verne's book *Les Enfants du capitaine Grant* (The Children of Captain Grant, 1867–1868, published in English as *A Voyage Round the World* in 1876), the character of Major McNabbs equates aboriginal Australians with monkeys. Tanenboym's adaptation, *Di ferlorene shif* (The Lost Ship, 1896, later reprinted as *Di vilde velt*, The Wild World, 1911), was based on an English-language translation; as in the English version, Tanenboym used the term "Negro" in relation to the aboriginals, something that did not appear in the French original. Apart from shortening the plot and changing McNabbs's name to Major Richardson, Tanenboym followed the English text, but omitted a sentence that derisively mimicked African American speech. Still, the Yiddish adaptation included Richardson's quip, "The Negroes say that apes are also people, but more skillful and abler than them [Blacks]. They're right. I don't see any a difference between the Negro and an ape." When the book's characters reach the South Atlantic Island of Tristan d'Acunha, both the French original and the English translation emphasize the "ugliness" of the female "Negroes and Cape Hottentots" who married English and American men, as well as the "disagreeable" physique of their mixed-race children. Here again, Tanenboym somewhat softened the language (about the women), as the Yiddish version reads, "the women are black as coal. The children are a mixture of Negroes and Europeans, [or] more accurately, very ugly half-Negroes."[7]

Tanenboym's reworking of Verne's adventure books communicated the dualism of the original texts in displaying the brutality and horrors of slavery while casting Black Africans as inferior. In *In vilden afrika* (In Wild Africa), Tanenboym adapted the second half of Verne's *Un capitaine de quinze ans* (1878, translated to English in the U.S. as

Dick Sand, A Captain at Fifteen, 1878). Like Verne, he illustrated in ghastly detail the torture of the enslaved, alongside African characters' savagery, drunkenness, and ignorance.[8] A more derogatory image of a Black man was relayed in Verne's 1886 novel *Robur le Conquérant* (Robur the Conqueror, published in English as *A Trip Round the World in a Flying Machine* in 1887), which Tanenboym published in 1899 under the title, *Di flih mashin* (The Flight Machine). In the French original and the early English translation, Frycollin, the African American servant of the patrician Uncle Prudent (president of a flight enthusiasts' institute), is a racist caricature: "A true South Carolina negro. . . . A clown, glutton, sluggard, and above all a superb coward." When Robur kidnaps Prudent, his secretary Phil Evans, and Frycollin and takes them aboard his flight machine, Frycollin becomes hysterical and cries out, as his "brain was as weak as his stomach was strong." Throughout the book, the Black servant remains a clownish, terrified figure, whose cowardice leads him to abandon Prudent by escaping first from the flight machine.[9]

Whereas Tanenboym retained many of Frycollin's laughable traits from the English translation, he left out some of the offensive physical description. In his text, Frycollin is called Jim Brown, and he is "a tall, robust Negro" rather than Verne's "doltish head on a scrawny little body." Tanenboym also left out Verne's references to Frycollin/Brown deserving to be a slave and to his monkey-like features. Tanenboym did add examples of Brown's cowardice: "[H]e was such a coward, that he was afraid of a cat," and "if he were white, he would have turned pale as limestone, but since he was black as coal, his red lips turned blue." Tanenboym's adaptation followed the English translation in depicting Brown's childish fear onboard Robur's flight machine, as he is the only one who screams, has convulsions, and keeps begging for help. Another addition by Tanenboym, which appeared neither in the French original nor in the English translation, is in the passage when Prudent and Evans reunite with Brown, who escaped and left them behind. In Tanenboym's rendition, both men call out together, "Bravo, Brown! You are a real American!" Apart from showing the Black servant as capable of a daring act, Tanenboym—as other Yiddish writers in the late nineteenth century—often idealized the American national character as tolerant and industrious, differentiating between Americans and other Gentiles.[10]

Tanenboym was also a prolific essayist, especially in the *Yidishes tageblat* and *Morgen zhurnal*. It is important to note that his talent and knowledge notwithstanding, Tanenboym was not necessarily a coherent thinker, as demonstrated in his texts about racial issues. Nonetheless, if we can trace a common theme in his writings as an essayist about African Americans, it would be that sociocultural conditions, not immutable biological attributes, were at the root of what he saw as Black ignorance and laziness. In 1898, Tanenboym called for racial equality in America, asking why the developed race, the white race, was unable to civilize other races like the Black, Chinese, and American Indian. Tanenboym argued that if "half-wild Irish, ignorant Italians and completely crass Slavs" had civilized themselves, so could the others. In 1906, following the shooting incident that involved Black soldiers in Brownsville, Texas, Tanenboym argued, "The Negro is now a free citizen, but he is at such a low level of civilization and citizenship" that white Americans cannot see him as their equal. Writing about Southern states, where African Americans constituted half or more of the population, Tanenboym speculated, "It is possible that with time, let's say in 100–200 years, those Negroes will become more efficient and abler people, but for the time being they form a heavy burden" on those states. His solution was to populate those states with American whites and European immigrants. Yet in 1910, Tanenboym came out against racial segregation, sharply criticizing Baltimore's zoning law that banned African Americans from moving into blocks where whites made up the majority, and vice versa. Baltimoreans believe that "the Negroes are very bad, depraved, barbaric, brutal. But that is not true," Tanenboym wrote; "Not all Negroes are bad. . . . To a certain extent there are bad and good people in every nation." Tanenboym quoted Booker T. Washington and W. E. B. Du Bois's articles to prove the remarkable progress made by African Americans since the Civil War and concluded that racial segregation is as "nonsensical and unjust" as it is unconstitutional.[11]

John Paley and Editorial Colleagues

Lexicographer and historian Zalmen Reyzin argued that Tanenboym's works served as a "transition between pure schlock" and "more serious reading material." A writer considered less critically acclaimed than that was John Paley, who was not only the editor of the *Yidishes tageblat*, but also a highly successful writer. A yeshiva student from Byelorussia who also pursued secular education, he was rumored to be a *meshumed* (convert to Christianity) for a short period in Russia. Paley arrived in America at the age of seventeen (1888) and already aboard the ship managed to complete a novel for which he received a $50 honorarium. After less than four years in the country, he was editing widely circulating Yiddish papers in Philadelphia, and later moved to New York, developing a unique mixture of catering to Old-World traditionalism and shoddy sensationalism. Although Paley's cultural baggage was as light as his principles, he was endowed with a rare understanding of Jewish sensibilities. In 1902, after a few Jewish names were mentioned in connection to crime in New York, Paley wrote that Jewish thieves were not really Jews. According to him, these so-called Jewish swindlers were often actually "Catholic Poles, whose last names also end with a 'ski' or 'vich,' or Negroes, who carry biblical first names." Paley's vacillation on racial questions can be seen in two conflicting editorials. In 1906, he applauded the Afro-American Realty Company, which bought and leased houses to Black tenants as a countermeasure against white landlords who evicted their African American renters. Paley wrote, "The Negroes in New York gave the whites a taste of their own medicine and taught them a strong lesson." A year later (1907), however, Paley termed Blacks "an inferior race, which becomes wild when drunk."[12]

Undoubtedly, Paley's untimely death in 1907 at the age of thirty-six (which was widely rumored to be a suicide) cut short the productive career of one of the leading and highest-paid Yiddish writers in America. Circa 1900, Paley published the crime novel *Di shvartze khevre, oder nu york bay tog un bay nakht* (The Criminal Gang, or New York by Day and by Night), which aimed, as Paley boasted in the book's preface, to expose the malady of the underworld and "give the facts as they are." Whereas the book does not have any main Black characters—"shvartse" refers to criminality, not race—its representation of African Americans is illuminating. The book follows Rachel, an innocent young woman, who arrives in New York, expecting to marry Willie, the man who promised her marriage and a new life in America, not knowing that Willie is trafficking in women (termed a "white slaver" back then), who intends to sell her off to a brothel. The novel takes place in dance halls and dens of vice, including one where an actress, who is also the pianist, must "entertain the Nigers and sailors." Paley describes a rowdy music hall, where "a sailor tumbles and falls under a table with a Black prostitute" near the buffet. When Rachel reaches her lowest ebb, she sits in a brothel, and remains silent "when a Negro lays his head on her naked neck. Rachel Green has been defeated."[13]

It is noteworthy that Paley did not portray Black characters per se in a negative way. More than in *Yente Telebende*, nevertheless, African Americans in his book symbolize the brash and dangerous influence of the American street and culture on Jewish immigrants. In a dance hall populated by "thieves, bandits, scoundrels, prostitutes . . . a Niger usually plays the entire musical program." Another place is a smoke-filled dive, in the middle of which stands a huge barrel "and on it a Niger with a fiddle, Niger women, white women, Chinese and Italians danced together so madly." At one point, Willie threatens Rachel that if she does not comply, the eponymous owner of the notorious "McGurk's Suicide Hall" will get her involved "with Nigers, Chinese, and Indians." To be sure, the references to various ethnic groups apart from African Americans reveal that, for Paley, they were all part of a perilous environment; brutal and antisemitic Irish hoodlums and policemen had a particularly menacing presence in Paley's New York. Yet again, Rachel's ultimate degradation and "defeat" was when a Black man had his way with her.[14]

Paley's colleagues at the *Yidishes tageblat*, such as Getsil Zelikovitsh and Tashrak, also utilized race to excoriate what they saw as the drawbacks of vulgar or hasty assimilation. We have already seen Zelikovitsh's travel impressions from Sudan, or his jokes about Black people shedding ink tears. In 1912, he published a short sketch "The Sermon about the Fiddle," in which he praised Jewish violinist Efrem Zimbalist after attending his concert at Carnegie Hall, calling him the "Shakespeare of fiddle." Zelikovitsh extolled Zimbalist for playing soulful Hasidic music at a time when "our Jewish daughters in America are ashamed of playing 'kike-music'—Jewish melodies—on the piano." Zelikovitsh complained that as they were ashamed of "kike-music," Jewish youth was "enchanted" by "a piece of worthless coon nonsense such as *Alexander's Ragtime Band*," without mentioning it was written by a fellow Russian Jew, Irving Berlin. Whereas the early twentieth-century "coon songs" often entailed grotesque portrayals of African Americans, in this context, for Zelikovitsh, it was emblematic of the Jewish younger generation's self-negation and adoration of inferior aspects of American life.[15]

Paley's and Zelikovitsh's associate, the Yiddish humorist Tashrak, was best known for his short comic stories, feuilletons, and satirical pieces, which illustrated some of the absurdities of Jewish life in America. In fact, in the early 1900s, some observers termed Tashrak "A Jewish Mark Twain" or a "Ghetto Mark Twain." While Irish Americans and German Americans received much more attention in his writings, in 1918 Tashrak published a feuilleton that included an African American character by the name of coarse/fat (*grobe*) Lizzy. Like many other feuilletons by him, it takes place in *Blotetown* (Rubbish/Smut/Nonsense Town), which was Tashrak's nickname for New York City, and was titled "A Hanukah Miracle in Rubbish Town." The narrator tells of a party at his home to celebrate both Hanukah and his wife's birthday, for which they called "coarse Lizzy," who sometimes helps them with housekeeping. Since Lizzy has a two-year old toddler and nobody with whom to leave him, "she brings the little Niger with her to where she works." As the party started, the Black infant did not want to go to bed and "pestered us a little"; therefore, Lizzy took the child, "gave him a good beating for his nerve, and from the blows the little Niger fell asleep." At the end of party, after all the guests left, one of them returns in a hurry—it turns out that by mistake Lizzy took his daughter and left him "with her little devil." The host and the guest rush to Lizzy's home, "barely manage to wake her up" and switch back the toddlers.[16] Like Zelikovitsh and Paley, Tashrak focused on what he saw as the superficiality and assimilatory side of American Judaism. The first half of the feuilleton takes place at "Congregation Temple Jacob," where the rabbi is called "reverend" and where "our honorable Alderman Paddy Fitzpatrick" (a recurring figure in Tashrak's sketches) is the one who gives a Hanukah speech, arguing that the Maccabees were Irish due to the "Mac" in their name. For Tashrak, Fitzpatrick's speech and "coarse/fat" Lizzy's rough behavior serve as comic examples of the role of non-Jews in Jewish life; yet in Lizzy's case, it also matches American stereotypes about Black women as unfit mothers due to ingrained immorality.[17]

Dovid Hermalin

An author who dedicated much attention to racial questions was the Romanian-born Dovid M. Hermalin, who came to New York in 1885 at the age of twenty. Hermalin made some of his early steps in Yiddish journalism under the editorship of Getsil Zelikovitsh at the weekly *Der folksadvokat*, and soon gained immense popularity as the author of advice columns on topics such as family life, religion, and moral issues. Those columns were usually signed "H." and critics often termed them, sometimes derisively, as "women's editorials"; an adverse Yiddish journalist determined that Hermalin enjoyed "a great success among the women and non-intelligent male readers." Like the writers above, Hermalin adapted works by European authors such as Arthur Conan Doyle, William Shakespeare, and Leo Tolstoy (among many others), while also composing original books that dealt with subjects such as "Free Love" and "Hypnotism."[18]

Circa 1900, Hermalin published the historical novel *Di geheymnise fun dem shpanish-amerikanishen krieg* (The Secrets of the Spanish-American War), which featured heroic Cubans and Americans (among them several Jews) alongside treacherous and cruel Spaniards. The plot includes two minor Black characters—one of them is "a Black giant" by the name of Vortego, who is "a Negro over six feet tall with a face of a devil, or more accurately, the devil could have only wished to have such a face." Vortego has "a pair of lips as big as two black apples" and teeth like that of "a wild animal." The evil Magdalena Martinez wants to humiliate and murder her stepsister, Rose, since the man Magdalena loved yearned for Rose. After kidnapping Rose, Magdalena calls Vortego, who met her sister previously, and asks whether he would like to have "a good time" with Rose. The Black giant "bared his teeth as a wild beast" and later shows his "bestial mien," yet the rape plan is foiled when Rose's savior shoots Vortego to death.[19]

Whereas Vortego is a base animalistic stereotype, a dignified Black character appears later in the story and plays a more significant role. Enter Alfredo Sanchez, "a little Negro," who is a courageous Cuban soldier, willing to sacrifice his life for Cuba and carry out any order by his commander, General Antonio Maceo (a real figure, who is a celebrated hero of Cuban independence). Sanchez is extremely loyal, willing to endure flogging and a near suicide mission, and Maceo calls him "a brave and clever Negro." Undeniably, Sanchez's characterization bears the hallmarks of the period: Despite his bravery and battle skills, he remains a docile, happy-go-lucky man. Moreover, throughout the novel, Sanchez is always mentioned as "the Negro" or "the Negro Sanchez." Still, Sanchez is one of the freedom-loving Cubans and Americans, which Hermalin contrasts with the tyrannical and antisemitic Spaniards.[20]

Hermalin's name appeared in another book that came out circa 1900, titled *Di vilde menshen* (The Savage People). Although the author is one John P. Rensler, and Hermalin was listed as the translator from English, it seems that Hermalin wrote the book himself, borrowing ideas from Jules Verne's plotlines; and from popular English-language novels about Africa, such as H. Rider Haggard's *She: A History of Adventure* (1886–1887), which also featured African cannibalism. *The Savage People* follows the adventures of three European explorers and presents a host of African characters, such as the Zulu fighters who accompany the explorers as they come upon a cannibalistic tribe. The narrator remarks that the Zulu men were such "an example of manly strength" that "a bullet from an old-type revolver would probably bounce off from them." The explorers encounter a couple of cannibals, and as in several memoirists' accounts, they are depicted "black as a magnificently polished boot"; the same words describe the skin color of Agichaka, the African cannibal queen, who also has "big teeth but very white." The queen's court is shown in all its pomp and savagery: As a gesture of goodwill, Agichaka's men invite the travelers to eat the cannibals whom the Europeans shot and killed earlier, since it is better "to eat them while they're warm." Agichaka intends to sacrifice one of the Europeans, a German professor, whom she married just a short while beforehand.[21]

At that point, however, other African characters in the novel, whom Hermalin renders as wonders of nature, come into play. Princess Sartsele, a member of a rival tribe whom Agichaka imprisoned, helps the Europeans escape. She is portrayed as having a "tall and beautiful stature . . . slender waist, and well-developed bosom"; in short, "a truly wonderful dame" (*froyentsimer*). But then even the gorgeous and friendly Sartsele shows her bloodthirstiness to the extent that the travelers fear her. During their stay with the cannibals, the Europeans encounter Kharyl the sorcerer, who is "strong and tall," but "so ugly that in Europe a painter would have paid him a lot of money to serve as a model of the devil." Later Kharyl kills Ayusha, one of the wives of Sartsele's father, and when he is caught, his death sentence—to be burned alive—is revealed to him; Kharyl is so frightened that the narrator comments, "If a Negro can turn pale, then Kharyl became pale." The correlation between ugliness, depravity, and race, deeply ingrained in nineteenth-century literature, is surely noticeable in the plot, especially in the depictions of Agichaka and Kharyl. Yet Hermalin also utilized other conventions, such as the "noble savage" or "nature's children," to cast in a positive light the Zulu fighters, Sartsele, and Ayusha. The narrator details Ayusha's skin color as "brown but not black" with "a wonderfully attractive face," and wishes himself a wife like her, but only if he is "destined to endure the world without a white wife." There was hardly a nineteenth-century literary trope about savagery, race, and appearance that Hermalin did not apply.[22]

As the other writers above, Hermalin was neither a systematic nor a coherent thinker. Still, in his copious journalistic career, especially in *Di varhayt* and *Der tog*, Hermalin confronted racial questions and repudiated racism in America more than the above authors. Although a comprehensive examination of Hermalin's concepts about race is beyond our scope, a few examples of his contradictory approach should suffice. On the one hand, he repeatedly decried racism, violence against African Americans, and segregation, arguing (1906) that the criminal justice system was biased against anyone who "came to this world in the form of a Niger." A white woman who stabbed her biracial husband was sentenced to ten days in prison, Hermalin noted (1913), while a Black woman who tied her husband to their bed and jumped up and down on him was sentenced to seven years. After watching D. W. Griffith's *The Birth of a Nation* (1915), Hermalin termed it "a piece of racial hatred, persecution and prejudice" which helps explain not only why Leo Frank was lynched, but also why "a Southern dog can expect more justice than a Negro."[23]

On the other hand, even though he was well ahead of his time on some racial issues, Hermalin expressed contemporary attitudes about race, as his above literary works demonstrate. In 1908, as he deplored racism and commended "highly educated" African Americans, such as Booker T. Washington, Hermalin was concerned about the "disproportionate number of Jewish names" in the movement for racial equality. He saw it as "a Jew [who] pushes himself in a fight that is not his"; according to him, Jews in both the South and the North "feel no more sympathy for the Nigers than the rest of the white population" and "Jews only want to make a 'show' so people will say they champion the oppressed." More significantly, Hermalin believed that Jews' advocacy for racial equality would increase antisemitism among whites, and that no good will come of that movement, since Africans Americans "who are still 90 percent slaves, must work themselves out of their slavish habits."[24]

Black characters did not appear only in the writings of popular pulp authors. Yiddish anarchist poet Dovid Edelshtat, who died (1892) of tuberculosis at the age of twenty-six, published in 1891 a melodramatic short story titled *Di undankbare negerin* (The Ungrateful Negress). James Armstrong, a widowed Southern plantation owner, is swayed by abolitionism and decides to liberate all his slaves but one before the Civil War. He does not free young Maggie, who is his son's governess, because his son, Charlie, became very attached to her after his mother's death. After the war, Maggie feels sad and lonely as the only remaining slave and begs Armstrong, with "hot tears rolling down her black cheeks," to free her. Armstrong is enraged, telling her that Charlie might die without her and calling her ungrateful; angrily, he orders her to leave. Though upset by his rage, Maggie smiles and sings an old slave song that her mother sang when picking cotton and then leaves the plantation. After a couple of months, Charlie's health deteriorates, he yearns for Maggie, does not want any "other Negresses," and refuses to eat. Armstrong sends people to look for Maggie, but she is nowhere to be found, and Charlie eventually dies. As the bereaved father sits alone at night next to his son's coffin, Maggie shows up, crying, "Where is my child?" while "madly pulling out her black scattered locks." The father calls her "snake, ungrateful Negress," blaming her for Charlie's death. Maggie falls to her knees before the little coffin and starts singing a "heartrending song . . . wild sorrow, the suppressed pains of a thousand-year slavery were heard in that Negro song." As the song fades, the astonished father approaches Maggie and sees "the ungrateful Negress was dead."[25] The story articulates a genuine and moving spirit of solidarity. As critics have noted, nonetheless, it is also sentimental and simplistic, where Maggie is a canvas on which Edelshtat drew his ideological identification with the downtrodden. At any rate, *The Ungrateful Negress* was reprinted many times, and Edelshtat's poetry left a deep mark on Jewish anarchists, who formed Edelshtat's groups in Chicago, Boston, and other cities, as well as an Edelshtat singing society in New York in the decade after his death.[26]

The Young Ones

If Edelshtat's portrayal of the young Black woman was humanizing yet laden with doctrinarian sentimentalism, other Yiddish authors stressed entirely different aspects of African American women. An example can be found in a short story by Dovid Ignatov (Ignatoff). He was part of a group of young Yiddish writers who immigrated to the United States in the first decade of the twentieth century and established in 1907–1908 a literary movement called *Di yunge*—the young ones. Rebelling against both lowbrow, commercialized literature and against politically mobilized writing, *Di yunge* sought to appeal to the cultured Yiddish reader. Ignatov immigrated to New York in 1906, and soon attracted considerable critical acclaim. In 1918, Ignatov published a short story titled *Es regent* (It's Raining), in which a man by the name of Kaplan uses the morning of a (rainy) day off to visit a brothel. The madam calls her assistant, "a buxom Negress," Cadie, to show him "the girls." Cadie, "with a smeared smile on her thick lips" presents him some of the sex workers, but Kaplan does not like any of them. Then Cadie stops, "measures me from head to toe with the large whites of her eyes, and she rolls up her black lips, so her red gums take turns with her white teeth and she gives me a sneaky smile: 'alright, come!'" Cadie takes him up to the top floor, and on the way, she stops again, looks at him "and constantly smiles sneakily"; she finds Kaplan a woman that truly bedazzles him. Despite the story's brevity, Cadie's sexuality is not manifested only through her appearance and work at a brothel, but her innate understanding—conveyed via racial attributes—of what a man is looking for.[27]

A fellow writer associated with *Di yunge* was the aforementioned Yoysef Opatoshu, a renowned and highly praised writer, who had immigrated to New York in 1907 at the age of twenty-one. Critic Yitskhok Rontsh claimed that of all Yiddish prose authors, Opatoshu was "artistically the most distinctive in bringing forth the horrible situation" of African Americans. That assertion certainly captures the intention of the famed writer, who painfully illustrated in various stories the horrors of lynching and the reign of terror unleashed on Black families. In *Fir neger*

(Four Negroes, 1920), four Black inmates sit in a prison cell besieged by a white mob that wants to lynch one of them, John. The prisoners know that if the rioters break through, all of them will be murdered. As the menacing shouting of "Hang him!" and "The beast is in the basement!" get nearer and louder, the other three "see death before their eyes," so they open the cell door and throw out John "as you throw a calf or a horse to a pack of wolves only to escape and save your own life." In another story, *Negers* (Negroes, 1928), after a white farmer was found shot to death, local whites are hunting down Black men; an eight-year-old Black child, Fred, witnesses his father escaping the family's cabin when three white men come looking for him. Fred watches them with fear and hate as they interrogate his mother and lock her up in a hog pen.[28]

Opatoshu's focus on human brutality and animosity, ever-present in his works, serves as a powerful protest against the abuse of African Americans by the surrounding white society. Still, there is a gap between Opatoshu's sympathy for the suffering Black characters and the way he pictures their physical appearance (and at times also their behavior). We already saw his ambivalence in a short play he published in 1922. A more notable example is the story *Lintsheray* (Lynching), first published in book form in Warsaw in 1923. In its blood-curdling plot, a young African American, Bookert (whose name was perhaps fashioned after Booker T. Washington), attacks a white man's daughter after the father sexually assaulted Bookert's fourteen-year-old sister. A bloodthirsty white mob searches for Bookert, and after catching him, the story provides in horrific detail how Bookert is tied up and burned alive, surrounded by a jeering crowd. Opatoshu shows how the taunting throng was no longer made up of "Americans, Germans, Italians, and Slavs," but rather all became part of "the white race that came to get even with the Black guy." The only ones against the lynching are "a Yankee," a Jewish cobbler, and Mr. Levi, a Jewish immigrant storeowner. Levi tries to forbid his son, Harry, from joining the lynch mob, saying "A Jew should not mix in!" and "today they lynch a Negro and tomorrow a Jew!" Harry tells the cobbler that Levi believes "the whole village should be lynched, not the Negro"; the cobbler tells him that "[o]nly goyim" can burn someone alive.[29]

At the same time, *Lintsheray* opens with a description of Bookert's grandfather, Jim. Jim has "a short, flat nose with wide-open nostrils, the curls on his head which reached his eyebrows . . . all of that reminded one of an old Orangutan." Many flies "as big as bees" stand on his hairy hands and buzz around his nose, but the old man does not care, and keeps daydreaming in his "dense brain" about other times and stories he heard. There is a startling dissonance between the apelike imagery used to describe Jim and the way he honorably stands before the Sheriff; Jim reminds the officer that he carried him around as a child and bitterly says that even if "a Negro isn't trustworthy," the Bible is, and Jim swears on the holy book that Bookert has not returned home yet. The disparity between Jim's decency and his depiction as an orangutan reflects a bifurcated pattern in Opatoshu's treatment of Black characters, a decoupling between the moral and the esthetical: African Americans can be virtuous yet portrayed as simians.[30]

A similar characterization is conspicuous in a short story that Opatoshu published in 1925, titled *A ger* (A Convert to Judaism). A young African American who belongs to a Black Israelite community, Bookert (yet again), has worked as a driver for a Jewish boss, Shapiro, since he was sixteen. Bookert is deeply in love with Shapiro's daughter, Bessie, but knows that the father will never allow any relations between them. Following a car accident, nevertheless, Shapiro is bedridden, and Bookert makes himself indispensable to the family, to the point that the wife says he is "more devout than the Jewish goyim [non-observant Jews]" and Shapiro replies, "obviously, he belongs to the 'Israelites,' half a Jew." Patient and resolved, Bookert courts Bessie for months, and after a long time, she falls for him and even Shapiro, despite his misgivings, agrees that the two will marry. Bookert converts to Judaism and becomes increasingly pious, yet congregants at the local synagogue ridicule the Black convert. Finally, things heat up when, during an anniversary of a person's death, a family member does not want Abraham (Bookert's new name) for *minyen*—traditionally, a prayer quorum of ten male adults—since he wants "a real Jew." The Black convert goes to that member and smacks him. The story ends with that scene, when "the scuffle started." There is hardly a doubt that Opatoshu paints Bookert as a persistent man whose love and dedication win over the whole family and casts the congregants as racist. Bookert's physical features, however, are portrayed as follows: "The Negro ugliness, that lies in the restless lips, flattened nose and amber-colored eyes—made him surprisingly more handsome"; in another place, Opatoshu refers to Bookert's "persistence, hard as his skull." This gap between the decency of Black characters and their physical attributes is perhaps the most evident marker of Opatoshu's contradictory approach to race.[31]

"The Same Crude, Coarse Features on Their Faces": Borekh Glazman and the Menacing Presence of Black Characters

While in Opatoshu's work African Americans are often victims, in Borekh Glazman's stories they have more of a volatile and menacing presence or exhibit strong eroticism. In a sense, Glazman was the most Americanized writer among all of those under review in this chapter. Glazman arrived in America in 1911 at the age of eighteen, did odd jobs, worked as a house painter, traveled across the country (especially in Southern states), studied at Ohio State University, and served in the U.S. Military. In a letter to S. Niger (1926), Glazman wrote, "To this day, the language of my most intimate thoughts, feelings, and experiences is English," and "even *speaking* fluently is easier for me in English." As one critic argued, to the much-described New York's East Side, Glazman added "the far away 'South' with its exoticism" but later he abandoned those themes, fearing that "the erotic" will drown out all other aspects.[32]

In 1919, Glazman wrote *A nakht in a dorem-shtot* (A Night in a Southern Town), which was published in 1927 in book form. The story follows Ore, a Jewish bricklayer, who recently moved to Augusta, Georgia. As he walks through the streets at night, he suddenly hears such a "wild singing" that it draws him in. His feet lead him to the Black quarter, where the small houses' windows were closed during the day "as if wild orgies were constantly going on there"; but at night, all the doors are open "like in an African village." Someone is playing a "lustful" ragtime song, as young men and women are dancing in the street. They dance with "all limbs, all body parts," at times slow "like a dog who howls outside a door and begs to be let in" and at times "animalistically fast." As a popular tune, "Hesitation Blues," plays in the background, couples break away from the dancing crowd now and then, and "twisted together drag themselves to a side den somewhere." Young female bodies curve, and "smoke—as from flesh that has been singed in the heat" fills the air. Before Ore notices, "his pounding breast is pressed against the elongated and pointed breasts of a Negro lady, and they throw each other around in a dance." Suddenly a bell rings somewhere, and Ore is awakened, as if from "a heavy dream," spits, and breaks free from the dancing throng. As he walks away, Ore feels good, "freed from something sinful and ugly."[33]

If Glazman emphasized in this story what he saw as the animalistic, wild, and oversexed nature of Black music and gyrating Black bodies, it was another story that displays not only the sexuality of a Black woman, but also her ultimate peasant traits. *Af di felder fun dzhordzhia* (In the Fields of Georgia) signals how the representation of African Americans contained both Old-World imagery and New World vocabulary. The story was first published in 1921 in New York, and later republished in slightly different versions in the Soviet Union in 1925 and in Poland in 1927. It features a traditional Jewish peddler, with his horse and wagon, who is stuck on a December night in a field in rural Georgia. His wife and children are in New York and he misses them dearly, but his livelihood is on the road. Looking for a place to spend the night, he sees a small house with a broken window; he knocks on the door and when it opens, the peddler sees "two rows of pearl-white teeth" and then "a pair of shining eye whites." The friendly (unnamed) woman who opens the door is "a Negress, a full-bodied, heavy Negress," who says, "Not you I was expecting" but invites him in. The peddler enters cautiously, since you can never know "what's going on behind a Negro face and what thoughts are hidden there, especially if they're shady"; but you can know "even less what's going on behind a white face." The table inside is set for a festive dinner for two, and the peddler realizes that it is Christmas Eve. The woman tells him that although she is waiting for her husband every evening, he recently left her and will not return. They dine together, and the woman is depicted, "Black was she, and grew in the middle of a field, like a heavy tree." She had heard a lot about Jews and their customs from the preacher in her church, and roars with "a loud laughter, like thunder" when mentioning that "Our father Abraham, the Jewish father, had a Negro wife, Hagar, and even had a child with her."[34]

After their meal, the woman goes out for a moment and when she comes back, Glazman pictures her as "a large, bodily, heavy piece of earth," who is holding an "unusually large watermelon." The peddler is tired, and when he retires to a separate room, the woman looks at the "red, juicy blood" of sliced watermelon, as if it is telling her, "Here, look. . . . I was cut open and left untouched." The watermelon metaphor becomes clearer during the quiet night, in which both cannot sleep. The woman rolls in her bed, groaning and wondering, "what kind of a man is he . . . or maybe my black flesh disgusts him." She is astonished that "a man is staying under one roof with me and wouldn't want her next to him." She believes that "if one of her brethren [a Black man] would have come to her alone at night he wouldn't have spent the night" away from her. Glazman describes how "a heavy bodily scent starts to wrap itself around her, like a piece of black plowed land." Her blood begins to flow violently, and she turns to God, "I have waited for a man throughout a whole evening . . . the Jew came. Isn't he a man? Is he holy?" And now, as it is Christmas Eve, "a child, a holy child will be born to you." The peddler smells "the sharp, charming scent [that] carries itself to his nostrils" from her room and becomes anxious that soon he will not be able to leave. "Burning up, with a pounding heart," the peddler slips away before sunrise. In her room, the woman is falling asleep, "with a quiet hopeful idea, like a dream, on her thick lips—at dawn, very early, she will get up, sneak into his room, sit down on his bed and beg him: He should be good to her! She will already know how to reward him in return." With that thought she falls asleep, "her thick lower lip hanging down," smiling, "She'll have a child with the pious man. And the child will not be so dark like her, dark as night, but lighter, like twilight." At dawn she finds the empty bed; she "wallowed in it with her heavy body, groaned and gasped like a buffalo, ripped the pillow covers" and "broke out in a howling lament over an empty bed."[35]

Yitskhok Rontsh interpreted this story as one that "evokes a sympathetic feeling" toward the Black woman, since "She is genuine and good, and a woman of the people in the full sense of the word." That reading seems to be aligned with the gist Glazman meant to infuse into the plot. During the 1920s, Glazman flirted with communism, his books came out in the Soviet Union, and his works dealt with the lower classes, even though he wrote privately that he was "very far from Marxist ideology"; the folksy characterization of the Black woman, therefore, could fit well within a socialist ideological framework.[36] Regardless of Glazman's leftist orientation and Rontsh's assessment, nonetheless, *In the Fields of Georgia* often reads as a catalog that merges many of the attributes associated with both peasant women in the Old World and African American women in the New World. Her weight is constantly linked to her embodiment of "a heavy piece of earth" or a "heavy tree." Her rustic, peasant-like qualities present her as indigenous and autochthonous, and even her bodily scent is that of plowed land. In that respect, her innate erotic urge that leads to emanating a scent is part of a wider trope about intrinsic and unrestrained Black sexuality: The woman knows that a Black man would not have stayed away from her, and she would figure out how to reward the peddler (the cut-up juicy watermelon metaphor is another signifier). At the same time, her rusticity, roaring laughter, and childlike expectation of having a holy child with the Jewish man also amalgamate the imagery of the peasantry with that of African American women. The perceived free sexual allure of young Gentile women, especially peasants, has been a recurring theme in the works of Yiddish writers such as Isaac Bashevis Singer.[37]

Glazman's contradictory attitude toward African Americans reached its starkest manifestation in a 1922 novella titled *A binele, a binele (un damols iz gekumen . . .)* (A Little Bee, A Little Bee [And Then Came . . .]), which was published in New York in 1923. Later it appeared with small modifications in Moscow under the title *Black on White* (1925) and in Poland under the title *The Dance of the Negroes* (1928).[38] The main character is a Jewish businessman, Bernard Cowan, who travels back to his home in North Carolina aboard a ship from New York. Whereas Cowan was born Jewish and grew up on the Lower East Side, he is alienated from his past; he changed his name from Cohen to Cowan, since the latter "is more Irish than Jewish." Even though he is married with children, in his business trips to New York he enjoys participating in "the wildest and most unbelievable orgies," where he relishes causing pain to young women. Cowan had many Black mistresses in his North Carolina town, preferring married women, due to an incident when he impregnated the family's maid, a biracial seventeen-year-old girl, Cora. As Cora refused to get an abortion, Cowan used his clout to have her sent away from the public maternity hospital where she stayed, and she died shortly after giving birth at home. Cowan ignored the child, and once, when his mixed-race son came to the store and said, "You're my father," Cowan beat him so badly that the teenager was thrown out bleeding. Despite his later regret, Cowan is indeed an anti-hero, if not a villain altogether.[39]

The novella's timeline oscillates between Cowan's recollection of his past, and the travel aboard a ship, where he feels sick, vomits, and hallucinates. In the novella's defining scene, late at night, after all the white passengers are done dancing and retire to their cabins, African American servants, kitchen workers, deck hands, and students from a Black college's glee club gather in the ship's main ballroom. Some play the piano, others bring in guitars and banjoes, and many start to dance; the dance soon becomes wilder and noisier, more passionate, and the nauseous Cowan, whom a Black attendant saved from falling overboard, is seated in a chair nearby, trembling with fear that the friendly attendant might murder him. As the dance intensifies, white passengers wake up, come out of their cabins "with disheveled hair," wearing pajamas and nightgowns, and stare from the balconies at the Black dancing crowd below. Critics have lauded Glazman's profound understanding of human psyche and racial hatred; and explained that scene as a symbol of Black protest against their daily oppression, a temporary inverted world, where healthy, lively, and musically gifted Black men are contrasted not only with the ailing Cowan, but all white passengers, who fear Black vitality. Due to his feverish stomach sickness, Cowan believes his mixed-race son is onboard and plans to kill him; in his remorse about Cora, feelings of self-disgust and delirium, he commits suicide, as the ship approaches the port in Virginia.[40]

Still, the portrayal of African Americans as oversexed and animal-like is not conveyed only through Cowan's perspective, but that of Glazman himself. Cowan used to change his Black mistresses frequently, since "Negro women's body in the South is cheap, free for the taking, and always willingly jumps into the hands of a white man." When Cowan visited a married woman, if the husband were around, the wife would give him Cowan's money to go to a saloon; if that would not work, the wife would use "harsh words" to send her husband away. She would order him to leave, saying "did you hear, n-n-nigger?" and "angrily hissing with her large white horse's teeth." When Cowan walks through the Black quarter of his town, he sees people in ragged clothes, naked toddlers "with soiled bottoms" were "playing on the street, like little dogs." On the street were "women with bare naked arms and breasts like pointed black pears." As he reminisces about Cora, Cowan invokes her "passionate lips, not beastly crude" like those of other Black women. In his description of the African American men who gather around the ballroom's piano, Glazman details the different colors of those "Black, brown-skinned, chocolate-skinned, and cacao-skinned." All of them have "the same crude, coarse features on their faces," as if they are made of the "same batter," but each is mixed with a different kind of fluid. He likens them to "a lined-up row of glasses," starting with "thoroughly black coffee," and the further a glass stands from the first, the "more milk is poured inside," the lighter their skin complexion becomes.[41]

The mesmerizing dance scene brings with it animalistic connotations of the dancers. There are only Black men in the ballroom, and they dance foxtrot together "like big, tropical orangutangs and gorillas" while others do the cakewalk. Groggy white passengers watch the dancers from their balconies, as if "sea monsters from the abyss sneaked in and took over the ship." The terrified passengers see the Black dancers "like orangutangs who broke out from their cages and would soon jump on them," snatching the women and taking them to "wild, ugly orgies"; then they will carry those halfdead women "under their hairy, animal armpits" and take them to one last dance on the deck before tossing the bodies into the ocean. In that particular depiction, it seems that Glazman was ridiculing the terrified white passengers' reflexive dread of Black men. Yet the other examples reveal not just the passengers or Cowan's perspectives but Glazman's own impressions of African American sexuality and volatility. As in other stories, Glazman indubitably set out to expose inherent racial inequity, directly presenting white hostility toward African Americans—Cowan's town officials that help to expel Cora from a public hospital, or white passengers who resent the fact that "stinking Negroes" (the glee club students) were even allowed to sit in the ballroom's corner when young white couples filled the dance floor. Concomitantly, not only did Glazman cast African Americans as an ominous presence or as displaying inborn, uncontrollable sexuality, he also pictured them as animal-like and repeatedly dwelt on their basic "crudeness." Glazman's social message against racism was formulated via an imagery that is deeply rooted in racist concepts.[42]

Sholem Ash and the Limitations of Humanism

During the same years Glazman penned and revised the above novella, one of the most successful and critically acclaimed Yiddish authors devised a more amiable and humane Black character, who still features typical racial conventions. Sholem Ash would have received a place of honor next to the triumvirate of classic Yiddish writers—Abramovitsh/Mendele Moykher Sforim, Sholem Aleichem, and I. L. Peretz—if it were not for his controversial writings. Apart from his works about the Jewish underworld, prostitution, pimps, and women trafficking, between 1939 and 1949 Ash published a trilogy about the lives of Jesus and Mary. Those books, which came out during and after the Holocaust, shocked and angered many Yiddish readers, and led to a widespread allegation that Ash was promoting conversion to Christianity.[43] In the mid-1920s, all that acrimony was still in the future. Between December 1924 and March 1925, Ash serialized in the *Forverts* his novel *Elektrik tsher* (Electric Chair), which came out in book form in Poland (1927) under the title *Toyt urteyl* (Death Sentence). The novel tells of a Jewish banker, Max Stone, who is imprisoned in Sing Sing's death row for killing a man. In prison, he hears from an adjacent cell the crying of a Black adolescent, Rep, who was also sentenced to death, in his case for killing a white woman. The woman fooled him, pretended to love him, and then stole his money. At night, Stone hears "a strange growl, as if a dog was wailing behind the wall." Later the wailing becomes weaker and weaker "like a drowsy child drops on his face and wants to sleep." During the daytime, Rep is in good mood and sings "Negro songs," but that changes at nightfall.[44]

Ash vividly illustrates how all death row's prisoners (besides Stone) loathe Rep, since his "awful sin was—the color of his skin." They keep telling Rep that soon he will be sent to "the inferno of 'Black dogs'" and are deeply offended by the absence of a separate electric chair for Black convicts. The inmates are surprised when "the banker" (Stone) befriends Rep and spends more time with him than with anyone else. Stone becomes close to the "forlorn Black boy" and "often he forgot about himself and pondered on the Niger." Stone prays to God to spare Rep; other prisoners, including himself, already experienced life, but Rep "still hasn't tasted anything." Stone sends a letter to the governor, begging him to commute Rep's death sentence, although that appeal might damage his own chances of avoiding execution. The banker, who has taken a liking to the Black teenager, keeps promising the childlike Rep that the governor will surely commute Rep's sentence. In reference to the dialog between Stone and Rep, Ash noted parenthetically that Rep called him "'boss' as he would have called him if they were" out of prison. Rep asks him, "Why are you so sure? Tell me 'boss,' God bless you, tell me 'boss.'" Rep keeps asking Stone, and falls to his knees, begging, "You know something 'boss' and don't want to tell me, oh, in God's name, tell me 'boss' . . . by God tell me or I die." Rep's bloodshot eyes "glaze" and almost "bounce out of the eyes sockets." Stone keeps assuring Rep that the governor's pardon will arrive, even when Rep is already seated in the electric chair. During Rep's last night, he does not cry anymore but chants church songs and prays to God. Stone lies face down in his cell and keeps praying to God to save the Black teenager, but in the morning, he learns that Rep was executed at dawn. People say Rep "smiled the whole time. Even when they put a cap on his head, he still believed that the 'pardon' comes." Ash certainly wanted to humanize Jewish-Black encounter and presented a naïve and likable Black character, who remains a pure soul despite his crime. However, Ash still operated within contemporary cultural precepts, utilizing several tropes about African American childlike behavior, hysterical wailing, and somewhat cartoonish physiognomy. Despite his good intentions, the famous author did not veer away from the period's assumptions.[45]

* * *

The construction of Black characters in Yiddish prose unmistakably underwent significant changes between the "booklets epidemic" of the 1890s and what critics regarded as more refined works of the 1920s. As writers in the 1890s and 1900s were hardly immune to existing stereotypes about Black people's savagery or backwardness, they were at times callous in ascribing offensive traits to them. It is noteworthy that simultaneously, those popular authors condemned racism and argued for improving the living conditions of African Americans. Avner Tanenboym, for example, omitted several detestable quips about Black characters from his adaptations of Jules Verne's novels, whether they appeared in the French original or in English translations, and attempted to show that deterministic racism was not scientific. Likewise, Dovid Hermalin deplored racism and wrote about its inhumane effects. Yet they and others in those years vacillated between condemnations of racism and creating Black characters who come across as beastlike, savage, brutal, or buffoonish. Oftentimes such renderings were an integral part of dime novels, a genre whose main purpose was to entertain the readership and attain commercial success.

By the 1920s, Yiddish authors applied more subtlety and variety in the portrayal of Black individuals, expressed growing sympathy for them, and showed the violence and cruelty they had to endure. That was mostly true of younger authors with more artistic aspirations and/or ideological commitment. By that decade, remonstrations about American racial inequities were becoming the bon ton, both in wider circles in American culture and among American Jews. For Yoysef Opatoshu, Borekh Glazman, Sholem Ash, and others, American racism and its devastating ramifications constituted a problem that they artistically addressed. Their works were a literary cry against the harshness of white society—Jewish characters included—toward African Americans. Concurrently, nevertheless, those authors did not refrain from casting Black characters as animal-like (even apelike), prone to violence, oversexed, childlike, or just happy-go-lucky people. The dichotomy between the authors' ethical opposition to racism and the often-negative esthetical portrayal of Black women and men is the most conspicuous—and telling—aspect of their characterization.

A common thread throughout the period was the delineation of African Americans as the incarnation of peasantry in the New World, which could yield both negative traits—violence, volatility, primitivity—and positive ones—simplicity, innocence, and straightforwardness. Such depictions were also linked to various writers' imagery of Black Americans as epitomizing the vulgar and dangerous dimensions of American life and their effect on Jewish immigrants, especially the vulnerable ones, such as women and children. Even when other ethnic groups were mentioned (Irish, Italians, etc.), the presence of African Americans still seemed to be the essential peril. Hence, as in other arenas of Yiddish culture in the 1920s, the ambivalence toward Black people hardly disappeared, even with the growing detail and depth in the overall description of Black characters.

Epilogue

In Search of a More Palatable Past

In the weeks following the onset of World War I (1914), the *Yidishes tageblat* explained to its readers who the belligerent sides were: The Slavs were "a wild, barbaric and inferior race," which cohabited Europe with the "Latin race" and the "Teutonic race," the last being "much more important" than the Latin race. The editorial (probably written by one of the two coeditors, Gedalya Bublik or Leon Zolotkof) asserted that the Teutonic and Latin races did a lot for "humanity and progress," while wondering, "What have the Russians, the Poles, the Bulgarians, and the Serbs done for civilization?" Yiddish poet and journalist Judd L. Teller, who came to New York as a child in 1921, recalled how "Poles and Ukrainians formed a disreputable little enclave" among Jewish immigrants in lower Manhattan, "Shuttling between mass and raucous saloons, they smelled of incense, vodka, and vomit." Apart from those immigrant groups, Yiddish accounts in numerous memoirs, autobiographies, oral history interviews, and the Yiddish press frequently cast Irish Americans as an even graver menace. In 1917, a pioneer of Jewish socialism in America (originally a Hasidic Yeshiva student from Warsaw), Benyomen Faygnboym, identified those whom Jewish immigrants viewed with most trepidation: "[W]hen a Jew thought about antisemitic troubles in America, the Irishman immediately appeared in his mind" and Jews "were especially afraid of the crude Irish masses." Many East European Jewish authors and memoirists of diverse background and virtually all the Yiddish newspapers characterized Irish Americans not only as drunk and antisemitic, but also as signifying an unadulterated kind of *goyishkayt* (Gentileness), a Gentile essence that was seen as the intrinsic opposite of Jewishness.[1]

Attesting to the influence of racial discourses on the Yiddish intelligentsia, those accounts also remind us that Yiddish-speaking Jews did not encounter only African Americans; they faced numerous ethnic groups upon arrival in America, including Germans, Irish, Italians, and those from the Slavic nations (e.g., Bohemians, Poles, and Ukrainians). Through the 1920s, most Jewish immigrants from Eastern Europe had much more contact with European immigrants and their American-born offspring than with Black Americans. Some of those groups were indubitably cast as the new country's peasantry, the lower-stratum Gentiles which Jews were used to dealing with. Yet whereas the racial status of the Irish, Italians, and Slavs was unstable during the late nineteenth and early twentieth centuries, those groups did not have black skin; they seldom occupied the role of the ultimate racial other.[2]

As we have seen, there was a dual source of influence on the depictions of Black people in Yiddish culture. The first was Old-World Yiddish folklore and social attitudes toward low-status gentiles, mostly the peasantry. Common characteristics associated with peasants were impulsiveness, violent behavior, crudeness, and insobriety, together with directness and simplicity. The second source was American racial attitudes and popular culture, which were rife with racist imagery and vocabulary, all of which left a profound mark on Yiddish culture. Socioeconomic conditions in the United States, where Jewish storekeepers, tavern owners, and peddlers had Black clients, and Jewish homeowners employed Black domestic workers and had Black tenants in their buildings, reinforced the images of Black Americans as America's peasantry. The coalescence of these two sources produced representations of Black women and men as carefree, sexually promiscuous, childlike, volatile, unruly, potentially menacing, and prone to violence. At times Yiddish writers drew certain parallels between the historical situation of African Americans in the South and Jews in the Russian Pale of Settlement; overall, though, in Jewish eyes, Black Americans were anything but "America's Jews."

Concomitantly, the passionate condemnations of lynching and the strong opposition to racial discrimination were sincere. At a time when few white Americans took any interest in the situation of African Americans, Yiddish writers were truly horrified by the violence and prejudice inflicted upon America's Black population, which sullied their vision of American justice; loyal to the codes of *mentshlekhkayt* (humanity) and *mentshlekhe bahandlung* (humane treatment), they despised the inhumanity of racism. Unquestionably, they were also gravely concerned that Jews might be next to bear the brunt of racial hatred. Simultaneously, despite the frequent manifestations of sympathy for the plight of Black Americans, Yiddish writers, journalists, and performers could not see them as their equals. Whereas deterministic racial concepts appeared occasionally, a much more common form was the argument that Black people were historically and culturally "backward" or "ignorant," yet were capable of improvement. There was undoubtedly an array of attitudes, where callousness and derision were also evident. More often than not, nonetheless, the Yiddish descriptions of Black women and men were more multifaceted, where identification coexisted with distance. That pattern reflects the compound character of racism. Rather than a binary, dichotomous concept, this book has shown that one could express genuinely anti-racist views while harboring racist judgments or imagery.

That phenomenon was markedly apparent among people who were—or at least considered themselves to be—well ahead of their time. Jewish leftists continually lambasted racism in the name of class solidarity and equality, parading what historian Eli Lederhendler has aptly termed "a programmatic concern for the underdog." Nevertheless, even the most emphatic critics of racism, such as Abraham Cahan, Karl Fornberg, Abraham Revusky, Sadie Vinokur, Borekh Charney Vladeck, and A. S. Zaks (to name but a few), paternalistically characterized African Americans as servile, backward, weak, and/or infantile. Armed with good intentions, ideological zeal, and preoccupation with group public image, left-wing Jews foreshadowed the mistakes of Jewish labor organizers and liberals/progressives a generation or two later: underestimating or being oblivious to the underlying power inequality, different historical circumstances, and the long-term impact of racism in America that separated the Jewish and Black experiences.[3]

Into the Great Depression

The 1930s would witness the perpetuation of those dynamics, yet with important variations. By the 1920s, there were increased nuance and overall improvement in Yiddish culture's portrayal of Black men and women, but it was far from complete, and the ambivalence hardly vanished. Indeed, relationships between Jewish and Black labor organizers, communists, performers, and musicians deepened and flourished during the Great Depression. Songwriter Sammy Cahn remembered seeing two Black performers singing Sholem Secunda's Yiddish number *Bay mir bistu sheyn* (To Me You're Beautiful) before a delighted Black audience at Harlem's Apollo Theater in 1935. The two might have been the duo Johnny Macklin and George MacLean, who performed (1937) *Bay mir* in the Catskills and New York City under the name "Johnnie and George." In those years, singer and dancer Cab Calloway recorded and performed Jewish writers' Yiddish-inflected songs such as "*A Bee Gezint*" (*abi gezunt*—As Long as You're Healthy) and "*Utt-Da-Zay*" (*ot azoy*—That's the Way). In a very different vein, the poetry of the communist writers' group *Proletarishe pen* (Proletarian Pen), abbreviated to *Proletpen* (1929–1938), exhibited keen interest in the fight for racial justice during its existence. Apart from the many references to the Scottsboro case, poets bleakly illustrated the cruelty inflicted upon African Americans. Yitskhok Rontsh's 1933 poem *A gutn dzhab gemakht* (Done a Good Job) is a graphically shocking depiction of a lynching from the perspective of the white lynch mob: After hanging and burning their Black victim, the mob proceeds to cut off his penis, "a souvenir for kids and grandkids," and on the next day one of them boasts, "I got a chocolate ear." Malka Li's poem of the same year, *Der niger in sobvey* (The Niger on the Subway) describes a young Black man who is clenching his fists, crying about his brother, whom white assailants hanged from a tree and now "he sees the murderer's picture in every white."[4]

At the same time, the 1930s witnessed more friction in Black-Jewish relations. Before the Great Depression, the topic of antisemitism among Black Americans rarely came up, but by the mid-1930s several Black agitators, such as Ira Kemp, Arthur Reid, and Sufi Abdul Hamid (whom the press dubbed "Black Hitler"), employed overtly anti-Jewish rhetoric. As the Jewish presence in Harlem declined to mostly landlords and storeowners, Black radicals attacked Jews as exploiters, and Hamid called for a "jihad" against them. After a campaign to boycott stores which did not hire Black clerks, a race riot erupted in Harlem (March 1935), in which African Americans rioters damaged over two hundred Jewish-owned stores. Exhortations against antisemitism by Black leaders such as Adam Clayton Powell Jr. and Robert W. Bagnall notwithstanding, a review of the Black press in the 1930s concluded that most writers were "either indifferent to German anti-Semitism or view with evident pleasure the degradation of a minority group other than their own." On their part, Jewish attitudes toward Black fellow citizens were not limited to responses to perceived or real antisemitism: At the Bronx's notorious "slave markets," many Jewish housewives engaged Black domestic workers on street corners or park benches, sometimes offering them extremely low pay. One domestic remembered that Jewish women used to feel the muscles of potential workers as if it were an "auction block" during the period of slavery. An awareness of common interest, and empathy toward the struggles of African Americans in general, did not always result in sympathy with the non-abstract Black woman or man.[5]

Yiddish culture continued to reflect conflicting opinions about the Black population. Apart from its reports about *shvartser hitler*, Yiddish newspapers attempted to demonstrate that reputable Black leaders condemned the demagogues and fought against them. After the Harlem riot of 1935, *Tog*'s journalist Y. Abramson reminded his readers, "Black workers are our brothers and must be treated as such." His colleague, Ben-Tsiyen Goldberg, argued that even if there is "a larger percentage" of African Americans who display "drunkenness and cursing," it is "our own fault"; the only solution is "to lift up the Negro" by giving him better education, housing, and means to make a decent living. Still, the daily termed the riot "a pogrom" and portrayed the fear and despair of Jewish small businessowners, whose stores were looted and destroyed, mentioning how a group of Black kids passed by a Jewish tailor whose store was robbed, and made fun of him. The *Tog* accused communist agitators who "exploit the ignorance of the Negro population" to control it and pointed to the Jewish last names of those arrested for fomenting the riots to show the culpability of Jewish communists. The *Forverts* echoed those accusations, printing a pre-riot letter from a Harlem storekeeper, R. B. Goldman, who wrote that for ages "there was no antisemitism among Negroes," but lately the communists incited Black Harlemites against Jewish businessowners "just as in old Russia and in other countries the peasant was incited against Jewish storekeepers." Four years later (1939), another Harlem storeowner, Yoysef Sorin, claimed that African Americans made Harlem crime-infested and described in the *Forverts* the many hold-ups that he experienced by Black perpetrators. Sorin also believed that Jewish communists worsened the situation by agitating Black Harlemites against "Jewish bloodsuckers."[6]

Yiddish literature also continued to reveal much ambivalence. If *Proletpen*'s poets expressed the most heartfelt identification with African Americans, others were more disparaging. Lithuanian-born Peysekh Markus was best known for his writings about the eminent rabbinic leader, the Vilna Gaon. Earlier in his career, Markus published (1932) a collection of stories titled *A brik ibern atlantik* (A Bridge over the Atlantic). Most of the characters in his work, whether white or Black, Jews or non-Jews, are negative; Markus's Black men are erotic, drunk, and corrupt. In the story "Negro Blood," the main character is Ralph Clark, a light-skinned African American man who can sometimes pass as white. Ralph hates Black people, saying, "A Negro isn't a human being at all," and later stabs "another Negro . . . an old, filthy man" that he caught with his wife. Though Ralph planned to participate in a car race, no "colored" are allowed. Disheartened, Ralph gets drunk, drives fast, and runs over a white woman. The story ends as a white mob gathers around Ralph's car and begins to beat him up and probably lynch him. In another story from Markus's collection, "A Negro Dies," the main character is Jackson, a Black man with "a flat nose . . . and swollen-thick lips"; since his face is not "pitch black," Jackson "could fool people by passing as an Indian, as Negroes do" when they want to be treated better by whites. Jackson boasts before Black teenagers how once, as he was raping a white woman, he roared at her, "white devil, have some Negro blood!" That story and others present Black society that is awash in alcohol, violence, and promiscuity.[7]

A few years after Markus, the Polish-born impressionistic author and critic, Shia Tenenboym (Joshua Tenenbaum), encapsulated many of Yiddish culture's contradictory approaches to race. Tenenboym came to America in 1934 after living for a few years in Belgium, and in 1937 he published a collection of evocative sketches titled *Bay der velt tsugast* (A Guest on Earth). "In Black Negro-Land" follows his visits to Harlem, where he laments white violence against African Americans and what European civilization has done to Africa's children. "Children" is a key term in his description: Blacks "are children, they are naïve, helpless, weak, and ignorant." Since they are "strangely naïve, like children," Black people eagerly took on "the evildoing of European civilization.

They take on capitalism, various Christian sects . . . syphilis, prostitution, and disease." Tenenboym commented, "In general Negroes are an ugly race, their eyes are completely black, filled with gasoline, as if intoxicated by infinite ecstasy. Their lips are fat, hanging down to boot." If such objectification of the Black body was not enough, Tenenboym added that in their "fight against ugliness," Black women constantly try to straighten their hair: "[T]hey want to escape from their peculiarity, from their origins." Markus, Tenenboym, and others divulge how many underlying and essentializing (though conflicting) assumptions about Black sexuality, criminality, childishness, ignorance, or submissiveness remained ingrained well into the 1930s.[8]

In Search of a More Palatable Past

On one level, this is a story of Americanization/acculturation. An immigrant group, Yiddish-speaking Jews, blended their own culture into the American racial vocabulary. The outcome exposes the ambivalence, anxiety, and the pull of clashing tendencies and influences. The fact that even a group which dedicated considerable energy and attention to racial justice was so enmeshed in prejudiced portrayals attests to the intensity and depth of popular American culture's racist imagery. The vacillation between sympathy and aloofness—often by the same person—also demonstrates the high stakes for Jews who felt the need to differentiate themselves as much as possible from American society's ultimate other.

Several scholars have pointed to historical parallels in the Black and Jewish diasporic experience, where dispersal, exile, and oppression have played a crucial role. According to that interpretation, both Blacks and Jews often had to describe themselves in opposition to European and American conceptions of who they are.[9] Others have noted that both African Americans and American Jews witnessed clashes between integrationists/assimilators and nationalists; and were in dispute over what term best described them—Hebrews, Israelites, of the Mosaic persuasion, or rather Jews; or in the case of Black Americans—Colored, Negro, Colored Americans, people of color, Blacks, Anglo-Africans, Afro-Saxon, Afro-Americans, or African Americans.[10] A different historical irony is that in Western thought and literature, Jews' dark skin and hair were used by their enemies to underscore their alleged foreignness, menace, and/or inferiority. While being victims of hatred, however, both Blacks and Jews still absorbed and articulated a negative imagery of another maligned group. It is a painful reminder that any facile conclusion about intergroup cooperation, shared values, or a "rainbow coalition" would fall short without considering the profound impact of surrounding racism and antisemitism.

Yiddish culture's representation of Black women and men illuminates a much wider phenomenon. It is not just the current advocates of Yiddish who essentialize it as infused with radical or left-wing consciousness. Since the mid-twentieth century (with some important nineteenth-century precursors[11]), a host of American rabbis and communal leaders not only devised a liberal/progressive type of Judaism, but also projected it back onto the Jewish past. Their version of Judaism and Jewish historical experience readily lends itself to terms such as social justice, *tzedakah*, and *tikkun olam*. Several generations of American Jews grew up deeply convinced that such boosterish and self-congratulatory renditions of Judaism and Jewish history were realistic and empirical.[12] Part of the motivation was surely to provide a sunnier, more palatable Jewish past and validate current values and sensibilities via a revered (though overstated if not largely invented) heritage.

Within such a framework, it became almost inevitable to use the past in service of the present and argue that Judaic values and a historical experience as a persecuted minority led Jews to identify with America's Black population. A perfect example was a remark by Murray Friedman, an admirable scholar and civil rights leader, who argued that the young Jews who went to the South in the early 1960s "were acting out, albeit unconsciously, a Jewish tradition." Those claims became the mainstay of most of the scholarship, where one historian has suggested that "by virtue of their suffering," African Americans "fell outside of the usual category of 'goyim.'" This kind of presentism—the interpretation of the past according to current views and needs—produced oversimplifications and inaccuracies.[13]

Presentism can operate in the opposite direction, too. Contemporary readers may be much less tolerant of nuance and ambiguity, and hence reach more condemnatory conclusions. While such an approach is understandable, this book has demonstrated that, as it often is with all human beings, the women and men under review featured conflicting judgments and inclinations; that complexity must be taken into account. Hopefully, this book, in tandem with several scholars who have already begun to offer new paradigms, will help to dispel many of those ahistorical assertions, even if it might also unnerve Jewish liberal or progressive sensibilities. Several decades ago, prominent historian Yosef Hayim Yerushalmi observed, "Many Jews today are in search of a past, but they patently do not want the past that is offered by the historian."[14] At a time of spiraling antisemitism (espoused, unfortunately, by several Black celebrities) and a historic national reckoning about racism, it is the historian's task to engage in neither the accusatory nor the apologetic; rather, it is to strive to investigate the past with all its incongruities and blemishes, and not just what befits contemporary tastes and preferences.

ACKNOWLEDGMENTS

I am deeply grateful to the numerous individuals and institutions that supported the publication of this book. At the Arizona Center for Judaic Studies at the University of Arizona, I am very fortunate to have colleagues such as Beth Alpert Nakhai, Anat Balint, David Diamond, David Graizbord, Leonard Hammer, Deborah Kaye, Tom Kovach, Uri Maimon, Naomi Tor, and J. Edward Wright. Our many conversations and lively companionship have served as a constant source of support and provided the much-needed social and intellectual atmosphere for conducting my research and preparing the manuscript. The Center's business manager, Martha Castleberry, and its program and outreach coordinator, Jackie Schmidt, offered much assistance that allowed me to focus on my research.

Over the years, I had the pleasure of meeting many scholars who offered valuable suggestions about my research, such as Steven J. Gold, Jeffrey S. Gurock, Dana Herman, Jonathan Karp, Ber Kotlerman, Eli Lederhendler, Alan T. Levenson, Antony Polonsky, Karen K. Seat, Nancy Sinkoff, Cornelia Wilhelm, and Gary P. Zola. When I organized and led an international conference, "Contradictions and Tropes of Antisemitism" (Tucson, 2020), I was privileged to host a remarkable group of scholars who offered many important insights into questions of antisemitism and race, among them Amy Elman, Miriam F. Elman, Aleksandra Gliszczyńska-Grabias, Günther Jikeli, Matthias Küntzel, Stephen H. Norwood, Eunice Pollack, Alvin H. Rosenfeld, and Philip Spencer.

Several journal editors, who worked with me on articles that pertain to this book, made useful suggestions and I am indebted to them. They include Joel Berkowitz, John J. Bukowczyk, Sonia Gollance, Chaya Halberstam, Steven T. Katz, Federica Schoeman, and Nick Underwood. In the past few years, the Scholars Working Group on the American Yiddish Press at the Center for Jewish History served as a helpful forum to discuss various aspects of Yiddish culture, including this project. I am grateful to Ayelet Brinn, Eric Goldstein, Ellen Kellman, William Pimlott, Rachel Rojanski, Daniel Soyer, Nina Warnke, and Saul Zaritt, among others, for those discussions.

During my year as the European Union's Marie S. Curie Senior Fellow at the Freiburg Institute for Advanced Studies (FRIAS, at the University of Freiburg, Germany), I was lucky to encounter an impressive group of scholars, who provided a convivial and intellectually stimulating environment: Christoph Durt, Kristen R. Ghodsee, John Kasianowicz, Bernd Kortmann, Clémence Ledoux, Sieglinde Lemke, Lisa McGirr, Benjamin Nathans, Kate Rigby, John C. Swanson, Roxana Willis, and Walther Zimmerli created a vibrant scholarly community.

Over the years, Arnon Gutfeld has supported many of my endeavors and I am greatly thankful to him. During my time in New York as a penniless graduate student, the late Yiddish poet and artist, Yoni Fayn, allowed me to live rent-free in his Brooklyn home's attic and helped to inspire in me a deeper appreciation of Yiddish culture. I would like to express my gratitude to the anonymous readers of my manuscript for their suggestions and support. Needless to say, all mistakes remain mine.

The support of several institutions and foundations enabled me to carry out my research and obtain serene writing periods, and I am obliged to them for their generosity. The Jacob Rader Marcus Center of the American Jewish Archives (Cincinnati) awarded me the Bernard and Audre Rapoport Fellowship to conduct preliminary archival research. Fordham University's Jewish Studies Program and the New York Public Library conferred on me a research fellowship to conduct on-site research at the Dorot Jewish Division of the New York Public Library (2018). In late 2019, the College of Social and Behavioral Sciences (SBS) at the University of Arizona awarded me a one-semester Junior (pre-tenure) Professional Development Sabbatical, which allowed me to conduct research, mostly in New York. The onset of the COVID-19 pandemic shuttered archives and libraries and significantly slowed down this project. Still, as mentioned above, the research leading to this book has received funding from the European Union's Horizon 2020 research and innovation program under the Marie Sktodowska-Curie grant agreement No. 754340. That period of the Marie S. Curie Cofund Senior Fellowship (2021–2022) took place at FRIAS. The Gerda Henkel Foundation granted me a five-month research fellowship (summer and fall of 2022), which helped me to continue my writing and defray further research costs. SBS awarded me a regular sabbatical (2022–2023) that enabled me to complete the manuscript. Finally, the Center for Advanced Study—Sofia (Bulgaria) awarded me the "Social Relevance of the Humanities" fellowship in the fall of 2024, which allowed me to put the finishing touches on the manuscript. I am grateful to the Center's Director, Diana Mishkova, and the research fellows for their feedback, and to Dimiter Dimov for facilitating my stay in Sofia.

The research for this book was made possible also thanks to the dedicated effort of the archivists and librarians at the American Jewish Archives, American Jewish Historical Society, Dorot Jewish Division of the New York Public Library, Klau Library at the Hebrew Union College—Jewish Institute of Religion, Institute for Jewish Research (YIVO), and the National Library of Israel. The advancement by leaps and bounds of digital archives greatly facilitated the access to varied historical materials for this book. The National Library of Israel and Tel Aviv University's Historical Jewish Press website is an indispensable source (https://www.nli.org.il/en/discover/newspapers/jpress), as is the Yiddish Book Center's online archive (https://www.yiddishbookcenter.org/). Other digital sources include Projekt Gutenberg (https://www.projekt-gutenberg.org/), and websites such as www.hebrewbooks.org and https://benyehuda.org/. I am grateful to Jennifer Hammer, Brianna Jean, Valerie Zaborski, and all those involved in the production of this book at NYU Press for their meticulous job in guiding me through the publication process. Jim Reilly deserves special thanks for his thorough copy editing.

The support of family and friends helped me immensely in the most challenging and joyous stages of writing this book. My friends Emmanuel Darmon, Ehud Eilam, Amy Feinstein, Yaron Kolton, Shay Koren, Yossi Niv, and Katja Vehlow were always ready to chat, offer a word of advice, or just take my mind off the project. Sheila Sommerman and Herb Schneider opened their homes and hearts to me on Manhattan's Upper West Side and on Long Island. The brothers Kenneth and Alan Sommerman, both of blessed memory, were always happy to discuss languages, especially German and Yiddish, and their various dialects.

My family kept taking me out of my proverbial shell and reminding me to hit the "off" button. My brother Effie and his spouse Galit, my niece Reut, and my two nephews, Eitan and Ela'ad, were always ready to cheer me up, whether face-to-face or remotely. My sister, Limor, and her partner, Oren, made sure that their travels and culinary experiments would offer me a pleasant distraction. Even though she is still unsure of what I do for a living, my mother, Bruria, was an endless source of (sometimes unsolicited) suggestions. I miss my late father, Eliezer (*z"l*), dearly, and wish he could have made one of his sardonic cracks about this book. When writing, I often thought of my Yiddish-speaking grandparents, Efraim and Zehava (Golda) Ribak and Gershon and Ahuva Yoel; while Efraim passed away before I was born, the others had a significant presence in my life.

Finally, my stepchildren, Benjamin and Mila, were frequently puzzled by what I do but helped to brighten up the day with their usual antics. My life partner, Tamara (aka the Kugl), has always been there as my anchor and my rock. Her love and support were vital for the completion of this book.

NOTES

INTRODUCTION

1 Unless otherwise noted, all the translations from the Yiddish, Hebrew, and German are mine. Sholem Aleichem, *In amerika: motl peisy dem khazns un andere mayses* (Varhayt, 1918), 72. In his excellent translation to English, Hillel Halkin omitted "crude creatures"—Sholem Aleichem, *The Letters of Menakhem-Mendl and Sheyne-Sheyndl* and *Motl, the Cantor's Son* (Yale University Press, 2002), 264. On *Motl*, see Dan Miron, "Bouncing Back: Destruction and Recovery in Sholem Aleykhem's 'Motl Peyse dem Khazns,'" *YIVO Annual of Jewish Social Science* 17 (1978): 119–84; and Jeremy Dauber, *The Worlds of Sholem Aleichem* (Schocken, 2013), 196–99, 299–301.

2 Albert J. Raboteau, "African-Americans, Exodus, and the American Israel," in *Strangers & Neighbors: Relations Between Blacks & Jews in the United States*, ed. Maurianne Adams and John Bracey (University of Massachusetts Press, 1999), 57–63; and Yvonne Chireau, "Black Culture and Black Zion: African American Religious Encounters with Judaism, 1790–1930, an Overview," in *Black Zion: African American Religious Encounters with Judaism*, ed. Yvonne Chireau and Nathaniel Deutsch (Oxford University Press, 2000), 13–32.

3 One can mention only a fraction of the studies on Black-Jewish relations (others are mentioned in subsequent endnotes): Marc Dollinger, *Black Power, Jewish Politics: Reinventing the Alliance in the 1960s* (Brandeis University Press, 2018); Herbert Hill, "Black-Jewish Conflict in the Labor Context: Race, Jobs, and Institutional Power," in *African Americans and Jews in the Twentieth Century*, ed. V. P. Franklin et al. (University of Missouri Press, 1998), 264–92; Seth Forman, *Blacks in the Jewish Mind: A Crisis of Liberalism* (New York University Press, 1998); Steven Hertzberg, *Strangers Within the Gate City: The Jews of Atlanta, 1845–1915* (Jewish Publication Society, 1978), 181–215. A succinct historiographical discussion is in Cheryl Lynn Greenberg, *Troubling the Waters: Black-Jewish Relations in the American Century* (Princeton University Press, 2006), 2–7. A dated bibliographical list is in Lenwood G. Davis, *Black-Jewish Relations in the United States 1752–1984: A Selected Bibliography* (Greenwood, 1984). For a standard popular history, see Murray Friedman, *What Went Wrong: The Creation and Collapse of the Black-Jewish Alliance* (Free Press, 1995).

4 Those quotes are from Hasia R. Diner, *In the Almost Promised Land: American Jews and Blacks, 1915–1935* (1977; repr. Johns Hopkins University Press, 1995),

67–68, 74; and Hasia R. Diner, "Drawn Together by Self-Interest: Jewish Representation of Race and Race Relations in the Early Twentieth Century," in *African Americans and Jews in the Twentieth Century*, ed. Franklin et al., 35. Similar assessments are in Michael Alexander, *Jazz Age Jews* (Princeton University Press, 2001), 8, 176–77, 181–82; George Bornstein, *The Colors of Zion: Blacks, Jews, and Irish from 1845 to 1945* (Harvard University Press, 2011), 68–69, 71–72, 126–27; Friedman, *What Went Wrong*, 60; and Hertzberg, *Strangers Within*, 185–86. A much more nuanced analysis is in Eric L. Goldstein, *The Price of Whiteness: Jews, Race, and American Identity* (Princeton University Press, 2006), 79–81, 153–54. See also Mark Slobin, *Tenement Songs: The Popular Music of the Jewish Immigrants* (1982; repr. University of Illinois Press, 1996), 51.

5 Just a few examples will suffice: Cornel West, "On Black-Jewish Relations," in *Blacks and Jews: Alliances and Arguments*, ed. Paul Berman (Delacorte, 1994), 146; Eric J. Sundquist, *Strangers in the Land: Blacks, Jews, Post-Holocaust America* (Belknap Press of Harvard University Press, 2005), 23–27; and David R. Roediger, *Working Toward Whiteness—How America's Immigrants Became White: The Strange Journey from Ellis Island to the Suburbs* (Basic Books, 2005), 98, 107–8.

6 Dollinger, *Black Power, Jewish Politics*; Jeffrey Melnick, *A Right to Sing the Blues* (Harvard University Press, 1999); and Michael Rogin, *Blackface/White Noise: Jewish Immigrants in the Hollywood Melting Pot* (University of California Press, 1996).

7 Among the few references to that similarity, see Milton Himmelfarb, "Negroes, Jews, and Muzhiks," in *The Ghetto and Beyond: Essays on Jewish Life in America*, ed. Peter I. Rose (Random House, 1969), 409–18; and Marc Caplan, "Yiddish Exceptionalism: Lynching, Race, and Racism in Opatoshu's *Lintsheray*," in *Joseph Opatoshu: A Yiddish Writer between Europe and America*, ed. Sabine Koller, Gennady Estraikh, and Mikhail Krutikov (Legenda, 2013), 187. On immigrant Jews and their Black clientele, see Arnold Shankman, "Friend or Foe? Southern Blacks View the Jew, 1880–1935," in *"Turn to the South": Essays on Southern Jewry*, ed. Nathan M. Kaganoff and Melvin I. Urofsky (American Jewish Historical Society, 1979), 105–23; Clive Webb, "Jewish Merchants and Black Customers in the Age of Jim Crow," *Southern Jewish History* 2 (October 1999): 55–80; and Marni Davis, *Jews and Booze: Becoming American in the Age of Prohibition* (New York University Press, 2012), 122–27, 162–64.

8 On East European Jews' ambivalent view of Black Americans as potential allies, see Gil Ribak, *Gentile New York: The Images of Non-Jews among Jewish Immigrants* (Rutgers University Press, 2012), 3–4, 184–87, 192–94. On American Jews and the concept of minority rights, see Carole Fink, *Defending the Rights of Others: The Great Powers, The Jews, and International Minority Protection, 1878–1938* (Cambridge University Press, 2004), 193–235; and Oscar I. Janowsky, *The Jews and Minority Rights, 1898–1919* (Columbia University Press, 1933), 264–309. On the wartime, Red Scare, and 1920s' crop of bigotry, see Todd J. Pfannestiel, *Rethinking the Red Scare: The Lusk Committee and New York's Crusade Against Radicalism,*

1919–1923 (Routledge, 2003), 123–33; Robert K. Murray, *Red Scare: A Study of National Hysteria, 1919–1920* (1955; repr. McGraw-Hill, 1964); and John Higham, *Strangers in the Land: Patterns of American Nativism, 1860–1925* (1955, new edition Atheneum, 1978), 234–99.

9 On Garvey's worsening attitudes toward Jews, see Robert A. Hill and Barbara Blair (eds.), "Introduction," in *Marcus Garvey Life and Lessons: A Centennial Companion to the Marcus Garvey and Universal Negro Improvement Association Papers* (University of California Press, 1987), lii–lx. On Garvey in the Yiddish press, see chapter 3.

10 On the importance of 1929 for the Jewish world, see Hasia R. Diner and Gennady Estraikh, "Introduction," in *1929: Mapping the Jewish World*, ed. Diner and Estraikh (New York University Press, 2013), 1–7. On the effect of the Scottsboro trial on Yiddish culture, see Amelia Glaser, "Speaking of Scottsboro," in *Proletpen: America's Rebel Yiddish Poets*, ed. Amelia Glaser and David Weintraub (University of Wisconsin Press, 2005), 133–34. See also Paul Buhle and Robin D. G. Kelley, "Allies of a Different Sort: Jews and Blacks in the American Left," in *Struggles in the Promised Land: Toward a History of Black-Jewish Relations in the United States*, ed. Jack Salzman and Cornel West (Oxford University Press, 1997), 205–9. On antisemitism among African Americans at the time, see Leonard Dinnerstein, *Antisemitism in America* (Oxford University Press, 1994), 202–6. On Jews during the riots in 1930s Harlem, see Jeffrey S. Gurock, *The Jews of Harlem: The Rise, Decline, and Revival of a Jewish Community* (New York University Press, 2016), 184–88; and Cheryl Lynn Greenberg, *"Or Does It Explode?": Black Harlem in the Great Depression* (Oxford University Press, 1991), 126–27.

11 Eric L. Goldstein, "The Struggle over Yiddish in Postimmigrant America," in Diner and Estraikh, *1929*, 142–44. On the decline in Yiddish papers' circulation, see N. Goldberg, "Di yidishe prese in di fareynikte Shtatn, 1900–1940," *YIVO Bleter* 18 (1941): 137–44. On the Yiddish theater's dwindling audience, see Irving Howe, with the assistance of Kenneth Libo, *World of Our Fathers* (1976; repr. Schocken, 1989), 491–92; and J. Hoberman, *Bridge of Light: Yiddish Film between Two Worlds* (Museum of Modern Art and Schocken Books, 1991), 157–59. Memoirists' recollection of the denigration of Yiddish are in Deborah Dash Moore, *At Home in America: Second Generation New York Jews* (Columbia University Press, 1981), 90, 104–6. On the East Bronx as a pocket of working-class Yiddish speakers, see Beth S. Wenger, *New York Jews and the Great Depression: Uncertain Promise* (1996; repr. Syracuse University Press, 1999), 93. For a parallel decline in Canada, see Rebecca Margolis, *Jewish Roots, Canadian Soil: Yiddish Cultural Life in Montreal, 1905–1945* (McGill-Queen's University Press, 2011), 124, 151, 170, 192.

12 Ben-Yehuda, writing in *Ha-'or*, April 6, 1910, p. 1 (emphasis in the original). See also, Marc Volovici, *German as a Jewish Problem: The Language Politics of Jewish Nationalism* (Stanford University Press, 2020), 173–99.

13 Max Weinreich, *History of the Yiddish Language*, trans. Joshua A. Fishman (University of Chicago Press, 1980), 252–56. S. Niger, *Di tsveyshprakhikayt fun unzer*

literatur (Luis Lamed fond far undzer literatur in bayder shprakhn, 1941), 12–14, 69–72.

14 Kenneth B. Moss, *Jewish Renaissance in the Russian Revolution* (Harvard University Press, 2009), 282–83. On language proficiency and alienation from Yiddish among modernizing Jews, including Yiddish writers, see Dan Miron, *A Traveler Disguised: A Study in the Rise of Modern Yiddish Fiction in the Nineteenth Century* (Schocken, 1973), 7–14; and Israel Bartal, "From Traditional Bilingualism to National Monolingualism," in *Hebrew in Ashkenaz: A Language in Exile*, ed. Lewis Glinert (Oxford University Press, 1993), 141–50. See also S. Dubnow, "From Jargon to Yiddish," in *Great Yiddish Writers of the Twentieth Century*, ed. and trans. J. Leftwich (J. Aronson, 1987), 519–27. On the alienation from Yiddish, mostly in the German lands, see Sander L. Gilman, *Jewish Self-Hatred: Anti-Semitism and the Hidden Language of the Jews* (Johns Hopkins University Press, 1986), 98–100, 261, 276–79. On "coon nonsense" and *Hesitation Blues*, see chapter 5.

15 On Yiddish-speaking Black Americans, see above. Analysis and examples of Yiddish-speaking Gentiles in Eastern Europe are in Ribak, *Gentile New York*, 18; Aleksander Harkavy, *Prakim me-chayay* (Hebrew Publishing, 1935), 6–7; I. J. Singer, *Fun a velt vos iz nishto mer* (Matones, 1946), 53; and Tuvya Bruk, "Goyim ke-yehudim," *Yeda-ʿam* 8 (1962): 84. On the Hebrew-Yiddish "language war," see Kalman Weiser, "Introduction," in *Czernowitz at 100: The First Yiddish Language Conference in Historical Perspective*, ed. Kalman Weiser and Joshua A. Fogel (Rowman & Littlefield, 2010), 1–9; and Naomi Seidman, *A Marriage Made in Heaven: The Sexual Politics of Hebrew and Yiddish* (University of California Press, 1997), 102–31. In a recent excellent study, Naomi Brenner has demonstrated how critical to both Hebrew and Yiddish literature was the contact with each other—*Lingering Bilingualism: Modern Hebrew and Yiddish Literatures in Contact* (Syracuse University Press, 2016).

16 For example, see attitudes in Chinese, Korean, and Russian cultures: Yinghong Cheng, *Discourses of Race and Rising China* (Springer, 2019), 14–17, 161–89; Jennifer Lee, *Civility in the City: Blacks, Jews, and Koreans in Urban America* (Harvard University Press, 2002), 79–80; and Allison Blakely, *Russia and the Negro: Blacks in Russian History and Thought* (Howard University Press, 1986).

17 On the term Kushite and its application over time, see David M. Goldenberg, *Black and Slave: The Origins and History of the Curse of Ham* (De Gruyter, 2017), 7, 11; and Abraham Melamed, *The Image of the Black in Jewish Culture: A History of the Other* (Taylor & Francis e-Library, 2003), viii, 24–25, 53–59. See also in chapter 1. Melamed also refers to the more recent negative connotation of "Kushi" in contemporary Hebrew, a topic that is beyond our scope. See also, Stephen Katz, *Red, Black, and Jew: New Frontiers in Hebrew Literature* (University of Texas Press, 2009), 128.

18 Aleksander Harkavy, *Yidish-english-hebreyisher verterbukh* (1928; repr. Yiddish Book Center, 1999), 322. Nakhum Stutchkov, *Der oytser fun der yidisher shprakh* (YIVO, 1950), 168. On *Arapy* in Russia, see Blakely, *Russia and the Negro*, 13–14.

19 Emily Miller Budick has claimed, "schwartzer is the Yiddish word Jewish Americans use to refer, usually condescendingly, to blacks," *Blacks and Jews in Literary Conversation* (Cambridge University Press, 1998), 14; Karen Brodkin has called it "a racist term," *How Jews Became White Folks and What That Says about Race in America* (Rutgers University Press, 1998), 17–18. Harry Golden, *The Right Time: An Autobiography* (G. P. Putnam's Sons, 1969), 23. See also Harry Golden, *Forgotten Pioneer* (World Publishing Company, 1963), 68–69; and Kimberly Marlowe Hartnett, *Carolina Israelite: How Harry Golden Made Us Care about Jews, the South, and Civil Rights* (The University of North Carolina Press, 2015).

20 Morrison is quoted in Nell Irvin Painter, *The History of White People* (W. W. Norton, 2010), 363. See also Sterling Stuckey, *Slave Culture: Nationalist Theory and the Foundations of Black America* (Oxford University Press, 1987), 198–200.

21 On the development of the term "nigger" in English, see Randall Kennedy, *Nigger: The Strange Career of a Troublesome Word* (Pantheon Books, 2002); and Jabari Asim, *The N Word: Who Can Say It, Who Shouldn't, and Why* (Houghton Mifflin, 2007), 9–11, 77–82. Keith Allan has argued, "Until the late eighteenth century nig(g)er was synonymous with Negro . . . thereafter and until the second half of the twentieth century the term nigger was essentially a colloquial synonym for Negro"—Keith Allan, "When Is a Slur Not a Slur? The Use of Nigger in 'Pulp Fiction,'" *Language Sciences* 52 (2015): 188. See also Johnnetta B. Cole, "Culture: Negro, Black and Nigger," *Black Scholar* 1 (June 1970): 40–44. On the term Neger in German, see Robbie Aitken and Eve Rosenhaft, *Black Germany: The Making and Unmaking of a Diaspora Community, 1884–1960* (Cambridge University Press, 2013), 9–10; and Timothy L. Schroer, *Recasting Race after World War II: Germans and African Americans in American-Occupied Germany* (University Press of Colorado, 2007), 92.

22 On the orthography of the term Niger and the "nun word," see Eli Bromberg, "We Need to Talk about Shmuel Charney," *In Geveb: A Journal of Yiddish Studies*, October 2, 2019, https://ingeveb.org. Scholars who also saw Niger's name as derived from solidarity with African Americans include Melnick, *Right to Sing the Blues*, 98–102, 235n15; and Benjamin Harshav, *Marc Chagall and his Times: A Documentary Narrative* (Stanford University Press, 2004), 327. Other sources are mentioned in Bromberg's article.

23 Niger's diary entry, August 27, 1933, 224–25, in Papers of Shmuel Niger, RG 360 (YIVO Institute for Jewish Research, hereafter YIVO), box 113, folder 3057. His letterhead in the 1920s appears in many collections of correspondence—see for instance, in the Papers of Yisroel-Yankev (I. J.) Schwartz, RG 649 (YIVO), folder "Letters from S. Niger." On Niger's role in the creation and dissemination of Yiddish high culture, see Barry Trachtenberg, *The Revolutionary Roots of Modern Yiddish, 1903–1917* (Syracuse University Press, 2008), 82–107.

24 There are many examples of both Niger and Neger used in the same news item, at times describing the same person: "14 geshosen fun a Niger," *Yidishe velt*, Sep. 2, 1902, 1. On that paper, see Lucy S. Dawidowicz, "Louis Marshall's Yiddish News-

paper, *The Jewish World*: A Study in Contrasts," *Jewish Social Studies* 25 (1963): 102–32. See also, "A vilder Neger," *Yidishe velt*, Aug. 19, 1903, 1; "A shrekens nakht," *Forverts*, Aug. 24, 1900, 1; "Villen nit varten oyfen gezets," *Forverts*, Nov. 1, 1901, 1; "A Niger gelyntsht," *Forverts*, March 11, 1902, 1; "Niger dershlogt alte froy tsum toyt," *Forverts*, Oct. 20, 1912, 1; "A Niger vet zingen yidish in bronzvil," *Forverts*, Feb. 14, 1918, 2; "In di amerikaner theatere," *Forverts*, March 17, 1922, 3 (Williams). On Williams, see Louis Chude-Sokei, *The Last "Darky": Bert Williams, Black-on-Black Minstrelsy, and the African Diaspora* (Duke University Press, 2006). "Vayse un Negers halten milkhome," *Morgen zhurnal* (hereafter *MZ*), Aug. 8, 1907, 8; "Root elektet tsherman fun der konvenshon," *MZ*, June 19, 1912, 1; "Meshugener Neger toytet fier menshen in shikago," *MZ*, July 19, 1916, 5. "Ermordet fun a Niger," *Yidishes tageblat* (hereafter *YT*), Jan. 19, 1906, 1; "Dr. Theodor Herzl's filozofishe felitonen, skitsen, un noveleten: Fun vin biz budapest," *YT*, June 15, 1919, 8. "Zeks froyen patshen a Niger," *Varhayt*, Oct. 14, 1907, 2; "Niger befalt a maydel," *Varhayt*, Oct. 20, 1908, 5; "Yid ermordet fun a Niger," *Varhayt*, March 4, 1912, 1. "Regirung shikt militer eyntsushtelen rasen-rayots in omaha," *Tog*, Sep. 29, 1919, 1. See also Gil Ribak, "'Negroes Must Not Be Likened to Jews': The Attitudes of Eastern European Jewish Immigrants toward African Americans in a Transnational Perspective," *Modern Judaism* 37 (October 2017): 271–96.

25 Bromberg, "We Need to Talk about Shmuel Charney," n40. See also the annotated translation of Dik's introduction by Eli Rosenblatt, "Slavery or Serfdom," In geveb, November 2015, https://ingeveb.org. The historical Jewish press website is a joint project of the National Library of Israel and Tel Aviv University, https://www.nli.org.il/en/discover/newspapers/jpress. The headline "A 19-year-old Niger shoots his young wife in cold blood" is in *Forverts*, Sep. 29, 1897, 1; "A rabbi stabbed by a Niger" *Forverts*, July 5, 1899, 1; "Crazy Niger shoots 2 people," *Forverts*, Oct. 11, 1911, 8; "East-Side Jew murdered by a Niger in the west," *Forverts*, Aug. 9, 1915, 1; "Crazy Niger stabs 2 men," *YT*, Sep. 15, 1921, 7. See also news reports that included, "A wild Niger jumps from a corner with a revolver in his hand," *YT*, March 20, 1907, 10; another "wild Niger" who shot people at a church in Tampa, Florida, *MZ*, July 17, 1910, 4. See also headlines such as "Wild Niger holds up in forest," *MZ*, June 3, 1913, 1; "A Niger stabs a white girl," *Morgen tsaytung*, March 12, 1906, 8; "A Niger kisses also the white bride," *Varhayt*, Sep. 22, 1907, 1; "Jew murdered by Niger," *Varhayt*, March 4, 1912, 1; "A Niger bandit stabs three Jews," *MZ*, Nov. 26, 1909, 7. Examples of discussions of the "Negro question" (either in the headline or the text) are in *MZ*, Nov. 1, 1906, 5; *Forverts*, July 7, 1914, 2; *Varhayt*, Nov. 20, 1916, 3; *Tog*, July 19, 1917, 5.

26 *Ha-pisgah*, April 4, 1890, 2. *Varhayt*, Sep. 24, 1906, 4 (the editorial was probably written by Miller). *Di yidishe bine*, Dec. 10, 1909, 2. Other examples are in Bromberg, "We Need to Talk about Shmuel Charney." On Grand Museum, see Rachel Shteir, *Striptease: The Untold History of the Girlie Show* (Oxford University Press, 2004), 61–62. On Miller and *Varhayt*, see Y. Khaykin, *Yidishe bleter in amerike* (Published by the author, 1946), 175–95, 218–31; and Ehud Manor, *Louis Miller and*

"Di Warheit" ("The Truth"): Yiddishism, Zionism and Socialism in New York, 1905–1915 (Sussex University Press, 2012). On Sheldon's play and subsequent movie, see Cedric J. Robinson, *Forgeries of Memory and Meaning: Blacks and the Regimes of Race in American Theater and Film before World War II* (University of North Carolina Press, 2007), 215–22. On the concept of intelligentsia in the context of Yiddish culture, see Delphine Bechtel, "The Russian Jewish Intelligentsia and Modern Yiddish Culture," in *Nationalism, Zionism, and Ethnic Mobilization of the Jews in 1900 and Beyond*, ed. Michael Berkowitz (Brill, 2004), 213–26; and Howe, *World of Our Fathers*, 15–20.

27 Cahan's quote appear in his autobiography, *Bleter fun mayn lebn* (Forward Association, 1931), 5:569 (quotes in the original). Cahan explained that he had many notes remaining from 1914 (when he covered the trial), which he used for his autobiography. Zisl Kornblit's quote is in *Forverts*, May 16, 1923, 6 (parentheses and quotes in the original). On Frank's innocence and Jim Conley's letters in the context of the trial, see Steve Oney, *And the Dead Shall Rise: The Murder of Mary Phagan and the Lynching of Leo Frank* (Pantheon, 2003), 390–400, 414–17, 430–37, 612–13, 644–49; and Leonard Dinnerstein, "The Fate of Leo Frank," *American Heritage* 46 (1996): 98–107. Jeffrey Melnick has touched on Cahan's coverage of the case in *Black-Jewish Relations on Trial: Leo Frank and Jim Conley in the New South* (University Press of Mississippi, 2000), 35–38, 84–85. See also Eugene Levy, "'Is the Jew a White Man?': Press Reactions to the Leo Frank Case, 1913–1915," *Phylon* 35 (1974): 212–22. On another piece by Kornblit, see Gil Ribak, "'Beaten to Death by Irish Murderers': The Death of Sadie Dellon (1918) and Jewish Images of the Irish," *Journal of American Ethnic History* 32 (Summer 2013): 52.

28 For the transliteration of "nigger," see *Der vorshteher* ("The Representative") of St. Louis, which prided itself as "The greatest Jewish daily west of New York City," Nov. 16, 1908, 1; and Dec. 14, 1908, 1. In "We Need to Talk about Shmuel Charney," Bromberg argues that "the one gimel spelling of ניגער [might have] influenced some Yiddish speakers to spell the English slur with one "g." On the capitalization of Black and Negro, see Nancy Coleman, "Why We're Capitalizing Black," *New York Times*, July 5, 2020, https://www.nytimes.com. Cf. Nell Irvin Painter, "Capitalize 'White,' too," *Washington Post*, July 23, 2020, A19.

29 Y. E. Rontsh, "Der Neger in unzer literatur," *Amerike in der yidisher literatur* (Rontsh bukh komitet, 1945), 203–55. Irena Klepfisz, "Queens of Contradiction: A Feminist Introduction to Yiddish Women Writers," in *Found Treasures: Stories by Yiddish Women Writers*, ed. Frieda Forman et al. (Second Story Press, 1994), 31. On Jewish women's literacy in Eastern Europe, see Shaul Stampfer, *Families, Rabbis and Education: Traditional Jewish Society in Nineteenth-Century Eastern Europe* (Liverpool University Press, 2010), 167–189. On the relative neglect of shund and a call to reevaluate Yiddish cultural history, see Saul Zaritt, "A *Taytsh* Manifesto: Yiddish, Translation, and the Making of Modern Jewish Culture," *Jewish Social Studies* 26 (2021): 186–222. See also Khone Shmeruk, "Le-toldot sifrut ha-shund be-yidish," *Tarbitz* 52 (1983): 325–54; and Ellen Kellman, "Entertain-

ing New Americans: Serialized Fiction in the *Forverts* (1910–1930)," in *Jews and American Popular Culture*, ed. Paul Buhle (Praeger, 2007), 2:199–211.

30 On chapbooks and their popularity, see David G. Roskies, *A Bridge of Longing: The Lost Art of Yiddish Storytelling* (Harvard University Press, 1995), 56–58. The transatlantic Yiddish book industry is discussed in Hagit Cohen, *Nifla'ot ba-'olam he-ḥadash: sefarim ve-kor'im be-yidish be-'artsot ha-berit, 1890–1940* (Ha-Universiṭah ha-petuḥah, 2016), 56–102, 385; Eric L. Goldstein, "A Taste of Freedom: American Yiddish Publications in Imperial Russia," in *Transnational Traditions: New Perspectives on American Jewish History*, ed. Ava F. Kahn and Adam D. Mendelsohn (Wayne State University Press, 2014), 105–39; Jeffrey Veidlinger, *Jewish Public Culture in the Late Russian Empire* (Indiana University Press, 2009), 83–85, 99–105, 156; and Yisroel Tsinberg, *Di geshikhte fun der literatur bay yidn* (Tomor, 1935), 8: 191–92.

31 Shmuel Niger et al., eds., *Leksikon fun der nayer yidisher literatur* (Altveltlekhen yidishn kultur congress, 1956–1981), 8:733–45; Iris Parush, *Reading Jewish Women: Marginality and Modernization in Nineteenth-Century Eastern European Jewish Society* (Brandeis University Press, 2004), 150–54; Justin Cammy, "Judging *The Judgment of Shomer*: Jewish Literature versus Jewish Reading," in *Arguing the Modern Jewish Canon: Essays on Literature and Culture in Honor of Ruth R. Wisse* (Harvard University Press, 2008), 85–127; Shmeruk, "Le'toldot sifrut ha'shund," 329–32; and Sofi Grace-Pollack, "Reshito shel shomer be-yidish," *Chulyot* 2 (1994): 69–87. The quotes from the competitors' book covers are in A. Litvak, *Vos geven: etyudn un zikhroynes* (Kletskin, 1925), 71, 75. On the mass attendance at Shomer's funeral in New York (1905), see Arthur A. Goren, *The Politics and Public Culture of American Jews* (Indiana University Press, 1999), 30–34.

32 Rontsh, "Der neger," 225–55. The quote from Leyvik's poem is translated by Jessica Kirzane (who also challenges facile generalizations) in her article, "The 'Yiddish Gaze': American Yiddish Literary Representations of Black Bodies and Their Torture," in *Judaism, Race, and Ethics: Conversations and Questions*, ed. Jonathan K. Crane (Pennsylvania State University Press, 2020), 124–60 (quote is on p. 139). Other scholars who have explored such ambivalence in Yiddish poetry are Merle L. Bachman, *Recovering "Yiddishland": Threshold Moments in American Literature* (Syracuse University Press, 2008), 114–73; Amelia Glaser, "From Jewish Jesus to Black Christ: Race Violence in Leftist Yiddish Poetry," *Studies in American Jewish Literature* 34 (2015): 44–69; and Colleen McCallum-Bonar, "Black Ashkenaz and the Almost Promised Land: Yiddish Literature and the Harlem Renaissance" (PhD diss., Ohio State University, 2008), 64–66, 122, 140–42, 171–72.

33 The quotes are from Y. Y. Schwartz, *Kentoki* (Mayzl, 1925), 11, 86. Parts of the poem were published in *Di tsukunft* between 1918 and 1924. Avraham Novershtern, *Kan gar ha-'am ha-yehudi: sifrut yidish be-'artsot ha-berit* (Magnes, 2015), 116. Critics who praised the poem for its identification with African Americans are Menachem Ribalow, *Tsukunft* (March 1926): 184–86; and Hertzberg, *Strangers Within*, 186. On the discrepancies between the Yiddish original and the English transla-

tion by Gertrude Dubrovsky, see Papers of Yisroel-Yankev (I. J.) Schwartz, RG 649 (YIVO), box 2, folder "Kentoki—Dubrovsky tr." See also Julian Levinson, *Exiles on Main Street: Jewish American Writers and American Literary Culture* (Indiana University Press, 2008), 132–38.

34 Mani Leyb, "Tsum goyishn poet," in *The Penguin Book of Modern Yiddish Verse*, ed. Irving Howe, Ruth R. Wisse, and Khone Shmeruk (Penguin Books, 1988), 139 (my translation). The quote by Howe, Wisse, and Shmeruk is in "Introduction," *Penguin Book*, 45. The quote by Rapaport is in his letter (June 19, 1926) to Shmuel Niger, Papers of Malka Li, RG 367 (YIVO), folder 7. See also Jordan Finkin, "To Organize Beauty: The Sonnets of Mani Leyb," *Studies in American Jewish Literature* 34 (2015): 79–80.

35 In *World of Our Fathers*, Irving Howe demonstrates many writers' leaning toward socialist and radical Yiddish culture. The following is an incomplete sample—Moses Rischin, *The Promised City: New York's Jews 1870–1914* (Harvard University Press, 1962), especially 115–30; Gennady Estraikh, *Transatlantic Russian Jewishness: Ideological Voyages of the Yiddish Daily "Forverts" in the First Half of the Twentieth Century* (Academic Studies Press, 2020); Gennady Estraikh and Mikhail Krutikov, eds., *Yiddish and the Left* (Legenda, 2001); Gerald Sorin, *The Prophetic Minority: American Jewish Immigrant Radicals, 1880–1920* (Indiana University Press, 1985); Tony Michels, *A Fire in Their Hearts: Yiddish Socialists in New York* (Harvard University Press, 2005); Daniel Katz, *All Together Different: Yiddish Socialists, Garment Workers, and the Labor Roots of Multiculturalism* (New York University Press, 2011); and Ronald Sanders, *The Downtown Jews: Portraits of An Immigrant Generation* (Harper & Row, 1969). In recent years, scholars such as David E. Fishman pointed to the divisive role and instrumental use of Yiddish by a leftist organization such as the Jewish socialist Bund—*The Rise of Modern Yiddish Culture* (University of Pittsburgh Press, 2005), 48–61.

36 Joshua Shanes, *Diaspora Nationalism and Jewish Identity in Habsburg Galicia* (Cambridge University Press, 2012); Itzik Nakhmen Gottesman, *Defining the Yiddish Nation: The Jewish Folklorists of Poland* (Wayne State University Press, 2003); Joshua M. Karlip, *The Tragedy of a Generation: The Rise and Fall of Jewish Nationalism in Eastern Europe* (Harvard University Press, 2013); Cecile Esther Kuznitz, *YIVO and the Making of Modern Jewish Culture: Scholarship for the Yiddish Nation* (Cambridge University Press, 2014); and Kalman (Keith) Weiser, *Jewish People, Yiddish Nation: Noah Prylucki and the Folkists in Poland* (University of Toronto Press, 2011).

37 On those beliefs, see Jeffrey Shandler, *Adventures in Yiddishland: Postvernacular Language and Culture* (University of California Press, 2006), 87–88, 187–90; Ilan Stavans and Josh Lambert, "Preface: The Old in the New," in *How Yiddish Changed America and How America Changed Yiddish*, ed. Stavans and Lambert (Restless Books, 2020), unpaginated; and Edward S. Shapiro, "Introduction," in *Yiddish in America: Essays on Yiddish Culture in the Golden Land*, ed. Edward S. Shapiro (University of Scranton Press, 2008), xix. Ruth R. Wisse, "Yiddish:

Past, Present, Imperfect," *Commentary* (Nov. 1997): 38. Markus Krah has shown how post-Holocaust Jewish leftists elevated Yiddish "to the status of a secular mystique"—*American Jewry and the Re-Invention of the East European Jewish Past* (De Gruyter, 2018), 159–61.

38 Ellison is quoted in Steve Pinkerton, "Ralph Ellison's Righteous Riffs: Jazz, Democracy, and the Sacred," *African American Review* 44 (2011): 192.

39 Stuart Hall, "New Ethnicities," in *Selected Writings on Race and Difference*, ed. Paul Gilroy and Ruth Wilson Gilmore (Duke University Press, 2021), 248–49 (emphasis in the original). On Western notions of African cannibalism, see Jan Nederveen Pieterse, *White on Black: Images of Africa and Blacks in Western Popular Culture* (Yale University Press, 1992), 113–22. On literacy levels among Black Southerners, see Robert A. Margo, *Race and Schooling in the South, 1880–1950: An Economic History* (University of Chicago Press, 1990), 6–12.

40 On cultural historians and representation, see Peter Burke, *What Is Cultural History?* (2004; 3rd edition, Polity Press, 2019), 78–83. The school of "invention" owes much to Benedict Anderson, *Imagined Communities: Reflections on the Origin and Spread of Nationalism* (Verso, 1983). Werner Sollors, ed., *The Invention of Ethnicity* (Oxford University Press, 1989), ix–xx. A more moderate position is that of Kathleen Neils Conzen et al., "The Invention of Ethnicity: A Perspective from the U.S.A.," *Journal of American Ethnic History* 12 (1992): 3–41. A critique of that school of thought is in Michael Stanislawski, *Zionism and the Fin de Siecle: Cosmopolitanism and Nationalism from Nordau to Jabotinsky* (University of California Press, 2001), xvii–xviii. See also Matthew Frye Jacobson, *Special Sorrows: The Diasporic Imagination of Irish, Polish, and Jewish Immigrants in the United States* (Harvard University Press, 1995), 7, 220–21; and Jonathan Boyarin and Daniel Boyarin, *Powers of Diaspora: Two Essays on the Relevance of Jewish Culture* (University of Minnesota Press, 2002), 10–18.

41 David Lowenthal, *The Past Is a Foreign Country* (Cambridge University Press, 1985), xvi–xvii. Ab. Cahan, *Historye fun di fereynigte shtaaten* (Forverts, 1910), 1:108, 400. Cahan's description was affected by Joachim Heinrich Campe's adventure book, *Die Entdeckung von Amerika* (The Discovery of America, 1782)—see chapter 1. The news item with the "gorilla" mention is in *Forverts*, March 15, 1921, 1 (parentheses in the original). On Cahan's folksy and colloquial mixture of Americanism and socialism, see Moses Rischin, ed., *Grandma Never Lived in America: The New Journalism of Abraham Cahan* (Indiana University Press, 1985), xvii–xlii; Ribak, *Gentile New York*, 62, 82–83; Howe, *World of Our Fathers*, 537–43; Seth Lipsky, *The Rise of Abraham Cahan* (Nextbook/Schocken, 2013), 35–38, 100–101; and Estraikh, *Transatlantic Russian Jewishness*, 8–10, 98–105, 113–16.

42 On the changing attitudes toward "Yankees," the Irish, and other groups, see Ribak, *Gentile New York*. See also above.

43 The first quote is in Mendele Moykher Sforim, "Fishke der krumer," *Geklibene verk* (YKUF, 1947), 3:135. See also David Aberbach, *Realism, Caricature, and Bias:*

The Fiction of Mendele Mocher seforim (Littman Library of Jewish Civilization, 1993), 48–64 (the second quote is in Aberbach, 60).

44 The "Talented Tenth" was Black scholar and leader W. E. B. Du Bois's famous call (1903) to train a Black American elite—see Francesca R. Gentile, "Marketing the Talented Tenth: W. E. B. Du Bois and Public-Intellectual Economies," *Rhetoric Society Quarterly* 47 (2017): 131–57.

45 Yankev Magidov, *Der shpigl fun der ist sayd* (pub. by author, 1923), 28–29; and Dovid Shub, *Fun di amolike yorn: bletlekh zikhroynes* (Cyco, 1970), 349, 351–52. See also Roskies, *Bridge of Longing*, 93; and Tony Michels, "'Speaking to Moyshe': The Early Socialist Press and its Readers," *Jewish History* 14 (2000): 51–82.

46 Ayelet Brinn, *Revolution in Type: Gender and the Making of the American Yiddish Press* (New York University Press, 2023), 18–20, 208–9, 217–18; Nurit Orchan, *Yots'ot me-arba' 'amot: nashim kotvot ba-'itonut be-yidish ba-'imperyah ha-rusit* (Merkaz Zalman Shazar, 2013), 19–20, 24, 50–52; and Shmuel Werses, "Kol ha'isha ba'shevu'on be'yidish 'kol mevaser,'" *Khulyot* 4 (1997): 53–82. See also Judith R. Baskin, "*Women of the Word*: An Introduction," in *Women of the Word: Jewish Women and Jewish Writing*, ed. Judith R. Baskin (Wayne State University Press, 1994), 18–19; and Anita Norich, "Women in the Literary Canon and Classroom," *Conference Proceedings: Di Froyen: Women and Yiddish—Tribute to the Past, Directions for the Future* (National Council of Jewish Women, 1997), 69–72.

47 George M. Fredrickson, *The Black Image in the White Mind: The Debate on Afro-American Character and Destiny, 1817–1914* (Harper & Row, 1971), 250–54, 274–80; Sander L. Gilman, "Black Bodies, White Bodies: Toward an Iconography of Female Sexuality in Late Nineteenth-Century Art, Medicine, and Literature," in *"Race," Writing, and Difference*, ed. Henry Louis Gates, Jr. (University of Chicago Press, 1986), 223–61; Kali N. Gross, *Colored Amazons: Crime, Violence, and Black Women in the City of Brotherly Love, 1880–1910* (Duke University Press, 2006); Beverly Guy-Sheftall, *Daughters of Sorrow: Attitudes toward Black Women, 1880–1920* (Carlson, 1990); bell hooks, *Black Looks: Race and Representation* (Routledge, 2015), 61–77, 87–113; and Pieterse, *White on Black*. See also, Frantz Fanon, *Black Skin, White Masks* (1952, trans. Richard Philcox, repr. Grove Press, 2008), 138-144, 157.

48 The following is a partial list: a key study is by Matthew Frye Jacobson, *Whiteness of a Different Color: European Immigrants and the Alchemy of Race* (Harvard University Press, 1998). See also David R. Roediger, *The Wages of Whiteness: Race and the Making of the American Working Class* (Verso, 1991); Noel Ignatiev, *How the Irish Became White* (Routledge, 1995); Thomas A. Guglielmo, *White on Arrival: Italians, Race, Color, and Power in Chicago, 1890–1945* (Oxford University Press, 2003). Studies of Jewish immigrants from that perspective are Brodkin, *How Jews Became White Folks*; Melnick, *A Right to Sing the Blues*; and Rogin, *Blackface/White Noise*. For critique of Whiteness Studies, see Eric Arnesen, "Whiteness and the Historians' Imagination," *International Labor and Working-Class History* 60 (2001): 3–32; and Goldstein, *Price of Whiteness*, 4–5.

49 Eli Lederhendler, *Jewish Immigrants and American Capitalism, 1880–1920: From Caste to Class* (Cambridge University Press, 2009), 82–84.

50 Comprehensive studies of American Jews' racial status and attitudes toward race include Goldstein, *Price of Whiteness*; and Jacobson, *Whiteness of a Different Color*, 164–66, 171–87. See also Adam Zachary Newton, "Jews on America's Racial Map," in *The Cambridge History of Jewish American Literature*, ed. Hana Wirth-Nesher (Cambridge University Press, 2015), 505–24. The feuilleton appeared in *Yudishe gazeten*, Aug. 12, 1892, 12. See also chapter 3.

51 On cooperation between Jews and African Americans as a story of elites, see David Levering Lewis, "Parallels and Divergences: Assimilationist Strategies of Afro-American and Jewish Elites from 1910 to the Early 1930s," *Journal of American History* 71 (1984): 543–64; Goldstein, *Price of Whiteness*, 216–17; Hill, "Black-Jewish Conflict," 264–92; and Terrence L. Johnson and Jacques Berlinerblau, *Blacks and Jews in America: An Invitation to Dialogue* (Georgetown University Press, 2022), 122–23.

52 Miller and Goodall are quoted in Shankman, "Friend or Foe?," 107, 116. Booker T. Washington, *The Future of the American Negro*, Projekt Gutenberg, accessed April 27, 2023, https://www.gutenberg.org. Richard Wright, *Black Boy: A Record of Childhood and Youth* (1937; repr. Harper & Row, 1966), 70–71. See also Raboteau, "African-Americans, Exodus, and the American Israel," 57–63; and Louis R. Harlan, "Booker T. Washington's Discovery of Jews," in *Booker T. Washington in Perspective: Essays of Louis R. Harlan*, ed. Raymond W. Smock (University Press of Mississippi, 1988, reissued as non-paginated e-book, 2006). Interestingly and incidentally, Washington echoed Jewish conceptualization of lower-class Gentiles, dismissing non-Jewish European immigrants as "beggars, anarchists or superstitious peasants"—Washington is paraphrased by Shankman, "Friend or Foe?," 108.

53 On Bierfield, see "Double Lynching of a Jew and a Negro," in *A Documentary History of the Jews in the United States, 1654–1875*, ed. Morris U. Schappes (Citadel, 1950), 515–17. On Weinberg, see Shankman, "Friend or Foe?," 117–18. Ford's newspaper is quoted in Albert Lee, *Henry Ford and the Jews* (Stein and Day, 1980), 29. On the Nazi "Degenerate Music" exhibition, see Pamela M. Potter, *Art of Suppression: Confronting the Nazi Past in Histories of the Visual and Performing Arts* (University of California Press, 2016), 26–28. The white segregationist is quoted in Clive Webb, *Fight against Fear: Southern Jews and Black Civil Rights* (The University of Georgia Press, 2001), 50.

54 On "Eli, Eli," see chapter 4; and Edna Nahshon, ed., *New York's Yiddish Theater: From the Bowery to Broadway* (Columbia University Press, 2016), 69, 251. On Black performers and "Eli, Eli," see Melnick, *A Right to Sing the Blues*, 179–81, 259n50. Maya Angelou, *Singin' and Swingin' and Gettin' Merry Like Christmas* (Bantam, 1977), 18. On Black musicians and Yiddish as "jive," see Jonathan Z. S. Pollack, "'Ovoutie Slanguage Is Absolutely Kosher': Yiddish in Scat-Singing, Jazz Jargon, and Black Music," in *The Song Is Not the Same: Jews and American Popular Music*, ed. Bruce Zuckerman, Josh Kun, and Lisa Ansell (Purdue University Press,

2011), 71–87. See also Jonathan Karp, "Performing Black-Jewish Symbiosis: The 'Hassidic Chant' of Paul Robeson," *American Jewish History* 91 (2003): 53–81; and Stephen J. Whitfield, *In search of American Jewish culture* (University Press of New England, 1999), 145–60.

55 One can mention only a few studies that focus on historical racial stereotyping and popular culture and engage with some of the insights of critical race scholarship: Chude-Sokei, *The Last 'Darky'*; Lynn Abbott and Doug Seroff, *Ragged but Right: Black Traveling Shows, 'Coon Songs,' and the Dark Pathway to Blues and Jazz* (University Press of Mississippi, 2007); Brenda Dixon Gottschild, *Waltzing in the Dark: African American Vaudeville and Race Politics in the Swing Era* (Palgrave Macmillan, 2000); J. Stanley Lemons, "Black Stereotypes as Reflected in Popular Culture, 1880–1920," *American Quarterly* 29 (1977): 102–16. See also the classical study by Fredrickson, *Black Image in the White Mind*; and Mia Bay, *The White Image in the Black Mind: African-American Ideas about White People, 1830–1925* (Oxford University Press, 2000).

CHAPTER 1. "MOTHERS SELL THEIR LITTLE CHILDREN"

1 All dates are given according to the Gregorian calendar. *Kol mevaser*, April 27, 1871, 6–7; May 4, 1871, 7 (quotes are from this part); May 11, 1871: 6–7. Shpiegelthaler served as the paper's agent in Nikolayev. It seems that Shpiegelthaler wrote some parts of the text himself (the original author's name does not appear). This translation might have also used materials from E. Quaas, "Die Szuri's, die Kuli's und die Sclaven in Zanzibar," *Zeitschrift für Allgemeine Erdkunde* (Dietrich Reimer, 1860), 9:421–60; and from James Christie's report about the abysmal treatment of slaves in Zanzibar in "Notes on the Cholera Epidemics in East Africa," *The Lancet* (Jan. 28, 1871): 113–15; and (Feb. 11, 1871): 186–88. See also James Christie, "Slavery in Zanzibar as It Is," in *The East African Slave Trade*, ed. H. A. Fraser et al. (London: Harrison, 1871), 31–64. Other sources of influence were the books by popular Yiddish writer Ayzik Meyer Dik (discussed in this chapter). A comprehensive study of *Kol mevaser* is by E. R. Malachi, "Der *kol mevaser* un zayn redaktor," in *Der pinkes far forshung fun der yidisher literatur un prese*, ed. Shlomo Bikl (Altveltlekhen yidishn kultur kongress, 1965), 49–121. See also Alexander Orbach, *New Voices of Russian Jewry: A Study of the Russian-Jewish Press of Odessa in the Era of the Great Reforms, 1860–1871* (E. J. Brill, 1980), 54–71, 108–23.

2 The quotes are from Diner, *In the Almost*, 20–23, 236; and Alexander, *Jazz Age Jews*, 8, 181–82. Examples of such discourse are in Michael Lerner and Cornel West, *Jews and Blacks: Let the Healing Begin (G.P. Putnam's Sons, 1995)*; Lenora E. Berson, *The Negroes and the Jews* (Random House, 1971), 123–24; and Bornstein, *Colors of Zion*, 68–69. See also Dollinger, *Black Power, Jewish Politics*, 27–28; Forman, *Blacks in the Jewish Mind*, 10–13, 65–66; and Greenberg, *Troubling the Waters*, 4–5, 43–45. For a critique of such concepts, see Ribak, *Gentile New York*, 2, 188–89; Kenneth D. Wald, *The Foundations of American Jewish Liberalism* (Cambridge University Press, 2019), 31–40; Jonathan Krasner, "The Place of Tikkun

Olam in American Jewish Life," *Jewish Political Studies Review* 25 (2013): 59–98; and Eli Lederhendler, *American Jewry: A New History* (Cambridge University Press, 2017), 269–78.

3 On the Black population in Tsarist Russia, see Robert Fikes, "In the Land of Czars and Commissars: African Americans in Russia, the Soviet Union, and Post-Soviet Russia," Black Past, June 4, 2015, accessed August 2, 2021, https://www.blackpast.org/; and Blakely, *Russia and the Negro*, 13–49.

4 On the diet and hunger among East European Jews, as well as the famine in Lithuania (1867–1869) and the cholera epidemic in Poland (1869) as the beginning of substantial Jewish immigration from Eastern Europe to America, see Israel Bartal, *The Jews of Eastern Europe, 1772–1881* (trans. Chaya Naor, University of Pennsylvania Press, 2005), 122, 150–51; Louis Greenberg, *The Jews in Russia: The Struggle for Emancipation* (Yale University Press, 1944–1951) 1:160–61; and Salo W. Baron, *Steeled by Adversity: Essays and Addresses on American Jewish Life* (Jewish Publication Society, 1971), 276–77.

5 An excellent overview of the genres of premodern Yiddish literature is in David G. Roskies, "The Genres of Popular Yiddish Literature, 1790–1860," *Working Papers in Yiddish and East European Jewish Studies* 8 (1975): 1–30. On the question of Judaizing and narrative changes in translations into Yiddish, see Rebecca Wolpe, "Judaizing Robinson Crusoe: Maskilic Translations of *Robinson Crusoe*," *Jewish Culture and History* 13 (2012): 42–67. On Friday's racial identity in Jewish adaptations of *Robinson Crusoe*, see Iris Idelson-Shein, *Difference of a Different Kind: Jewish Constructions of Race during the Long Eighteenth Century* (University of Pennsylvania Press, 2014), 173-175.

6 See in chapter 2 below.

7 The prosecutor's quote is also in Justin Cammy, trans., "The Judgment of Shomer, or The Jury Trial of All of Shomer's Novels," *Arguing the Modern Jewish Canon*, 137–38. My translation is based on S. Niger, *Shalom aleichem: 'iyunim be-yetsirato* (1928; trans. Zvi Arad, Ha-kibuts ha-me'uchad, 1968), 11–12.

8 Dauber, *Worlds of Sholem Aleichem*, 99–106. On the question whether Tevye's quotations are actually misquotes, see Ken Frieden, *Classic Yiddish Fiction: Abramovitsh, Sholem Aleichem, and Peretz* (State University of New York Press, 1995), 165–66. See also Veidlinger, *Jewish Public Culture*, 70–73.

9 On the term Kushite and its application over time, see Goldenberg, *Black and Slave*, 7–11. On the historical debate about the interpretations of the "Curse of Ham" and the above verses from *Jeremiah*, *Amos*, and the *Song of Songs*, see David M. Goldenberg, *The Curse of Ham: Race and Slavery in Early Judaism, Christianity, and Islam* (Princeton University Press, 2003), 1–4, 22–25, 37–38, 79–82, 157–70, 198–200; Harper's disparaging statement about the Ethiopians is quoted in Goldenberg, *Curse of Ham*, 22. Goldenberg has discussed the centuries-long debate about why, though Ham sinned, Canaan was cursed, and demonstrates that many scholars have confused the myth of dark skin with the myth of slavery. See also Frank M. Snowden, Jr., *Before Color Prejudice: The Ancient View of*

Blacks (Harvard University Press, 1983), 80–108. Cf. Melamed, *Image of the Black*, 43–44, 56–57, 78–91, 179–85. See also Gene Rice, "Was Amos a Racist?" *Journal of Religious Thought* 35 (1978): 35–44; and Jill M. Munro, *Spikenard and Saffron: The Imagery of the Song of Songs* (Sheffield Academic Press, 1995), 37–38, 76.

10 The quotes are in David M. Goldenberg, "The Curse of Ham: A Case of Rabbinic Racism?," in Salzman and West, *Struggles in the Promised Land*, 31, 35. See also Bernard Lewis, *Race and Slavery in the Middle East: An Historical Inquiry* (Oxford University Press, 1990), 34–36, 51–53, 92, 101–2; and Harold David Brackman, "The Ebb and Flow of Conflict: A History of Black-Jewish Relations Through 1900" (PhD diss., University of California-Los Angeles, 1977), 88–93. An incomplete list of scholars who did such "ransacking" according to Goldenberg includes Thomas F. Gossett, *Race: The History of an Idea in America* (1963; 2nd edition Oxford University Press, 1997), 4–5; Robert Graves and Raphael Patai, *Hebrew Myths: The Book of Genesis* (1963; electronic edition RosettaBooks, 2014), 91–93; Winthrop D. Jordan, *White over Black: American Attitudes toward the Negro, 1550–1812* (1968; 2nd edition University of North Carolina Press, 2012), 18, 36–37; Edith Sanders, "The Hamitic Hypothesis; Its Origin and Functions in Time Perspective," *Journal of African History* 10 (1969): 521–32; St. Clair Drake, *Black Folk Here and There: An Essay in History and Anthropology* (Center for Afro-American Studies, University of California, 1990), 2:17–30; and Joseph R. Washington, *Anti-Blackness in English Religion, 1500–1800* (E. Mellen Press, 1984), 11, 15.

11 Rabbi Moses Ben-Maimon (Maimonides), *Moreh ha-nevochim*, 3:51, trans. to Hebrew Yosef Kafach (1970), accessed Sept. 10, 2021, http://www.daat.ac.il. See also Melamed, *Image of the Black*, 122–48. Jonathan Schorsch, *Jews and Blacks in the Early Modern World* (Cambridge University Press, 2004), 108–9, 133–34. A. D. Ogez, *Kitser moreh nevoykhim oder vos der 'moreh nevoykhim' lerent* (n.p., 1935), 7.

12 On the importance of the *Mikra'ot*, see Barry Levy, "Rabbinic Bibles, 'Mikra'ot Gedolot,' and Other Great Books," *Tradition; A Journal of Orthodox Jewish Thought* 25 (1991): 65–81. On the continued effect of the *Mikra'ot* on traditional Jews, see the novel by Chaim Potok, *In the Beginning* (Alfred A. Knopf, 1975), 271–84. See also Barry D. Walfish, "An Introduction to Medieval Jewish Biblical Interpretation," in *With Reverence for the Word; Medieval Scriptural Exegesis in Judaism, Christianity, and Islam*, ed. Jane Dammen McAuliffe, Barry D. Walfish, and Joseph W. Goering (Oxford University Press, 2003), 3–12.

13 The references to the verse from Amos in *Mikra'ot gedolot* and to the verse from Song of Songs are in https://www.mgketer.org, both accessed October 21, 2021. See also Melamed, *Image of the Black*, 45–46; Schorsch, *Jews and Blacks*, 20–21, 34–35; Goldenberg, *Black and Slave*, 112–14; and Goldenberg, *Curse of Ham*, 22–25, 48, 56.

14 One can mention only a few of the many studies of *Tsene-rene*: Chava Turniansky, "Iberzetsungen un baarbetungen fun der Tsene-rene," in *Sefer Dov Sadan: ḳovets mecḥkarim mugashim biml'ot lo shiv'im ve-cḥamesh shanah*, ed. Shmuel Werses, Natan Rotenstreich, Chone Shmeruk, et al. (ha-Ḳibuts ha-Me'uchad, 1977), 165–

90; Chone Shmeruk, *Sifrut yidish be-Polin: Meḥkarim ve-ʻiyunim historiyim* (Y. L. Magnes, 1981), 147–64; Morris M. Faierstein, "A Guide to the Ze'enah U-Re'enah: Correcting Some Misconceptions," *In geveb*, February 2019, http://ingeveb.org; Chava Weissler, *Voices of the Matriarchs: Listening to the Prayers of Early Modern Jewish Women* (Beacon Press, 1998), 38–44; and Dov-Ber Kerler, *The Origins of Modern Literary Yiddish* (Oxford University Press, 1999), 101–13.

15 The references to Amos are included in the *haftore* for the Torah portion "Acharei Mot," which is usually read around May, and page numbers sometimes correspond to the particular *haftore*. The said editions are: *Chamisha chumshey tora bi-leshon ʻashkenaz: tse'enah u-re'enah benot tsiyon be-ʻatarah* (Amsterdam: Chaim Druker, 1711), 96 (Hebrew pagination); *Chamisha chumshey tora bi-leshon ʻashkenaz: ʻim kol haftarot ve-chamesh megilot ve-tirgum le-megilot ʻasher yechuneh be-shem tse'enah u-re'enah* (Vilna and Grodno: The Partners, 1827), 22; *Tse'enah u-re'enah min chamisha chumshey tora* (Warsaw: Baumberg, 1849), 181 (Hebrew pagination); *Chamisha chumshey tora: ʻim kol haftarot ve-chamesh megilot ve-tirgum le-megilot bi-leshon ʻashkenaz ʻasher yechuneh be-shem tse'enah u-re'enah* (Warsaw: Gershon and Pesach Lebensohn, 1859), 142 (Hebrew pagination). For editions that did not include that quote, see *Chamisha chumshey tora ʻim kol haftarot ve-chamesh megilot: ve-tirgum le-megilot ʻasher yechuneh be-shem tse'enah u-re'enah* (Vilna: Yosef Reuven min Ram, 1865); and *Sefer tse'enah u-re'enah* (Vilna: Avraham Zvi Rosenkranz and Menachem Mendel Shriftzetser, 1895). Cf. *Tse'enah u-re'enah ʻim kol haftarot ve-chamesh megilot* (Lublin: Nechama Hershenhorn, Shloyme Shimen Shtreizberger, and Menachem Mendel Shnaydmeser, 1910), 224. Ibn Ezra's quote and doubts about its origin are in Melamed, *Image of the Black*, 175–76, 183. On ideologically motivated modern changes and omissions to *Tsenerene*, see Chava Turniansky, "Yayin chadash be-kankan yashan: Girsa'ot maskiliot shel ze'enah u-re'enah," in *Let the Old Make Way for the New: Studies in the Cultural and Social History of Eastern European Jewry, Presented to Emanuel Etkes*, ed. David Assaf and Ada Rapoport-Albert (Zalman Shazar Center, 2009), 2:313–44. On Yefet ben Eli, see Sivan Nir and Meyera Polliack, "'Many Beautiful Meanings Can Be Drawn from Such a Comparison': On the Medieval Interaction View of Biblical Metaphor," in *Exegesis and Poetry in Medieval Karaite and Rabbinic Texts*, ed. Joachim Yeshaya and Elisabeth Hollender (Brill, 2016), 40–79. See also Lewis, *Race and Slavery*, 52.

16 The quote is from the 1895 Vilna edition, 57. That quote is identical to the 1865 Vilna edition, 18. A similar reference appears in the 1910 Lublin edition, yet "kushim" is replaced by "Moors"—*Tse'enah u-re'enah*, 20. On Ham's sex in the ark and the term "narap" for Blacks, see Goldenberg, *Curse of Ham*, 102–4, 314n86. See also Stutchkov, *Oytser*, 168.

17 Rashi's text is in https://www.mgketer.org, accessed on October 21, 2021. The references to Moses's wife are included in the Torah portion of *Beha'alotkha*, *Chamisha chumshey tora* (Vilna & Grodno, 1827), 20; *Chamisha chumshey tora ʻim kol haftarot* (Zhitomir: Khonine Lipe and Yehoshua Shapiro, 1859), 234; *Chamisha* *chumshey tora* (Lemberg: P. Balaban, 1865), no pagination; *Chamisha chumshey tora* (Vilna, 1865), 238; *Chamisha chumshey tora tse'enah u-re'enah* (Warsaw: Tursha, 1890), page number illegible; *Sefer tse'enah u-re'enah* (Vilna, 1895), 150. The 1827 edition added the term "Moor" after Kushite, whereas the Lemberg and Warsaw editions added the term "Narap." On rabbinic sources' different interpretations of Numbers 12, see Goldenberg, *Curse of Ham*, 52–59. Cf. Melamed, *Image of the Black*, 115–20. On gypsies as thieves in Yiddish folklore, see Stutchkov, *Oytser*, 168. A positive attitude toward Romani is in the memoir of Romanian-born ethnographer, Konrad Bercovici, *It's the Gypsy in Me* (Prentice Hall, 1941).

18 Yosef Hayim Yerushalmi, *Haggadah and History: A Panorama in Facsimile of Five Centuries of the Printed Haggadah* (Jewish Publication Society of America, 1975), 61–62 and Plate 47. On the circulation of the Venetian Haggadah and its many reprints, see Diane Wolfthal, *Picturing Yiddish: Gender, Identity, and Memory in the Illustrated Yiddish Books of Renaissance Italy* (Brill, 2004), 207. Melamed, *Image of the Black*, 217–20. Chone Shmeruk, *Ha-'iyurim le-sifrei yidish ba-me'ot ha-16–17: ha-tekstim, ha-temunot ve-nima'aneyhem* (Akademon, 1986).

19 The text is taken from a bilingual (Old Yiddish original and Hebrew translation) edition, Ariela Krasni, trans., *Mayse bukh: sipurim 'u-ma'asiyot mi-masoret yehudei 'ashkenaz* (Bashaar, 2018), 1:290–93. See also the tale about the Black royal couple and their white baby, in Krasni, *Mayse bukh*, 2:500–501. Sara Zfatman, "Mayse bukh: kavim li-demuto shel zhaner be-sifrut yidish ha-yeshanah," *Ha-Sifrut* 28 (1979): 126–52. Claudia Rosenzweig, "'Getlekhe un Nisht Getlekhe Mayses': The 'Mayse-bukh' and Its Readership," *Jewish Studies Quarterly* 26 (2019): 203–23. A list of the tales is in Boris Kotlerman, "Mafteach shalem le-sipurei ha-'mayse bukh,'" *Chuliyot* 10 (2006): 291–328. Weissler, *Voices of the Matriarchs*, 37, 41–42. Tsinberg, *Di geshikhte*, 6:210–26.

20 Eldad's quote as well as a discussion of the various manuscripts of his writings are in Abraham Epstein, *Eldad ha-Dani* (Vienna: Ch. D. Lippe, 1891), xlviii–li, 23. On Eldad's book's dissemination among Yiddish readers, see Zalmen Reyzin, "Tsu der geshikhte fun der yidisher folks-literatur," *YIVO-bleter* 3 (1932): 252. Mendele Moykher Sforim, *Masoes benyomen ha-shlishi*, in *Geklibene verk* (YKUF, 1946) 2:168, 170. On the influence of such folklore, see Shmuel Werses, "Ha-'agadot 'al 'aseret ha-shevatim ve-darchey klitatan be-sifrutenu ha-chadasha," *Jerusalem Studies in Jewish Folklore* 9 (1986): 38–66. On the impact of Eldad's accounts on the way Europeans viewed Africa, see Tudor Parfitt, *Black Jews in Africa and the Americas* (Harvard University Press, 2013), 13–17. On Abramovitsh's portrayal of the synagogue backbenchers, see Miron, *Traveler Disguised*, 99–100, 131–35. See also Dan Miron and Anita Norich, "The Politics of Benjamin III: Intellectual Significance and Its Formal Correlatives in Sh. Y. Abramovitsh's 'Masoes Benyomin Hashlishi,'" in *The Field of Yiddish: Studies in Language, Folklore, and Literature*, ed. Marvin I. Herzog et al. (Institute for the Study of Human Issues, 1980), 4:1–115.

21 *Sefer masa'ot shel R. Binyamin zal*, annotated by Marcus N. Adler, https://www.hebrewbooks.org, 62 (Hebrew pagination), accessed July 3, 2022. On the geographical dimensions of Benjamin's travel in Africa, see François-Xavier Fauvelle-Aymar, "Desperately Seeking the Jewish Kingdom of Ethiopia: Benjamin of Tudela and the Horn of Africa (Twelfth Century)," *Speculum: A Journal of Medieval Studies* 88 (2013): 383–404; Martin Jacobs, "'A Day's Journey': Spatial Perceptions and Geographic Imagination in Benjamin of Tudela's 'Book of Travels,'" *Jewish Quarterly Review* 109 (2019): 203–232; and Melamed, *Image of the Black*, 154–58. On another legendary traveler, David Reubeni, who might have been Yemenite or Ethiopian, see Alan Verskin, ed. and trans., *Diary of a Black Jewish Messiah: The Sixteenth-Century Journey of David Reubeni through Africa, the Middle East, and Europe* (Stanford University Press, 2023).

22 On the spread of Benjamin's *Travels* and their translation to Yiddish, see Shlomo Berger, *Translation between Language and Culture: Benjamin of Tudela's Travels in Yiddish (Amsterdam 1691)* (Vossiuspers-University of Amsterdam, 2005), 5–22. J. J. Benjamin II, *Drei Jahre in Amerika, 1859–1862* (by the author, 1862), 1:91–92. In his introduction to the English translation, Oscar Handlin provides historical background about Benjamin's life, in Israel Joseph Benjamin, *Three Years in America* (1862; trans. from the German by Charles Reznikoff and repr. Jewish Publication Society, 1956), 1:1–36. Benjamin was much harsher in his depiction of American Indians and Chinese—see Ribak, *Gentile New York*, 36–37.

23 Benjamin II, *Drei Jahre*, 1:47. Mendele Moykher Sforim, *Masoes benyomen hashlishi*, in *Geklibene verk*, 2:161–62. On gender aspects in *Benjamin III*, see Seidman, *Marriage Made in Heaven*, 42–43, 53–56. See also Leo Wiener, *The History of Yiddish Literature in the Nineteenth Century* (Charles Scribner's Sons, 1899), 31, 159–60.

24 Shomer is quoted in Parush, *Reading Jewish Women*, 140. On chapbooks and the popularity of books such as *A Thousand and One Nights*, see Roskies, *Bridge of Longing*, 56–58. On the continued attraction of both religious and secular popular works among Yiddish readers throughout the nineteenth century, see Tsinberg, *Di geshikhte*, 8:191–92. See also the description of "four hundred monstrous women," who "were exceedingly black; they were the Devil's companions," in another Yiddish translation, the sixteenth-century *Vidvilt*, which was translated into Yiddish from a German medieval epic—see Jerold C. Frakes, ed. and trans., *Early Yiddish Epic* (Syracuse University Press, 2014), 181–84, 227.

25 The quotes are from an early 1900s translation to Yiddish—H. D. Nomberg, trans., *Toyzend un eyn nakht: shekherezade's mayselekh* (Yiddish Publishing, undated), 1:5–8, 30, 68–72 (quotes are on 70–71). That translation follows two heavily Germanized nineteenth-century Yiddish editions that came out in Warsaw and Lublin. On the portrayal of Blacks in *A Thousand and One Nights*, see Tarek Shamma, "Women and Slaves: Gender Politics in the *Arabian Nights*," *Marvels & Tales: Journal of Fairy-Tale Studies* 31 (2017): 239–60; and Ulrich Marzolph and Richard van Leeuwen, *The Arabian Nights Encyclopedia* (ABC-CLIO, 2004), 500. Interestingly, the references to the slave's lips and Blacks being more elevated than whites appeared in the English-language translation of *Arabian Nights*, but not

in the German translation by Gustav Weil (circa 1839–1842)—see https://www.projekt-gutenberg.org, accessed on November 14, 2021. On Nomberg, see Ruth R. Wisse, *I. L. Peretz and the Making of Modern Jewish Culture* (University of Washington Press, 1991), 37–40.

26 Avrom Ber Gotlober, *Zikhronot ʻu-masaʾaot*, ed. Reuben Goldberg (Bialik, 1976), 2:15–17. Z. Reyzin, "Campes 'Antdekung fun amerike' in yidish," *YIVO bleter* 5 (1933): 35–36. Zohar Shavit, "Literary Interference between German and Jewish Hebrew Children's Literature during the Enlightenment: The Case of Campe," *Poetics Today* 13 (1992): 41–61. Idelson-Shein, *Difference*, 154–56. David Brion Davis, *The Problem of Slavery in Western Culture* (1966; reissued Oxford University Press, 1988), 457–58.

27 Joachim Heinrich Campe, *Sämtliche Kinder und Jugendschriften: Entdeckung von Amerika* (Braunschweig: Schulbuchhandlung, 1807), 1:186, 298. Moses Mendelsohn-Frankfurt, *Metsiʾat ha-ʾarets ha-chadasha* (Altona: by the author, 1807), 108, 163–65. See also Rebecca Wolpe, "From Slavery to Freedom: Abolitionist Expressions in Maskilic Sea Adventures," *AJS Review* 36 (2012): 55–57. On Mendelsohn-Frankfurt and his translation of Campe, see Ken Frieden, *Travels in Translation: Sea Tales at the Source of Jewish Fiction* (Syracuse University Press, 2016), 139–72.

28 Khaykl Hurvits, *Sefer tsofnas paneyakh* (Berditshev: Israel B"k, 1817), 51 (Hebrew pagination). I used an edition from Lemberg (1857) that is nearly identical to Guenzburg's: *Tsofnas paneyakh hu' sefer kolumbus* (Lemberg: H. Zuker, 1857), 1:18th story (no pagination). Wolpe, "From Slavery," 57–58. Reyzin, "Campes 'Antdekung fun amerike,'" 29–40. S. Niger Charney, "America in the Works of I. M. Dick (1814–1893)," *YIVO Annual of Jewish Social Science* 9 (1954): 63.

29 Isaac Satanov is quoted in Schorsch, *Jews and Blacks*, 280. Helpful studies about such reasoning among maskilic abolitionists are Idelson-Shein, *Difference*, 85–89; and Wolpe, "From Slavery," 45–46. On Satanov, see Nancy Sinkoff, *Out of the Shtetl: Making Jews Modern in the Polish Borderlands* (2004; reissued Brown Judaic Studies, 2020), 38–39.

30 Ayzik Meyer Dik, *Di shklaveray oder di laybeygenshaft* (Vilna: Romm, 1868). Roskies, *Bridge of Longing*, 66–98. Parush, *Reading Jewish Women*, 144–50. On Dik's wide-ranging source material, see David G. Roskies, "An Annotated Bibliography of Ayzik-Meyer Dik," in Herzog, *Field of Yiddish*, 4:117–84.

31 Niger Charney, "America," 69. John MacKay, "The First Years of *Uncle Tom's Cabin* in Russia," in *Transatlantic Stowe*, ed. Denise Kohn, Sarah Meer, and Emily B. Todd (University of Iowa Press, 2006), 67–80. David Hecht, "Russian Intelligentsia and American Slavery," *Phylon* 9 (1948): 265–69.

32 The question to what extent 1881–1882 signaled a turning point is disputed by historians: see Jonathan Frankel, "The Crisis of 1881–82 as a Turning Point in Modern Jewish History," in *The Legacy of Jewish Migration: 1881 and Its Impact*, ed. David Berger (Brooklyn College Press, 1983), 9–22. Cf. Eli Lederhendler, *The Road to Modern Jewish Politics* (Oxford University Press, 1989), 146–53; Benjamin

Nathans, *Beyond the Pale: The Jewish Encounter with Late Imperial Russia* (University of California Press, 2002), 8–9; and Michael Stanislawski, *For Whom Do I Toil? Judah Leib Gordon and the Crisis of Russian Jewry* (Oxford University Press, 1988), 146–47.

33 Dik, *Shklaveray*, 3–4, 182, 184. Studies that deal with Dik's attitude toward slavery and Blacks in this book are Wolpe, "From Slavery," 60–70; and Eli Rosenblatt, "Enlightening the Skin: Travel, Racial Language, and Rabbinical Intertextuality in Modern Yiddish Literature" (PhD diss., Graduate Theological Union and the University of California-Berkeley, 2017), 1–47, 127–35. See also the annotated translation of Dik's introduction by Eli Rosenblatt, "Slavery or Serfdom," *In geveb*, November 2015, https://ingeveb.org. Jessica Kirzane, "Teaching Guide for Dik's 'Slavery or Serfdom' (trans. Rosenblatt)," *In geveb*, October 2016, https://ingeveb.org; and Rachel Rubinstein, "'Strange Rendering': *Uncle Tom's Cabin* in Yiddish and the Staging of Race at the Turn of the Twentieth Century," *American Jewish History* 101 (2017): 37–38.

34 I. M. Dik, *'Iyey hayam* (Romm, 1856), 11. Rebecca Wolpe has argued that Dik made "an uncharacteristically harsh comment about the black Africans" in this book, which does not repeat in any of his other writings, "From Slavery," 65. Mendelsohn-Frankfurt, *Metsi'at*, 108, 163–65. Another book, *A Wondrous Tale of the Unfortunate Aminodov*, might have been Dik's rendering (1847, reissued 1855) of an eighteenth-century story by German author Johann Jakob Dusch (via a Hebrew version). In that book, "Black savage people" (Shvartse vilde mentshn) chase the unfortunate protagonist and a European island dweller called Clorus, but the two manage to kill many of the assailants. The Black savages who live on a nearby island continue to wage wars against the two, until reinforcements help Clorus and Aminodov defeat them, capture many, and even civilize a few—*Eyn sheyne vunderlekhe historye fun dem umgliklekhn Aminodov* (Warsaw: Lebensohn, 1855), 17–21. On the controversy about whether Dik authored that book, see Zeev Gries, *The Book in the Jewish World, 1700–1900* (The Littman Library of Jewish Civilization, 2007), 167–69. Cf. Roskies, "Annotated Bibliography," 137.

35 Attributed to Ayzik Meir Dik, *Di vistenay zahara* (Vilna: Romm, 1868), 11–12, 14.

36 *Vistenay zahara*, 21–24, parentheses in the original for "plain," "un visend (prost)."

37 *Vistenay zahara*, 19–20, 26–27, 30, 35–36, 67. On sexualized descriptions of the Black body in nineteenth-century Western culture, see Gilman, "Black Bodies, White Bodies," 223–61; and Sieglinde Lemke, *Primitivist Modernism: Black Culture and the Origins of Transatlantic Modernism* (Oxford University Press, 1998), 97–102. On the imagery of Black men as cowards, see Darlene Clark Hine and Earnestine Jenkins, "Black Men's History: Toward a Gendered Perspective," in *A Question of Manhood: A Reader in U.S. Black Men's History and Masculinity*, ed. Darlene Clark Hine and Earnestine Jenkins (Indiana University Press, 1999), 1: 44, 47–48.

38 *Ha-tsefirah*, Sep. 16, 1875, 285–86; Sep. 22, 1875, 295; Sep. 28, 1875, 303–4; Oct. 5, 1875, 311. On that newspaper, see Ela Bauer, "Constructing the Shrine of Our

People's History": *Hatsefirah* and the Historiography of Polish Jewry," *Polin; Studies in Polish Jewry* 29 (2017): 41–60.

39 *Kol mevaser*, Oct. 23, 1862, 1. May 4, 1865, 237. *Ha-melits*, May 22, 1862, 492. Malachi, "Der *kol mevaser* un zayn redaktor," 64. Between 1869 and 1872, *Kol mevaser* came out as an independent publication, and in 1873 Tsederboym tried unsuccessfully to revive it.

40 Resser's article is in *Kol mevaser*, May 18, 1865, 275–78. It seems that Resser conceivably conflated the names of two German newspapers—*Die Illustrirte Zeitung* and *Über Land und Meer*, whose subtitle was *Allgemeine Illustrirte Zeitung*. On Resser, see Zalmen Reyzin, *Leksikon fun der yidisher literature, prese un filologye* (Kletzkin, 1929), 4:422–26. The other reference is in *Kol mevaser*, Sep. 1, 1870, 260. See also the dismay over the cruelty of slavery and white Southern behavior, *Kol mevaser*, Aug. 24, 1865, 475–76; June 27, 1872, 173–74. In 1879, Hebrew socialist poet Yehalel (Yehuda Leib Levin) compared the ruling elites' economic use of Jews in Russia to that of African Americans—quoted in Eliyahu Stern, *Jewish Materialism: The Intellectual Revolution of the 1870s* (Yale University Press, 2018), 161.

41 *Kol mevaser*, July 1, 1869, 171; July 15, 1869, 187. Vohliner should not be confused with Yiddish Journalist and critic A. Voliner (pen name of Eliezer Landoy), who was born later. On Yiddish adaptations of Verne's works, see chapter 5, and Nathan Cohen, *Yiddish Transformed: Reading Habits in the Russian Empire, 1860–1914* (Berghahn, 2023), 78–80, 88, 274–75. On matchmaking in traditional Jewish society, see Parush, *Reading Jewish Women*, 40–41, 46–56; and ChaeRan Y. Freeze, *Jewish Marriage and Divorce in Imperial Russia* (University Press of New England for Brandeis University Press, 2002).

42 *Ha-melits*, June 7, 1870, 153–54. Whereas Shaykevitsh claimed the story appeared in the *Times*, it is highly questionable whether he read English in his early twenties, and he might have written it himself—see Rose Shomer-Bachelis and Miriam Shomer-Zunser, *Undzer foter shomer* (IKUF, 1950), 38–40; and Grace-Pollack, "Reshito shel shomer be-yidish," 69–87. Such stories about West Africa filled English-language papers to an extent that makes it difficult to determine an exact source, which Shaykevitsh probably read in German. Similar stories appeared in *Times*, Dec. 2, 1867, 10; *The Israelite* (Cincinnati), May 17, 1867, 5; and *Philadelphia Inquirer*, July 25, 1867, 7. On Shomer's immense popularity and the debate over his literary deficiencies, see Justin Cammy, "Judging *The Judgment of Shomer*," 85–127; and Alyssa Quint, "'Yiddish Literature for the Masses?' A Reconsideration of Who Read What in Jewish Eastern Europe," *AJS Review* 29 (2005): 61–89.

43 Shomer, *Halb mentsh halb affe, oder vu zukht man dem emes? eyne vahre ertseylung* (Vilna: Romm, 1888), 6, 10, 18, 33 (all parentheses in the original). In the foreword, Shomer characteristically assured his readers that Fiktel was his acquaintance, and he "could show the documents" of the case to anyone interested. On wicked women in Shomer's work, see Parush, *Reading Jewish Women*, 152. On the circulation of racial concepts in Tsarist Russia, see Marina Mogilner, *A Race*

for the Future: Scientific Visions of Modern Russian Jewishness (Harvard University Press, 2022), 14–17.

44 Shomer, *Halb mentsh*, 8–10. On Shomer as the writer of "new reading women," see Parush, *Reading Jewish Women*, 150–51. On the influence of Social Darwinism and deterministic racism on the Jewish intelligentsia, see Yaacov Shavit and Jehuda Reinharz, *Darvin ve-kamah mi-bney mino: 'evolutsiah, geza', svivah ve-tarbut* (Ha-kibbutz ha-me'uchad, 2009), 103–52. Mitchell B. Hart, "Jews and Race: An Introductory Essay," in *Jews & Race: Writings on Identity and Difference*, ed. Mitchell B. Hart (Brandeis University Press, 2011), xvi–xviii. Black people were hardly the only group that was likened to apes—Asians and Irish shared that fate. Silvia Sebastiani, "A 'Monster with Human Visage': The Orangutan, Savagery, and the Borders of Humanity in the Global Enlightenment," *History of the Human Sciences* 32 (2019): 80–99. Bay, *White Image in the Black Mind*, 95, 134–35.

45 The estimated number of bookshops is in Jeffrey Brooks, *When Russia Learned to Read: Literacy and Popular Literature, 1861–1917* (Princeton University Press, 1985), 110. On bookshops and libraries among Jews in Russia, see Veidlinger, *Jewish Public Culture*, 24–113; Hagit Cohen, *Be-hanuto shel mokher ha-sefarim: ha-nuyot sefarim yehudiyot be-mizrah Eropah ba-maḥatsit ha-sheniyah shel ha-me'ah ha-tesha-'esreh* (Magnes, 2006), 24, 107–10, 145. On the marketing innovations, see in chapter 5 below. Cammy, "Judging *The Judgment of Shomer*," 85–127; Quint, "Yiddish Literature," 61–89; and Goldstein, "A Taste of Freedom," 108–9. Shomer's daughters mentioned commercial and familial reasons for his move to America—Shomer-Bachelis and Shomer-Zunser, *Undzer foter shomer*, 110–11.

46 Yoysef Sheynhak (Joseph B. Schönhak), *Sefer toldot ha-'arets: toldot ha-chayim* (Warsaw: Baumberg, 1841), 214 (Hebrew pagination, parentheses in the original). *Ha-tsefirah*, July 24, 1862, 196. Aaron David Bernstein, *Natur-visenshaftlikhe folks-bikher*, trans. to the Yiddish by A. Frumkin and M. Shapira (L. Friedman, 1910), 11:30–31. While a Hebrew translation of Bernstein came out in 1880, a Yiddish translation appeared in Warsaw in 1889—see Cohen, *Be-hanuto*, 101n30, 105. See also the books' advertisement in *Fraye arbeter shtime* (hereafter FAS), Jan. 20, 1906, 7. On the wide reputation of Bernstein's books among maskilim in Eastern Europe, see Dov Sadan, *Ka'arat egozim* (in the chapter "Moshav letsim"), Ben-Yehuda, accessed Dec. 22, 2021, https://benyehuda.org; and *MZ*, Sep. 23, 1909, 4. See also Idelson-Shein, *Difference*, 146.

47 Avrom Reyzin, ed., *Yudishe khrestomatiye: a leze bukh far shul un hoyz* (Progress, 1908), 32–33. Reyzin's poem appeared in *Forverts*, Dec. 29, 1917, 8. Scholars who discussed that poem referred to a later, redacted version—Bachman, *Recovering "Yiddishland,"* 160–62, 173; and Kirzane, "Yiddish Gaze," 130–34. On Reyzin's influence on later generations of Jewish socialists and communists, see the lecture by East German musicologist Inge Lammel, in Inge Lammel Collection, S 0135, Center for Popular Culture and Music, Albert Ludwig University of Freiburg (Germany), undated lecture (Hanover), box 5, folder "Vortrag Jiddische Lieder,"

7. See also Nathan Cohen, “No More ‘Little Jews without Beards’: Insights into Yiddish Children’s Literature in Eastern Europe Prior to World War I,” *Modern Judaism* 41 (2021): 92–109.

48 The story about Ibrahim is in *Ha-melits*, March 27, 1887: 649–50 (quotes in the original). A slightly different version appeared in G. Zelikovitsh, *Tsiyure-masa‘: reshimot masa‘ be-midbar ’erets kush* (Tushiyah, 1910), 41–44. The second piece is in *Ha-melits*, July 18, 1886, 836. The claim about Kitchener is quoted in Reyzin, *Leksikon*, 1:1105. On the Nile Expedition, see Edward M. Spiers, *The Victorian Soldier in Africa* (Manchester University Press, 2004), 112–31.

49 The first episode is in *Ha-melits*, Aug. 26, 1886, 1188–1190; and in Zelikovitsh, *Tsiyure-masa‘*, 21–23. In his imagery of the woman’s breasts, Zelikovitsh used the terminology of Song of Songs, 4:5, 8:6. The description of Karima and Halima is in *Ha-melits*, Oct. 28, 1887, 2393–2394; and in Zelikovitsh, *Tsiyure-masa‘*, 54–56. The third quote is in *Ha-melits*, July 18, 1886, 836. See also *Ha-magid*, March 25, 1886, 93–94. On Zelikovitsh’s writings as a woman and his gendered columns, see Brinn, *Revolution in Type*, 33–39, 118–28. On Zelikovitsh’s erotic novels, see Ze’ev Goldberg, “Getsil Zelikovitsh ve-sifrut ha-shund’: reshito shel ha-roman ha-balashi ve-haroman ha-’eroti be-yidish,” *’Alpayim* 19 (2000): 170–96. See also David Biale, *Eros and the Jews: From Biblical Israel to Contemporary America* (Basic Books, 1992), 160–61, 167–68.

50 On the success of American Yiddish writers in Eastern Europe, see Goldstein, “A Taste of Freedom,” 105–43. Hagit Cohen, “Sachar ha-sfarim ha-trans-‘atlanti, u-tsmichato shel merkaz tarbut ha-yidish be-‘artsot ha-brit, 1890–1939,” *‘Iyunim bi-tkumat yisrael* 20 (2010): 437–66.

51 *‘Ivry anokhi*, Feb. 12, 1875, 145 (Hebrew pagination). *Ha-magid*, May 12, 1880, 155. *Ha-magid*, Oct. 11, 1882, 316. On Montefiore and the Chalukah system in the Old Yishuv, see Abigail Green, “Rethinking Sir Moses Montefiore: Religion, Nationhood, and International Philanthropy in the Nineteenth Century,” *American Historical Review* 110 (2005): 631–58. On the debate among Jews in Russia whether to immigrate and if so, whither, see Frankel, “The Crisis of 1881–82,” 9–22; and Israel Klausner, *Be-hit’orer ’am* (Zionist Library, 1962), 105–42.

52 Sokolow wrote in *Ha-tsefirah*, Feb. 20, 1883, 45. An earlier and more derogatory portrayal of Black Africans by Sokolow appeared *Ha-tsefirah*, Jan. 10, 1877, 5–6 (translated from the Russian). On Sokolow, see Ela Bauer, “‘We Call Him Mister (Pan) Editor’: Nahum Sokolow and Modern Hebrew Literature,” *Studia Judaica* (Kraków) 18 (2015): 85–104. Elyashev wrote in *Der yud*, Feb. 21, 1901, 2. On Elyashev, see N. B. Minkov, *Zeks yidishe kritiker: aleksander tsderboym, y.y. lerner, y.h. ravnitski, yoel Entin, bal makhshoves, s. niger* (Yidbukh, 1954), 227–90. Ahad Ha’am, “Altneuland,” Ben-Yehuda, accessed Jan. 13, 2022, https://benyehuda.org. Levin wrote in *Ha-Zeman*, March 30, 1903, 7. On Levin, see Judah M. Bernstein, “A Preacher in Exile: Shemaryahu Levin and the Making of American Zionism, 1914–1919,” *American Jewish History* 102 (2018): 323–50. On the quarrel between Herzl, Ahad Ha’am, and their disciples, see Yossi Goldstein, “Eastern Jews vs.

Western Jews: The Ahad Ha'am—Herzl Dispute and Its Cultural and Social Implications," *Jewish History* 24 (2010): 355–77.

53 *Kol mevaser*, Nov. 3, 1864, 638. See also *Ha-yoy'ets le-bet yisroel be-rumenye*, March 14, 1888, 3; March 22, 1890, 2. *Der yud*, Sep. 26, 1901, 7. See also *Ha-tsefirah*, July 7, 1875, 7, where Eliahu Wolf Rabinovitsh argued Black Jews had "different facial features" from their Black neighbors. On Faitlovitch and his activity, see Emanuela Trevisan Semi, "The Ideology of 'Regeneration' and the 'Beta Israel' at the Beginning of the XXth Century," *REEH; Revue Européenne des Etudes Hébraïques* 2 (1997): 141–54; Rachel Baron-Bloch, "The Racial Politics of the Alliance Israélite Universelle," *Jewish Quarterly Review* 114 (2024): 109-140; and Parfitt, *Black Jews*, 85, 145–46. See also James Arthur Quirin, *The Evolution of the Ethiopian Jews: A History of the Beta Israel (Falasha) to 1920* (University of Pennsylvania Press, 1992), 11–15.

54 On the Saint Petersburg-based *Fraynd*'s beginning, character, popularity, and circulation, see Chaim Dov Hurvitz, "Unzer ershte teglikhe tsaytung," in *Der pinkes: yohrbukh far der geshikhte fun der yidisher literatur un shprakh, far folklor, kritik, un bibliografye*, ed. S. Niger (B. A. Kletskin, 1912–1913), 243–64. Sarah Abrevaya Stein, *Making Jews Modern: The Yiddish and Ladino Press in the Russian and Ottoman Empires* (Indiana University Press, 2004), 23–54, 85–122, 229n83. Veidlinger, *Jewish Public Culture*, 84, 99, 105–8. D. Druk, *Tsu der geshikhte der yudisher prese in rusland un poylen* (No publisher mentioned, 1920), 25–32.

55 *Fraynd*, Aug. 30, 1905, 2–3; Sep. 1, 1905, 2–3; Oct. 12, 1908, 3 (the feuilleton was unsigned). *Haynt*, Aug. 11, 1908, 1. On the disagreement between Faitlovitch and Nahum, see *Haynt*, Sep. 8, 1908, 1. On Subbotniks, see Nicholas Breyfogle, "The Religious World of Russian Sabbatarians (Subbotniki)," in *Holy Dissent: Jewish and Christian Mystics in Eastern Europe*, ed. Glenn Dynner (Wayne State University Press, 2011), 359–92. On *Haynt*, see Joanna Nalewajko-Kulikov, "'Who Has Not Wanted to Be an Editor?': The Yiddish Press in the Kingdom of Poland, 1905–1914," *Polin; Studies in Polish Jewry* 27 (2015): 273–304.

56 Shlomo Lambroza, "The Pogroms of 1903–1906," in *Pogroms: Anti-Jewish Violence in Modern Russian History*, ed. John D. Klier and Shlomo Lambroza (Cambridge University Press, 1992), 191–247. Monty Noam Penkower, "The Kishinev Pogrom of 1903: A Turning Point in Jewish History," *Modern Judaism* 24 (2004): 187–225. Steven J. Zipperstein, *Pogrom: Kishinev and the Tilt of History* (Liveright, 2018).

57 *Fraynd*, Aug. 30, 1903, 7–8, 11–12. See also, *Fraynd*, July 17, 1903, 1. On the depiction of America in that newspaper, see Ribak, *Gentile New York*, 45–47. On Lincoln's changing attitude toward African Americans and slavery, see Eric Foner, *The Fiery Trial: Abraham Lincoln and American Slavery* (W. W. Norton & Co., 2010). On the 1903 lynching and race riot in Delaware, see Yohuru R. Williams, "Permission to Hate: Delaware, Lynching, and the Culture of Violence in America," *Journal of Black Studies* 32 (2001): 3–29.

58 *Fraynd*, Aug. 29, 1904, 2; Sep. 27, 1904, 1; Aug. 7, 1905, 1. Aleksandrov's critique of Reconstruction governments is *Fraynd*, Sep. 2, 1904, 1. Aleksandrov was one of

the pioneers of Yiddishism in America—see Z. Reyzin, "Fun dem yivo-oytser," *YIVO bleter* 5 (1933): 137–51. On Washington's claims about literacy, see Rutledge M. Dennis, "The Situational Politics of Booker T. Washington," in *The Racial Politics of Booker T. Washington*, ed. Donald Cunnigen, Rutledge M. Dennis, and Myrtle Gonza Glascoe (Elsevier, 2006), 3–21.

59 Multatuli's text appeared in *Fraynd*, June 28, 1910: 2–3. Podruzhnik's article is *Fraynd*, June 20, 1913, 14–15. See also the comparison between pogroms in Russia and race riots in America, *Fraynd*, Aug. 23, 1908, 1. On Podruzhnik, see Reyzin, *Leksikon*, 2:842–45.

60 *Neue Freie Presse*, Sep. 11, 1910, 3. *Fraynd*, Sep. 12, 1910, part II, 2. On the *Neue Freie Presse*, see Steven Beller, *Vienna and the Jews, 1867–1938: A Cultural History* (Cambridge University Press, 1989), 38–45, 149–53, 196–200. See also Booker T. Washington, *My Larger Education: Being Chapters from My Experience* (Doubleday, Page, and Co., 1911), 239–61. On the American Yiddish press's celebration of Black leaders and achievements, see Diner, *In the Almost*, 50–62.

61 U. Katzenelenbogen, "I See a Colored Man for the First Time . . . ," *Opportunity: Journal of Negro Life* 6 (1928): 261–62. Though Katzenelenbogen does not provide an exact date, it seems the circus performance took place in the late 1890s, *Moment*, April 21, 1912, 3. Elias Newman, *William Wiener Oral History Library of the American Jewish Committee* (New York Public Library Dorot Division, hereafter NYPL), 18.

CHAPTER 2. THE NEGRO TOOK THE PLACE OF THE PEASANT

1 Peter Wiernik, "The Jew in Russia," in *The Russian Jew in the United States*, ed. Charles S. Bernheimer (John C. Winston Co., 1905), 21 (emphasis added). This article was written prior to the Kishinev pogrom (April 1903). Lesin wrote in *Tsukunft* (Jan. 1923): 2. On Wiernik's negative attitude toward all things Russian, see the memoir of a journalist who worked with him, Yankev Magidov, *Shpigl fun der ist sayd*, 42–44; and Joseph Hirsch, "Peter Wiernik and His Views" (DHL diss., Yeshiva University, 1974), 306, 312. On Lesin, see below and in Ribak, *Gentile New York*, 12, 62–63, 107–8, 163, 166, 169, 185.

2 See, for example, the distinction between the Polish lord, Ukrainian peasantry, and a Russian colonel in Mordkhe Spektor, *Mayn lebn* (Achisefer, 1927), 1:50–51, 67; 2:51–63; Chaim Zhitlovsky, *Zikhroynes fun mayn lebn* (Zhitlovsky's Jubilee Committee, 1935), 1:160–67; Israel Bartal, "Non-Jews and Gentile Society in East European Hebrew and Yiddish Literature 1856–1914," *Polin* 4 (1989): 53–69; Ewa Morawska, "Polish-Jewish Relations in America, 1880–1940: Old Elements, New Configurations," *Polin* 19 (2007): 71–86; Ewa Morawska, *Insecure Prosperity: Small-Town Jews in Industrial America, 1890–1940* (Princeton University Press, 1996), 15–17, 24–25, 40–44, 243–44; David G. Roskies, *Against the Apocalypse: Responses to Catastrophes in Modern Jewish Culture* (Harvard University Press, 1984), 163–72; David G. Roskies, *The Jewish Search for a Usable Past* (Indiana University Press, 1999), 45–46; Walter P.

Zenner, "Middlemen Minority Theories and the Jews: Historical Survey and Assessment," *Working Papers in Yiddish and East European Jewish Studies* 31 (1978): 1–30.

3 On American Jews and the concept of minority rights, see Fink, *Defending the Rights of Others*, 193–235; and Janowsky, *Jews and Minority Rights*, 264–309. On East European Jews' view of Blacks as potential allies, see Ribak, *Gentile New York*, 3–4, 184–87, 192–94. On the 1920s and their crop of bigotry, see Higham, *Strangers in the Land*, 264–99.

4 The most illuminating studies of East European Jewish folklore are in Yiddish. The quotes are from I. L. Cahan, *Der yid: vegn zikh un vegn andere in zayne shprikhverter un rednsortn* (YIVO, 1933), 25–32; Stutchkov, *Oytser*, 167–68; Yudl Mark, "A zamlung volksfarglaykhen," *Yidishe sprakh* 5 (1945): 99–140; and Amos Funkenstein, "The Dialectics of Assimilation," *Jewish Social Studies* 1 (1995): 1–13. See also B. Borokhov, "Di oyfgaben fun der yidisher filologye," in Niger, *Der pinkes*, 11; Dov Sadan, *Ka'arat tsimukim* (Mordecai Newman, 1952), 395–411; Ignatz Bernshteyn, *Yudishe shprikhverter un rednsarten* (1908; repr. Fourier, 1988), 53; and Chaim Schwartzboym, "Yisrael ve-'umot ha-'olam be-'aspaklariyat ha-folklor," *Yeda-'am* 15 (1971): 56–61.

5 The Israeli Folktale Archive (IFA) has many examples of such accounts. See the story by Fishl Sidr, in *Sipurey-'am me-borislav*, ed. Otto Schinzler (IFA, 1968), 23–27; and the story by Shmuel Zanvel Pipe, in *Sipurey-'am me-sanuk*, ed. Dov Noy (IFA, 1967), 20–21. See also story #2787 (IFA), told by a Galician Jew to Moshe Soyfer Federman; and story #5409 (IFA). See also the story by Dvora Fus in *Folktales of the Jews*, ed. Dan Ben-Amos (Jewish Publication Society, 2007), 2:229–230; S. An-ski, "Der yidisher folks-gayst un zayn shafung," in *Gezamlte shriftn* (Farlag An-ski, 1925), 15:23–24. Danusha V. Goska has conflated Jewish attitudes toward peasants with what she has termed "anti-Polonism" among Jews—*Bieganski: The Brute Polak Stereotype, Its Role in Polish-Jewish Relations and American Popular Culture* (Academic Studies Press, 2010), 57–65, 83–84.

6 Gotlober, *Zikhronot u-masa'aot*, 1:114–15. Avrom Lesin, *Geklibene verk: zikhroynes un bilder* (Cyco, 1954), 24. Singer, *Fun a velt*, 208. See also Meyer Kushner, *Lebn un kamf fun a kloakmakher* (published by a committee from local 9, International Ladies' Garment Workers Union, 1960), 56; Velvel Ze'ev Lefkovitsh, "Der mark zuntik," in *Bobroysk: yizker-bukh far bobroysker kehille un umgegent*, ed. Yehuda Slutsky (Tarbut ve-chinukh, 1967), 1:638–40. One can mention only a handful of similar recollections: Avrom Pinkhes Unger, *Mayn heymshtetl strykov* (Arbeter Ring, 1957), 49–50; Shneyer Yafe, *Epizodn fun mayn lebn* (pub. by the author, 1953), 24. Elizabeth Hasanovitz, *One of Them: Chapters from a Passionate Autobiography* (Houghton Mifflin, 1918), 4, 9.

7 Hirsh Abramovitsh, "Onvayzungen un bamerkungen," *Yidishe shprakh* 12 (1952): 122–23. Harkavy, *Yidish-english-hebreyisher verterbukh*, 365. See the negative portrayal of Polish and Lithuanian peasants aboard a ship to America, *Yudisher emigrant*, Jan. 28, 1909, 10. See also Avraham Drori, "Mukraya-Kaligurka," *He-'avar*

19 (1972): 231; Chaim Schwartzboym, "Yisrael ve-'umot ha-'olam be-'aspaklariyat ha-folklor," *Yeda-'am* 15 (1971): 56–61.

8 Cahan, *Der yid*, 25–32; Stutchkov, *Oytser*, 167–68; Israel Steinberg, *Mi-ma'ayan ha-khokhma shel am israel* (I. L. Peretz, 1962), 80–81. See also the piece by Hertz Ha-cohen Naymanovitz, *Varshoyer yudishe tsaytung*, May 3, 1867, 138.

9 Irving Chait, *Voices from Ellis Island* (Library of Congress), 116:8; Maurice Hindus, *Green Worlds: An Informal Chronicle* (Doubleday & Co., 1947), 70–71; Louis J. Horowitz and Boyden Sparkes, *The Towers of New York: The Memoirs of a Master Builder* (Simon and Schuster, 1937), 5–6. See also the memoir of Anna Rosenthal in *Di yidishe sotsyalistishe bavegung biz der grindung fun 'bund,'* ed. Elias Cherikover et al. (YIVO, 1939), 426; Morawska, "Polish-Jewish Relations," 75.

10 Reference to African Americans as the New-World incarnation of peasant folk is in Himmelfarb, "Negroes, Jews, and Muzhiks," 409–18. On immigrant Jews and their Black clientele, see Shankman, "Friend or Foe?," 105–23; Webb, "Jewish Merchants and Black Customers," 55–80; Davis, *Jews and Booze*, 122–27, 162–64; Hasia R. Diner, "Between Words and Deeds: Jews and Blacks in America, 1880–1935," in Salzman and West, *Struggles in the Promised Land*, 94–99; and Goldstein, *Price of Whiteness*, 76–79.

11 The quotes about Pearlman's adventures were told by his relatives some sixty years after his death—Louis Schmier, "'For Him the "Schwartzers" Couldn't Do Enough': A Jewish Peddler and His Black Customers Look at Each Other," *American Jewish History* 73 (1983): 45. Frieden's memoir was translated from Hebrew—Lee Shai Weissbach, ed. and trans., *A Jewish Life on Three Continents: The Memoir of Menachem Mendel Frieden* (Stanford University Press, 2013), 230. Sam Carasik, *American Jewish Autobiographies Collection* (YIVO) #173: 64. See also the account of Isaac Donin, who went to a barbershop run by a Black man upon his arrival in Galveston, Texas— *American Jewish Autobiographies Collection*, (YIVO), #100: 25. Hasia R. Diner, *Roads Taken: The Great Jewish Migrations to the New World and the Peddlers Who Forged the Way* (Yale University Press, 2015), 91, 102–3, 137.

12 Zvi Scharfstein, *'Arba'im shanah be-'amerika* (Masada, 1956), 50–51. Malka Li, *Durkh kindershe oygen* (Yidbukh, Geselshaft far veltlekhe shuln in argentine, 1955), 161. See also Brackman, "Ebb and Flow," 448–49.

13 Robert G. Weisbord and Arthur Stein, *Bittersweet Encounter: The Afro-American and the American Jew* (Negro Universities Press, 1970), xxiv; Seth M. Scheiner, *Negro Mecca: A History of the Negro in New York City, 1865–1920* (New York University Press, 1965), 121–25, 133. See also Gilbert Osofsky, *Harlem: The Making of a Ghetto* (Harper Torchbooks, 1968), 46–52.

14 Tsipin wrote in *Varhayt* (Truth), July 2, 1914, 4. Estimates of New York's Jewish and Black populations are in Walter Laidlaw, ed., *Population of the City of New York, 1890–1930* (Cities Census Committee, 1932), 243, 275, 289, 292; and The Official Website of the City of New York, www.nyc.gov (accessed on June 18, 2023). See also Marcy S. Sacks, *Before Harlem: The Black Experience in New York City before World War I* (University of Pennsylvania Press, 2006), 1, 76, 85; Arthur A.

Goren, *New York Jews and the Quest for Community: The Kehillah Experiment, 1908–1922* (Columbia University Press, 1970), 17–18. Kenneth Waltzer, "East European Jewish Detroit in the Early Twentieth Century," *Judaism* 49 (2000): 291–309; and Robert A. Rockaway, "The Detroit Jewish Ghetto before World War I," *Michigan History* 52 (1968): 28–36.

15 Hertzberg, *Strangers Within*, 187–88; the *Savannah Tribune* is quoted in Shankman, "Friend or Foe?," 111; Goldstein, *Price of Whiteness*, 76–78.

16 Ira Rosenwaike, *Population History of New York City* (Syracuse University Press, 1972), 85. Jeffrey S. Gurock, *When Harlem Was Jewish* (Columbia University Press, 1979), 50, 146–49, 166–68. Osofsky, *Harlem*, 70–127. Mary White Ovington, *Half a Man: The Status of the Negro in New York* (1911; repr. Schocken, 1969), 43–44.

17 Thomas Jesse Jones, *The Sociology of a New York City Block* (Columbia University Press, 1904), 23–24, 103, 106. Steven Bloom, "Interactions Between Blacks and Jews in New York City, 1900–1930, As Reflected in the Black Press" (PhD diss., New York University, 1973), 165–70. Scheiner, *Negro Mecca*, 30. The ad is in *YT*, Dec. 28, 1914, 6. See also Jeffrey S. Gurock, "Harlem's Jews and Blacks," *Jewish Digest* 24 (1978): 42–47. An excellent overview of the Jarmulowsky family is by Rebecca Kobrin, "Destructive Creators: Sender Jarmulowsky and Financial Failure in the Annals of American Jewish History," *American Jewish History* 97 (2013): 105–37.

18 Gurock, *Jews of Harlem*, 166–74. Irving Louis Horowitz, *Daydreams and Nightmares: Reflections on a Harlem Childhood* (University Press of Mississippi, 1990), 5. Irving Cutler, *The Jews of Chicago: From Shtetl to Suburb* (University of Illinois Press, 1996), 71, 98, 198–99. Philip P. Bregstone, *Chicago and Its Jews: A Cultural History* (pub. by the author, 1933), 180.

19 Isaac M. Rubinow, "Economic and Industrial Condition," in Bernheimer, *The Russian Jew*, 105 (quotes in the original). *Forverts*, Oct. 2, 1917, 4. Israel Goldstein, *My World as a Jew* (Cornwall Books, 1984), 1:25. His later quote is in Israel Goldstein, *William Wiener Oral History Library of the American Jewish Committee* (NYPL—Dorot), 37–38.

20 *Yidishe Velt*, Oct. 18, 1904, 1; Oct. 19, 1904, 4; *Forverts*, Sep. 9, 1904, 1; Oct. 20, 1904, 4; *YT*, Oct. 18, 1904, 1, 8; Oct. 19, 1904, 8 (Fromenson's quote is also from *YT*); Oct. 20, 1904, 8; Oct. 21, 1904, 8; See also *New York Times*, Oct. 24, 1904, 9; Selma C. Berrol, *Immigrants at School: New York City, 1898–1914* (1967; repr. Arno, 1978), 85–91; Diane Ravitch, *The Great School Wars: New York City, 1805–1973* (1974; repr. Basic, 1988), 176. On Fromenson's career, see *American Jewish Year Book* 5665 (1904/5): 99–100; and Jeffrey S. Gurock, *American Jewish Orthodoxy in Historical Perspective* (Ktav Publishing House, 1996), 181–99.

21 Harry Roskolenko, *The Time That Was Then: The Lower East Side 1900–1914, An Intimate Chronicle* (Dial, 1971), 13. Michael Gold, *Jews Without Money* (International Publishers, 1930), 174–75. "Incredulity" is in Roberta S. Gold, "The Black Jews of Harlem: Representation, Identity, and Race, 1920–1939," *American Quarterly* 55 (2003): 180. *WPA Federal Writers' Project* (New York Municipal Archives), reel #164, folder "Black Jews." See also Edward Wolf, "Negro 'Jews': A Social Study," *Jewish Social Service Quarterly* 9 (1933): 314–19; Jacob S. Dorman, *Chosen People: The Rise of American Black Israelite Religions* (Oxford University Press, 2013), 115, 121; and Howard Brotz, *The Black Jews of Harlem* (1964; repr. Schocken, 1970), 11–12.

22 Konrad Bercovici, "The Black Blocks of Manhattan," *Harper's Magazine*, Oct. 1, 1924: 613–14, 618. Gold, "Black Jews," 179–225 (quote from the *Sun* is on p. 179). See the relatively positive report about Harlem's Black Jews in *MZ*, Jan. 16, 1929, 6. See also Parfitt, *Black Jews*, 82–94; Bruce D. Haynes, *The Soul of Judaism: Jews of African Descent in America* (New York University Press, 2018), 77–80; and Goldstein, *Price of Whiteness*, 146–47. On the attitude toward Ethiopian Jews, see the American Jewish Committee, *Ninth Annual Report* (1916): 17–18; *Varhayt*, April 15, 1911, 6; May 13, 1911, 4–5.

23 Ovington, *Half a Man*, 163. Katz, *All Together Different*, 81–83 (Schlesinger's quote), 110–14, 145–46. Diner, *In the Almost*, 199–235. Nancy Joan Weiss, *The National Urban League, 1910–1940* (Oxford University Press, 1974), 53–54, 155.

24 Katz, *All Together Different*, 81–83. Diner, *In the Almost*, 210, 221, 224–29 (first quote from *Fortshrit*). Drobkin wrote in *Fortshrit*, Dec. 7, 1917, 8. On interethnic relations within Jewish-led unions and the Jewish labor movement, see Ribak, *Gentile New York*, 101–25, 146–47, 159, 182–83. See also Charles L. Lumpkins, *American Pogrom: The East St. Louis Race Riot and Black Politics* (Ohio University Press, 2008).

25 London's speech is in *Congressional Record*, 67th Congress, 2nd Session, 1365–66. The Yiddish news item that quoted London is in *Forverts*, Jan. 19, 1922, 1. On that speech, as well as on London's preference for English over Yiddish, see Gordon J. Goldberg, *Meyer London: A Biography of the Socialist New York Congressman, 1871–1926* (McFarland & Co., 2013), 44, 243. See also Harry Rogoff, *An East Side Epic: The Life and Work of Meyer London* (Vanguard, 1930), 249–50.

26 Revusky wrote in *Tsukunft* (April 1926): 190–94 (quotes in the original). On the different stages of his life in Russia, the Land of Israel, and the U.S., see Reyzin, *Leksikon*, 4:405–8. On Fort-Whiteman, see Joy Gleason Carew, *Blacks, Reds, and Russians: Sojourners in Search of the Soviet Promise* (Rutgers University Press, 2008), 32–33, 179–83.

27 Quotes with "Mr." are in Arnold Shankman, *Ambivalent Friends: Afro-Americans View the Immigrant* (Greenwood, 1982), 114. See also Arnold Shankman, "Friend or Foe?," 105–23. The storeowner's quote is in Webb, "Jewish Merchants," 66. The historian's quote is by Eli N. Evans, *The Provincials: A Personal History of Jews in the South* (1973; repr. University of North Carolina Press, 2005), 276. See also Stella Suberman, *The Jew Store* (Algonquin Books, 1998), 63. Jack Nusan Porter, "John Henry and Mr. Goldberg: The Relationship between Blacks and Jews," *Journal of Ethnic Studies* 7 (1979): 80–81.

28 Mark Twain, "Concerning the Jews," Internet History Sourcebooks Project, accessed Feb. 15, 2022, https://sourcebooks.fordham.edu. Schmier, "'For Him the

'Schwartzers,'" 47–49. Hertzberg, *Strangers Within*, 184–85. Goldstein, *Price of Whiteness*, 76–78. On the 1906 riot, see Davis, *Jews and Booze*, 122–27; Webb, "Jewish Merchants," 65; and Rebecca Burns, *Rage in the Gate City: The Story of the 1906 Atlanta Race Riot* (2006, rev. edition, University of Georgia Press, 2009).

29 Edwin Emerson Jr., "The New Ghetto," *Harper's Weekly*, Jan. 9, 1897, 44. The scholar is Brackman, "Ebb and Flow," 450. On Emerson's later career in the service of Nazi Germany, see Arnie Bernstein, *Swastika Nation: Fritz Kuhn and the Rise and Fall of the German-American Bund* (St. Martin's Press, 2013), 24–25.

30 Frieden's memories are in Weissbach, *A Jewish Life*, 227 ("niggars" originally in quotes), 230–31 ("black" originally in quotes), 233–34, 264–66. On Norfolk's Jewish community, see the *Encyclopedia of Southern Jewish Communities*, Goldring/Woldenburg Institute of Southern Jewish Life, accessed March 12, 2022, https://www.isjl.org. On similar attitudes by a Southern Jewish storeowner, see James McBride, *The Color of Water: A Black Man's Tribute to His White Mother* (Riverhead, 1996), 58–59.

31 Borekh Tsukerman, *Zikhroynes* (Yidisher kemfer, 1962), 1: 282–84. On customer peddlers, see Jacob Rader Marcus, *United States Jewry, 1776–1985* (Wayne State University Press, 1993), 4:263–64. On Tsukerman's journalistic and political career, see Rachel Rojanski, "The Rise and Fall of 'Die Zeit' (Di Tsayt): The Fate of an Encounter between Culture and Politics," *Jewish History* 14 (2000): 83–107.

32 Levin wrote in *Tog*, Oct. 11, 1916, 8 (emphasis in the original). *The Voice of the Negro* and Bowling are quoted in Shankman, "Friend or Foe," 122. See also the report of prominent Jewish anarchist Shoel Yanovsky, *FAS*, Feb. 3, 1928, 3. On the establishment of *Der tog*, see Khaykin, *Yidishe bleter*, 231–40; and Howe, *World of Our Fathers*, 545–49.

33 The reference to Savannah's police chief is in Vladeck, "Autobiography," quoted in Franklin Jonas, "The Early Life and Career of B. Charney Vladeck, 1886–1921: The Emergence of an Immigrant Spokesman" (PhD diss., New York University, 1972), 94. All the other quotes are in *Forverts*, March 22, 1911, 5 ("white" in quotes in the original). On Vladeck's prominence in the Jewish labor movement and Yiddish intelligentsia, see Yephim Yeshurun, ed., *B. vladeck in der opshatsung fun zayne fraynd* (Forverts Association, 1936).

34 Cahan, *Bleter fun mayn lebn*, 4:134 (cakewalk); 5:356–57; *Forverts*, March 22, 1914, 6. Leo Frank thanked Cahan for sending him copies of the *Forverts*; in a letter on March 31, 1914, Frank praised Cahan's reportage's "literary value, and attention to truthful detail," Papers of Abraham Cahan, RG 1139, series IV, box 5, folder 158 (YIVO). Melnick, *Black-Jewish Relations on Trial*, 35–38, 84–85. On the cakewalk, see Brooke Baldwin, "The Cakewalk: A Study in Stereotype and Reality," *Journal of Social History* 15 (1981): 205–18.

35 Cahan, *Bleter fun mayn lebn*, 5:356–57, 384–85, 389, 428, 430. See also Cahan's coverage of the Leo Frank trial in *Forverts*, March 22, 1914, 6; March 26, 1914, 6; April 2, 1914, 6. On Frank's innocence, see Oney, *And the Dead Shall Rise*, 132–37, 430–37, 612–13, 644–649; Dinnerstein, "The Fate of Leo Frank," 98–107; Melnick,

Black-Jewish Relations on Trial, 7; Albert S. Lindemann, *The Jew Accused: Three Anti-Semitic Affairs (Dreyfus, Beilis, Frank), 1894–1915* (Cambridge University Press, 1991), 254–57. Outside scholarly circles, some still believe that Frank was the culprit—their motives can be seen at Leo Frank Case Archive, accessed March 3, 2022, https://www.leofrank.org, a website which claims Jewish "Anti-Gentilism" is a problem in contemporary America.

36 Entin wrote in *Tog*, April 19, 1924, 11; April 20, 1924, 9 ("race problem" and "decadents" originally in quotes). Entin wrote under the pseudonym "a guest for a while." On Entin's literary and public career, see N. B. Minkoff, *Zeks yidishe kritiker*, 171–223.

37 Blum and Lesin wrote in *Tsukunft* (Oct. 1920): 576–79. Blum's later article appeared in *Tsukunft* (June 1921): 357–61. On the *Tsukunft*, see chapter 3.

38 Max (Mordecai Z.) Raisin, *Dapim me-pinkaso shel rabi* (Shulsinger, 1941), 151, 153–55. On Raisin's life and career, see Michael A. Meyer, "Two Anomalous Reform Rabbis: The Brothers Jacob and Max Raisin," *American Jewish Archives Journal* 68 (2016): 1–33; and Cipora O. Schwartz, *An American Jewish Odyssey: American Religious Freedom and the Nathan Barnert Memorial Temple* (Ktav, 2007), 47–57.

39 "Reminiscences of Jonah J. Goldstein" (Dec. 10, 1965), Columbia University Oral History Research Office Collection, 3: 600. Davis substituted for the Alliance's director, Dr. David Blaustein. On the Educational Alliance, see the minutes of a meeting of the Education Committee (Jan. 6, 1913), *Educational Alliance Papers* (YIVO), reel #266.3; *Alliance Review* (May 1901), 61–63; S. P. Rudens, "A Half-Century of Community Service: The Story of the New York Educational Alliance," *American Jewish Year Book* 46 (1944), 73–86; Howe, *World of Our Fathers*, 230–35; and Rischin, *Promised City*, 101–3.

40 Em Jo Basshe and Bernard Smith, "The Jew and the Negro," *The Reflex* 2 (April 1928): 78–81. S. M. Melamed, "The Wronged Negro," *The Reflex* 2 (May 1928): 58–59. On that monthly, see Charles A. Madison, *Jewish Publishing in America: The Impact of Jewish Writing on American Culture* (Sanhedrin Press, 1976), 226. On Melamed's wartime writings, see Ribak, *Gentile New York*, 136, 145. On his career in Yiddish and other languages, see Reyzin, *Leksikon*, 2:436–37. See also the quote by rabbi Julian Morgenstern in Jeffrey Gurock, "The 1913 New York State Civil Rights Act," *AJS Review* 1 (1976): 106–7.

41 The quote is from Lewis, "Parallels and Divergences," 547. Similar interpretations appear also in Diner, *In the Almost*, 3, 95–96. Friedman, *What Went Wrong*, 64–66. Forman, *Blacks in the Jewish Mind*, 10–11. Steven Cassedy, "The Question of Human Rights in American Yiddish journalism: The Example of *Di tsukunft*," in Estraikh and Krutikov, *Yiddish and the Left*, 10–14. Berson, *Negroes and the Jews*, 31. See also Greenberg, *Troubling the Waters*, 28, 45.

42 Levy quotes the lawyer and the Anglo-Jewish press, "'Is the Jew a White Man?,'" 212, 214, 219–22. Levy analyzes the responses of the African American newspapers, as does Bloom, "Interactions Between Blacks and Jews," 55–62. See chapter 3.

43 Higham, *Strangers in the Land*, 264–99. Gil Ribak, "'You Can't Recognize America': American Jewish Perceptions of Antisemitism as a Transnational Phenomenon after World War I," in *American Jewry: Transcending the European Experience?*, ed. Christian Wiese and Cornelia Wilhelm (Bloomsbury, 2017), 281–304. Neil Baldwin, *Henry Ford and the Jews: The Mass Production of Hate* (Public Affairs, 2001). Leo P. Ribufo, "Henry Ford and the International Jew," *American Jewish History* 69 (1980): 437–77. Heywood Broun and George Britt, *Christians Only: A Study in Prejudice* (Vanguard Press, 1931), 72–124, 203–45.

44 Isaac Babel, "17 September 1920: The Killers Must Be Finished Off," in *1920 Diary*, ed. Carol J. Evins, trans. H. T. Willetts (Yale University Press, 1995), 106. See M. Sadikov's account of the pogroms, *In yene teg* (n.p., 1926), 32–43. Committee of Jewish Delegates, *The Pogroms in the Ukraine Under the Ukrainian Government, 1917–1920* (John Bale, Sons & Danielson, 1927). Jeffrey Veidlinger, *In the Midst of Civilized Europe: The Pogroms of 1918–1921 and the Onset of the Holocaust* (Metropolitan Books, Henry Holt and Company, 2021).

45 On the relief efforts during and after World War I, see Daniel Soyer, *Jewish Immigrant Associations and American Identity in New York, 1880–1939* (1997; repr. Wayne State University, 2001), 161–89. On Jewish unions and civil rights activists, see Diner, *In the Almost*, 118–63, 199–235. Weiss, *National Urban League*, 53–54, 155.

46 Israel Bartal, "Ha-lo yehudim ve-chevratam be-sifrut ivrit ve-yidish be-mizrach eropa bein ha-shanim 1856–1914" (PhD diss., Hebrew University, Jerusalem, Israel, 1980), 4–5, 257–59; Morawska, "Polish-Jewish Relations," 71–86; Morawska, *Insecure Prosperity*, 15–17, 24–25, 40–44, 243–44; Roskies, *Jewish Search for a Usable Past*, 45–46; Ribak, *Gentile New York*, 12–27.

47 Claims about Jews who allegedly viewed African Americans as "America's Jews" are in Diner, *In the Almost*, 74–76; Sundquist, *Strangers in the Land*, 23–27; and Bornstein, *Colors of Zion*, 71–72, 126–27. See also, Katz, *Red, Black, and Jew*, 116-17, 139, 165.

CHAPTER 3. "THEY DESERVE ALL THE POLITICAL AND ECONOMIC RIGHTS"

1 *Folksadvokat*, Aug. 31, 1888, 6. On that weekly's success, see Khaykin, *Yidishe bleter*, 63. The author of those jokes was probably Getsil Zelikovitsh, who co-edited this weekly in those years, and published an identical joke under his name in *Yudishe gazeten*, Jan. 15, 1892, 7. *Tsukunft* (July 1928): 412–13 (emphasis in the original). On Pirozhnikov's career, see Reyzin, *Leksikon*, 2:905–8. On the history and character of the *Tsukunft*, see Zrubavl (Yankev Vitkin), "Etapn in der *Tsukunft*," *Tsukunft* (Nov.–Dec. 1962): 429–34; and Steven Cassedy, ed., *Building the Future: Jewish Immigrant Intellectuals and the Making of the Tsukunft* (Holmes & Meier, 1999), 1–20.

2 Arthur A. Goren, "The Jewish Press," in *The Ethnic Press in the United States: A Historical Analysis and Handbook*, ed. Sally M. Miller (Greenwood, 1987), 205–6, 216. Mordecai Soltes, *The Yiddish Press: An Americanizing Agency* (1925; repr. Arno & New York Times, 1969), 19–29. Michels, "Speaking to Moyshe," 51, 71n4.

3 Hutchins Hapgood, *The Spirit of the Ghetto* (1902; repr. Harvard University Press, 1967), 178. About Hapgood's background and views, see Sanders, *Downtown Jews*, 218–25. Robert E. Park, *The Immigrant Press and Its Control* (Harper & Brothers, 1922), 89. When circulation calculation is per capita, the Yiddish press surpassed any other foreign-language press already in 1910—see Goldberg, "Di yidishe prese," 129–44.

4 B. Gorin, *Di geshikhte fun yidishen teater* (Literarisher ferlag, 1918), 2:8–9. Goldstein, "A Taste of Freedom," 105–39. Howe, *World of Our Fathers*, 518–19, 529–30. Soltes, *Yiddish Press*, 15. Park, *Immigrant Press*, 97–99. Michels, "Speaking to Moyshe," 53, 73n14—Michels notes that there were varying levels of literacy in Yiddish, affected by generation, class, and gender.

5 The scholar is Diner, *In the Almost*, 31, 36–50, 74–76, 81 (the quotes are on pp. 31, 74, 81). See also Diner, "Between Words and Deeds," 87–106; Sundquist, *Strangers in the Land*, 17–30; Bornstein, *Colors of Zion*, 71–72, 126–27; Hertzberg, *Strangers Within*, 185–86. Friedman, *What Went Wrong*, 60. A more nuanced analysis is by Goldstein, *Price of Whiteness*, 80–81, 140–43, 153–54. Philip S. Foner has claimed (inaccurately) that the Yiddish press paid "little attention" to African Americans—"Black-Jewish Relations in the Opening Years of the Twentieth Century," *Phylon* 36 (1975): 362n18.

6 Diner, *In the Almost*, 35–88. Diner, "Drawn Together by Self-Interest," 27–39. Diner has also mentioned the sensationalism of covering crimes perpetrated by African Americans. Though helpful, many mistranslations and inaccuracies have marred Diner's analysis—in several cases (e.g., *In the Almost*, 51–52, 63), the primary sources' meaning is opposed to Diner's rendering.

7 On the convergence of those events in Jewish eyes, see Ribak, "You Can't Recognize," 281–304. Ribak, *Gentile New York*, 156–57, 184–85, 192–93. See also chapter 2.

8 *Folksadvokat*, Aug. 17, 1888, 3. On the rabbi's career, see Abraham J. Karp, "New York Chooses A Chief Rabbi," *Publications of the American Jewish Historical Society* 44 (1955): 129–98; and Jeffrey S. Gurock, *Orthodox Jews in America* (Indiana University Press, 2009), 113–18. Examples of Lefkowitz's advertisement are in *Yudishe gazeten*, March 3, 1893, 7; April 14, 1893, 10; June 30, 1893, 5; Aug. 4, 1893, 13; Sep. 15, 1893, 5; Oct. 13, 1893, 15. By Dec. 15, 1893, 8, the ad mentioned large size clothing that can fit the "largest man." See also, *Yudishe gazeten*, March 29, 1895, 20. On that weekly, see E. R. Malachi, "Der baginen fun der yidisher prese in amerike," in *Pinkes far der farshung fun der yidisher literatur un prese*, ed. Chaim Boaz (Congress for Jewish Culture, 1972), 253–93; Moyshe Shtarkman, "Di yidishe prese in amerike, 1875–1885," in *Zamlbuch lekhvod tsvei hundert un fuftsiksten yoyvl fun der yiddisher prese 1686–1936*, ed. Y. Shatski (Amopteyl fun yidishn visenshaftlekhn institut, 1937), 126–35; and Khaykin, *Yidishe bleter*, 53–58, 98.

9 The feuilleton is in *Yudishe gazeten*, Aug. 12, 1892, 12.

10 *Yudishe gazeten*, April 16, 1880, 5. *YT*, Aug. 16, 1900, 1, 4; *FAS*, Aug. 24, 1900, 6; *Forverts*, Aug. 17, 1900, 1. *YT*, Nov. 29, 1906, 4; Aug. 23, 1908, 4. On the 1900 race riot, see Sacks, *Before Harlem*, 39–42. On Tillman, see Stephen Kantrowitz, *Ben*

Tillman and the Reconstruction of White Supremacy (University of North Carolina Press, 2000).

11 *Forverts*, April 25, 1903, 4 (quotes in the original). *Yidishe velt*, July 7, 1903, 4. *FAS*, June 27, 1903, 1. On Miller's career, see Herts Burgin, *Di geshikhte fun der yidisher arbeter bavegung in amerike, rusland un england* (Fareynikte yidishe geverkshaftn, 1915), 143, 373–75, 394–97, 404–5, 642–45; and Manor, *Louis Miller*. See also Williams, "Permission to Hate," 3–29.

12 *Teglikher herold*, Oct. 19, 1894, 1; April 27, 1895, 1. *MZ*, April 22, 1906, 5. March 8, 1910, 5. See also *Varhayt*, Oct. 4, 1909, 1–2; May 24, 1911, 5. On the *Teglikher herold*, see Moyshe Shtarkman, "Vikhtikste momentn in der geshikhte fun der yidisher prese in amerike," in *75 yor yidishe prese in amerike, 1870–1945*, ed. Y. Glatshtein et al. (Y. L. Peretz shrayber farayn, 1945), 40–41; Khaykin, *Yidishe bleter*, 62–63, 172. A penetrating overview of the American press's reportage about lynching is by Richard M. Perloff, "The Press and Lynchings of African Americans," *Journal of Black Studies* 30 (2000): 315–30. On German-American newspapers in Philadelphia and lynching, see Russell A. Kazal, *Becoming Old-Stock: The Paradox of German-American Identity* (Princeton University Press, 2004), 115–18.

13 On Krants's views, see his book *Di kulturgeshikhte: der mensh un zayn arbayt* (A. M. Yevalenko, 1900), 1:291–92; 3:274–77; his article "Kristentum, mukhamad'nism, un tsivilizatsion," *Minikes' peysakh blat* 14 (1910): 41–44; *Forverts*, Sep. 18, 1917, 3; and the book *Gants amerika: di geshikhte fun ale lender in der nayer velt* (Educational Committee of Arbeter Ring, 1915), 1:69–70, 79–80. Cahan's article is in *Arbeter tsaytung*, March 7, 1890, 3. See also Rogin, *Blackface, White Noise*, 121–22. On *Arbeter tsaytung*, see Jonathan Frankel, *Prophecy and Politics: Socialism, Nationalism, and the Russian Jews, 1862–1917* (Cambridge University Press, 1981), 131–32, 465–67; and Michels, *Fire in Their Hearts*, 95–104.

14 *Arbeter tsaytung*, Oct. 6, 1901, 4. See also *Arbeter tsaytung*, Oct. 23, 1891, 2; Sep. 15, 1901, 4. *Forverts*, Feb. 26, 1901, 1; Feb. 27, 1901, 1; June 24, 1908, 8. See also *Abend tsaytung*, April 17, 1906, 1; *FAS*, Jan. 5, 1907, 1; *Yidishe arbeter velt*, Dec. 25, 1908, 2. On Ward's lynching, see Tim Crumrin, *Hidden History of Terre Haute* (History Press, 2020), 75–82. On the social effects of lynching, see Amy Louise Wood, "The Spectacle of Lynching: Rituals of White Supremacy in the Jim Crow South," *American Journal of Economics and Sociology* 77 (2018): 757–88.

15 *Forverts*, July 5, 1899, 1. *YT*, Oct. 29, 1909, 1. *MZ*, Oct. 29, 1909, 1. Nov. 26, 1909, 7. *Groyser kundes* (hereafter *GK*), March 27, 1914, 8. Isidore Buzet was a known actor on the Yiddish stage—see *Forverts*, Sep. 6, 1918, 3. Zalmen Zilbertsvayg, *Leksikon fun yidishn teater* (Elisheva, 1931), 1:147–48. In 1927, Buzet became a co-owner of the McKinley Square Theatre (Bronx), which then turned into a Yiddish theater—Museum of Family History, accessed July 28, 2022, http://www.museumoffamilyhistory.com. On the *Kundes*, see Khaykin, *Yidishe bleter*, 210–14. There are many studies about the historical development of the concept of Black criminality in U.S. history—see Khalil Gibran Muhammad, *The Condemnation of Blackness: Race, Crime, and the Making of Modern Urban America* (Harvard University

Press, 2010); and Rayford W. Logan, *The Betrayal of the Negro: From Rutherford B. Hayes to Woodrow Wilson* (Collier, 1965).

16 *Varhayt*, May 19, 1911, 1, 4. See also *Varhayt*, June 27, 1906, 8. *Forverts*, July 1, 1921, 4. See also *Forverts*, May 9, 1919, 5; Dec. 18, 1923, 2; Feb. 3, 1926, 1. Diner, *In the Almost*, 62–66. On the *Varhayt*, see Khaykin, *Yidishe bleter*, 175–95; Manor, *Louis Miller*.

17 "Crazy Niger shoots 2 people," *Forverts*, Oct. 11, 1911, 8; "Crazy Niger stabs 2 men," *YT*, Sep. 15, 1921, 7; "A wild Niger jumps from a corner with a revolver in his hand," *Forverts*, March 20, 1907, 10; "Wild Niger holds up in forest," *MZ*, June 3, 1913, 1; "A Niger kisses also the white bride," *Varhayt*, Sep. 22, 1907, 1. On American newspapers and Black crime, see Muhammad, *Condemnation of Blackness*, 26, 187, 221; Logan, *Betrayal of the Negro*, 165–68.

18 *MZ*, Dec. 30, 1906, 4. See also *New York Times*, Dec. 6, 1906, 5; Dec. 20, 1906, 5; John D. Weaver, *The Brownsville Raid* (W. W. Norton, 1970). *YT*, May 18, 1921, 1. See also, *YT*, Oct. 15, 1917, 8.

19 *Forverts*, Jan. 31, 1918, 3 (Botvinik wrote under the pen name "lead pencil"). Cf. Diner, *In the Almost*, 63, who mistranslated the sketch and therefore sees it just as a protest against the inequities of the justice system. Botvinik wrote a short sketch with a stoic character of a Black porter whom a white passenger abuses, yet the former remains passive—*Forverts*, May 22, 1920, 3. On Botvinik's portrayal of a Black character in a Yiddish stage production, as well as his own play, see the chapter about the Yiddish theater. See also a short skit by playwright Osip Dymov, which has a similar portrayal of a Black defendant, *Tog*, June 24, 1919, 5. On the concept of inherent criminality among Black women in press reports, see Gross, *Colored Amazons*; and Muhammad, *Condemnation of Blackness*, 1–10.

20 *Forverts*, Jan. 12, 1922, 3. See also A. Philip Randolph's periodical's editorial about Boddy, *The Messenger* (January 1922): 336–37. The news item with the "gorilla" mention is in *Forverts*, March 15, 1921, 1 (parentheses in the original). West, "On Black-Jewish Relations," 146. See the report on the 1921 suspect in the African American paper, *New York News*, in Fredrick G. Detweiler, *The Negro Press in the United States* (University of Chicago Press, 1922), 236–37.

21 *YT*, Aug. 30, 1907, 6. *MZ*, Sep. 23, 1909, 4. See also Will Irwin, "The American Saloon," *Collier's Weekly* (May 16, 1908): 10, who mentioned Lee Levy and Company of St. Louis, MO, as the maker "of a vile, obscenely labeled gin largely sold to negroes," which led them to violence and rape. Davis, *Jews and Booze*, 127–30. Denise Herd, "The Paradox of Temperance: Blacks and the Alcohol Question in Nineteenth-Century America," in *Drinking: Behavior and Belief in Modern History*, ed. Susanna Barrows and Robin Room (University of California Press, 1991), 354–75. Austin K. Kerr, *Organized for Prohibition: A New History of the Anti-Saloon League* (Yale University Press, 1985).

22 *MZ*, July 23, 1919, 1. The historian who wrote about "enthusiasm," "positive," and "heroic terms" is Diner, *In the Almost*, 51–52, who confused what the paper quoted and what was its position. *YT*, July 29, 1919, 1. July 28, 1919, 1 ("reds" in

quotes in the original). On the "Red Summer" of 1919 in Washington, D.C., see Cameron McWhirter, *Red Summer: The Summer of 1919 and the Awakening of Black America* (Henry Holt, 2011), 96–115. On Chicago, see Jonathan S. Coit, "'Our Changed Attitude': Armed Defense and the New Negro in the 1919 Chicago Race Riot," *Journal of the Gilded Age and Progressive Era* 11 (2012): 225–56.

23 *Forverts*, June 2, 1921, 9. *MZ*, June 2, 1921, 1. The latter daily equated medieval Jewish ghettos with the Black section of Tulsa. *YT*, June 2, 1921, 1. June 3, 1921, 1. Kesner's column appeared *YT*, June 5, 1921, 6. The historian is Uri Schreter, "'The Most Awful Scenes': The Tulsa Massacre and Racist Violence in the Yiddish Press," *In Geveb*, June 25, 2021, https://ingeveb.org. On white rioters shooting at the firefighters and that charges against Rowland were subsequently dropped, see Randy Krehbiel, *Tulsa 1921: Reporting a Massacre* (University of Oklahoma Press, 2019), 50, 200, 237.

24 *Forverts*, Aug. 18, 1915, 4. *Bronzvil*, Aug. 20, 1915, 2. *GK*, Aug. 20, 1915, 3 (Marinov); Aug. 27, 1915, 3 (cartoon). See also *Naye velt*, Aug. 20, 1915, 1; and *Tog*, Jan. 19, 1915, 4. Avrom Lesin thought the lynching made Jews and Blacks "comrades in misfortune," but only in "certain aspects"—*Tsukunft* (Sep. 1915): 792. See also Ribak, *Gentile New York*, 129–30. Cf. Cassedy, "Question of Human Rights," 11–12. On Leon Israel's work, see Matthew Baigell, *Social Concerns and Left Politics in Jewish American Art, 1880–1940* (Syracuse University Press, 2015), 20–21, 28–29, 53–54, 100–103, 212; Lauren B. Strauss, "Images with Teeth: The Political Influence of Artwork in American Yiddish Periodicals, 1910s-1930s," in Shapiro, *Yiddish in America*, 28–45; and Edward A. Portnoy, "The Creation of a Jewish Cartoon Space in the New York and Warsaw Yiddish Press, 1884–1939" (PhD diss., Jewish Theological Seminary of America, 2008), chapter 3.

25 *Moment*, March 16, 1914, 3. *Frayhayt*, Oct. 3, 1923, 1. One can mention only a fraction of Yiddish dailies' references to Conley's race—*Varhayt*, Feb. 24, 1914, 1; April 9, 1914, 1; June 3, 1914, 1; Oct. 5, 1914, 1. *MZ*, March 15, 1914, 1; March 16, 1914, 5; Oct. 4, 1914, 2. *YT*, Feb. 24, 1914, 1; March 2, 1914, 1; June 30, 1915, 1. *Forverts*, Feb. 24, 1914, 1; Oct. 1, 1914, 1. The *Forverts* reported on an earlier case in Georgia, where a Jewish peddler was accused (yet acquitted) of a crime that a Black man purportedly committed—Aug. 24, 1915, 4. On those and other of Cahan's quotes, see chapter 2, and in Cahan, *Bleter fun mayn lebn*, 5:356–57, 384–85, 389, 428, 430; *Forverts*, March 26, 1914, 6. April 2, 1914, 6. Melnick, *Black-Jewish Relations on Trial*, 61–62, 111–12.

26 For examples of the weekly's rebuke of white racism, see *FAS*, Aug. 24, 1900, 6; June 27, 1903, 1; Feb. 9, 1907, 4; July 9, 1910, 4–5; July 14, 1917, 5. The article by "Dril." is in *FAS*, Sep. 18, 1915, 2, 6. On Yanovsky and the *Fraye arbeter shtime*, see Reyzin, *Leksikon*, 1:1219–24; Khaykin, *Yidishe bleter*, 255–60; Anna Elena Torres, *Horizons Blossom, Borders Vanish: Anarchism and Yiddish Literature* (Yale University Press, 2024), 16, 22, 30, 35, 48-49, 131-33, 232–34; and Paul Avrich, *Anarchist Portraits* (Princeton University press, 1988), 187–99.

27 The Quotes are in Diner, *In the Almost*, 74–76. Similar arguments are made in Sundquist, *Strangers in the Land*, 23–27; Roediger, *Working toward Whiteness*, 98; Bornstein, *Colors of Zion*, 71–72, 126–27; and Alexander, *Jazz Age Jews*, 8, 147, 176–77, 181–82.

28 *YT*, April 25, 1900, 4. In 1911, Zolotkoff became the editor of the *Yidishes tageblat*. On his career, see Niger, *Leksikon*, 3:525–27.

29 *Forverts*, Nov. 26, 1903, 4 (emphasis in the original). On Fornberg, see Ribak, *Gentile New York*, 95–96, 109, 136, 174; and Moshe Shtarkman, "Di tsukunft 1892–1942," *Tsukunft* (May–June 1942): 267–68.

30 *Forverts*, June 16, 1904, 4 (quotes in the original). On the press coverage of the Elias affair, see J. A. Rogers, *Sex and Race: A History of White, Negro, and Indian Miscegenation in the Two Americas* (1942; repr. Helga M. Rogers, 1970), 2:380–88. See also the article in *Der arbeter* (The Worker), July 30, 1910, 4–5, where M. Landa praised African American achievements, but argued that white workers in the North do not treat Blacks worse than they treat Italian or Slavic immigrants.

31 *Varhayt*, Sep. 24, 1906, 4. When using the term "Niger," it is in quotes in the original. See also, Lambroza, "Pogroms of 1903–1906," 191–247.

32 *Dos folk*, Jan. 15, 1908, 11. On Syrkin's brand of Zionism, see Borekh Tsukerman, *Afn veg* (Yidisher kemfer, 1956), 59–118; and Frankel, *Prophecy and Politics*, 288–328. Vortsman wrote in *Tog*, July 19, 1917, 5. On Vortsman, see Reyzin, *Leksikon*, 1:915–17.

33 Tsivyen wrote in *Forverts*, May 2, 1917, 3 (Liberia in quotes in the original). See his description of Southern Blacks in *Di naye velt*, May 21, 1920, 15. On Tsivyen and fellow Bundists' views on Zionism in that period, see Estraikh, *Transatlantic Russian Jewishness*, 65–67. On *lehavdl* language, see Weinreich, *History of the Yiddish Language*, 193–94. On Brandeis and the rise of American Zionism in those years, see Ben Halpern, "Brandeis Becomes a Zionist," *Modern Judaism* 6 (1986): 227–43; and Melvin I. Urofsky, *American Zionism from Herzl to the Holocaust* (Anchor, 1975), chapters 4–6.

34 *Tog*, April 12, 1917, 5. Peretz Hirshbeyn, *Felker un lender: rayse-ayndrukn fun nayzeland, avstralye, dorem-afrike, 1920–1922* (B. Kletskin, 1929), 98, 127, 129. Hirshbeyn returned to the South in the 1940s and interviewed local Blacks—see *Neger in di dorem-shtatn*, undated manuscript in Papers of Peretz Hirschbein, RG 833, folder 110 (YIVO). On Hirshbeyn's travel writings, see Mariusz Kałczewiak, "Anticolonial Orientalism: Perets Hirshbeyn's Indian Travelogue," *In Geveb*, July 8, 2019, https://ingeveb.org.

35 Zaks wrote in *Tog*, Oct. 7, 1919, 8; July 14, 1919, 4. See also chapter 2 for Meyer London's reference to African Americans; and Ch. Sher's analysis of the "Pogroms against the Negroes in America," *Tsukunft* (Sep. 1919): 543–46, where he argued, "the man has awakened in the Negro." See also another article by Sher, *Tsukunft* (June 1919), 360–62. On Zaks in that period, see Herman Frank, *A. S. Zaks: Kemfer far folks-oyflebung* (A. S. Zaks Gezelshaft, 1945), 230–38.

36 *Forverts*, March 27, 1928, 6. On that ditty, see Kristina DuRocher, *Raising Racists: The Socialization of White Children in the Jim Crow South* (University Press of Kentucky, 2011), 78–79.

37 *Forverts*, July 4, 1926, 10; May 27, 1928, 13. On the Jewish obsession with public imagery, see Gil Ribak, "'The Jew Usually Left Those Crimes to Esau': The Jewish Responses to Accusations about Jewish Criminality in New York, 1908–1913," *AJS Review* 38 (2014): 1–28; Lila Corwin Berman, *Speaking of Jews: Rabbis, Intellectuals, and the Creation of an American Public Identity* (University of California Press, 2009), 168–73; and Diner, *In the Almost*, 64–65. On Rogoff's career in the *Forverts*, see Khaykin, *Yidishe bleter*, 200–201, 269, 347, 349. On the Harlem Renaissance and the New Negro movement, see George Hutchinson, *The Harlem Renaissance in Black and White* (The Belknap Press of Harvard University Press, 1995); and David Levering Lewis, *When Harlem Was in Vogue* (Alfred A. Knopf, 1981).

38 Fromenson's article and quotes from *The Modern View* appeared in *YT*, May 11, 1906, 8. On the *Modern View*, see Walter Ehrlich, *Zion in the Valley: The Jewish Community of St. Louis, Vol. I, 1807–1907* (University of Missouri Press, 1997), 244–45, 391–92. The editorial was published in *YT*, March 21, 1906, 6. The editorial probably referred to (and misquoted) a 1906 article by Washington—see Louis R. Harlan and Raymond Smock, eds., *The Booker T. Washington Papers: Volumes 1 through 14 Complete* (University of Illinois Press, 1979; digital edition, 2014) 8:551. *Yidisher rekord*, Aug. 30, 1912, 4. See also the joke about Reform Judaism that used Washington's blackness, in the Orthodox monthly *Yidisher vekhter* (The Jewish Guard), May 1, 1912, 58.

39 Moyshe Kats's eulogy for Washington is in *Tog*, Nov. 18, 1915, 4. *MZ*, Nov. 16, 1915, 4. Khaykin's comparison that favored Du Bois's strategy over Garvey's is in *Tog*, Nov. 25, 1921, 4. There are numerous examples of lionization of Black successes—see Benyomen Faygnboym's eulogy to Booker T. Washington, *Tsukunft* (Dec. 1915): 1088–91. See also praise for Black advancements in *Forverts*, Sep. 17, 1917, 3; and *MZ*, Aug. 10, 1920, 4. Cf. Diner, *In the Almost*, 50–62.

40 "Negro Moses" is in *Forverts*, Feb. 3, 1925, 1. Goldberg wrote in *Tog*, Feb. 6, 1925, 4. Critic Mordkhe Danzis defended Garvey's vision, *YT*, Aug. 7, 1922, 4. See the positive description of Garvey and his followers in the Zionist Hebrew weekly *Ha-Doar* (The Post), August 22, 1924, 2. On Garvey's anti-Jewish outburst against the judge and district attorney as "damned dirty Jews" after he was found guilty (1923), see Colin Grant, *Negro with a Hat: The Rise and Fall of Marcus Garvey* (Oxford University Press, 2008), 371–72. Diner, *In the Almost*, 54–55, 64, 76.

41 Kremer's story was published in the *Forverts*, May 22, 1919, 3. He noted that there were workers of other nationalities who joined the Jews and "even Polish workers." On Kremer's career see Reyzin, *Leksikon*, 3:787. See also the sketch in *Forverts*, June 29, 1919, 2 about a Black homeless man who is abused by white train workers. Brainin wrote in *YT*, Dec. 21, 1920, 4. On Black Yiddish-speakers, see in *Der kibitser* (The Joker), Dec. 26, 1913, 5. On that theme in *Forverts*'s "Yente

Telebende" sketches by humorist B. Kovner (pen name of Yankev Adler), and in theater productions based on that character, see below and in chapter 4. On Yiddish-speaking Gentiles in Eastern Europe and the 1919 mass protests in New York, see Ribak, *Gentile New York*, 18, 169–70.

42 Lesin wrote in *Tsukunft* (Oct. 1920): 579. *MZ*, Aug. 10, 1920, 4. See also the article by Abe Goldberg, *Yidishe folk*, Nov. 21, 1919, 3; and Ribak, *Gentile New York*, 156–57, 180–87.

43 *Tog*, June 4, 1920, 7 (the report was signed by "E. P-N). *YT*, Aug. 4, 1920, 4. *Forverts*, April 15, 1923, 4. April 22, 1923, 9 ("intellectuals" and "enlighten the people" in quotes in the original). See also, *FAS*, July 6, 1923, 5. On the context of Russian populism, see Mark Kiel, "The Jewish Narodnik," *Judaism* 19 (1970): 295–310. On Randolph and Jewish organizations, see Paula F. Pfeffer, *A. Philip Randolph, Pioneer of the Civil Rights Movement* (Louisiana State University Press, 1990), 11, 91–92, 109–10, 209, 229–31, 234, 293–94; and Katz, *All Together Different*, 80–82, 111–12.

44 *Frayhayt* used "Niger" when describing a Black prisoner, identified only as "Freeman," who claimed Jim Conley gave him a woman's handbag that might have been Mary Phagan's—Oct. 3, 1923, 1. Lilliput's articles are in *Frayhayt*, May 19, 1922, 5; April 19, 1923, 5. See also William Gropper's cartoon against racism in the response to the Mississippi Delta floods of 1927 and 1929, *Morgn frayhayt*, March 20, 1929, 8, quoted in Strauss, "Images with Teeth," 49–51. On the communist Yiddish press in the U.S., see Gennady Estraikh, "The Yiddish-Language Communist Press," in *Dark Times, Dire Decisions: Jews and Communism*, ed. Jonathan Frankel and Dan Diner (Oxford University Press, 2004), 68–72; and Matthew Hoffman, "The Red Divide: The Conflict between Communists and Their Opponents in the American Yiddish Press," *American Jewish History* 96 (2010): 1–31. On Olgin and the public trials, see Melech Epstein, *The Jew and Communism: The Story of Early Communist Victories and Ultimate Defeats in the Jewish Community, U. S. A., 1919–1941* (Trade Union Sponsoring Committee, 1959), 245–47, 384. On Blacks and Jews in the Communist Party, see Mark I. Solomon, *The Cry Was Unity: Communists and African Americans, 1917–36* (University Press of Mississippi, 1998), 12–13, 96, 101, 107–8, 138, 282. On *Shuffle Along*, see David Krasner, *A Beautiful Pageant: African American Theater, Drama, and Performance in the Harlem Renaissance, 1910–1927* (Palgrave Macmillan, 2002), 239–88.

45 *Hamer* (Sep. 1926): 3; (Dec. 1926): 63–64. The poems by Hughes and others are *Hamer* (Oct. 1928): 16–19. See the poems by Li and Faynberg, *Hamer* (June 1927): 18; (Sep. 1928): 12–13. On the *Hamer*, see Henry Felix Srebrnik, *Dreams of Nationhood: American Jewish Communists and the Soviet Birobidzhan Project, 1924–1951* (Academic Studies Press, 2010), 2–3, 7.

46 *Frayhayt*, April 13, 1923, 6; April 14, 1923, 8. *Forverts*, March 16, 1919, 3. Civil rights leader and journalist Ida B. Wells commented on the "elevator cage" that many Black workers occupied—Wells is quoted in Karen Sotiropoulos, *Staging Race: Black Performers in Turn of the Century America* (Harvard University Press,

2006), 28. On the ubiquity of Black elevator operators, see James R. Grossman, *Land of Hope: Chicago, Black Southerners, and the Great Migration* (The University of Chicago Press, 1989), 128, 141.

47 The teaser ads are in *Forverts*, Nov. 17–21, 1919, 2. Other Aunt Jemima ads are *Forverts*, Jan. 14, 1920, 2; Dec. 11, 1920, 12; Oct. 12, 1926, 2; Nov. 12, 1929, 7. *GK*, April 18, 1919, 16. FLIT ad is in *Forverts*, Sep. 6, 1927, 2; the soap ad is *Forverts*, Nov. 6, 1927, 21. *MZ*, Jan. 17, 1929, 3 (Cantor); Jan. 24, 1929, 9 (Jolson). Ayzman's sketch is in *Tog*, Oct. 28, 1927, 8 (quotes in the original). Goldstein, *Price of Whiteness*, 140–43 (also refers to the ads with Cantor and Jolson). A nuanced analysis of Cantor's use of blackface without a "dialect" and specific clothing as a way of Judaizing the character is in David Weinstein, *The Eddie Cantor Story: A Jewish Life in Performance and Politics* (Brandeis University Press, 2018), 22–30. See also Brian D. Behnken and Gregory D. Smithers, *Racism in American Popular Media: From Aunt Jemima to the Frito Bandito* (Praeger, 2015), 23–32, 35–36; Kerri P. Steinberg, *Jewish Mad Men: Advertising and the Design of the American Jewish Experience* (Rutgers University Press, 2015), 60-61; and M. M. Manring, *Slave in a Box: The Strange Career of Aunt Jemima* (University Press of Virginia, 1998).

48 One version for Adler's pen name is that the *Forverts*'s longtime editor, Abraham Cahan, joked by giving a Galitsyaner such as Adler the name of a Litvak/Lithuanian Jew (Kovno/Kaunas). According to another version, Cahan wanted to erase Adler's real name, under which he previously ridiculed the *Forverts* when working at satirical Yiddish newspapers. Henry D. Spalding, ed., *A Treasure-Trove of American Jewish Humor* (1976; rev. edition Jonathan David Publishers, 1978), 82; Khaykin, *Yidishe bleter*, 192; Reyzin, *Leksikon*, 1:42–43.

49 On the meaning of Yente's name, see Harkavy, *Yidish-english-hebreyisher verterbukh*, 106, 255, 528. Henry Sapoznik, *Klezmer! Jewish Music from Old World to Our World* (Schirmer Trade Books, 1999), 84–85.

50 The earlier skit is in *Forverts*, Sep. 20, 1919, 3. The second is *Forverts*, Jan. 17, 1920, 10 (quotes in the original). On Yente's success among Jewish audiences, see the numerous letters and memoirs in Papers of Jacob Adler (B. Kovner), RG 473, (YIVO), folders 23 and 27. See also Gil Ribak, "My Mom Drank Ink: The 'Little Negro' and the Performance of Race in Yente Telebende's Stage Productions," *In Geveb*, April 2023, https://ingeveb.org.

51 On the imagery of the *sheygets* in Yiddish folklore, see Stutchkov, *Oytser*, 168, 619–20, 668; Mark, "A zamlung volksfarglaykhen," 99–140; and Ribak, *Gentile New York*, 17. On the relationship with *shkotsim*, see Singer, *Fun a velt*, 38, 48–50, 72, 179, 205–24; Yafe, *Epizodn fun mayn lebn*, 24, 26–27; and Morris Rosenfeld, "Mayn shoten un ikh," *Shriftn fun Morris Rosenfeld* (Literarishn ferlag, 1908), 3: 70–76. At certain contexts, *sheygets* could also be a term of endearment. On the Black kid as a "pickaninny" in the stage production of *Yente*, see chapter 4.

52 Condemnations of lynching and white racism (an incomplete list) are in *GK*, July 13, 1917, 1; July 30, 1919, 3, 8; May 6, 1921, 4 (Congo); Feb. 13, 1925, 9. On the *Kundes* and its circulation, see Aaron Rubinstein, "Devils & Pranksters: *Der groyser* *kundes* and the Lower East Side," *Pakn treger* 47 (2005): 17–20; Khaykin, *Yidishe bleter*, 210–14; and Strauss, "Images with Teeth," 24–45. Already in 1908, the satirical magazine *Der kibitzer* spoofed whites' idea of civilization and barbarism—see the cartoon in Goldstein, *Price of Whiteness*, 80.

53 *GK*, April 7, 1916, 11; June 29, 1917, 12; April 2, 1920, 12; Aug. 13, 1926, 7. On the prevalence of cannibal jokes in mass culture, see Curtis Keim and Carolyn Somerville, *Mistaking Africa: Misconceptions and Inventions* (1999; 5th ed., Routledge, 2022), 113–14; and Jennifer Brown, *Cannibalism in Literature and Film* (Palgrave Macmillan, 2013).

54 An overview of this subject is in Ribak, *Gentile New York*, 13–20. See op. cit. in chapter 2 above.

55 *GK*, Sep. 26, 1919, 14; Nov. 24, 1922, 5. See also the joke about the "Black philosopher," *GK*, May 6, 1921, 6.

56 "How they played and danced" cartoon is in *GK*, Dec. 25, 1925, 7. The "Summer tragedy" cartoon is in *GK*, Aug. 6, 1926, 12. On those who saw jazz music and modern dancing as "jungle music," see Kathy J. Ogren, *The Jazz Revolution: Twenties America & the Meaning of Jazz* (Oxford University Press, 1989), 153–59; and Kurt Gartner, "Musicians and Entertainment," in *Jazz Age: People and Perspectives*, ed. Mitchell Newton-Matza (ABC-Clio, 2009), 93–107.

57 *Forverts*, March 11, 1910, 5. *Varhayt*, Oct. 29, 1918, 5. *MZ*, June 7, 1921, 1. On Tulsa and the "Curious Reporter," see Schreter, "'The Most Awful Scenes.'"

58 *Varhayt*, Jan. 27, 1911, 5 (quotes in the original). Hermalin's article is *Varhayt*, Jan. 22, 1911, 4. On Hermalin and his views, see the chapter on Yiddish literature below.

59 *FAS*, July 20, 1918, 6. Other examples for Rosen's writing about Anglo-Saxons and Slavs are *FAS*, Nov. 8, 1913, 5; June 22, 1918, 2. On Rosen's career, see Reyzin, *Leksikon*, 4:100.

60 Diner, *In the Almost*, 28–31, 89, 236–37. Diner, "Drawn Together by Self-Interest," 27–39.

61 A discussion of that theme is in Ribak, "Negroes Must Not Be Likened to Jews," 271–96; Hertzberg, *Strangers Within*, 191; and Himmelfarb, "Negroes, Jews, and Muzhiks," 409–18.

62 On *mentshlekhe bahandlung*, see Nancy L. Green, *The Pletzl of Paris: Jewish Immigrant Workers in the "Belle Epoque"* (Holmes & Meier, 1986), 132–33, 146; Susan A. Glenn, *Daughters of the Shtetl: Life and Labor in the Immigrant Generation* (Cornell University Press, 1990), 174–75; and Howe, *World of Our Fathers*, 645.

CHAPTER 4. "MY MOM DRANK INK"

1 See my article "My Mom Drank Ink." The quotes are in Y. Adler/B. Kovner, "Yente telebende: a komedy in 4 akten" (undated), 21–22, Papers of Jacob Adler (B. Kovner), RG 473, (YIVO), folder 72. In that copy, the names of Joseph Rumshinsky (composer) and Louis Gilrod (lyricist) are not mentioned. See also Joseph Rumshinsky, Louis Gilrod, and Isidore Lillian, "Yente telebende: vashington,

lincoln un moyshe rabeiny and arayn geganen sich aus gedreit" (Hebrew Publishing Co., 1916), notated music (the text is Latinized in this sheet). Retrieved from the Library of Congress,, Music Division, Heskes Collection, box 10–708, accessed Sept. 20, 2022, https://www.loc.gov. On Gilrod's career, see the article by Zalmen Zilbertsvayg, *Forverts*, March 14, 1930, 3, 8. I am grateful to Gary P. Zola, who sent me a copy of the Library of Congress's sheet. On that song, see Gary Phillip Zola, ed., *We Called Him Rabbi Abraham: Lincoln and American Jewry, A Documentary History* (Southern Illinois University Press, 2014), 294–96. Mar wrote in *Tsukunft* (Dec. 1925): 715.

2 *Litvakes* are Lithuanian Jews, whom Yiddish folklore describes as dry, skeptical, and rationalist; *Galitsyaners* are Jews from a Habsburg province in today's Southeast Poland/West Ukraine, who are depicted as emotional, superstitious, and even as swindlers. Examples of that folklore are in Ignaz Bernstein, *Jüdische Sprichwörter und Redensarten* (1908; repr. Fourier, 1988), 141–42; Stutchkov, *Oytser*, 165; Yishaya Zlotnik, *Khumesh-folklor ale folkstimlikhe diburim, glaykhvertlekh, halatsos, anekdoten un folkstaytshen vas betseyhen zikh oyfen humash* (Polonia, 1937), 9, 31; Moshe Kopstein, *Dos folk un zayn oytser* (Shalom, 1979), 30, 33, 48. See also Michael Wex, *Born to Kvetch: Yiddish Language and Culture in All of Its Modes* (Harper Perennial, 2006), 56–57; and Rachel Manekin, "Galitsianer," The YIVO Encyclopedia of Jews in Eastern Europe, accessed Aug. 30, 2022, https://yivoencyclopedia.org/.

3 Gorin, *Geshikhte*, 1:21–27, 150–203. A. Mukdoyni, *Teater* (A. Mukdoyni Yubilei-Komitet 1927), 26–33. Communal leaders pressured Yiddish actors not to tarnish Jewish reputation in America—see the memoir of stage star Boris Tomashevsky, *Mayn lebns-geshikhte* (Trio, 1937), 76–78. Nina Warnke, "The Child Who Wouldn't Grow Up: Yiddish Theater and Its Critics," in *Yiddish Theater: New Approaches*, ed. Joel Berkowitz (Littman, 2003), 201–16. Faina Burko, "The American Yiddish Theater and Its Audience Before World War I," in Berger, *Legacy of Jewish Migration*, 85–96. David S. Lifson, *The Yiddish Theater in America* (Thomas Yoseloff, 1965), 44–51. Hapgood, *Spirit of the Ghetto*, 118–35. On the use of Germanized Yiddish on stage, see Leon Kobrin, *Mayne fuftsik yor in amerike* (YKUF, 1966), 264–66.

4 Mark Slobin, "From Vilna to Vaudeville: Minikes and 'Among the Indians' (1895)," *The Drama Review: TDR* 24 (Sep. 1980): 18. Elsewhere Slobin argued, "The black character himself is a rare visitor within the Yiddish theater," *Tenement Songs*, 51. See also Paul Klapper, "The Yiddish Music Hall," *University Settlement Studies Quarterly* 2 (Dec. 1906): 19–23. On the commercialization and lowbrow character of the Yiddish theater in America, see Joel Berkowitz, "This Is Not Europe, You Know: The Counter-Maskilic Impulse of American Yiddish Drama," in Shapiro, *Yiddish in America*, 135–65.

5 One can mention only a fraction of the literature about the portrayal of African Americans in American popular culture in the nineteenth and early twentieth centuries. W. Fitzhugh Brundage, "Working in the 'Kingdom of Culture': African

Americans and American Popular Culture, 1890–1930," in *Beyond Blackface: African Americans and the Creation of American Popular Culture*, ed. W. Fitzhugh Brundage (University of North Carolina Press, 2011), 1–42. Dale Cockrell, "On Soundscapes and Blackface: From Fools to Foster," in *Burnt Cork: Traditions and Legacies of Blackface Minstrelsy*, ed. Stephen Johnson (University of Massachusetts Press, 2012), 55–59. M. Alison Kibler, *Censoring Racial Ridicule: Irish, Jewish, and African American Struggles over Race and Representation, 1890–1930* (University of North Carolina Press, 2015), 23, 28, 131–33. Eric Lott, *Love and Theft: Blackface Minstrelsy and the American Working Class* (1993; 2nd edition, Oxford University Press, 2013). Fredrickson, *Black Image in the White Mind*, 53–58, 102–28, 275–91. Robert C. Toll, *Blacking Up: The Minstrel Show in Nineteenth Century America* (Oxford University Press, 1974). On the role of Jews in the reproduction of such images as performers and managers, see Pamela Brown Lavitt, "First of the Red Hot Mamas: 'Coon Shouting' and the Jewish Ziegfeld Girl," *American Jewish History* 87 (1999): 253–90. Melnick, *A Right to Sing the Blues*, 103–14. Rogin, *Blackface/White Noise*, 5–6, 16–17, 67–70. On the imagery of the peasantry in Yiddish folklore, see op. cit.

6 The first quote is in Goldstein, *Price of Whiteness*, 79. Goldstein based his assertion on the findings of Fred Somkin, "Zion's Harp by the East River: Jewish-American Popular Songs in Columbus's Golden Land, 1890–1914," *Perspectives in American History*, New Series, 2 (1985): 189n18. The quote about *Yente* is in Diner, *In the Almost*, 67–68.

7 The lyrics appeared in *Kol mevaser*, Dec. 10, 1868, 350. On that play, see Gorin, *Geshikhte*, 1:151. Alyssa Quint, "The Botched Kiss and the Beginning of the Yiddish Stage," in *Culture Front: Representing Jews in Eastern Europe*, ed. Benjamin Nathans and Gabriella Safran (University of Pennsylvania Press, 2008), 79–102. On Mogulesko's role, see Zilbertsvayg, *Leksikon*, 1:291. On Kotzebue's play, see Christopher B. Balme, *Pacific Performances: Theatricality and Cross-Cultural Encounter in the South Seas* (Palgrave Macmillan, 2007), 14, 62–66. In her book, Alyssa Quint has criticized the notion of Goldfaden as the "father of the Yiddish theater," *The Rise of the Modern Yiddish Theater* (Indiana University Press, 2019), 40–41. See also Wiener, *History of Yiddish Literature*, 236.

8 The quotes are from Avrum Goldfaden, *Shulamis, oder bas-yerushalayim* (New York: Hebrew Publishing Company, undated), 9, 41–42. Goldfaden's letter is quoted in Y. Shatsky, "Avrum goldfaden un zayn teater," *Tsukunft* (March 1926): 157. On *Shulamis* and *Bar Kochba*, as well as on critics' view of Goldfaden, see Seth L. Wolitz, "*Shulamis* and *Bar Kokhba*: Renewed Jewish Role Models in Goldfaden and Halkin," and Mirosława M. Bułat, "From Goldfaden to Goldfaden in Cracow's Jewish Theaters," both in Berkowitz, *Yiddish Theater*, 87–104, 139–55. Tsingitang's name possibly derives from "tongue." Alyssa Quint has interpreted Tsingitang as Avsholem's "undisciplined id," *Rise of the Modern Yiddish Theater*, 167.

9 Avrum Goldfaden, *Bar Kokhba, oder di letste teg fun yerushalayim* (Warsaw: Y. Alapin, 1887), 25, 27. Part of Kalish's memoir appeared in *Tog*, May 13, 1925: 5. On

Kalish's memoir, see Nina Warnke, "Thomashefsky, Kalich, and Adler: Female Self-Enactment in Memoirs," in *Women on the Yiddish Stage*, ed. Alyssa Quint and Amanda Miryem-Khaye Seigel (Legenda, 2023), 10–14, 28–35. On productions in the 1930s, see Wolitz, "*Shulamis* and *Bar Kokhba*," 87–104; and Bułat, "From Goldfaden to Goldfaden," 151–54. One critic in Krakow even assailed (1939) *Shulamis* for the "utterly grotesque emphasis on the . . . black equal rights movement" in its recreated role of Tsingitang, Bułat, 154.

10 On Jewish actors in blackface in those productions, see Rubinstein, "Strange Rendering," 49. A clipping of the 1898 poem is in the Abraham Goldfaden Collection, RG 219 (YIVO), folder 51. As a translator, Goldfaden was interested in how best to convey Hebrew terms—see his handwritten notebook's translation of "Niger" and "Shvartz," Abraham Goldfaden Collection, RG 219 (YIVO), folder 108, pages 191, 286. On Goldfaden's life and career in America and various critics' view of him, see Zilbertsvayg, *Leksikon*, 1:328–67. On the ban, see John Klier, "'Exit, Pursued by a Bear': The Ban on Yiddish Theater in Imperial Russia," in Berkowitz, *Yiddish Theater*, 159–74. On the connection, if any, between "Bar Kokhba" and the ban, see Nahma Sandrow, *Vagabond Stars: A World History of the Yiddish Theater* (Harper & Row, 1977), 62.

11 Gorin, *Geshikhte*, 2:36–86 (quote on p. 41). The text by Hurvits is taken from a handwritten manuscript, *Shloymeh ha-meylekh, oder, di liebe fon shir ha-shirim*, 7, **P (Ms. Yid. 1112, NYPL—Dorot). Ads for that theater show are in *Folksadvokat*, Jan. 4, 1889, 8. *Arbeter tsaytung*, Aug. 8, 1890, 6; April 6, 1894, 7. *Teglikher herold*, Dec. 6, 1894, 3. On the early theater in New York, see Y. S., "A barikht vegn yidishn teater in nu york fun 1894," in *Arkhiv far der geshikhte fun yidishn teater*, ed. Yankev Shatsky (YIVO, 1930), 1:446–49. David Pinsky, "The Yiddish Theater," *Jewish Communal Register of New York City, 1917–1918* (Kehillah of New York City, 1918), 572–77. On Hurvits's early career, see Zalmen Zilbertsvayg, *Avrom goldfaden un zigmunt mogulesko* (Elisheva, 1936), 47–52. See also Ilana Bialik, "Audience Response in the Yiddish 'Shund' Theatre," *Theatre Research International*, 13 (1988): 97–105.

12 On the leading ethnic acts in vaudeville, including Jews, see Robert W. Snyder, *The Voice of the City: Vaudeville and Popular Culture in New York* (Oxford University Press, 1989), 48, 52–53, 110–14 (Baker's quote is on p. 112). Harley Erdman, *Staging the Jew: The Performance of an American Ethnicity* (Rutgers University Press, 1997), 71–83, 99–100. Liebowitz's letter is in *Ha-pisgah*, April 4, 1890, 2 (also mentioned in the introduction above). On African American, Irish, and Jews' struggle against negative stage characters, see Kibler, *Censoring Racial Ridicule*.

13 The play's content is quoted in an unsigned review, *Menshenfraynd*, Sep. 4, 1891, 14. The ad with Tomshevsky is in *Teglikher herold*, Sep. 2, 1896, 2. On the play's success and Marks's career, see in Zilbertsvayg, *Leksikon*, 2:1269–73. On Perlmutter, see *Leksikon*, 3:1838.

14 Kh. Y. Minikes, *Tsvishen indianer, oder der kauntri pedler* (Katzenelenbogen, 1895), 11–12, *ZP-563 (NYPL—Dorot), stage directions originally in parentheses.

See also the depiction of Blacks and Indians in the attached parody, "Di hagode fun'm kauntri pedler," in Minikes, *Tsvishen indianer*, 20–21. A translation of Minikes's play appears in Slobin, "From Vilna to Vaudeville," 17–26. See also, Slobin, *Tenement Songs*, 108–13.

15 Ash is quoted in Slobin, "From Vilna to Vaudeville," 17. Niger's critique appeared in *Tog*, April 5, 1932, clipping in the Papers of Shmuel Niger, RG 360 (YIVO), box 85, folder 1888. See also, Reyzin, *Leksikon*, 2:418–20; and Rachel Rubinstein, *Members of the Tribe: Native America in the Jewish Imagination* (Wayne State University Press, 2010), 43–45.

16 M. Zeyfert, "Di geshikhte fun yudishen theater: in dray tsayt perioden," in *Di yidishe bihne*, ed. Khonen Y. Minikes (Katzenelenbogen, 1897), unpaginated. On Adler, *Othello*, and the competition in the mid-1890s, see Joel Berkowitz, *Shakespeare on the American Yiddish stage* (University of Iowa Press, 2002), 77–86; Tomashevsky, *Mayn lebns-geshikhte*, 295–301; and Lulla Adler Rosenfeld, *The Yiddish Theater and Jacob P. Adler* (Shapolsky, 1977; rev. edition, 1988), 274–75, 278. See the ads for *Queen of Sheba* in *Varhayt*, Oct. 29, 1906, 3; Jan. 8, 1907, 3. On the racial discourse among the Yiddish intelligentsia in those years and the use of the term "Hottentots," see Ribak, *Gentile New York*, 87. On the imagery of Hottentots through the nineteenth century, see Linda E. Merians, *Envisioning the Worst: Representations of "Hottentots" in Early-Modern England* (University of Delaware Press, 2001).

17 John Paley, "Mit'n ponim tsum publicum, oder ver iz shuldig?," in Minikes, *Di yidishe bihne*, unpaginated. In his autobiography, composer Joseph Rumshinsky recalled a Yiddish play by Latayner titled "The Four Hundred Years" that was shown in Philadelphia, where Yankev Veksler played a Black slave—*Klangen fun mayn lebn* (Biderman, 1944), 468–69. S. Niger wrote about Zeyfert as a shundist, though noting it is a "matter of taste"—*Tog*, Oct. 5, 1924, 10.

18 Berkowitz, *Shakespeare*, 74–75, 120–21. Leon Zolotkoff parodied the way a simple Jewish tailor watched and understood Othello in *Yudishe gazeten*, Dec. 11, 1896, 4.

19 See ads for both productions in *Forverts*, April 29, 1901, 3; May 8, 1901, 3. See also *FAS*, May 4, 1901, 8. The details about Thalia's songs and the hissing audience are in Edna Nahshon, "Overture: From the Bowery to Broadway," in Nahshon, *New York's Yiddish Theater*, 29. On the cancellation of *Uncle Thomashefsky's Cabin* (1915) at Astor Theater, see *Variety* 37 (Feb. 12, 1915): 5; (Feb. 20, 1915): 14. Pamela Brown Lavitt has conflated that production with Tomashevsky's Yiddish productions a decade earlier—see her article "Vaudeville," in Buhle, *Jews and American Popular Culture*, 2:27.

20 Yankev Gordin, "Rayze bilder," *Ale shriften fun yankev gordin* (Hebrew Publishing Company, 1910), 3:25–26 ("gentleman" originally in quotes). On Gordin's life and career, see Barbara Henry, *Rewriting Russia: Jacob Gordin's Yiddish Drama* (University of Washington Press, 2011). Gordin traveled to Germany and Austria-Hungary in 1907 both to gain some control over the unauthorized circulation of his texts, and to receive treatment for the cancer that claimed his

life in 1909—Henry, *Rewriting Russia*, 152, 159. The feuilleton is in *Varhayt*, Feb. 1, 1906, 5. On Gordin's difficulty with Yiddish, see Gorin, *Geshikhte*, 2:109; Sandrow, *Vagabond Stars*, 132–35; Howe, *World of Our Fathers*, 467–68. "Yahudi" is probably a corruption of the Hebrew term for Jew, "Yehudi," as a parody of Westernized Jews' stilted (and colloquial at times) use of Hebrew. Selma C. Berrol, "In Their Image: German Jews and the Americanization of the *Ost Juden* in New York City," *New York History* 63 (1982): 417–33.

21 On Yente's success among Jewish audiences, see the numerous letters and memoirs, Papers of Jacob Adler (B. Kovner), RG 473, (YIVO), folders 23 and 27. See also the third chapter above and Ribak, "My Mom Drank Ink." The announcements on the upcoming stage production and ads are in *Forverts*, Oct. 12, 1917, 3; Oct. 26, 1917, 3; Nov. 16, 1917, 3–4; *Tog*, Nov. 3, 1917, 4; *MZ*, Nov. 7, 1917, 7; Nov. 22, 1917, 7; *Varhayt*, Nov. 13, 1917, 6; *YT*, Nov. 14, 1917, 6.

22 Y. Adler/B. Kovner, "Yente telebende: a komedy in 4 akten," 21–22; Rumshinsky, Gilrod, and Lillian, "Yente telebende: vashington, lincoln un moyshe rabeiny and arayn geganen sich aus gedreit." Randall Kennedy has mentioned the pervasiveness of the "Eeny-meeny-miney-mo" as a children's rhyme in *Nigger*, 15–16. See also Ribak, "'Negroes Must Not Be Likened to Jews,'" 279–80.

23 On Black characters in American popular entertainment in those years, see op. cit. On Pickaninnies, see Robin Bernstein, *Racial Innocence: Performing American Childhood from Slavery to Civil Rights* (New York University Press, 2011), 34–35, 49–55. On the commercialization and lowbrow character of the Yiddish theater in America, see Gorin, *Geshikhte*, 2:9–10, 203ff; and Berkowitz, "This Is Not Europe," 135–65.

24 On "goo-goo eyes," minstrelsy, and racial hatred, see Bill Doggett, "The Intersections of Early Recorded Sound 1900–1901, Race and Racial Terror ~ In Memory of Tulsa 1921 to George Floyd 2020," bdoggett55 (blog), accessed Jan. 26, 2021, https://bdoggett55.wordpress.com. On Jewish adoption of white, mainstream vocabulary, see Andrew R. Heinze, "'Is It 'Cos I's Black?' Jews and the Whiteness Problem," *David W. Belin Lecture in American Jewish Affairs* (2007), accessed Jan. 26, 2021, https://www.fulcrum.org.

25 See the first chapter above for a discussion of the *Song of Songs*; and Goldenberg, *Curse of Ham*, 79–82. Cf. Melamed, *Image of the Black*, 43–47.

26 On the Baltimore production, see *Forverts*, Dec. 14, 1917, 3. On the show in Toledo, see *Varhayt*, Jan. 12, 1918, 8; *MZ*, Jan. 25, 1918, 2—one of the actors in the piratic productions was no other than Louis Gilrod. The ad for the Massachusetts shows is in *Tog*, June 2, 1918, 2.

27 On La Rue's career, see Henry Sapoznik, "Thomas La Rue Jones: The Black Cantor" (blog post), July 21, 2020, accessed Oct. 6, 2022, https://www.henrysapoznik.com. Nahma Sandrow has written that La Rue "began his Yiddish career in the successful musical comedy *Yente Telebende*, produced in 1917 at Boris Thomashefsky's National Theater" in her article, "Popular Yiddish Theater: Music, Melodrama, and Operetta," in Nahshon, *New York's Yiddish Theater*, 73. I found no

mention of him in the 1917 production, and it seems that Sandrow has conflated the first (1917) and later (1921–1922) theater productions of *Yente Telebende*. Gorin wrote in *MZ*, Oct. 31, 1921, 7. Advertisements for the "great attraction," the Black Cantor at Liberty Theater are in *MZ*, March 19, 1920, 13; *Forverts*, Feb. 14, 1918, 2; *Forverts*, March 21, 1920, 17; *YT*, March 26, 1920, 14.

28 The "extra treat" is in *MZ*, Dec. 21, 1922, 8. Reviews of La Rue are in *Tog*, Jan. 13, 1922, 3 (B. Y. Goldstein); and *Forverts*, Jan. 20, 1922, 3 (Cahan). Later critique of La Rue is in *Tog*, Dec. 26, 1924, 3.

29 The quote about "special relations" and reference to the cartoon are in Diner, *In the Almost*, 67–68. Kovner's piece is in *Forverts*, Jan. 17, 1920, 10. The cartoon on the left is in *Forverts*, May 16, 1920, 5. The cartoon on the right is also in *Forverts*, March 31, 1922, 3. The cantor ("Samson") in the cartoon on the left was probably Meyer Kanewsky (Kanevsky), who did perform at the Manhattan Opera House—see *Musical Courier: Weekly Review of the World's Music* 81 (July 1, 1920): 24, 31. See also Edna Nahshon, "Tevye der Shvartzer Khazn," *Tablet*, June 16, 2022, accessed Feb. 15, 2023, https://www.tabletmag.com.

30 Rolland is quoted in *MZ*, April 21, 1922, 8. On Rolland's career in the Yiddish theater, see Brooklyn Jewish Historical Initiative, accessed Oct. 6, 2022, https://brooklynjewish.org. Tashrak's feuilleton, "Naye tsayten—naye strashunkes" is in *Minikes peysekh blat* (April 1923): 19–20. On Tashrak's career, see Gil Ribak, "Reportage from Blotetown: Yisroel-Yoysef Zevin (Tashrak) and the Shtetlization of New York City," *East European Jewish Affairs* 50 (Fall 2020): 57–74.

31 Erdberg wrote under the pen name S. Rubinzon, *YT*, June 28, 1920, 4; Sep. 20, 1920, 4. On those cantors, see Henry Sapoznik, "How a Century-Old Recording Revealed the Lost World of African-American Cantors" (blog post), July 7, 1920, accessed Feb. 15, 2023, https://www.henrysapoznik.com. Sapoznik mentions also Harlem pianist Willie "The Lion" Smith. See also Henry Sapoznik, "Goldye, Di Shvartze Khaznte" (blog post), Aug. 25, 2020, accessed Feb. 15, 2023, https://www.henrysapoznik.com. See ads for Goldye's shows in *Tog*, Jan. 20, 1925, 2; *Forverts*, June 13, 1925, 6. On Erdberg's imagery of Africa when he still lived in Poland, see his *Fort a yid nokh erets yisroel: rayze bilder* (n.p., 1926), 190–91.

32 Ethel Waters with Charles Samuels, *His Eye is on the Sparrow: An Autobiography* (1950; digital edition, Da Capo Press, 1992), 204. *YT*, Sep. 20, 1920, 4. Kristol wrote in *FAS*, Jan. 23, 1925, 3 (quotes in the original). See also Angelou, *Singin' and Swingin'*, 18.

33 Though it is unclear who William Hughes was, he played the Black kid at both the Lyric Theater and the Lenox Theater productions—Abraham Cahan mentioned that Hughes remained as the Black kid in *Forverts*, Jan. 20, 1922, 3. In a large advertisement for the play, it seems that Hughes is a white actor in blackface—see *YT*, Dec. 30, 1921, 13.

34 Cahan's review is in *Forverts*, Jan. 20, 1922, 3. The cartoon that shows actress Diana (Dina) Goldberg as Pine and "his little Niger" (unnamed) is in *Tog*, Jan. 13, 1922, 3. The dialogue is in the Papers of Jacob Adler (B. Kovner) (YIVO), folder

72, typed copy of "Mendel vert poter fun yenten," 6. The same archive, folder 73, contains another version of the 1917 play, but it is only three acts, and omitted the duet about Washington, Lincoln, etc. In the same folder, there is a typed copy of the play with the duet's lyrics crossed out by a blue highlighter line (pp. 21–22). As the 1917 production ran as a four-act show, the song was included in it, and it is unclear whether the song was cut altogether or moved elsewhere in the 1921–1922 productions. Another song that mentions Pine as a rock thrower is the song by Jacob Jacobs and Louis Cohen, "Yente Telebende and Pine, the Candy Kid" (Goldberg and Jacobs Amusement Co., 1922), notated music, accessed Oct. 6, 2022, https://loc.getarchive.net. For more details, see Ribak, "My Mom Drank Ink."

35 The fact that the partner-in-crime, the window repairman, is "Mike the Italian" has to do with Yiddish sources' description of Italian immigrants—see Ribak, *Gentile New York*, 83–86, 180–85. Cf. Rudolf Glanz, *Jew and Italian: Historic Group Relations and the New Immigration (1881–1924)* (Ktav Publishing House, 1971), 9–11. See also the comments by Rudolf Glanz and Lawrence Fuchs in Jean A. Scarpaci, ed., *The Interaction of Italians and Jews in America: Proceedings of the Seventh Annual Conference of the American Italian Historical Association* (American Italian Historical Association, 1975), 101, 107–8; and Richard Juliani and Mark Hutter, "Research Problems in the Study of Italian and Jewish Interaction in Community Setting," in Scarpacci, *Proceedings*, 43–52. On Twain and that motif, see Janet Holmgren McKay, "'An Art So High': Style in the *Adventures of Huckleberry Finn*," in *New Essays on "Adventures of Huckleberry Finn,"* ed. Louis J. Budd (Harvard University Press, 1985), 61–81; and Eric J. Sundquist, *To Wake the Nations: Race in the Making of American Literature* (Belknap Press of Harvard University Press, 1993), 225–70.

36 For studies of Yiddish folklore and its relation to perceived peasant traits, see above op. cit. See also Funkenstein, "Dialectics of Assimilation," 1–13; and Ribak, *Gentile New York*, 12–18.

37 A copy of the play (1920) is in Collection of Yiddish Plays, RG 114 (YIVO), folder 1.1., quotes from pages 3–4, 34, 36. On Botvinik and this play, see Zilbertsvayg, *Leksikon*, 1:119–20. Reviews of *Shayke* that imply the Black kid was cut out of the show are in *YT*, Feb. 3, 1922, 4 (Erdberg). See also B. Y. Goldstein's review in *Tog*, Feb. 11, 1922, 3, which mentions the whole cast sans Washington. Botvinik himself referred to it in *Forverts*, Feb. 3, 1922, 3. According to one advertisement, the play was shown (1923) in Boston, too—*Tog*, April 21, 1923, 2. Analysis and examples of Yiddish-speaking Gentiles in Eastern Europe are in Ribak, *Gentile New York*, 18; Harkavy, *Prakim me-chayay*, 6–7; and Bruk, "Goyim ke-yehudim," 84.

38 Abraham Schomer, "Stayl: drama in 4 akten fun avrom shomer," typed manuscript in the Papers of Jacob P. Adler, RG 1177 (YIVO), folder 1, pages 98, 107. On that play's success, see *YT*, Feb. 11, 1916, 10; and Zilbertsvayg, *Leksikon*, 3:2107–08. Later George Broadhurst adapted this play into English under the title *To-day* and made it into a Broadway show and two film versions (1917, 1930). See also an early

adaptation based on Broadhurst's text by Richard Parker, *To-Day: A Novel* (Macaulay, 1914). An earlier example of a Black woman who is a paragon of normalcy in comparison to neurotic, squabbling Jews is in *Forverts*, Aug. 19, 1908, 4.

39 My translation is based on a typed manuscript in the Papers of Osip Dymov, RG 469 (YIVO), folder 2, pages 37–37A (37A is handwritten). See a different translation and introduction by Nahma Sandrow, ed. and trans., *God, Man, and Devil: Yiddish Plays in Translation* (Syracuse University Press, 1999), 261–63, 287, 292. She does not include the exchange between the insect and Aunt Jemima. Landoy wrote in *Naye velt*, Jan. 16, 1920, 19–20. Cahan wrote in *Forverts*, Jan. 5, 1920, 5 (parentheses in the original). On Apel's career, see Mukdoyni, *Teater*, 120–26; and Zilbertsvayg, *Leksikon*, 1:83–84. The mention of Sullivan in the Astor Theater's cast is in *The Billboard*, April 22, 1922, 21. Raskin's caricature is in *GK*, May 19, 1922, 5. On the play's social criticism and the less successful production at Astor Theater, see Ted Merwin, *In Their Own Image: New York Jews in Jazz Age Popular Culture* (Rutgers University Press, 2006), 97–102.

40 Cahan wrote in *Forverts*, Jan. 5, 1920, 5. On Rumshinsky's work with Picon, see Rumshinsky, *Klangen fun mayn lebn*, 621–25, 683–90; and Hankus Netsky, "Breaking the Silence on American Yiddish Popular Music," in Shapiro, *Yiddish in America*, 194–96.

41 The actor's depiction as "vaudeville Negro" is in *Unzer teater*, Oct. 1, 1921, 30. Friedman wrote in *YT*, Oct. 21, 1921, 7 (quotes in the original). Botvinik wrote (as "A Theater Patriot") in *Forverts*, Nov. 11, 1921, 3 (quotes in the original). See also, *Forverts*, Oct. 2, 1927, 21. A feuilleton in *Tog* claimed there was a competing show, "Shmendrik in Brownsville," which had three Black actors singing and looking more respectable than the original show's Black actor—*Tog*, Nov. 29, 1921, 5. On Edelstein, see Rumshinsky, *Klangen fun mayn lebn*, 574–79. Interestingly, in 1929, William Siegel wrote (March 2, 1929) to Kovner, telling him that he saw *Yente* beforehand at the Lenox Theater, and asked Kovner about turning it into a movie, Papers of Jacob Adler (B. Kovner), folder 23. The term "Shmendrik" was popularized in Yiddish by Avrum Goldfaden's 1877 operetta by that name—see Quint, *Rise of the Modern Yiddish Theater*, 52, 99.

42 See Botvinik's play above and his sketches in *Forverts*, Jan. 31, 1918, 3; May 22, 1920, 3; and chapter 3 above.

43 The quotes are from the original play that appeared first in *Tsukunft* (March 1922): 158–59. All stage directions are in parentheses.

44 See chapter 5. See also Y. Opatoshu, "Lintsheray," *Gezamlte verk fun Y. Opatoshu* (Kletzkin, 1927), 5:8–9; Caplan, "Yiddish Exceptionalism," 184–98; and Jessica Kirzane, "Introduction to 'Lintsheray,'" *In Geveb*, June 21, 2016, https://ingeveb.org.

45 A copy of the drama school's May 1922 program is in Papers of Joseph Opatoshu, RG 436 (YIVO), folder 399. On Opatoshu's "stillborn child" with both productions in New York and Warsaw, see Leon Kusman's review in *MZ*, Dec. 8, 1922, 10. On the production in Warsaw, see *Teater un kunst* (Lodz), Nov. 9, 1922, 1, 5.

On the emergence of Schwartz and the Yiddish Art Theater, see Edna Nahshon, "Maurice Schwartz and the Yiddish Art Theater Movement," in Nahshon, *New York's Yiddish Theater*, 152–56.

46 In 1925–1926, the National Theater performed a successful operetta titled *Models fun libe* (Models of Love), written by Louis Freyman (pseudonym of Leyzer Genyuk), starring Aren Lebedev (Aaron Lebedeff). In a small role of "a Negro" was a young actor by the name of Yankev Rekhtsayt, who still spoke as an East Side Jew, but performed race jokes which, as one reviewer noted, even "Broadway discarded long time ago"—Hillel Rogoff, *Forverts*, Nov. 27, 1925, 3. See also B. Y. Goldstein, *Tog*, Nov. 20, 1925, 3.

47 The quote is taken from the earliest publication of the play—Leon Kobrin, "Riversayd drayv: drame in dray akten," *Tsukunft* (Feb. 1928): 76. An identical text is in the manuscript (dated March 5, 1927) of *Riversayd drayv*, Papers of Leon Kobrin, RG 376 (YIVO), folder 70, page 10. An analysis of that play is in Berkowitz, "This Is Not America," 159–65; it includes a bibliography of critical reviews of Kobrin's work (159n40). An earlier discussion of Kobrin's qualities as a writer with quotes from many critics is in *FAS*, Nov. 20, 1936, 6. On Kobrin's radical background and focus on the dislocations caused by immigration and poverty, see Kobrin, *Mayne fuftsik yor*, 166–240; and Mikhail Krutikov, *Yiddish fiction and the crisis of modernity, 1905–1914* (Stanford University Press, 2001), 132–44.

48 On the decline of the Yiddish theater in those years, see Hoberman, *Bridge of Light*, 103, 157; and Sandrow, *Vagabond Stars*, 291–95.

49 The quote is by Lederhendler, *Jewish Immigrants*, 82–84. He refers to scholars such as Brown Lavitt, "First of the Red Hot Mamas," 253–90; Melnick, *A Right to Sing the Blues*, 103–14; Rogin, *Blackface/White Noise*, 5–6, 16–17, 67–70; Jacobson, *Whiteness of a Different Color*; and Roediger, *Working toward Whiteness*, 93–130. Cf. Weinstein, *Eddie Cantor Story*, 22–30. The cartoon with the Jew holding out his hand to Jolson is in *GK*, May 28, 1926, 7. On Jolson's resignation from the exclusive Westchester Biltmore Country Club, see Jewish Telegraphic Agency, accessed May 4, 2023, https://www.jta.org. See also Annie Poland and Daniel Soyer, *Emerging Metropolis: New York Jews in the Age of Immigration, 1840–1920* (New York University Press, 2013), 235–37.

50 That point is made by Erdman, *Staging the Jew*, 184n12. Nahma Sandrow has argued that most Yiddish theater audiences viewed artistically and intellectually ambitious theater as "goyish" *Vagabond Stars*, 408–10.

51 See for example, Howe, *World of Our Fathers*, 204, 495–96; Goldstein, *Price of Whiteness*, 153–54; and Bachman, *Recovering "Yiddishland,"* 126.

52 On that "epidemic," see in Khaykin, *Yidishe bleter*, 75–84; Goldstein, "A Taste of Freedom," 109–10; and in chapter 5 below.

CHAPTER 5. "A HEAVY BODILY SCENT"

1 The story first appeared in *Tog*, July 4, 1929, p. 5. See also Y. Opatoshu, "Zind," *Gezamlte verk*, 12:68–73. On the Young Workers League, see Paul C. Mishler, *Rais-*

ing Reds: The Young Pioneers, Radical Summer Camps, and Communist Political Culture in the United States (Columbia University Press, 1999), 30–31, 42–44.

2 Rontsh, "Der neger," 209–10. It is noteworthy that the story appeared before the riots. On the fissures among Jewish socialists and communists in the U.S. over the Arab riots, see Gennady Estraikh, "The Stalinist 'Great Break' in Yiddishland," in Diner and Estraikh, *1929*, 46–48; Epstein, *The Jew and Communism*, 223–33; and Naomi Wiener Cohen, *The Year after the Riots: American Responses to the Palestinian Crisis of 1929–30* (Wayne State University Press, 1988).

3 That phenomenon is discussed in Cohen, *Nifla'ot*, 56–102, 385; Veidlinger, *Jewish Public Culture*, 83–85, 99–105, 156; and Goldstein, "Taste of Freedom," 105–39.

4 One can mention only a few of the works that deal with the "booklet epidemic"—Khaykin, *Yidishe bleter*, 75–84; Eliahu Shulman, *Geshikhte fun der yidisher literatur in Amerike, 1870–1900* (A. W. Biderman, 1943), 84–103; Alyssa Quint and Eric Goldstein, "Pop 'Em in Yiddish: The Subterranean World of Yiddish Pulp Fiction," *Guilt and Pleasure* 7 (2008): 110–13; Shmeruk, "Le-toldot," 335–38; and Cohen, "Sachar ha-sfarim," 441–46. Many critics dismissed such literary production—see Max Raisin's letter in *Ha-melits*, Jan. 10, 1898, 3.

5 On Tanenboym's life and career, see Niger, *Leksikon*, 4:25–27; Reyzin, *Leksikon*, 1:1159–64 (includes Kotik's quote); and Gil Ribak, "The Organ of the Jewish People: The *Yidishes Tageblat* and Uncharted Conservative Yiddish Culture in America," *Jewish Quarterly Review* 112 (2022): 815–16. On his success in Eastern Europe, see Veidlinger, *Jewish Public Culture*, 100–101; Cohen, *Yiddish Transformed*, 79–80, 312; and Litvak, *Vos geven*, 71. On his popularity among Jewish radicals, see Ezra Mendelsohn, *Class Struggle in the Pale: The Formative Years of the Jewish Workers' Movement in Tsarist Russia* (Cambridge University Press, 1970), 121. Tanenboym appears as a character in Matan Hermoni's novel *Hibru poblishing ḳompani* ('Or Kineret Zemorah-Bitan, 2011).

6 An excellent overview of Verne's treatment of race is by Peter Aberger, "The Portrayal of Blacks in Jules Verne's *Voyages Extraordinaires*," *French Review* 53 (1979): 199–206.

7 Verne's original French text is at Projekt Gutenberg, accessed Nov. 1, 2022, https://www.gutenberg.org. I am grateful to Emmanuel Darmon for his assistance with translating the original text. Jules Verne, *A Voyage Round the World: Australia* (London and New York: George Routledge and Sons, 1877), 19, 203. A. Tanenboym, *Di ferlorene shif, oder, a rayze arum di velt a visenshaftlikher roman in dray theyl* (New York: Y. Sapirshteyn, 1896), 203, 266, 270.

8 Interestingly, in Tanenboym's version, the five African Americans who are trapped in a flooded ant nest together with the others become hysterical and scream, "Water! Water is pouring in!" They "became restless and wanted to flee," while Dick Sand and Benedict the entomologist remain calm and figure out ways to survive—A. Tanenboym, *In vilden afrika: fun zhul vern* (New York: Hebrew Publishing Company, undated), 26–28. See his use of biblical verses, *In vilden afrika*, 52. On *Dick Sand* and the differentiation between Black Africans and African

Americans in Verne's work, see Aberger, "Portrayal of Blacks," 200, 204–6. See also Sebastian Schulman, "The Extraordinary Voyages of the Yiddish Jules Verne," online event at Yiddish Book Center, recorded January 7, 2021, https://www.yiddishbookcenter.org.

9 Jules Verne, *A Trip Round the World in a Flying Machine* (no translator mentioned, Chicago: M. A. Donohue, 1887), 39, 50, 64, 99–101, 150–52. On this and other translations, see Alex Kirstukas, introduction to *Robur the Conqueror*, ed. Arthur B. Evans, trans. Alex Kirstukas (Wesleyan University Press, 2017), xvi–xviii. In many respects, Verne's French original is more racist, mentioning that Frycollin "hardly deserved anything better than slavery," and "There was something of the monkey about him," *Robur the Conqueror*, 34–35, 236n2.

10 A. Tanenboym, *Di flih-mashin, oder, a rayze arum der velt in a luft shif* (Hebrew Publishing Company, c. 1899), 13–14, 18, 23–24, 32, 40–41, 67. For a racialized description of Black physique in an original work by him, see A. Tanenboym, *Tsvishen himel un vaser: ayn interesante rayze beshraybung* (Hebrew Publishing Company, 1925), 2. On the idealization of Americans among East European Jews, see Ribak, *Gentile New York*, chapters 2 and 3.

11 *YT*, Nov. 25, 1898, 5. *MZ*, Nov. 19, 1906, 5; Dec. 23, 1910, 4. See also Tanenboym's serialized adaptation of Thomas Mayne Reid's Western novel, *The War Trail: The Hunt of the Wild Horse* (1857), in *MZ*, Sep. 3, 1907, 2. On the incident in Brownsville, Texas, see chapter 3. On Baltimore's zoning law, see Garrett Power, "Apartheid Baltimore Style: The Residential Segregation Ordinances of 1910–1913," *Maryland Law Review* 42 (1983): 289–328.

12 The quote on Tanenboym is in Reyzin, *Leksikon*, 1:1160. On crime and Jewish names, see *YT*, July 16, 1902, 4. On the realty company, see *YT*, Aug. 6, 1906, 4. On drunkenness, see *YT*, Aug. 30, 1907, 6 (see also chapter 3 above). Although those editorials (apart from the 1902 piece) are unsigned, Paley wrote nearly all editorials until his death in 1907. On Paley's life and career, see Reyzin, *Leksikon*, 2:859–62; Khaykin, *Yidishe bleter*, 89, 101, 114–20; Shulman, *Geshikhte*, 61–62; and Ribak, "Organ of the Jewish People," 805–7. On the Afro-American Realty Company, see James Weldon Johnson, "Harlem: The Culture Capital," in *Afro-American Writing: An Anthology of Prose and Poetry*, ed. Richard A. Lang and Eugenia W. Collier (Pennsylvania State University Press, 1985), 295–96.

13 Yohan Paley, *Di shvartse khevre, oder nu york bay tog un bay nakht* (New York: Hebrew Publishing Company, undated), iv, 15, 35, 94. An analysis of this novel's moralism as a narrative of exposure is in Esther Romeyn, *Street Scenes: Staging the Self in Immigrant New York, 1880–1924* (University of Minnesota Press, 2008), 18, 22–25. On Paley's rumored suicide, see Ribak, "Organ of the Jewish People," 805n36. On Paley's salary, see the 1905 correspondence between Paley and the Industrial Removal Office (IRO) about his $1,000 honorarium for writing a book about the U.S., Records of the Industrial Removal Office, I-91, (AJHS), box 91, folder 41. On women trafficking, see Edward J. Bristow, *Prostitution and Prejudice:*

The Jewish Fight against White Slavery, 1870–1939 (Schocken, 1982); and Ribak, "The Jew Usually Left Those Crimes to Esau," 1–28.

14 Paley, *Shvartse khevre*, 13, 52, 90–91. On the Irish as the embodiment of the New World's Gentile peasantry, see Ribak, "Beaten to Death by Irish Murderers," 41–74.

15 On Zelikovitsh's other writings, see chapters 1 and 3. "Di droshe af'n fidl" appeared in *YT*, Dec. 17, 1912, 5 (quotes in the original in "kike music"). An abridged version of that sketch appeared in G. Zelikovitsh, *Geklibene shriften fun prof. g. zelikovitsh* (Zelikovitsh yubileum komite, 1913), 246–48. On the ubiquity of the term "coon song" in popular culture, see Raymond Knapp, *The American Musical and the Formation of National Identity* (Princeton University Press, 2005), 73–76. On Berlin, "coon songs," and "Alexander's Ragtime Band," see Charles Hamm, *Irving Berlin—Songs from the Melting Pot: The Formative Years, 1907–1914* (Oxford University Press, 1997), 68–136.

16 The feuilleton was published in *Minikes' yontef bleter* (Nov. 1918): 54–55. Communal activist Bernard G. Richards termed Tashrak "A Jewish Mark Twain," *Boston Evening Transcript*, Sep. 21, 1910 (copy does not show page number). "Ghetto Mark Twain" appears in *Baltimore News*, January 9, 1911, 2, newspaper clipping in Papers of Tashrak, RG 1502 (YIVO), folder 27. On Tashrak's treatment of Irish and German characters, see Ribak, "Reportage from Blotetown," 57–74. On Paley, Zelikovitsh, Tashrak, and other writers, see the memoir by Miriam Shomer-Tsunzer, "Fun yidishn literarishn nu-york baym onheyv yorhundert: zikhroynes arum a bild fun yor 1905," *YIVO bleter* 33 (1949): 168–82. See also Tashrak's feuilleton about the black-faced cantor in chapter 4 above.

17 Guy-Sheftall, *Daughters of Sorrow*, 41–45.

18 On Hermalin's career, see Reyzin, *Leksikon*, 1:866–70; Niger, *Leksikon*, 3:205–6; and Ribak, *Gentile New York*, 54, 84, 91, 97–98, 150, 159, 170. On Hermalin as a "women's writer," see Brinn, *Revolution in Type*, 111–13, 163–64. The journalist, who also tells an anecdote about Hermalin's popularity, is Dovid Shub, *Fun di amolike yorn*, 1:349, 351–52. See also the joke about Hermalin's readership (old women) in *GK*, Feb. 20, 1914, 8.

19 D. M. Hermalin, *Di geheymnise fun dem shpanish-amerikanishen krieg* (New York: Hebrew Publishing Company, undated), 135–36. On Yiddish-speaking immigrants in America during the Spanish-American War, see Ribak, *Gentile New York*, 59–60; and Jacobson, *Special Sorrows*, 141–76.

20 Hermalin, *Shpanish-amerikanishen krieg*, 156–59, 205, 459–60, 473–75. See also the character of the loyal Black servant, Bruno— *Shpanish-amerikanishen krieg*, 226–28. Interestingly, Hermalin hardly refers to Maceo's biracial ancestry, apart from one mention of his "half-black face" on p. 88. On racial identity, the Cuban revolution, and Maceo's blackness, see Jennifer L. Lambe, "Filial Phantasmagoria: The Apocryphal Sons of Antonio Maceo (Father of the Cuban Nation)," *New West Indian Guide* 93 (2019): 5–40.

21 Attributed to John D. Rensler, Dovid M. Hermalin, trans., *Di vilde menshen: a natur-geshikhtlikhe shilderung iber dem leben fun di vilde in afrika und*

farshidene yogden mit vilde thire (New York: Meir Chinsky, undated), 3, 19, 21, 39–45. *Vilde menshen* was advertised by M. Chinsky in *Arbeter tsaytung*, April 22, 1900, 7, and July 29, 1900, 2 without an author's name. The book came out in Warsaw in 1910–1911 under the title *Tsvishen Vilde menshen*—see *Haynt*, Feb. 24, 1911, 1. On black skin as a "polished boot" or polished shoe, see chapter 2, and the novel by M. M. Dolitsky, *Di finstere herrshaft biz minister mirsky: kriminal roman* (Hebrew Publishing Company, circa 1904), 561. On *She* and Haggard, see Brown, *Cannibalism in Literature and Film*, 26–30. Accusation of Hermalin as a plagiarizer came up (March 1915) in a correspondence between the editor of *Der tog*, Herman Bernstein, and Hermalin, in Papers of Herman Bernstein, RG 713 (YIVO), folder 170.

22 *Vilde menshen*, 53–54, 61, 66, 84–85. There are numerous works on savagery, appearance, villainy, and race—see Idelson-Shein, *Difference*, 157–58, 170–71; Ela Przybylo and Sara Rodrigues, "Introduction: On the Politics of Ugliness," in Przybylo and Rodrigues, eds., *On the Politics of Ugliness* (Springer International Publishing and Palgrave Macmillan, 2018), 1–30; Charles W. Mills, *The Racial Contract* (Cornell University Press, 1997), 60–62; and Ter Ellingson, *The Myth of the Noble Savage* (University of California Press, 2001).

23 *Varhayt*, June 27, 1906, 8; July 3, 1913, 8; *Tog*, Aug. 17, 1915, 8. Hermalin called American Jews to help Ethiopian Jews survive as Jews—*Varhayt*, April 15, 1911, 6. His support for racial integration in public schools is *Varhayt*, Jan. 22, 1911, 4. On Griffith's movie, see Melvyn Stokes, *D. W. Griffith's The Birth of a Nation: A History of "The Most Controversial Motion Picture of All Time"* (Oxford University Press, 2007).

24 *Varhayt*, Jan. 11, 1908, 4 ("show" in quotes in the original). See also his article in *Minikes' yontef bleter* (Oct. 1908): 29–30. Hermalin wrote about the racial aspects of World War I in *Tog*, March 2, 1917, 8; May 1, 1917, 8. On Jewish support for early civil rights organizations, see Nancy J. Weiss, "Long-Distance Runners of the Civil Rights Movement: The Contribution of Jews to the NAACP and the National Urban League in the Early Twentieth Century," in Salzman and West, eds., *Struggles in the Promised Land*, 123–52; and Diner, *In the Almost*, 119–42.

25 Edelshtat published the story in *FAS*, June 12, 1891, 5. Advertisements for competing collections of his writings with this story are in *Forverts*, Feb. 12, 1904, 2. *FAS*, Feb. 20, 1904, 6. On Edelshtat's life and work, see B. Y. Byalostotski, ed., *Dovid Edelshtat gedenk-bukh tsum zekhtsikstn yortsayt, 1892–1952* (Dovid Edelshtat komitetn, 1952). On Edelshtat's limited command of Yiddish, see Kalman Marmor, *Dovid Edelshtat* (koperativer folks farlag, 1942), 32.

26 One critic is Rontsh, "Der neger," 205–6. Zalmen Reyzin commented that not a single poem by Edelshtat avoided a political message—*Leksikon*, 2:719–20. On Edelshtat's influence on Jewish anarchists, see Avrich, *Anarchist Portraits*, 177–79, 184–85; and the comments by Shoel Yanovsky and Emma Goldman in Byalostotski, *Doṿid Edelshṭaṭ*, 185–88.

27 Dovid Ignatov, *Tsvishen tsvey zunen: a bukh in fir teylen* (M. N. Mayzel, 1918), 119–22. On *Di yunge*, see Ruth R. Wisse, "Di Yunge: Immigrants or Exiles?," *Prooftexts* 1 (1981): 43–61; and A. Leyeles, *Unzer vort*, June 1, 1917, 15–17.

28 Y. Opatoshu, "Fir neger," *Gezamlte verk*, 5:67–71. Opatoshu, "Negers," *Gezamlte verk*, 12:164–69. Rontsh, "Der neger," 205–9. On Opatoshu's rich career, see Nakhman Mayzel, *Yoysef opatoshu, zayn lebn un shafn* (Literarishe bleter, 1937); and the editors' "Joseph Opatoshu's Search for *Yidishkayt*," in Koller, Estraikh, and Krutikov, eds., *Joseph Opatoshu*, 1–17. See also a cartoon that claimed Opatoshu was self-aggrandizing, *GK*, June 5, 1925, 9.

29 Opatoshu, "Lintsheray," in *Gezamlte verk*, 5:7–41 (quotes are on pp. 20, 32, 35). It is unclear when the story was first published: while Rontsh mentions it as written in 1915 ("Der neger," 208), the Warsaw daily *Der moment* began serializing the story on Aug. 30, 1922, 2, before it came out in a book form (1923). However, a review of Opatoshu's work by Aren Glants in early 1921 already mentioned "Lintsheray"—*FAS*, April 8, 1921, 5–6. An analysis of that story is by Caplan, "Yiddish Exceptionalism," 184–98; and Kirzane, "Yiddish Gaze," 146–49. Jessica Kirzane translated the story to English, *In Geveb*, June 21, 2016, https://ingeveb.org. On Opatoshu's play, see chapter 4.

30 Opatoshu, "Lintsheray," 8–9, 14–15. Both Bookert and his mother cross themselves when they hear bad news, or when preparing for the worst ("Lintsheray", 13, 33)—as Marc Caplan has argued, that gesture might characterize Polish or Ukrainian peasants more than African Americans—"Yiddish Exceptionalism," 187. On Opatoshu's admiration for Yehoash, who also wrote about lynching, see an undated manuscript, Papers of Joseph Opatoshu, RG 436 (YIVO), folder 382. On apelike imagery, see Fredrickson, *Black Image in the White Mind*, 85–87, 188–89, 277; Sebastiani, "Monster with Human Visage," 80–99; and David Bindman, *Ape to Apollo: Aesthetics and the Idea of Race in the 18th Century* (Reaktion, 2002).

31 The story was published in *Tog*, March 21, 1925, 6 ("Israelites" in quotes in the original). On Opatoshu's ability to portray peasant characters, see the article by Hillel Rogoff, *Forverts*, July 3, 1921, 2. See also another short story by Opatoshu, *A gneyve* (A Theft), *Tog*, Oct. 15, 1944, 11.

32 Glazman's quotes are from his letter to S. Niger (Dec. 7, 1926), Papers of Shmuel Niger; RG 360 (YIVO), box 9, folder 126 (stress under "speaking" in the original). The critic is B. Byalostotski, *FAS*, Nov. 23, 1945, 5–6 ("South" in quotes in the original). On Glazman's Yiddish, see Aren Bekerman, *Borekh glazman: a monografye fun borekh glazman mit a biblyografye fun zayne verk* (Ivangoroder branch 130 of the A.N.A.P., 1944), 18–20. See also Reyzin, *Leksikon*, 1:577–79; and Rontsh, "Der neger," 210–15.

33 Borekh Glazman, "A nakht in a dorem-shtot," *Geklibene verk fun borekh glazman: af di felder fun dzhordzhia*, (Kletskin, 1927) 4:135–40. Glazman quoted part of *Hesitation Blues*—on the origins and popularity of that song, see Lynn Abbott and Doug Seroff, "'They Cert'ly Sound Good to Me': Sheet Music, Southern Vaudeville, and the Commercial Ascendancy of the Blues," in David Evans, ed., *Ramblin'*

on My Mind: New Perspectives on the Blues (University of Illinois Press, 2008), 88–89. On mixed-sex dancing in the works of various American Yiddish writers, see Sonia Gollance, *It Could Lead to Dancing: Mixed-Sex Dancing and Jewish Modernity* (Stanford University Press, 2021), 83–91, 138–45, 151–62.

34 Borekh Glazman, *Baginen: Novelen* (Kultur, 1921), 81–90. Cf. the later versions, Glazman, *Shteynvebs* (Shul un bukh, 1925), 162–72; Glazman, *Geklibene verk fun borekh glazman*, 4:7–18. Jessica Kirzane has briefly discussed the interracial sexual encounter in this story, but not Glazman's use of American racial tropes about Black women—Kirzane, "What Kind of a Man Are You? Interethnic Sexual Encounter in Yiddish American Narratives," in Lisa Grushcow, ed., *The Sacred Encounter: Jewish Perspectives on Sexuality* (CCAR Press, 2014), 197–200. On Hagar's race, see Nyasha Junior, *Reimagining Hagar: Blackness and Bible* (Oxford University Press, 2019); and Melamed, *Image of the Black*, 108–9.

35 Glazman, *Baginen*, 87–90. The sentence "I was cut open and left untouched" appears only in the 1925 and 1927 versions (p. 169 and p. 15, respectively). On Glazman's use of the watermelon as a metaphor for the woman's sexuality, see Mikhail Krutikov, "Der rase-inyen in der yidisher literatur," *Forverts*, April 27, 2012; and Kirzane, "What Kind of a Man," 198.

36 Rontsh, "Der neger," 214. Glazman's quote about Marxism is in his letter to S. Niger (Dec. 7, 1926), Papers of Shmuel Niger, box 9, folder 126. In 1930, the communist *Morgn frayhayt* formally denounced Glazman as someone who attempts to "entice Jewish workers into the webs of bourgeois ideology," *Morgn frayhayt*, Dec. 1, 1930, 2, 5. On that episode, see also S. Niger's diary, Papers of Shmuel Niger, box 113, folder 3057, entry of Dec. 3, 1930: 162.

37 On the imagery of Black women's sexuality and mammies, see Carolyn M. West, "Mammy, Sapphire, and Jezebel: Historical Images of Black Women and Their Implications for Psychotherapy," *Psychotherapy* 32 (1995): 458–66; K. Sue Jewell, *From Mammy to Miss America and Beyond: Cultural Images and the Shaping of US Social Policy* (Routledge, 1993), 36–47, 202; and Gilman, "Black Bodies, White Bodies," 223–61. On the imagery of the peasantry, see above, and in Gil Ribak, "Getting Drunk, Dancing, and Beating Each Other Up: The Images of the Gentile Poor and Narratives of Jewish Difference among the Yiddish Intelligentsia, 1881–1914," in Leonard J. Greenspoon, ed., *Wealth and Poverty in Jewish Tradition: Studies in Jewish Civilization, Volume 26* (Purdue University Press, 2015), 203–24. On Singer and the sexuality of peasant women, see Bonnie Lyons, "Sexual Love in I. B. Singer's Work," *Studies in American Jewish literature* 1 (1981): 69–73; Roskies, *Bridge of Longing*, 293. See also Joshua N. Lambert, *Unclean Lips: Obscenity, Jews, and American Culture* (New York University Press, 2014), 118–23.

38 Borekh Glazman, "A binele, a binele (un damols iz gekumen . . .)," *Af a hor: novelen* (N. Mayzel, 1923), 47–82. That is the story title in the table of contents. The title on the page preceding the story is "Un damols iz gekumen di bin" (And Then Came the Bee). Glazman, "Shvarts af vays," *Shteynvebs*, 264–317. Glazman, "Der tants fun di negers," *Geklibene verk fun borekh glazman: af yener zayt okean*,

3:5–65. My quotes and page numbers relate to the 1923 edition, but I also refer to certain sentences or words that appeared only in later versions.

39 Glazman, "A binele," 50, 53–54, 77–79. As in other stories by Glazman, the novella includes many American popular songs. The novella's title derives from a folksong with the line "And then there came a bumblebee," since Cowan recalls that tune from the time he spent with Cora in a meadow. On that song, "The Frog He Would A-Courting Ride," see Robert W. Halli Jr., ed., *An Alabama Songbook: Ballads, Folksongs, and Spirituals*, collected by Byron Arnold (University of Alabama Press, 2004), 86–90.

40 Glazman, "A binele," 63–74, 82. The critics are Rontsh, "Der neger," 211–12; and Bekerman, *Borekh glazman*, 67–68. Cf. S. Niger's critique, *Tog*, Jan. 28, 1923, 7.

41 Glazman, "A binele," 59–60, 64. The addition "angrily hissing with her large white horse's teeth" does not appear in the 1923 edition but rather in the 1925 and 1928 editions: Glazman, "Shvarts af vays," 283; Glazman, "Der tants fun di negers," 27. The phrases "like pointed black pears," "soiled bottoms" and "like little dogs" appear only in the 1925 and 1928 editions (pp. 284 and 27–28, respectively).

42 Glazman, "A binele," 67, 70–72. The 1923 edition has it, "like big, tropical orangutangs." In the 1925 and 1928 editions, the sentence is "like big, tropical orangutangs and gorillas" (pp. 298–99 and 44, respectively). See also that the ship's Black stewards and kitchen workers are described as "rugged, clumsy figures," who leaned on each other, "looking like a herd of driven together, shiny horses"—"A binele," 64. On the early modern role of animal metaphors in racial discourse, see Francesca Royster, "'Working Like a Dog': African Labor and Racing the Human–Animal Divide in Early Modern England," in *Writing Race Across the Atlantic World: Medieval to Modern*, ed. Philip D. Beidler and Gary Taylor (Palgrave Macmillan, 2005), 113–34. See also Linda G. Tucker, *Lockstep and Dance: Images of Black Men in Popular Culture* (University Press of Mississippi, 2007).

43 On Ash's career and works, see Anita Norich, "Sholem Asch and the Christian Question," in *Sholem Asch Reconsidered*, ed. Nanette Stahl (Yale University Press, 2004), 251–65; Hannah Berliner Fischthal, "Reactions of the Yiddish Press to *The Nazarene* by Sholem Asch," in *Sholem Asch Reconsidered*, 266–78; and Ben Siegel, *The Controversial Sholem Asch: An Introduction to His Fiction* (Bowling Green University Popular Press, 1976). On Ash's response to the protest against those novels, see Sholem Asch, *One Destiny: An Epistle to the Christians*, trans. Milton Hindus (G. P. Putnam's Sons, 1945). See also Gil Ribak, "'Mexicans Are Just Like Every Oriental People': The Southwest in Sholem Asch's Yiddish Writing," *Legacy: Newsletter of the New Mexico Jewish Historical Society* 32 (Spring 2018): 1, 4–5.

44 Sholem Ash, *Toyt-urteyl* (Kultur Lige, 1927), 97–98, 127–29. See also Rontsh, "Der neger," 217–19. Dan Miron has interpreted the novel as an expression of Ash's alienation and disgust with America—"God Bless America: Of and Around Sholem Asch's *East River*," in Stahl, *Sholem Asch Reconsidered*, 179.

45 Ash, *Toyt-urteyl*, 127–30, 134–42 ("Black dogs," "boss," and "pardon" are in quotes in the original). See also Ash's rather neutral portrayal of Stone's Black chauffer,

Toyt-urteyl, 7–8. On Black characters' childlike behavior and religiosity in popular culture, see Carolyn Dean, "Boys and Girls and 'Boys': Popular Depictions of African-American Children and Childlike Adults in the United States, 1850–1930," *Journal of American and Comparative Cultures* 23 (Fall 2000): 17–35; and Fredrickson, *Black Image in the White Mind*, 102–15, 121–28, 285–91, 327–29.

EPILOGUE

1 *YT*, Aug. 3, 1914, 3. See also *YT*, July 27, 1914, 4; July 30, 1914, 4; Dec. 6, 1922, 5. Judd L. Teller, *Strangers and Natives: The Evolution of the American Jew from 1921 to the Present* (Delacorte, 1968), 6. Faygnboym wrote in *Forverts*, Nov. 7, 1917, 4. Earlier negative images of the Irish by Jewish socialists appeared in *Arbeter tsaytung*, Dec. 2, 1894, 6; and *Forverts*, May 27, 1899, 2. On Jewish and Slavic immigrants, see Ribak, *Gentile New York*, 133–43, 154–55, 165–70; Ewa Morawska, *Insecure Prosperity*, 15–17, 24–25, 40–44, 243–44; and Morawska, "A Replica of the 'Old-Country' Relationship in the Ethnic Niche: East European Jews and Gentiles in Small-Town Western Pennsylvania, 1880s–1930s," *American Jewish History* 77 (1987): 27–86. On Jewish immigrants' images of Irish Americans, see Ribak, "Beaten to Death by Irish Murderers," 41–74. See also Rudolf Glanz, *Jew and Irish: Historical Group Relations and Immigration* (pub. by the author, 1966), 97–98, 102–3; and Scott Cline, "Jewish-Ethnic Interactions: A Bibliographical Essay," *American Jewish History* 77 (1987): 135–54.

2 On that theme, see Jacobson, *Whiteness of a Different Color*; Noel Ignatiev, *How the Irish became White* (Routledge, 1995); Russell A. Kazal, "The Interwar Origins of the White Ethnic: Race, Residence, and German Philadelphia, 1917–1939," *Journal of American Ethnic History* 23 (2004): 78–131; and Guglielmo, *White on Arrival.*

3 Lederhendler, *American Jewry*, 185. On labor organizers in the context of intergroup conflict, see Friedman, *What Went Wrong?*, 154–55; and Hill, "Black-Jewish Conflict," 264–92. On the paternalistic approach of Jewish liberals in the mid-twentieth century, see Dollinger, *Black Power, Jewish Politics*, 22–23, 27; and Greenberg, *Troubling the Waters*, 70, 102–3. See also Harold Brackman, "African Americans, Ambivalence, and Antisemitism," *Journal for the Study of Antisemitism* 5 (June 2013): 260–61.

4 On Cahn, *Bay mir bistu sheyn*, "Johnnie and George," and Cab Calloway, as well as on Café Society, Abel Meeropol, "Strange Fruit," and Billie Holiday, see Whitfield, *In Search of American Jewish Culture*, 1–2, 147, 158–60; and Pollack, "Ovoutie Slanguage Is Absolutely Kosher," 76–79. On Proletpen, see Gennady Estraikh, *In Harness: Yiddish Writers' Romance with Communism* (Syracuse University Press, 2005), 97–101; and Dovid Katz, "Introduction: The Days of Proletpen in American Yiddish Poetry," in Glaser and Weintraub, *Proletpen*, 3–25. The poems' translations to the English are by Amelia Glaser, *Proletpen*, 145–51, 160–63.

5 Quotes by Powell and Bagnall and the quote about the Black press are in Lunabelle Wedlock, "The Reaction of Negro Publications and Organizations to

German Anti-Semitism," *Howard University Studies in the Social Sciences* 3 (1942): 54, 57, 76–78, 83. On anti-Jewish demagogues, the riots in 1930s Harlem, and the Bronx "slave markets," see Dinnerstein, *Antisemitism in America*, 203–6; Gurock, *Jews of Harlem*, 184–88 (includes the domestic worker's quote); Greenberg, *"Or Does It Explode?,"* 121–27; and Ella Baker and Marvel Cooke, "The Bronx Slave Market," in Adams and Bracey, *Strangers and Neighbors*, 369–74. On the situation in Chicago, see St. Claire Drake and Horace R. Cayton, *Black Metropolis: A Study of Negro Life in a Northern City* (1945; revised edition, University of Chicago Press, 1993), 194–95, 244, 249, 273, 432, 446–48, 452–53. See also Kenneth B. Clark, "Candor about Negro-Jewish Relations," *Commentary* 1 (1945), https://www.commentary.org.

6 Abramson and Goldberg wrote in *Tog*, March 22, 1935, 8; March 24, 1935, 6. The report about the children and the editorial are *Tog*, March 21, 1935, 6–7. Goldman's letter and similar claims by journalist L. Fogelman are in *Forverts*, March 22, 1935, 6. Sorin's letter in *Forverts*, Oct. 27, 1939, 4, was in response to Fogelman's article (*Forverts*, Oct. 13, 1939, 4, 6), where "intelligent Negroes" presented their complaints against Jewish landlords and storekeepers. On communists as the instigators of the riot, see also *MZ*, March 21, 1935, 6. Cf. *FAS*, April 5, 1935, 4, which warned against blaming just the communists for the riot. In 1937, Lilliput (Kretshmer) assured his readers that Black Harlemites "shook off the false prophets . . . the Black Hitlers" and all race baiters, *Forverts*, Oct. 25, 1937, 2–3. See the word game about the color of the "Black Hitler" in *MZ*, Jan. 21, 1935, 4. Linguist Max Weinreich explained to a Vilna audience that like other Americans, African Americans reject radicalism—*Yidishe shtime* (Vilna), April 15, 1935, 5. On Jewish communists in Harlem, see Mark Naison, *Communists in Harlem during the Depression* (University of Illinois Press, 1983), 49, 55n57, 121–22, 137, 149, 171, 214.

7 Peysekh Markus, "Neger blut," *A brik ibern atlantik* (Biderman, 1932), 67–75. Markus, "A neger shtarbt," *A brik ibern atlantik*, 150–63. See also Rontsh, "Der neger," 220–21; and the critique by Isaac Bashevis Singer (under pseudonym Varshavsky) of Markus's book about the Vilna Gaon, *Forverts*, July 6, 1952, 5 (2nd section). Between the 1920s and the 1940s, Markus published his literary works in the communist *Morgn frayhayt*.

8 S. Tenenboym, *Bay der velt tsugast: dertseylungen un reportazshn* (Literarishe bleter, 1937), 58–59, 62. See also the story "The Negress of 'Sacré-Coeur,'" *Bay der velt tsugast*, 136–42. On Tenenboym, see Sol Liptzin, *A History of Yiddish Literature* (Jonathan David Publishers, 1972), 459–60. A similar erotic objectification of the Black body in those years appeared in Judd L. (I. L.) Teller's poem *Tsu a neger-meydl* (To a Negro Girl) in *Lider fun der tsayt* (n.p., 1940), 109. See also how poet Rose Nevadovska echoed the image of Black submissiveness: in the poem *Tsu di shvartse froyen* (To Black Women), she commiserates with Black women's hardship, toil, and poverty; however, Nevadovska ends the poem with a question, "Why is your step so servile-slavish?" Rose Nevadovska, *Azoy vi ikh bin: lider fun rose nevadovska, 1933–1936* (Rosa neṿadoṿsḳa bukh-ḳomiṭeṭ, 1936), 10.

9 Paul Gilroy, *Black Atlantic: Modernity and Double Consciousness* (Harvard University Press, 1993), 205–17; and Robert Philipson, *The Identity Question: Black and Jews in Europe and America* (University Press of Mississippi, 2000).

10 Ezra Mendelsohn, *On Modern Jewish Politics* (Oxford University Press, 1993), 133–39; and Lewis, "Parallels and Divergences," 543–64. See also Stuckey, *Slave Culture*, 198–200.

11 Leora Batnitzky, *How Judaism Became a Religion: An Introduction to Modern Jewish Thought* (Princeton University Press, 2011), 183–91; and Michael A. Meyer, *Response to Modernity: A History of the Reform Movement in Judaism* (1988; 2nd edition, Wayne State University Press, 1995), 10–74, 132–42, 264–76.

12 On American Jews' beliefs that liberalism and Judaism are inseparable, see Charles S. Liebman and Steven M. Cohen, *Two Worlds of Judaism: The Israeli and American Experiences* (Yale University Press, 1990), 96–99, 109–14; Michael Walzer, "Liberalism and the Jews: Historical Affinities, Contemporary Necessities," in *Studies in Contemporary Jewry*, vol. 11, ed. Peter Y. Medding (Oxford University Press/Institute of Contemporary Jewry, Hebrew University of Jerusalem, 1995), 3–10; Lederhendler, *American Jewry*, 269–78; Jack Wertheimer, *The New American Judaism: How Jews Practice Their Religion Today* (Princeton University Press, 2018), 38–42, 45; and William Spinrad, "Explaining American-Jewish Liberalism: Another Attempt," *Contemporary Jewry* 11 (1990): 107–19. Cf. Norman Podhoretz, *Why Are Jews Liberals?* (Doubleday, 2009), 280–90. A popular book that has essentialized Judaism but in an opposite direction is by Jonathan Neumann, *To Heal the World? How the Jewish Left Corrupts Judaism and Endangers Israel* (All Points Books, 2018).

13 Friedman is quoted in Berson, *Negroes and the Jews*, 123–24. The second quote is by Diner, "Between Words and Deeds," 91. See also Forman, *Blacks in the Jewish Mind*, 10–11. Jonathan D. Sarna has shown that Jewish organizations, lay and rabbinic alike, did not become deeply involved in civil rights issues before World War II—*American Judaism: A History* (Yale University Press, 2004), 308–9. See also, Sherman Labovitz, *Attitudes toward Blacks among Jews: Historical Antecedents and Current Concerns* (R and E Research Associates, 1975), 3, 16.

14 Yosef Hayim Yerushalmi, *Zakhor: Jewish History and Jewish Memory* (1982; repr. University of Washington Press, 1996), 97–98. Scholars who offer new paradigms include Goldstein, *Price of Whiteness*; Kirzane, "The 'Yiddish Gaze'"; and Caplan, "Yiddish Exceptionalism," to name a few.

INDEX

Page numbers in italics indicate Figures or Photos.

ABOUT THE AUTHOR

Gil Ribak is the Shirley D. Curson Associate Professor in the Arizona Center for Judaic Studies at the University of Arizona.